Our Wounded Wilderness

The Great Boundary Waters Canoe Area Wilderness Storm

Jim Cordes

Foreword by Mike Link

Printed By
MENNE PRINTING & GRAPHICS, INC.

Forest Lake and North Branch, Minnesota

měnně
printing & graphics

Publisher
Jim Cordes

Editor
Tom Fiero

Cover Design
Karen Hoeft

Book Design and Production
Karen Hoeft

Text © 1999, 2000 Jim Cordes
Second Edition, 2001

ISBN 0-9711160-0-8

Cover Photos
BWCA Lightning Strike Fires - USFS
Evacuation from Alpine Lake - Jan Fiola
Tourists Clearing the Gunflint Trail - Bearskin Lodge
Eagle in Broken Norway Pine - USFS
Storm Damage - Sommers Scout Camp Staff
Sawyer Viewing Damage and Beauty - USFS

Back Cover Photo
USFS Wilderness Ranger Brandee Wenzell - Roger Hahn

For further information visit canoecountry.com/stormbook
or Jim Cordes, Box 135, Lutsen, MN 55612

Contents

THE STORMS

THE FOREST SERVICE AND PUBLIC OFFICIALS:
A CALL TO ACTION

Hydro Sawyer - Ontario **C56**

Thunder Bay Chronicle Journal

Latrine in tree **C20**

USFS

THE DAMAGE

ncloud on Lake Saganaga **C1**

John Rose

Frank Stewart near Arrow Lake, Ontario **C18**

Thunder Bay Chronicle Journal

BWCA WEST

BWCA CENTRAL

BWCA CENTRAL

BWCA EAST

*Circled numbers refer to story location on map.
See the following 2 pages.*

USFS Beaver Aircraft loading Hotshot crew

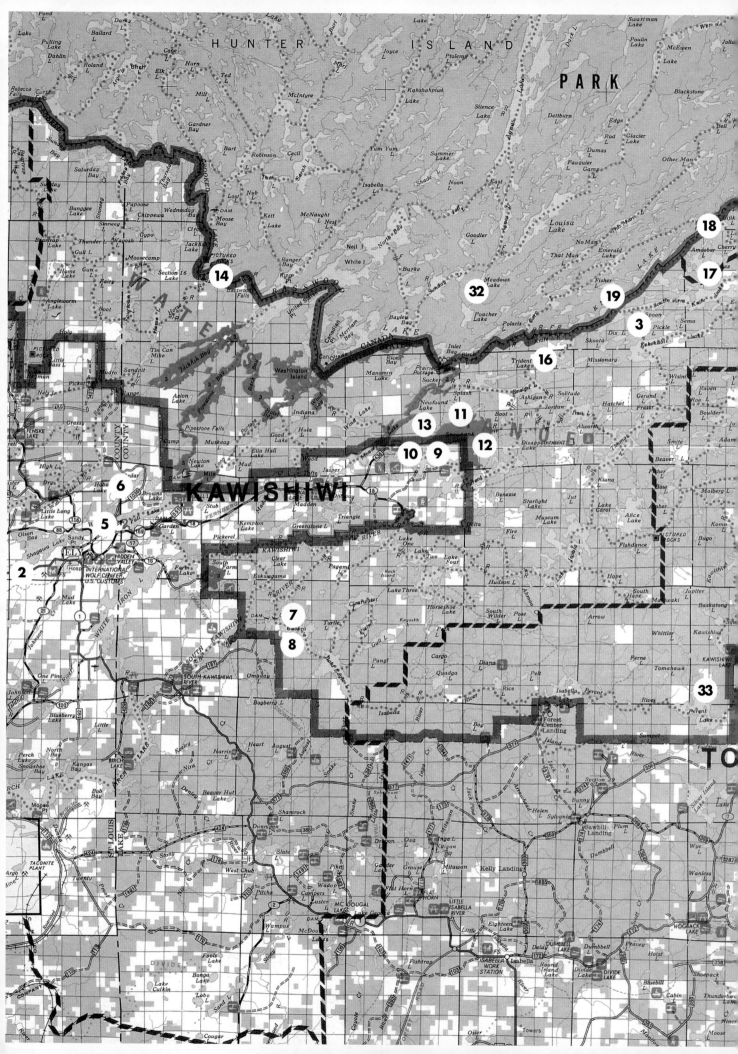

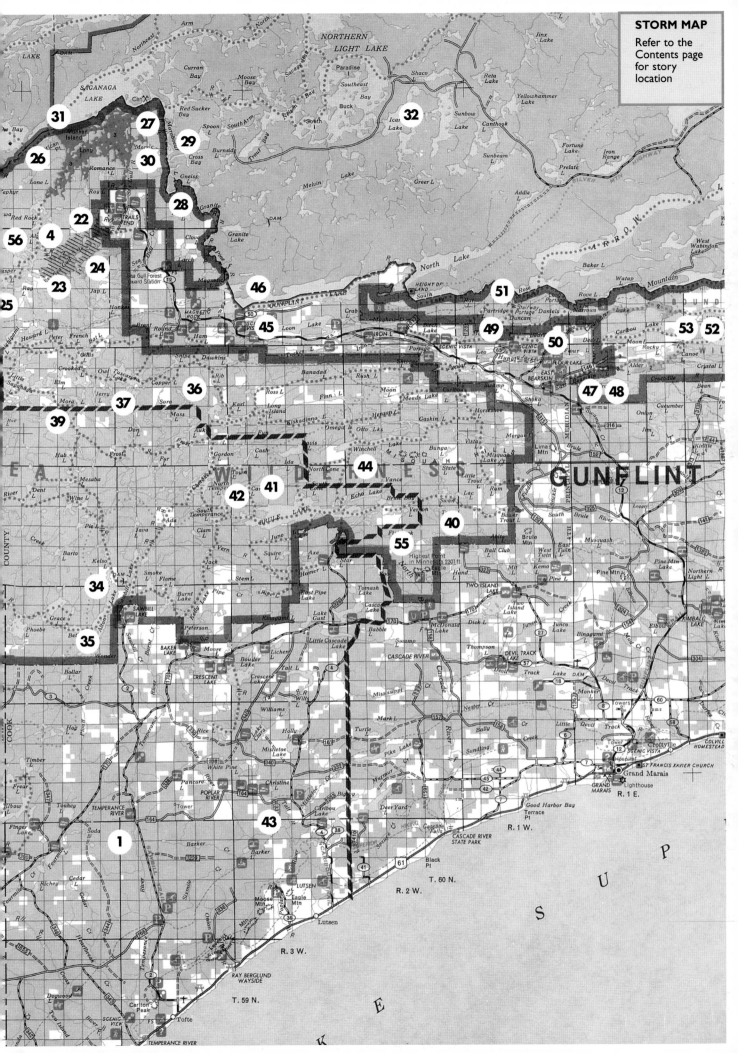

Introduction

On July 4 and 5, 1999, northern Minnesota experienced devastating winds and rainstorms that destroyed property and timber valued in the many millions of dollars. It blew down or snapped off 40 million trees. Miraculously, no lives were lost – although dozens of people were injured, some seriously.

The terrible winds originated in northwestern Minnesota. By the time they reached the Boundary Waters Canoe Area they topped 120 MPH, leveling 140,000 acres and millions of trees within the wilderness. The storm traveled on through Quetico Provincial Park and spent itself near Thunder Bay, Ontario. The rain damage that followed the next day was the worst seen in recent memory, washing out hundreds of roads and causing flooding and massive erosion, turning Lake Superior muddy brown.

In the Superior National Forest, especially the Tofte, Isabella and Gunflint Ranger Districts, all major roads were blocked. Highway 61 was closed in several areas between Two Harbors and Grand Marais. Also closed were Highway 1 to Ely; and the Echo,

Jim Cordes - Tofte Ranger Station

Kia Donais

Sawbill, Caribou, Gunflint and Arrowhead trails. Most other county and Forest Service roads were either washed out or blocked by the blowdown. Some roads were covered with hundreds of trees, taking days to clear. It required a Herculean effort from private, county, state and federal people to clear the roads. The Gunflint Trail lost nearly 250 electric power poles, causing a 14 day power outage in some locations during the busiest time of the year.

The BWCA lost an estimated 25 million trees. The heaviest devastation occurred generally in a path 4 to 12 miles wide and 35 miles long, beginning northeast of Ely at Jackfish Bay and paralleling the border area – including Basswood, Knife, Saganaga, Seagull, Gunflint, and Clearwater Lakes, to Pine Lake on the east end. Much of the rest of the wilderness had isolated winds as well. Lakes Insula, Polly and Brule were outside the worst blowdown

area but had injuries and medical evacuations.

Campers characterized the affected area as a "war zone," and all agreed that it was a "miracle" that no one was killed. Campers were capsized, hurled through the air, crushed under trees and pinned under their canoes. Forest Service pontoon aircraft were kept busy evacuating the badly injured. Others were brought out by canoe or motorboat, then by helicopter or by ambulance once roads were cleared of trees; to Duluth, Ely, Babbitt, Grand Marais, Two Harbors and other area hospitals.

Many campers were within inches of death. It is inconceivable that there were no fatalities. Heroism was commonplace. Nearly 200 persons were hastily recruited to search for and rescue campers. Working 12 hour days, these people obtained a rare special approval to use chainsaws in the BWCA. Working hard under very dangerous conditions, they cleared 551 portages and 1,520 campsites in short order.

There were probably 2,500 campers in the wilderness that day. An estimated 300 to 400 groups were in the path of the storm. Their stories often tragic, sometimes humorous and always interesting – needed to be told.

Some campers acknowledged their traumatic feelings for the first time while putting their memories on paper, and called it a therapeutic experience. All of them that I have talked to, including those with terrible injuries, say they will return to the BWCAW.

Many questions remain about the wilderness, the healing of the forest, the wildlife, future camper quotas, rules and regulations and forest fire potential. It will be interesting to see how it will all play out.

With this book, it is also my intention to put into perspective the <u>actual</u> damage done to our wilderness; and to correct misconceptions which may have been created by media coverage, so that we can make informed decisions about our future use of the BWCAW.

Foreword

How does a person reflect upon an event like the July 4th storm? Do we treat it like the disastrous tornados that devastated St. Peter, Minnesota in 1998, like Hurricane Andrew, the Yellowstone fires, or the San Francisco earth quake? We have a fascination with the devastating - we do not have a 24 hour cable weather channel because we want to observe average weather conditions throughout the world.

This book collects the human perspectives, the newspaper articles and the stories of human tragedy and heroism. These are stories to read and reflect on. Considering the number of people in the wilderness; the very small amount of serious injury it is amazing. Through the eye witness accounts we can share in the experiences of others and understand the drama that the canoers lived. This book also includes editorials and letters, items written in the anxiety, heat, and anger of the events. They were written, they were stated, and they create an honest perspective on the human responses, but in hindsight that does not make the opinions accurate.

As a nation of second guessers we can take a football game that lasts three hours on Sunday, and fill talk radio stations with "what-if's" and complaints 24 hours a day, until the next weekends game. When there are decisions made by representatives of the federal government we are particularly prone to bicker, quibble, and judge.

The July fourth windstorm encompassed two of our nation's passions - complaining about the weather and the government (Forest Service). We are quick to jump to conclusions and positions just because it is our normal way of filling time at the café, the gas station, and the church dinner. "Wasn't that windstorm awful?" "Why are the feds leaving the trees lay there?" "Isn't somebody going to do something?" Who wants to be the person who doesn't have an answer?

To this mix we add another Americanism - the prediction of disaster. Does anyone remember Y2K? Do you remember when Reagan blew a fuse over the Yellowstone fires and predicted a lifeless park. What about the news coverage on Mount St. Helen. They told us we would not see life return during our lifetime.

We have information, lots of information. We know about forest fires, downed timber, and loads of biomass so we immediately predict and react to the worst possible fire scenario. What is the best answer? I do not know. Read the material in this book as a source for reflection, not an answer. Hear the fear and the anguish, the hidden agendas of those who want to bring out the timber, understand the broader perspective of those in charge of managing the land, and step back to reflect before jumping to a conclusion.

Disasters are not just fascinating in their awesome display of power, they are also opportunities to learn. So while you reflect upon the human landscape and its recreational and economic perspectives, think also about the planet and the ecological experiment that is now before us.

When Mount St. Helen erupted the country was captivated by the drama and we were amazed by the power and the bleak landscape that followed. Today the wildlife roams an emerging forest and the land is rich and varied, aesthetic and inspiring. When Yellowstone burned it took a forest that was becoming sterile and converted it to a richly diverse natural system that could better sustain the myriad life forms that make this the world's greatest national park.

Today, the Boundary Waters - the world's greatest recreational wilderness - has a chance to provide us with another unfolding story. When we see the BWCAW by itself, the event that took place looks immense. When we see it as part of the boreal forest complex that winds itself around Hudson Bay, up to the Arctic Circle, west to the prairie and east to Canada's Atlantic provinces, the wind storm, for all its fury, affected a small portion of the whole.

We know fire is part of the natural landscape of the north, we know that growth is slow, and our human lifetimes are small snapshots on the ecological timescale. Here is a place to see the interaction of weather, biology, and geology. This is the laboratory that wilderness was designed to provide.

I am grateful that Jim Cordes pulled all of these materials together, that he has collected the history of this moment. Remember that the study of the environment is "Natural History" and when we combine nature and social history and distill the lessons that are involved, we are all better off. And after all the reflections, pick up a paddle and become an observer yourself.

Mike Link
Audubon Center of the Northwoods
Sandstone, MN
March 2000

Acknowledgements

Thank you, all of you who work and play in the Superior National Forest and BWCAW, who wouldn't allow this memorable snapshot in time to slip away without some recognition.

I am especially indebted to you campers and Superior National Forest visitors who were in the path of the storm, endured it and later told me about it; so that we all in some measure can comprehend your terror, exhilaration in surviving, your bewilderment and sense of loss.

I applaud the patience shown me by affected business owners, and the many extremely busy Forest Service people who helped – especially Gunflint District Ranger Jo Barnier, Cartographic Technician Tom McCann, the Wilderness Rangers and the three Beaver aircraft pilots. Thanks also go to my typist and editor Tom Fiero of Grand Marais, and designer, producer Karen Hoeft of Two Harbors for their many suggestions and timely support.

The *Ely Echo, Duluth News-Tribune, Cook County News-Herald, Minneapolis Star-Tribune* and *Thunder Bay Chronicle* have been valuable sources of information, and I am grateful to them for their generous permission to reprint articles related to the storm.

It would be impossible to name everyone who contributed to this project; help came from so many sources. Talking with the friendly and resourceful people of northeast Minnesota, many of whom interrupted their work to speak with me, or invited me into their homes, has been a deeply rewarding experience.

Thank you!

Tofte Ranger Station
July 4

Kia Donais is a frontliner, a Forest Service employee who issues BWCA permits at the Tofte Ranger Station. Her husband Shawn is the assistant Park Manager at Temperance River State Park.

Kia worked at the station on Independence Day. Here, in her own words, is how her day went:

by Kia Donais

I worked at the Tofte Ranger Station that Sunday the Fourth from 11:45 AM to 8:15 PM. Roberta and I were talking as it was slow and there had been very few people in the office. I was wishing that I could attend the Tofte parade at 1 PM. We were talking when Roberta looked up and said, "Oh my gosh, it's so dark! What is going on?"

We both looked outside and started towards the door. It was as dark as night outside. I thought something serious was happening as there were vehicles lined up on Hwy. 61. They all had their lights on. There was a police vehicle just beyond our view stopping traffic. We could see its lights flashing. Then I realized that the vehicles were stopped due to the parade in Tofte, not the strange mid-day darkness. I looked at the clock right then. It was exactly 12:50 PM. Roberta and I headed outside and gawked at the sky and the clouds for a few seconds before it began to rain...just a few drops at first and some wind. There was a group picnicking at the tables and we yelled at them to come inside. They were busy gathering coolers and heading for their vehicles. (They left without coming in.) Roberta had begun taking down the flag but the wind and rain picked up with such force that we ran back inside. We both got soaked in the few steps it took to get from the flag pole (with the flag half down and blowing wildly in the wind) to the entry way.

Roberta ran inside and began shutting windows in the office. I gawked at the storm for a minute and then decided to get the flag which had become unhooked and was flapping loosely. I got REALLY wet - wet hair and soaked uniform - in the few seconds it took to rein in the flag.

We sat down again and were remarking on how dark it was just a few minutes before. The wind was blowing outside but it didn't seem too bad to me. Probably because we were inside sitting at a desk where there were few windows. At this time I realized that the storm might have caused some damage and that we might want to try getting hold of the Wilderness Rangers. I was feeling intimidated to be on the radio if there were going to be emergencies. Just then, about 1:30 PM, Carrie Anderson and her family came in to dry off. They had been at the parade and had gotten completely soaked. At about this time we began hearing reports on the radio from the Fernberg repeater on the Fernberg Road (near Ely). Carrie was attempting to contact Gary

Shawn and Kia Donais

Robinson, who was the only ranger scheduled to be in the wilderness on the 4th in the Tofte District.

At one point I remember someone, a Forest Service person, saying "There are no trees standing here" and "I can't believe it" and "We need to get the Fernberg Road closed - there are live power lines across the road." Later, I remember a dispatcher attempting to get some information from a Wilderness Ranger about the conditions on a lake near the Fernberg. The Wilderness Ranger said he was sorry but he wouldn't be able to get to the lake. He was stuck on a portage with a group who had taken refuge under their canoe and there were "too many trees between here and there - it will take me hours just to cut out to the lakeshore." Then we heard about the Beaver planes and how they wouldn't be able to get out as there was more weather on the way. And we heard about a "serious head injury - we'll need a medivac and a life flight from Duluth." After that, we realized how bad the storm was. I went home knowing that the summer would not be the same!

Steve Schug, the Wilderness Ranger supervisor, came in at 3 PM. Roberta stayed until then. We had one group out of Cherokee Lake that afternoon. They'd made it OK but said there were a lot of trees down, especially on the last 10 rod portage near the entry point. I spoke to a woman calling from Crooked Lake Resort who had spoken to a party at Kawishiwi entry point. They were stranded there. There were too many trees down on the road and she wondered when we'd be out to clear them.

By the time I left that night those groups had been cut out of Kawishiwi with chainsaws. (I think - we were getting a lot of bad information.) Jerry J., a sawyer, was near Toohey Lake. His crew cut through the grade road to the Sawbill Trail by that afternoon. Shawn and I watched the fireworks at BlueFin Bay that night and we heard over his rescue radio that all the known injuries had been taken out of the BWCA and Cook County. That was encouraging.

I went to bed that night imagining groups stuck out there on portages, in ruined tents, with injuries, waiting sleeplessly (through the storms we had later) for morning to come, knowing they'd have another whole day of portaging through downed trees to get their injured members to an entry point.

That morning my husband called from Temperance River State Park (where they'd had about 20 trees come down - no injuries but lots of damage - in a path following the river valley) and told me to drop what I was doing, bring the camera and come see the river. It was at flood stage. After seeing the river last summer at its lowest in years, the change was remarkable.

It was quite the event – one I'll always remember.

THE STORMS

The Independence Day
Windstorm

This story, in the July 12 issue of the *Cook County News-Herald,* said it best:

July Fourth Storm Hits Area

It smashed through the region like a runaway boulder, leaving in its wake thousands of acres of destroyed and wounded wilderness. It trapped hundreds of people inside the Boundary Waters Canoe Area Wilderness, injuring many. It dropped trees on roofs, cars and tents, and blasted electrical and telephone lines to the ground, leaving most of the Gunflint Trail area in darkness.

According to Mike Steward, the meteorologist in charge at the Duluth National Weather Service, the fourth of July storm hit Cook County between 12:50 and 1:40 on Sunday afternoon. It brought with it winds that ranged between 80 and 100 miles per hour and torrential rains.

To put those winds into perspective, Bill Carroll of the National Weather Service said that a 70 mile per hour wind can knock a semi truck off the road.

"What we had that day was amazing," said Steward. "I was impressed with the storm, and we knew we had some problems."

Steward said that the National Weather Service was able to get warnings out in time, but that watching the storm rip through the BWCAW and Cook County gave those in the weather service an uncomfortable feeling.

"Usually, when a storm like that hits, people can get into their houses and basements," he said. The fact that the storm rampaged through the BWCAW, however, meant that many people would be camping and not have the sort of protection a house would give.

"People may have heard about the storm, but what could they do? It was a very uncomfortable situation," said Steward.

The Duluth Office of the National Weather Service provided the radar image taken at 1:27 PM on July 4.

Robert Henson, an acclaimed meteorologist and storm chaser, vividly describes a

similar but smaller scale wind in the article "Falling Skies," in the May-June 1999 issue of *Audubon Magazine.*

Falling Skies

Hell-bent winds that crash to earth - downbursts - can mow down huge swaths of trees like blades of grass and open the door for death and disease.

by Robert Henson

A June evening hurtled toward dusk as I drove west into the teeth of a High Plains thunderstorm near Akron, Colorado. A wall of wind-driven dust, perhaps 1,000 feet high, rose from the horizon at the storm's front edge. The gust turned over on itself like a wave while russet-colored vortices spun to life along it, forming and vanishing and reforming in seconds. I quickly pulled over, jumped out of my car, and dived face-down into a field.

In moments, the storm – moist and cool, but free of rain – was upon me. My ears popped as the wind revved from calm to nearly 100 miles an hour, driving needles of grit into my hair and skin. Half-exhilarated, half-terrified, I yelled into the prairie emptiness. In 5 minutes that seemed more like 30, the screams of the wind gradually settled into a soft moan. I got up, brushed off the dirt, and reclaimed my dignity. I had experienced the ferocity of a downburst.

A few acres of wheat fell to the wind from that particular storm, but the impact was short-lived compared to what a down-burst can do to a forest: Dense stands of old-growth trees can be mowed down in seconds like blades of grass, leaving forest inhabitants homeless and trees vulnerable to fire and disease. **C13**

The terrible winds originated in Northwestern Minnesota. In Park Rapids they

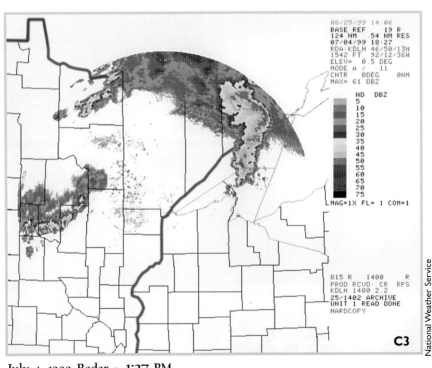

July 4, 1999 Radar - 1:27 PM

Reference to "C" throughout the book indicates a color photo in mid-section.

blew at 60+ mph for 30 minutes, knocking down trees and blowing a gable off a log house construction. According to one person there, the wind and rain began at 10:30 AM. He measured 6 inches. The thunder was so constant it sounded like a motor running.

By the time the winds reached the BW they topped 130 miles per hour, leveling 172,000 acres and 25 million trees within the wilderness. The storm traveled on through Quetico Provincial Park and spent itself near Thunder Bay, Ontario. **C22**

State lands within the Superior national Forest lost 50,000 acres of trees from its 100,000 acre total.

In the Superior National Forest, especially the Tofte, Isabella and Gunflint districts, all major roads were blocked. The main artery, Highway 61, was closed in several places between Two Harbors and Grand Marais due to the torrential rains. Closed because of flooding and fallen trees were State Highway 1 to Ely, the Moose Lake Road; and the Echo, Sawbill, Caribou, Gunflint and Arrowhead trails. Most other county and Forest Service roads within the area were either washed out or blocked by blowdown. Some roads were covered with hundreds of trees and took many days to clear. **C24-25-27**

According to some sources the real heroes of the storm recovery were USFS employees John Olson and Steve Grimaldi, who were responsible for repairing and opening the Forest Service roads in the most heavily damaged areas of the Superior National Forest. **C5**

Many driveways, homes and resorts were badly damaged. The Gunflint Resort on Gunflint Lake had 10 to 15 trees on some buildings. Golden Eagle Resort had trees on 17 of 26 buildings - two were totaled. Dave Tuttle, owner of Bearskin Lodge, had 40 to 60 trees on his buildings. One party checked out because 10-12 trees came down on their cabin while they were in it. The guests thought they were going to die. Steven Kennedy with his wife and daughter, from Pekin, Illinois, spent 15 terrifying minutes under a table listening to trees snap and break. They saw two fall on their car.

Dick Smith of Gunflint Pines Resort jokes that his resort's name could be changed to "Gunflint Stumps." 15 to 17 campsites were occupied at his campground. "It was just a miracle that nobody was killed as campers and tents were smashed by flying trees."

According to Luana Brandt of Nor'wester Lodge, "The force of the rain was squirting rain through the walls. I watched as pine trees had their tops twisted and popped off just like dandelions."

Power was out throughout the area, putting businesses in the dark for as long as two weeks. There were 230 electric poles down along the Trail. Using generators, a

Logger, Doug Popham, unloading blowdown debris picked up from area roads.

couple of resorts remained open, but most closed down for as long as 10 days to clean up – during the peak of the tourist season.

I have traveled the Gunflint Trail often since the storm. The broken trees are scattered until you reach East Bearskin Lake; then they become more common, increasing in number as you proceed along the Trail. Along the upper Trail to its end, some areas have severe damage while other sections have changed little. **C17**

All campgrounds, resorts, outfitters and other businesses are now back in operation, taking reservations and looking forward to seeing you in the new millennium.

Jim Brandenburg, a well known wildlife photographer whose home is in the blowdown area, claims that the storm "may not be nature's work but a product of man's carelessness with the environment."

Dr. Lee Frelich, a University of Minnesota researcher, subscribes to this theory. He states that our *derecho* ("direct" or "straight ahead" in Spanish) storm was the product of dozens of downbursts which flowed together. There was also a scattering of isolated downbursts, for example those that affected parts of Polly and Brule lakes. One downburst may cover 2 to 12 square miles.

Not having felt severe wind themselves, most campers on Polly Lake were surprised by the Beaver plane evacuation of a woman hit by a tree on their lake.

The storm traveled at 65 mph, and was equivalent to a number 3 or 4 hurricane, with winds estimated as strong as 120 to 140 mph. In 1977 northern Wisconsin experienced a derecho which clocked at 157 mph and extensively damaged 20,000 to 30,000 acres.

Dr. Frelich claims that, "had the Forest Service allowed wildfires, there would have been a younger forest, less susceptible to wind." Old growth white and Norway pine are especially vulnerable to such winds.

As the wind swept in, there were 2500 campers in the wilderness. Except for the dark skies and distant thunder, there was no warning.

Campers were capsized, hurled through the air, crushed under the trees and pinned under their canoes. Forest Service aircraft were kept busy evacuating the badly injured. Other victims were brought out by canoe or motorboat, then by helicopter or ambulance (once roads were cleared), to hospitals in Ely, Grand Marais, Two Harbors and others in the area. Many people were within inches of death as trees fell on them, their tents, canoes, cars, camper

Dave and Nancy Seaton

Hungry Jack Outfitter Canoes

trailers and cabins. Canoes and boats were caught in open water and swamped in 10 foot seas. It is almost inconceivable that there were no deaths.

An estimated 300 to 400 groups were in the path of the storm. Ellen Hawkins, a veteran Forest Service Wilderness Ranger for the Tofte District, looked at the severe damage and remarked that "A friend died - many generations will not have the experience that we had." Another veteran, Nancy Pius of the Ely District, claims that in some areas, "It's like a clearcut. I've talked to a lot of my co-workers who used the big trees as landmarks. Now they're all gone."

Nancy Pius

Campers jumping to avoid a falling tree

The following are damage reports written by Forest Service employees just following the storm:

First Look: Wilderness Portages and Campsites

Tofte/Gunflint USFS Wilderness Ranger Supervisor Steve Schug's Status Reports, as furnished by Wilderness Rangers and others on July 5 and 6, give us a first look at storm damage to BWCA campsites and portages.

Report by Gary Robinson, Sawbill Lake to Cherokee Lake

The route I covered today was from Sawbill to Cherokee and Sawbill to Smoke. I was able to check all portages but only four campsites. I was also able to talk with four parties coming out of Cherokee. The portages from Sawbill to Cherokee had a total of 60 trees down (1/2 of them very large). I believe a crew of 4-6 people could have them cleared in 2 days. The portage to Smoke Lake could be opened in 2 hours.

I believe our big issue is going to be campsites. The four I looked at all had significant tree damage. I of 4 is totally closed. The 4 parties I talked to who had been on Cherokee each told of trees down on campsites. My gut feeling is we have weeks of work on campsites.

Notes from Wallstrom & Zisook on condition of the wilderness from Kawishiwi Lake to north part of Polly Lake

Kawishiwi Lake Road – small trees all the way down to Hog Creek. Chainsaws can clear.

Kawishiwi Lake, Square Lake, Kawasachong Lake – OK. 6 to 8 trees down on all sites.

Townline Portages- – ~6 trees down on portages, lots of erosion.

Polly Lake – 1/2 of sites with serious blowdown damage.

Malberg – (heard from visitors) at least 2 sites with multiple trees down.

Report by Wilderness Ranger Cathy Quinn and Brandee Wenzell on condition of the Brule Lake area

Campsites – half of the campsites observed were campable. These sites had no more than 5-10 trees down on the site, including the latrine trail. The other half of the campsites observed were completely leveled. These sites had so many trees criss-crossed that you could not walk. Tent pads, latrines and firegrates could not be found in most cases.

Brule to Lily Lake portage – this portage is approximately 30 rods long and is almost entirely impassable. A group of campers traveling from Winchell Lake to Brule stated that all of the portages were leveled and that the Brule to Lily Lake portage was one of the better portages along the way.

Our perspective

Boundary Waters

Wind as a reminder of wilderness

Every trip to the Boundary Waters is memorable in its own way. But when the windstorm of a lifetime blasts through one of summer's busiest weekends, the results are something many hundreds of campers might wish to forget.

If only they could. In tale after harrowing tale, they have described unsheltered encounters with a storm of unimaginable ferocity, followed by arduous journeys out of a territory that turned in an instant from pacific woodland to menacing obstacle course.

The dozens of injuries, many serious, add up to a sobering toll. But the photographs, looking more like the aftermath of a volcanic blast than of high wind, suggest that the tally could easily have gone much higher. With aerial surveys completed only yesterday morning, and lake-by-lake ground checks still underway, it may be some days before the storm's full measure in human suffering is known.

Even with relaxation of federal rules against motorboats, chainsaws and floatplanes, opening up the portages is no simple or short-term task. In many areas the blowdown timber is chest-high or higher, and a crew working all day may clear only a fraction of a mile. It will be weeks, at least, before all the portages are passable and all the campsites clear.

U.S. Forest Service employees describe scenes that most Americans might associate with natural disasters in developing countries: little knots of people cut off from the rest of the world, greeting survey planes with waves and thumbs-up signs, making the best of things while the food supply shrinks, grateful that the weather at least has turned from wet and windy to warmer and dry.

It is well to remember that the storm damage reaches well beyond the BWCA, that thousands of households are without electricity, that homes and roads and forests were damaged in a wide area of northeastern Minnesota. But it is also understandable that attention tends to focus on this recreation area that so many Minnesotans have come to know and love so deeply. The idea that perhaps a quarter of this million-acre woodland may have been flattened is difficult and painful to grasp.

We have all been reminded that despite our fond familiarity, the canoe country is not as benign as our back yards. It is a wilderness after all, subject to storms that are not merely misery makers but massively destructive.

That will be, and should be, high in the minds of visitors who are planning BWCA trips in the weeks to come. They will need to be especially attentive to the normal risks of back-country travel and also to certain post-storm concerns: obstructed routes, overburdened ranger staffs, trees that have been loosened but not yet toppled by the wind. As the storm has just made clear, a trip that puts civilization at a few days' remove makes rescue just as remote.

For more information on this subject, see the Web links available with the electronic version of this article in the Opinion section of

 startribune.com

Fire grate

Abandoned canoe site 13 proposed to close

Superior National Forest Wind Damage Estimates
of Jan. 1, 2000

According to Forest Service estimates, 375,795 acres or 19% of the Superior National Forest (SNF) inside the BWCA was damaged by the storm. Outside the BWCA, 121,151 acres or 5.9% of SNF acreage was damaged. The following chart indicates the different degrees of damage and estimates the SNF acreage affected, as of January 1, 2000.

	Acres Inside BWCAW	Acres Outside BWCAW
Light Damage	114,546 (5.8%)	52,894 (2.8%)
Moderate Damage	88,492 (4.5%)	39,201 (2.1%)
Heavy Damage	172,757 (8.7%)	20,056 (1%)

Note: "Light Damage" in an area means up to 1/3 of the trees damaged. "Moderate Damage" means 1/3 - 2/3 of trees damaged. "Heavy Damage" means more than 2/3 of trees damaged.

Latrine in tree **C20**

LETTERS TO THE EDITOR

No more pines?

To the editor:

It is heartbreaking for us to think "If" our beautiful north woods as we remember from our past camping expeditions, will eventually turn into an entirely different uncharacteristic northern landscape with aspen being the dominant trees! Will the magnificent majestic towering pines become obsolete in our northwoods?

Could the devastating July 4th storm that ripped through the BWCA really be a wake up call to all of us of how fragile our planet earth is becoming? Could this be a form of global warming caused by our carelessness of polluting mother earth by our greedy, lazy, throwaway societal habits?

Do we really care? Do we lack vision? Will we continue on our current path of total destruction of our environment? Are we becoming so motorized and computerized that we're on the fast track to self destruction of our minds, bodies, air, water and land? Are we so selfish that we do not care about the next generations' well being?

Will our future grandchildren be able to experience the same tranquility, solitude, spirituality and beauty of nature in the great northwoods wilderness as we have enjoyed in the past? It's crucial that important, wise decisions be made now to preserve the great diversity of our wilderness and wildlife for future generations to enjoy!

Could our tranquil northwoods quickly become and turn into noisy motorized tourist traps? Now is the time to restrict, not expand, motorized vehicle use on our land and lakes. How pathetic when so many people who go on vacation, use motors to get there, motors to go fishing and etc., when they return home, they go to the health spas for exercise!

Healthy no-motorized outdoor activities need to be encouraged. Perhaps now is the time to get involved to help expand on projects and activities to rejuvenate and practice earth day everyday. Perhaps it's possible, not only saving our mother earth, but also cut down on our mountains of trash that is the result of our throwaway, greedy, lazy society.

Alice and Ed Cowley
Becker, MN

The Independence Day Rainstorm

Cascade Lodge and Lake Superior

Gene Glader and his wife Laurene had just left the fireworks display at the Grand Marais harbor when the real fireworks began. The Gladers own the Cascade Lodge between Lutsen and Grand Marais one of the premier lodges of N.E. Minnesota.

"By the time we got to the lodge, rain was coming down in sheets and lightning was constant. It was still pouring when we went to bed.

"Our phone rang at 2:30 a.m. Guests in cabin 11 reported water rushing in."

The rain continued to fall. Gene couldn't believe his eyes - Cascade Creek, running between his cabins, had become a raging torrent, washing away trees, carrying huge boulders and now threatening his cabins.

Gene estimates that between 11:30 p.m. and 3:30 a.m. the area could have been hit with 7 - 7 1/2 inches of rain. The creek washed out a footbridge and flooded a large area. Gene believes that, had the power and lights gone out, panic could have overtaken his cabin renters. Had they attempted to cross the footbridges and flooded areas in the darkness, they could have been swept into Lake Superior. **C7**

He suggests that it was lucky for those in the wilderness blowdown area that the winds didn't come at night when tents were occupied, and when dodging the falling trees would have been a bit more difficult.

Morning light at the lodge revealed the devastation. Cascade Creek had overflowed its bank and cut a new channel. In the flooded area were mountains of debris. Highway 61 was badly damaged, undermined and littered with broken asphalt. A highway crew with a dump-truck and plow arrived to push debris off the road.

Higher back up the hill, culverts were washed out and the creek bed was cleansed of all soil - to bare rock. Where Highway 61 crosses the Cascade River, the river came within inches of overflowing the bridge.

Lake Superior took it all in. According to observers, as far as you could see the lake was a dirty brown.

These articles in the July 12 issue of the Cook County News-Herald describe the storm's impact on Lake Superior:

Storm Impacts Superior

No boaters were hurt or terrorized on Superior by the wind that raked the Boundary Waters and the Gunflint Trail, but the brown noose of sediment ringing the big lake is a distress signal in and of itself.

"Everyone ran for shelter right away," said Petty Officer Tom Brown, US Coast Guard stationed in Grand Marais on July 4. In this case, the running was on water.

"Brown said, some boats didn't have radios, so we were going out physically and telling them to get back to harbor." Brown said. He said they all made it in, even though the Coast Guard had only a 30-minute window to warn after hearing the forecast of heavy weather.

However, there were some unplanned adventures on Superior thanks to the storm. One small 14-foot boat was reported beached in the Big Bay area of Hovland, but the occupant was safe. Another boat, which was being towed due to a motor breakdown, slipped its towline in the blow.

Out on Isle Royale, staff at Windigo Ranger Station reported seas rough enough to bring the 65-foot Voyageur back after it set out for the mainland. Again, there were no injuries on the island due to the storm. All trails were open.

Anyone driving along the North Shore of Superior July 5 saw the bruise left by the storm in the sediment stain reaching far into the lake. In a related article, Soil and Water Conservation District Manager Rebecca Wiinanen says it will take centuries for the lake to "recharge" or the same amount of time it will take for a White Pine seedling planted this year to reach the height of the ones felled July 4, 1999.

Gene Glader

Rainstorm damage, Highway 61 Cascade Lodge

Superior took hit July 4

Erosion from one-time events such as last week cause a major portion of the sediment problems for Lake Superior. With increased development near Lake Superior, the problems are increasing. Planning for erosion control needs to account for these "worst scenario" events. This is an immense challenge considering the high percentage of steep slopes and erodable soils within the watershed. The Cook County Water Plan and Land Use Plans address these issues and need to be consulted whenever disturbance to vegetation or soils is planned.

Unfortunately the cleansing of the land that Cook County experienced last week washes the pollutants into Lake Superior. The Lake requires nearly 200 years to cleanse itself, so we need to do all we can to keep sediment and pollution out of the lake.
C6

Rain Damage

Cook County Sheriff Dave Wirt heard reports of 12 inches of rain locally. Runoff from the storm rushed across State Highway 61 in many locations, tearing out chunks of blacktop, undermining the roadbed and washing away the shoulders.

The Minnesota State Patrol reported the highway three miles south of Two Harbors was under a foot of water. There was heavy flooding between Tofte and Grand Marais. Travel to Two Harbors, Grand Marais or Virginia was impossible for a time.

Cook County engineer Chuck Schmit estimated that the cost to repair roads within the county could reach $850,000. Much of the damage was along the Gunflint Trail. Duluth received 2.90 inches, the old record was 1.61 set 90 years ago.

Repair estimates for St. Louis, Cook, Itasca and Lake counties totaled $2.5 million.

Wine Lake near Embarrass reportedly rose 8 feet - docks floated away. In Aurora and Embarrass most basements were flooded. The Knife and St. Louis rivers reached 40 year high levels.

Rainfall Reports, July 4-5, 1999 Northeastern Minnesota

Location	Amount in inches
Beroun	1.15
Embarrass	3.30
Marble Lake	3.02
Leech Lake	1.45
Grand Marais	3.60
Grand Portage	2.85
Lutsen	5.41
Grand Rapids	2.98
Marcell	6.30
Pokegama	3.89
Big Falls	0.53
Isabella	3.89
Snowbank Lake	1.35
Two Harbors	4.35
Wolf Ridge near Finland	3.21
7 NW Two Harbors	4.35
Babbitt	3.19
Brimson	3.78
Cotton	5.77
Ely	6.71
Eveleth	5.59
Duluth	2.92

Temperance River Rescue
by Shawn Donais

Well everyone is curious how things went and after napping and falling asleep on Kia four or five times today I think I have my mental wits (no comments from the peanut gallery allowed) back for at least a short time.

Well I think the best way to do this is in a time line like fashion.

Kia and I had just gotten back from our local video emporium (the gas station) and had settled in, freshly showered, for a long movie and a night on the couch.

Then a very familiar multi-toned sound came from the scanner on top of the microwave, paging the Tofte Rescue to assist a stranded canoeist on the Temperance River. Kia and I both had the same thought: who would even think of canoeing the Temperance at its current flood level? After all, the water was thirty feet higher than it was the day before as it came roaring through the gorge in the park.

Two local boys had convinced one another to shoot the rapids on the river in an open aluminum canoe without float bags. -So the call came and I got dressed. Not having a clue what would be needed, I threw stuff in my small pack - my fleece jacket and a few essentials - and headed out the door. The rescue squad was just pulling out on the road so I followed it up the Sawbill Trail for about six miles to where two people were frantically waving us down. The canoeist named John took off into the woods

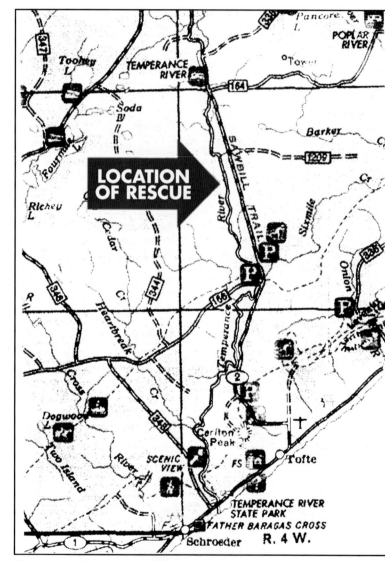

Temperance River Rescue Map

Kia Donais

down an old road (with four fresh ruts washed in it), saying his friend had been in the river for three hours already and needed help. We tried to stop him and get some info but it was too late. So the five of us that were there started grabbing stuff we thought we would need to pull his friend off the rocks, such as two ropes and a throw bag with a float attached. I grabbed my two life jackets and the body basket in case we needed to carry anyone back and took off after him.

The time was now 9:30 PM and it was getting dark in the woods. The rutted trail quickly ended about a half mile from the river so we were forced to bushwhack our way through, leaving an occasional glow stick hanging in hopes that the next crew would be able to follow our trail. At about 10 PM we hit the river and did not have a clue which way to go, up or down. We yelled and John finally yelled back from upstream.

What we were walking through was a combination of flooded woods and spruce swamp where every few steps involved someone sinking into knee-high mud. After a half hour of heading upstream, we finally could hear the other guy yelling over the rush of the river. We were standing ten feet away from the edge of the river, less than 60 feet from the stranded canoeist and could barely hear him. All that you could hear was the roar of the river. You practically had to yell just to talk to the guy a few feet from you. We were wondering where John went when we saw him heading out into the river. We yelled at him to wait until we had a safety line on him but he was too panicked to listen; he made it about ten feet from the edge of the river before the current took his feet out, and somehow he made it around a rock which was creating a current that pushed him out to his friend.

The five of us on shore thought oh *great, now we have two people to rescue.* After a few efforts we finally were able to throw a line out to the canoe which had become completely moulded around the rock it had hit. It was then we found out

Temperance River at full flood 7/5/99

Jan Fiola

across. Plus, I had the best life jacket. We rigged a harness and I tied myself to a safety line and we went about a hundred yards upriver for the attempt.

The furthest I ever made it was about one third of the way across before I was swept downstream, thankful for the life line and the two guys pulling on it who always pulled me back to shore. It was not going to work. I could not find a way across. Once the water got up to my waist my feet would get swept out and I would go shooting downstream. We really wanted to get a safety line across but without any access other than cutting through five miles of brush on the other side we were running out of time. Both of the canoeists were

what John had failed to mention. His friend's foot was caught in the canoe and was being crushed in the worst spot it could be in: right in the fold where the aluminum gunwale was wrapped around the rock.

After finally getting a life line tied around the two victims, we didn't have enough rope to send anyone else out so we had to rely on their poor judgement. They wanted us to try to winch the canoe in hopes of freeing his foot. It did not work and we were lucky that it didn't. All we managed to do was tear whatever we tied the rope around off the canoe. Later I realized we never would have gotten his foot out and if we had freed the canoe the guy would have died.

We knew we needed more equipment and would have to wait for it. We tried to call out on our radios but could not pick up anybody. After about 10 minutes we finally got out on a different channel and were able to relay our needs and position as best we could guess to the next crew. The determination was that we needed to try to get a safety line across the river first before we could do anything.

After waiting over an hour for equipment to make it in to us we started to put our plan into action. Looking around at the two old guys, the skinny guy and the guy with a limp, and realizing I probably had the most experience reading rapids, I volunteered to try to get the line

shivering from being in the water for almost seven hours already. I said that the only way to do it was for me to follow John's route into the river and make it to the other side of the big rock and ride the same current to the canoe that he had.

With little other option, that's what we did. I inched my way out into the river, somehow keeping my feet under me until I was almost directly upstream from the canoe. When my feet went out, I swam as hard as I could, making it to the other side of the rock on which they were stuck, where I grabbed the tip of the canoe and swung myself into the eddy behind the rock. Catching my breath, I found that both the canoeists were in pretty good shape for being in the river so long. Then I found out how bad his foot was stuck and realized if the canoe came loose he would go with it.

Holding my line tight, we slid a pry bar down the line. I worked my way around to the upstream side of the rock where the current held me in place, and started prying with all my might. The front of his boot was crushed right in the middle of the fold. Every time I pried he would scream as the aluminum flexed around his foot. The problem was that I could not get the pry bar into the fold, and prying anywhere else just increased the pressure on his foot. We had to find a way to punch some holes in the canoe to release some of the water pressure. In came the axe.

Although I did not realize it at the time I had been in the water for over an hour already. I started hacking at the canoe, making very little progress until finally I cracked through on one of the seams. I continued to try to chop the hole bigger under water. The pressure was eased slightly but as the pressure eased on one end of the canoe the pressure increased on the other side. Hacking a hole in that side helped to rebalance the pressure but his foot was still stuck.

Back to the pry bar. Now I could bend the fold slightly but doing so caused the whole canoe to start to move, and if the canoe went it would take him with it. I had very few choices left. We had tried to do many things without much success. I had to risk prying a little more in hopes of freeing his foot. Getting the bar just in front of his toes, I pulled. The bar came loose and bounced off my chin, leaving a pretty good mark on it. But as I felt my way around his foot, I was sure I had opened the crack a little. Then all of a sudden the canoe shifted, increasing the pressure on his foot, sending him yelling again. I was thinking there was no way I was going to get him out– I had been in the river for two hours and had not made much progress.

I looked at him and told him this was going to hurt a hell of a lot and asked him if he was ready. He said yes and I grabbed his foot and pulled as hard as I could. He screamed as I felt his boot move just a little. He said he could not take any more. I told him it was the only way and to tell me when he was ready. He took a deep breath and said OK. I grabbed his boot and pulled and twisted it with all my might. It moved an inch. It took three more tugs to pop his foot out of the fold in the canoe.

With his foot free from the fold his ankle was still caught between the gunwale as his boot would not fit through the gap. I needed to cut his boot off and yelled for a pair of EMT shears (a type of strong scissors used to cut through seat belts). On shore they frantically started looking through the supplies. We did not have one. I remembered my Leatherman in my pocket. I had started to hand it to a guy when I first went in the water but then thought maybe I might need it to cut my rope if it got tangled, and shoved it in my pocket.

I opened the blade and slid my fingers into the boot so I could keep my fingers between the knife and his foot, and slowly started cutting. Poking into my thumb a few times, I managed to cut down the seam and tear the back of his boot open. His foot had swelled up so that it was still stuck in the boot and I could not cut the whole boot off with my knife, so it was back to the pull and yank method. I could get my hands wrapped around his ankle now and was relieved to find it in good shape. I grabbed and pulled and out popped his foot.

I had been in the water for over two hours. The light from the shore hit his white foot and everyone cheered. Now we just had to get back to shore. Without a safety line the only choice was to tie the two canoeists together and let them go, letting the current pull them to the side of the river, held by their lifelines. They inched around the canoe, let go and both went under water, carried by the big rapids created by the rock we were stuck on. Then they came up and were pulled to the shore.

Now it was my turn. I inched myself over the canoe, making it halfway before the current that was holding me against the rock caught me and pulled my hand loose. Taking a deep breath and panicking for a second, I shot downstream before I felt my life line tighten and swing me around on my back. They had done a good job tying me in and I was easily pulled to shore, no worse for wear other than a leg that was cramping up from the cold water. (We were lucky that it actually was not too cold.)

We strapped the injured man into the stretcher and started the two mile haul by hand back to the road. His foot looked pretty good. The cool water had kept the swelling down and it looked like his ankle was OK. The front of his foot may have been crushed. I was cold and since I had been the one in the river I excused myself from carrying duty. (We had several fresh people to help now.) I started walking back, clearing the trail as I went along with two other guys. I walked out onto the Sawbill Trail about 20 minutes after the sun came up. It had been over eight hours since we first went in.

Someone handed me a can of pop and I guzzled it down, went to my truck and took off some of my wet clothes and put on the warm fleece. All I could think about was that I could not believe we got him free. It was a major group undertaking and my favorite person was the guy who had hold of the other end of my life line. I got home, took a hot shower, crawled into bed and fell asleep.

I learned a lot by the whole experience– mostly involving trust and that a lot of people have done some pretty extraordinary things up here in the last few days. Almost everyone is a volunteer and even though we have all had some training what was most needed was people who were willing to help.

"In Wildness and caring is the Preservation of the World." - H. D. Thoreau.

THE FOREST SERVICE AND PUBLIC OFFICIALS: A CALL TO ACTION

Storm Related Headlines

$12 million more for forest damage

Compromising Wilderness

THURSDAY, JULY 15, 1999

BWCAW camping permits halted

Fire Restrictions To Be Placed On Boundary Waters Canoe Area Wilderness

"Narrowest Escape from Death"

Access limited while crews clear storm-damaged areas

BWCAW Fire Restrictions

THE ART OF CAT-HOLES

Grams assesses storm damage

4A   Tuesday, July 13, 1999

STORM '99

Ventura sees BWCAW,

North Arm camps have power returned

BWCA still open; searches continue

Off-Site Camping Areas in the BWCAW

Superior took hit July 4

Crews Make Headway Into Damaged BWCAW

FOREST SERVICE
U S
DEPARTMENT OF AGRICULTURE

Cook County News-Herald, Grand Marais, Minn.
August 30, 1999

BWCAW fires allowed Aug. 20

Why no itineraries?

Independence Day Blowdown

Oberstar takes tour of BWCAW devastation

Forest Service plots BWCAW fire strategy

STATE OF MINNESOTA
DEPARTMENT OF NATURAL RESOURCES

A4   THE CHRONICLE-JOURNAL   Thunder Bay   Monday, July 5, 1999

Thunder Bay picks up the pieces

Boy dead, dozens hurt after deluge, heavy winds

By John Myers
Road cleanup (so far) is $115,000

Permits halted, chainsaws allowed in aftermath
Permits halted, chainsaws allowed in storm aftermat

A Visit to Duluth Forest Service Headquarters

In early February 2000 I interviewed two key Forest Service recovery personnel: Storm Recovery Director Dennis Neitzke, and Public Relations Team Leader Mark Van Every.

The mood at the Superior National Forest "S.O." (Forest Supervisor's Office) was far from business-as-usual. The July 4th storm has affected all phases of the region's operations, from the initial search and rescue, evacuations and road clearing; to the ongoing timber sales and salvage efforts, and much more. The Forest Service work force, already operating with minimal personnel, was stretched thin.

The day of the interview, people were moving at a hectic pace. Priority was being given to preparation of a draft Environmental Impact Statement, in order to determine what kind of restrictions would apply to continuing "fuel reduction" work on USFS land in the Gunflint Trail Corridor; and whether to begin using "prescribed fires" within the BWCAW. An Environmental Assessment was also being done for affected areas outside the wilderness and the Gunflint Corridor.

Protection of life and property in and near the wilderness has been a Forest Service priority since the big storm.

The following transcription presents the significant issues discussed in our interview:

Q: What are your thoughts about the lack of fatalities in the storm?

A: **We were all amazed and thankful. It had to be by the Grace of God that no one was killed.**

SUPERIOR NATIONAL FOREST

Q: What is the hiking trail status?

A: **The Snowbank Trail is ready. The Border Trail has about 20 miles left to clear.**

Q: How many campsites were damaged beyond repair?

A: **Few sites will be closed permanently. Due to the lack of standing trees at some sites, we recommend using bear-proof canisters, which are available from some outfitters.**

Q: What were the results of the permit lottery held on Jan. 15?

A: **At the same point in 1999 we received 4850 requests. This year it was 6200. There was no special shift in entry points requested.**

Q: Will there be additional fire suppression resources?

A: **We have requested one additional Type 1 helicopter, a Type 1 air tanker, one more Beaver airplane pilot, and a significant increase in fire related personnel. We're considering installing loud speakers on Beaver aircraft.**

Q: Will there be more Wilderness Rangers in the blowdown areas?

A: **There will be an increase.**

Q: Was damage done to archeological sites in the wilderness?

A: **Tree root balls have exposed some artifacts. We have sent in survey crews to identify problem areas and to cut downed trees in order to tip root balls back into holes.**

Q: Will the Forest Service discourage campers from entering full blowdown areas and dead-end lakes?

A: **We have no specific plans to do this unless there are extreme weather conditions.**

USFS Incident Team Member - Ely

Q: Are you satisfied with progress made on fuel reduction on the Gunflint Corridor?

A: **The salvage operations have gone well. Prescribed burning– not so well, due to wet conditions. Staged brush piles along the Corridor were burned.**

Forest Service Storm Center, Ely, MN - July 1999   **C50**

USFS

Forest Facts:
The Superior National Forest

• The Superior National Forest spans 150 miles along the U.S. - Canadian border it contains approximately 3 million acres.

• Over 445,000 acres (695 square miles) of the Forest is water.

• There are 27 campgrounds on the Superior, with over 500 campsites and more than 250 primitive backcountry sites. It also contains over 2,000 miles of mountain bike trails.

• Quetico Provincial Park is comprised of 1.2 million acres.

The Boundary Waters Canoe Area Wilderness (BWCAW)

• The BWCAW has approximately 1500 miles of canoe routes, 2300 designated campsites and over 2000 lakes and streams.

• The BWCAW contains:
1.1 million acres
180 miles of portages
1200 miles of canoe routes
245 miles of hiking trails

• BWCAW Visitor statistics:
200,000+ campers per year
1,600,000 visitor days per year
2,000 - 3,000 campers on any given summer day
Up to 286 new group permits issued daily

US Senator Paul Wellstone, Jim Sanders and Jo Barnier   **C49**

Cook County News-Herald

Barb Soderberg saw the BWCA destruction from the air. She said the straight-line winds – clocked at 80 mph – cut a swath through the heavily wooded area up to 12 miles wide by 30 miles long.

"It's absolutely leveled. Trees are all broken off and uprooted," said Soderberg, wilderness program manager for the Superior National Forest. "At least from the air it looks like a prairie with trees laying down on top of it all facing the same way."

An Interview
With USFS Gunflint District Ranger Jo Barnier
Dec. 1, 1999

Q: Would you have wanted the Wilderness Rangers to be in the BWCA to help campers during the storm?

A: No, for their own safety. I'm not sure that they would have been in the right locations even if they had been there.

Q: Are you happy with the progress being made on fire protection?

A: Yes, I am satisfied with the timber sales. We have sold 1500 of 3000 acres targeted and are still selling. We have until December 24.

Some prescribed burning was approved in 1997 and should be taken care of in 2000.

DNR sales were complete in September. Superior National Forest sales were complete in October.

Additional mechanical treatment and prescribed burns could begin in the summer of 2000 subject to approval of our Environmental Impact Statement (EIS) now being prepared.

Q: Will the Forest Service be closing campsites due to no shade, no pack-hanging trees?

A: We are considering some closings but not all of those that are in that condition.

USFS wind damaged canoes

Jim Cordes

A: We will completely inform campers so that they can make informed decisions. Hiking trails will remain closed until completely cleared.

Q: Will you station fire fighting tanker aircraft closer to the Superior National Forest?

A: We are considering prepositioning tankers and/or water dropping helicopters or water scoopers such as the CL215.

Q: Will the Forest Service modify the wilderness to help prevent major forest fires?

A: One tool for management is ignited prescribed fire covered in the Fuels Risk Assessment. If approval is given, 2001 is the earliest that BWCAW treatment can begin.

Q: What blowdown did Canada experience?

A: Canada had severe blowdown on 150,000 acres, starting at the border and ending near Thunder Bay. Timber sales started very soon after the storm.

Q: Will there be reduced camper quotas for 2000?

A: No changes in 2000 - we will look at it again for 2001.

Q: Will you be discouraging campers from going into full blowdown areas?

A: We will be discouraging them early in the year, then possibly prohibit them later depending on fire conditions.

Q: Campstoves only?

A: We will approach 2000 like a normal year. Fire restrictions will depend on weather.

Q: Has the Forest Service authorized additional pilots or aircraft?

A: Not as far as I know. We may contract with private firms or Canada.

Q: Will primitive management areas, hiking trails or dead-end lakes be off limits?

Q: Are you predicting less interest by the public in the BWCA for 2000?

A: Not at this time. We will know for sure after the permit lottery scheduled for January 15th.

Q: Will the Forest Service be faster in the future to suppress wildfires in the BW regardless of the cause?

A: Until fuel treatment is accomplished in the wilderness we will be jumping right on fires closer than 15 miles to the borders of the BW rather than the previous 4 or 5 miles. The decision to suppress BWCAW fires will be made by our ranger districts and Forest Dispatch in Grand Rapids, MN.

Q: How many campers were in the BW during the storm?

A: The maximum would be 500 overnight permits or about 2000 campers, plus people on day-use permits.

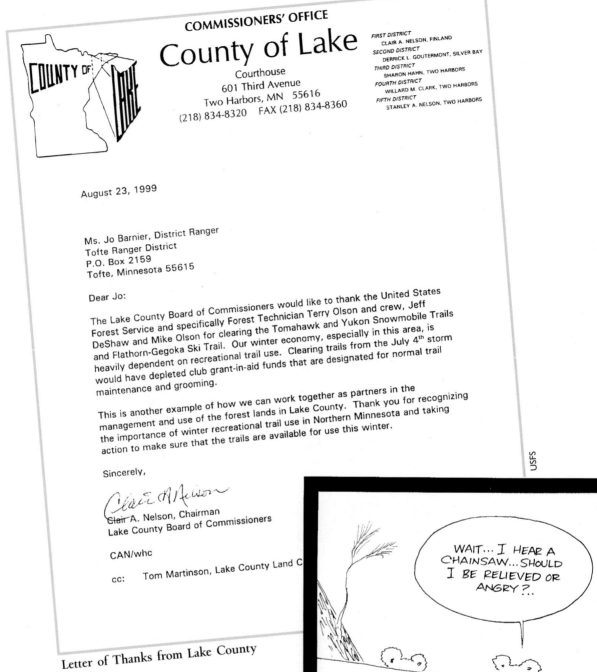

COMMISSIONERS' OFFICE

County of Lake

Courthouse
601 Third Avenue
Two Harbors, MN 55616
(218) 834-8320   FAX (218) 834-8360

FIRST DISTRICT
  CLAIR A. NELSON, FINLAND
SECOND DISTRICT
  DERRICK L. GOUTERMONT, SILVER BAY
THIRD DISTRICT
  SHARON HAHN, TWO HARBORS
FOURTH DISTRICT
  WILLARD M. CLARK, TWO HARBORS
FIFTH DISTRICT
  STANLEY A. NELSON, TWO HARBORS

August 23, 1999

Ms. Jo Barnier, District Ranger
Tofte Ranger District
P.O. Box 2159
Tofte, Minnesota 55615

Dear Jo:

The Lake County Board of Commissioners would like to thank the United States Forest Service and specifically Forest Technician Terry Olson and crew, Jeff DeShaw and Mike Olson for clearing the Tomahawk and Yukon Snowmobile Trails and Flathorn-Gegoka Ski Trail. Our winter economy, especially in this area, is heavily dependent on recreational trail use. Clearing trails from the July 4th storm would have depleted club grant-in-aid funds that are designated for normal trail maintenance and grooming.

This is another example of how we can work together as partners in the management and use of the forest lands in Lake County. Thank you for recognizing the importance of winter recreational trail use in Northern Minnesota and taking action to make sure that the trails are available for use this winter.

Sincerely,

Clair A. Nelson, Chairman
Lake County Board of Commissioners

CAN/whc

cc: Tom Martinson, Lake County Land C

Letter of Thanks from Lake County

USFS

The Damage is a "Natural Thing"

Terry Eggum, Assistant Ranger for Recreation and Wilderness for the Tofte/Gunflint Ranger Districts, explained his feeling about the damage to the wilderness.

"Personally there was the feeling that things were never going to be the same in those areas. Some of those areas were very beautiful and now look ragged, so there is a sense of loss. But I am used to the concept of wilderness and this is a natural thing, and should be accepted as such. That's part of the wilderness management philosophy."

© 1999 carson

Search and Rescue Operations

Sheriffs Dave Wirt, Steve Peterson, and Rick Wahlberg of Cook, Lake, and St. Louis Counties, took charge of the search and rescue operations in their respective areas.

Cleanup was a choice between machine and muscle - a difference between months or years. Blayne Hall, co-owner of Tom and Woods Outfitters at Moose Lake near Ely, urged the Forest Service to "use chainsaws – otherwise camping trips (to the BWCA) could be cut in half."

At least 164 persons were at work at one time for search and rescue, law enforcement, the DNR, Forest Service and other government agencies. Many chainsaw-qualified workers were recruited from the public.

Nancy Pius, an Ely area Wilderness Ranger who did search and rescue, recalls campers cheering as chainsaw crews "freed" them. Campers often wanted to help them but couldn't, for safety reasons. The biggest obstacle for campers trying to move through the blowdown wasn't the large tree trunks but the branches, which they subdued with axes and saws.

On about July 7 the Incident Command Team in Ely asked the National Interagency Coordination Center in Boise, Idaho to send professional firefighter personnel to help with the search and rescue operation. Promptly, three Hotshot crews were dispatched. These crews are highly trained professionals. Skilled with chainsaws, they were very effective in clearing portages and campsites of downed trees.

The Hotshots

The three Hotshot teams sent to work in the blowdown were: *the Bitterroot Team from the Bitterroot National Forest, stationed in Darby,

Clean up the mess

To the editor,

The whole mess left in the Northern Minnesota forests should not be left as it is. There need not be forest fires as a result of this storm. The area should be declared a disaster area and qualified for federal aid. Camps could be set up on the order of the Civilian Conservation Corps (CCC's) of the 1930's and early 40's. Portable saw mills, planers, and wood chippers could be set up at strategic places. The trees could be made into good lumber. The bad stuff could be made into wood shavings and wood chips. The brush stacked in medium sized piles to burn when the snow comes. If enough people could not be hired to man these camps, non-violent prison inmates could be brought in to do the job. It is easy to make a boom (flotilla) of logs in the lakes, if need be, and move them with a boat with a 15 to 25-horse motor. I feel I know what I am writing about because I owned a sawmill, planer, and lumber operation on an island in the area. I also operated a woodshaving and sawdust company in Miami, Florida. Also I worked in the CCC Camps in the Northern Minnesota forest.

Norman C. Horton, Sr.
St. Paul, MN

Cook County News Herald

Working our way out

Ken Hubert

Montana; *the Flathead Team from the Flathead National Forest, stationed in Hungry Horse, Montana; *the Sacramento Team.

The Sacramento crews had helped in the BW previously with fire suppression. Familiar with the area, the crews stayed in for 8 day stints and were resupplied with provisions by local outfitters via Beaver float planes. The work was hard, dangerous and stressful. Down trees under pressure could kill you if cut the wrong way. Fallen trees were sometimes cut from canoes, and often while standing in water.

Ellen Hawkins, a veteran Forest Service Wilderness Ranger, was impressed with the "Shots" chainsaw skill and work ethic.

Equipped by local outfitters, the Flathead and Bitterroot teams were just entering the wilderness when they were pulled out for fire suppression emergencies out west. The Shots and support personnel were thoroughly "bummed" by this sudden change. **C35&36**

The Sacramento Shots were flown into the wilderness and split into two-person crews, each led by a Wilderness Ranger or other Forest Service person. According to Ranger Cathy Quinn, at suppertime the guys would brag about who had the most dangerous saw cuts that day.

The staff at Wilderness Canoe Base told me that the most difficult portages to clear in their area were: (1)The 515 rod portage from Seagull Lake to Jap Lake. This portage was cleared by the Sacramento Hotshots on July 13, through rough terrain and 80% pure blowdown. (2)The 165 rod Seagull to Alpine Lake portage, running over ridge terrain and massive blowdown. It was a real challenge for the expert sawyers.

The search and rescue effort ended July 18, two weeks after the storm. The strong leadership provided by Sheriffs Wirt, Peterson and Wahlberg did not go unrecognized. The following is from a U.S. Forest Service news release:

County Sheriffs Dave Wirt, Steve Peterson and Rick Wahlberg of Cook, Lake and St. Louis counties, have been awarded the Forest Service Eastern Region Honor Award for their outstanding leadership during the search and rescue efforts following the July 4, 1999 wind and rain storm in northeastern Minnesota. They, or their representatives, will receive their awards from the Regional Forester on December 9 at a ceremony in Milwaukee.

"I am pleased that the county sheriffs are being recognized for their quick response, coordination and cooperation with other agencies during this emergency situation," said Forest Supervisor Jim Sanders. They were part of a major multi-agency search and rescue effort in and around the Superior National Forest. The efforts included a several-week, systematic search of all 2200 campsites, and over 400 miles of portage and trails, in the Boundary Waters Canoe Area Wilderness. Twenty medical evacuations were conducted without further injury, incident, or loss of life. In what has been described as "a miracle," no lives were lost as a result of this national disaster.

United States Department of Agriculture
Forest Service
Eastern Region

310 West Wisconsin Ave.
Suite 580
Milwaukee, WI 53203

Date: July 14, 1999

File Code: 2320
Route To:

Subject: Use of Motorized Equipment in the Boundary Waters Canoe Area Wilderness

To: Forest Supervisor, Superior National Forest

The windstorm that crossed northern Minnesota on July 4 was more powerful and extensive than any storm in recorded history. Two-thirds of the storm area lies within the Boundary Waters Canoe Area Wilderness (BWCAW). You have requested authority to use motorized equipment in the BWCAW for short term recovery efforts. I have reviewed the Minimum Requirements and Minimum Tools Analysis concerning this subject and personally visited the storm area. This letter documents my decision on your request.

I firmly believe that wilderness is a unique resource where man is a visitor, where one can observe the forces of nature. Not often do we have such a wonderful opportunity to observe a natural event of this magnitude. Some might argue that we should leave the affected area untouched and reduce public use to compensate for impassable portages and unusable campsites. However in this case we need to also consider the unique nature of the Boundary Waters. When the BWCAW was designated, it was already the object of high use by the public. The authorizing legislation (Public Law 95-495) and the Boundary Waters Plan provide for the continuation of this use. To maintain public use at the levels called for in the plan, I agree that the forest needs to reopen the trails, portages, and campsites. Otherwise the wilderness would suffer damage from overuse in other areas.

In consideration of the governing laws and my review, I hereby authorize you to use mechanized and motorized equipment to clear trails, portages and campsites *only where the use of non-motorized and non-mechanized equipment would be unsafe* (alternative 3 in the Minimum Tools Analysis, without the floatplanes). This authorization will terminate at the end of two operating seasons, no later than December 31, 2000.

My decision is consistent with Forest Service Manual 2326.1-5 b which provides for the use of motorized equipment to meet minimum needs for protection and administration of the area as wilderness when, "an essential activity is impossible to accomplish by nonmotorized means because of such factors as time or season limitations, safety, or other material restriction."

As you implement this decision, I ask that you keep safety in the forefront of your considerations and use the Job Hazard Analysis process in determining appropriate work technique and tools needed to recover storm damaged areas. Where non-mechanized and mechanized options are both viable, select the non-mechanized option. This approach will help to more fully meet the intent of wilderness.

/s/ *Robert T. Jacobs*
ROBERT T. JACOBS
Regional Forester

Caring for the Land and Serving People

Printed on Recycled Paper

USFS

Permitting motors in the wilderness

Portage clearing

USFS

BWCA Search and Rescue Status Meeting

The following are notes from a July 13 Forest Service meeting held to present staff with information on the status of search and rescue operations in the BWCAW.

NOTES 7/13

Search and rescue still underway; not all areas are covered. Looking at another 4-5 days.

• LNT (Leave No Trace) ethic

• Really need to stress using latrines and/or digging cat hole.

• Make sure the latrine hand-out is given to visitors and Wilderness Rangers to give to folks they encounter in BWCAW.

• Try to find designated campsite - if a site cannot be found, no campfires allowed.

• Large groups - 9 people - may have to split up and find a couple sites. (May need the stubs from permits to verify permits if checked by Ranger.)

SOME STATS:

• Portages: 70% of timber is down. 61% of portages checked.

79% passable.

• Total sites: 88% passable (passable meaning you can get through).

• Any gear left behind - if party is willing to go get gear that would be great - will have to get a permit.

• If the outfitters are willing to volunteer to go get gear that's between party leader and cooperators.

• No other crews planned to be brought in at the current time.

May not clear PMA's at all.

164 people on field. 233 total people on incident.

CLEAN UP:

Focusing on BWCAW.

• Areas outside BWCAW - specialists called in for water, soil, timber, etc.

• Timber Harvest in BWCAW? - Not going to happen.

Ground Crews Scour BWCA

The following article is reprinted from the July 19, 1999 issue of the Cook County News-Herald:

Crews make BWCAW headway

Ely Incident Command Post – Ground crews are working their way to each campsite and across every portage in the damaged sections of the Boundary Waters Canoe Area Wilderness after July 4th's windstorm. Search and rescue teams need to verify from the ground that no one was caught portaging during the storm. Despite the thorough aerial searching, tangles of blowdowns hindered a complete view of the portage routes.

Sawyer and swamper portage clearing **C57**

"We have over 160 individuals assigned to the wilderness search and rescue effort," said Mike Wurst, Operations Deputy for the Incident Command Team in charge of the effort." Of the 909 portages in the BWCAW, 546 have been checked by ground crews. Of those, 88% are currently passable." Wurst estimates that the effort may take an additional week before crews are able to get into all the damaged areas.

Bryce Berklund, crew member assigned to the effort said, "We cut one portage today that was 60 rods (990 feet) of pure blowdown. Others were barely touched by the storm." Berklund said that the crews are also trying to deal with the dramatic weather changes and packing extra supplies like gas and oil. 'Our chains on the saws go bad so fast - this is not normal cutting by any means. It is the hardest work I've done with a saw."

Aerial sketch mapping completed yesterday concluded that 478,000 acres were heavily impacted by the storm. Of that, 386,000 acres was forested land and 92,000 acres was primarily wet areas. Isolated pockets within that portion were untouched. Similarly, pockets in the relatively undisturbed portions of the wilderness area were heavily damaged. Nearly 48% of the total BWCAW area was affected by the storm.

(As time progressed, more accurate estimates were made of the blowdown; see the section on SNF wind damage estimates as of January 1, 2000.)

Sawyer in blowdown   **C58**

Brule to Juno portage

Sawyer in blowdown   **C53**

Search and Rescue crews

The following is from the *Ely Echo*:

"We're still in search and rescue mode," said Lake County Sheriff Steve Peterson. "Until all the portages are opened and the campsites have been checked we'll still be looking for people. We want to be 100 percent sure."

Peterson flew over the wilderness area the day after the storm with the Forest Service and said it was an amazing sight.

"I've never seen such a wide area of destruction in my life," he said. "You have to see it to believe it. It's amazing that no one was killed."

Hotshot crews were an important part of the search and rescue operation. The following, from the Hotshots agency, summarizes their work and training:

Interagency Hotshot Crews are professional wildland fire suppression teams specifically trained, organized and equipped for rapid response to wildfire situations anywhere in North America. We are a diverse team of career and temporary agency employees who work in the most difficult fire environments imaginable. Hotshots uphold a tradition of excellence and have solid reputations as diverse, multi-skilled professional firefighters.

The crews are employed by the U.S. Forest Service (52 crews), Bureau of Land Management (5 crews), National Park Service (2 crews), and various Native American Tribes (5 crews).

Hotshot Crews started in Southern California in the late '40s on the Cleveland and Angeles National Forests. the name was in reference to being in the hottest part of fires. Hotshot crews use pulaskis, chain saws and fire to create a "fuel break" between the fire and unburned fuel. Trees and brush are cut down and the ground is scraped to mineral soil to create a line the fire can not cross. Of course, this does not always work. Wind driven fires can cross almost any barrier including rivers and mountain ranges, so sometimes the crews just hold what they can and wait for the wind to die or the weather to change.

Forestry Hand Tool - Pulaski Tool
The Pulaski is an ideal tool for chopping, grubbing or trenching. The head is made from an alloy tool steel. The handle is a No. 1 hickory. Length is 36", weight of head 3 3/4 lbs. with overall weight 5 lbs.

Working on a Hotshot crew takes a lot of drive, initiative, and physical conditioning, as well as a sense of humor and ability to work with a diverse group of men and women who literally live with each other during the season. The crews travel throughout the west by truck, van or plane. To get to the more remote fire sites, crews either hike or are flown in by helicopter. Crew members pack all the water and supplies needed during a 12 hour (or longer) shift. Crew members sleep on the ground and are lucky to get a shower every couple of days.

All crews require that personnel be available 24 hours per day, 7 days a week during the fire season. Most crew members carry pagers or cell phones to stay in contact in case of a fire assignment. This means the summer is not theirs to enjoy; they do not have the time to view the local sites and do what most people do in the summer.

Hotshot crews are grouped according to geographic area:
Northern Rockies Hotshot Crews
Rocky Mountain Hotshot Crews
Pacific Northwest Hotshot Crews
Great Basin Hotshot Crews
California Hotshot Crews
Southwest Hotshot Crews
Southeast Hotshot Crews
Alaska Hotshot Crews
Training Crews

Sacramento Hotshots at Forest Service Station in Ely

Local experts Bert and Johnnie Hyde laid a bit of canoe orientation on the Sacramento Hotshots. "The Hotshots were up till about one in the morning," says Minnesota DNR's Ron Sanow, lead information officer for the incident. "They repacked their fire bags into the traditional green Duluth packs, and the first team of two hotshots and one canoe left in a floatplane about 11 a.m. Saturday."

Canoes, gear and Hotshots were loaded on Beaver floatplanes for their trip to the interior wilderness. "The sheriffs in three counties are at 99 percent certainty that we've rescued everybody who needs rescuing," said Sanow. "Until they are 100 percent sure, though, we'll keep on with the search and rescue operation."

From a Hotshot recruiting bulletin:

Interagency Hotshot Crews are Looking for Physically Fit Men and Women With Wildfire Suppression Experience Who Want to Fight Wildfire Throughout the United States and Canada.

Conveying tips to the Hotshots

Sacramento Hotshot Crews Help With Search & Rescue in Minnesota's Boundary Waters Canoe Area Wilderness

The Sacramento Interagency Hotshot Crew, who are based on the Lincoln National Forest in New Mexico, arrived on Friday, July 9 at the Incident Command Post in Ely, Minnesota. Having just come off the line on a fire in Colorado, they were requested through the National Interagency Coordination Center in Boise for assistance.

Information for Hotshot Applicants -
Hotshot crews are a national resource financed by federal resource agencies as primary wildfire suppression forces. Because of a Hotshot crew's organization, experience and training, it can perform a multitude of fire suppression tasks in addition to the construction of fire control lines. Burning operations, helicopter management, and the operation of pumps, engines and chainsaws are some of the specialized skills Hotshot crews perform.

These crews have earned an excellent reputation throughout the United States, Alaska and Canada as elite teams of professional wildland firefighters. A crew is organized into 1 Superintendent, 2 Assistants, 2 Module

Hotshot Fishing while waiting for aircraft   **C46**

USFS

Leaders for supervision and 20 crewmembers. Crews are dispatched to wildfires primarily in the West and on occasion to fires in the Eastern United States, Alaska and Canada. During fire assignments, the crews construct fireline and perform firing, holding and mop-up operations. Fire assignments are arduous, with a typical shift length in excess of 8 hours. The duration of an assignment may be several weeks before returning home. The crews average 90 days away from their home unit on assignment each summer. While away from home, crews live in fire camps, spike camps, and employ "coyotetactics" which involve eating and sleeping on the fireline with minimal provisions.

Worst of blowdown near Kekekabic Lake

USFS

Search and Rescue crews at Ely

USFS

Reference to "C" throughout the book indicates a color photo in mid-section.

Portage and Campsite Clearing

Climbing on Top of the Stacked Black Spruce 6-8 Ft. in the Air Chunkin in a Hole is Mighty Hairy Business
by Bruce Barrett

Jim, The following journal is from memory and therefore will contain minor errors in sequences. As I remember the July 4th weekend... the area north of Orr (I live @ Ash Lake) was a wet and stormy affair. I recall standing on the dock & looking south across the lake on the evening of Sun, July 4 and thinking "ole' Ma Nature is really putting on a show tonite". Nonstop cloud-to-cloud lightning w/ occasional cloud to ground arcs. This went on for over an hour. I was watching the cell that dropped upwards of 7 inches of rain on the Range. Not the best night for man-made fireworks when the real thing steals the show.

I was totally unaware of the "whoop-ass" that had occurred a mere 30 miles east of my home. Sunday had been blustery, w/ very scattered wind falls, but nothing exceptional. Certainly, nothing could prepare me for what I was to see for the next 2 weeks. Many times I was thankful that this wind event hadn't occurred in a populated area. A miracle yet, that lives weren't lost as it were.

Mon, 7/5 was a holiday & I went fishin' in the rain. When arriving home that eve, my wife relayed a message from Steve Jakala. Steve was in Ely as Operations Section Chief, the air evacuation was near completion & paddle crews were needed. Kurt Fogelberg (Lead Fire Tech) was contacted and a 6 person crew was notified to assemble & leave Voyageurs Nat'l. Park at 0700 on Tues. 7/6. We were in Ely by 0900. Had an assignment for the PM to assist in the clean-up @ the boat/canoe access on the Moose Lake chain out of Winton. I teamed w/ a 21 year old seasonal fire tech from NW MN going to school @ Crookston, named Derek Anderson. After cutting several vehicles/boat trailers out from under trees we returned to base in Ely & received another mission. After supper, it was off to Grand Marais. Arrived 2400 - Briefing & assign-

View of BWCA blowdown from Beaver Aircraft

USFS

ments @ 0700 - 7/6. I stayed partnered w/ my new young acquaintance and the others were sent out w/ Forest Service crews. I am an avid outdoorsman and because of experience was turned loose to work independently. Duane Cihlar got our radios cloned to forest frequencies, drew a circle on F-13 (Fisher map for N Gunflint/Bearskin) designating a general work area, gave directions to Devil's Track Beaver base & informed us outfitted grub/canoe/paddles/PFDs would be delivered for a 1000 flight. We all know how these things go so a 1500 departure was no surprise to me. Derek was in the "learning mode". The following is a brief description of what we saw, who we interacted with & my overall impressions on this experience:

1500 hrs. - 7/6/99 - Devil's Track Seaplane Base Dan Ross, whom I had worked w/ on fire in the past but hadn't seen in years, certainly had not changed. Retired MN CO, he still was a state pilot and about as much at home in a Beaver as most folks are in their easy chair. He lashed on the canoe, stowed our gear, gave the safety briefing and never once stopped telling stories. I put Derek in the co-pilot seat so he could see better. He hadn't ever been in an airplane before so again a first. The stories continued thru our headsets, to the much too quick drop point on the north central side on Winchell Lake. A group of 3 canoes (9 people) were on the lake and after Dan & the Beaver rumbled away leaving us & our gear in solitude, they paddled over and unleashed a barrage of questions. Most importantly, this group wondered if they could get out of Winchell thru Gaskin. I remember saying - "as near as I can tell - From the air - it looks like no one can go anywhere until these portages are cut". What an incredible scene it was looking out the Beaver window. Maybe like a nuclear blast, or the ray gun from some monstrous spaceship, I was reminded of eel grass in a swift flowing stream (all stems laying flat in the same direction). I noted the lead persons name; they paddled west & we never saw them again. We did see where they went - the portages were wasted. Set up camp - ate steaks w/ baked potato (only real food all trip) Checked a few sites near camp. Plan initially was to base out of Winchell, but realized it better to be mobile & cover more area than to backtrack (deadhead) all the time.

7/7 - Left camp set up and paddled to west end of Winchell - map showed 7 campsites (only found 6) The majority were in bad shape - no evidence of abandoned camps/gear. Called in progress & site conditions on a regular basis as required by the Forest Service. They needed to know if sites were usable & if parties needed assistance. Cleared to Omega - returned to camp/packed up & headed east. Checked remaining 5 sites - cleared portage to Gaskin. Checked 4 sites on SE shore - all totalled out.

- Cut Gaskin to Horseshoe - saw 2 groups on Gaskin - made contact w/ one - they were fine - tired of the rain - waiting to go out thru Winchell to Brule. We were in contact w/ a crew clearing portages north from Brule (Cathy Quinn) - informed group of their progress. Took down name of leader. Camped on SW site of Horseshoe.

7/8- Horseshoe Lake - another morning of drizzle - saw an outfitter paddling a recon route in order to ascertain conditions - had come from Poplar thru Caribou - gleaned some info from him on portage conditions - Checked to the south (4sites on Horseshoe) 1 site occupied - all OK - saw a nice bull moose in SE arm of Horseshoe (about a 48"er) - cut to Vista/checked 3 sites (remember Vista seemed odd in that we had to look àt a black wall of cedar root wads all along the north shore- the portage was a stream (as were many due to heavy rains during the storm) it felt that somehow Vista was elevated (Derek said " like an alpine lake - high in the mountains") We lost our map on the portage into Misqua/had to paddle back a ways & search / found under a slash pile (Last time Derek holds the Map) Paddled back to Horseshoe camp & spent the nite.

7/9- Paddled N up Horseshoe - checked 3 site (2 useable) - walked portage to Caribou/OK - Cut to Allen/1 site - Back into Gaskin thru Jump- Looked ~ remaining 5 sites on Gaskin- Cut to Henson/mosquitos are terrible but Derek refuses to use repellent /camped ~ 3rd site in narrows - nice camp- became base for several days- sand beach - good drainage in tent pads- southern exposure (hope is to dry our damp bedding/gear) Question is "do ya dear leave out the fart sack while we leave for work" Trend is - even if it's sunny/dry in morn, it will rain sometime soon so... No way do we chance it - hang @ camp long enough to dry gear/reorganize. Explore/check remain-

ing 3 sites on Henson & 2 on Otto (nice out of the way lake-noted old burn) While paddling into camp this eve - got a call from dispatch to check on a group in the Omega area-relatives were concerned - Grandfather/son/grandson (forget name/home area) Superior NF may have records- they had an intense experience

7/10- Left camp on Henson daylight -0500- cut into Omega & began search for ? party/4 sites on Omega -they were in the second one- Derek & I spoke w/ them only briefly from the canoe - Here's the story: They were camped on the western most campsite of Omega on the fateful fourth. The camp was set up & somehow none heard the wind coming. Being 1100 hr.-ish the father & his son were lounging near a 12" spruce (I checked out the site later) Granddad was over tinkering w/ something by the firegrate. The canoe was pulled up on the ledgerock in front of camp. Each took turns telling a portion of the story As it was told to us (difficult to believe) instantly a deafening roar & tremendous winds tipped over everything on the shallow soil ledge that held the camp-the root wad from the 12" spruce rose up off the ground the boy (12-13 yrs..) was picked up by the wind & carried several feet thru the air before his Dad could jump up and grasping a leg return him to earth. As the boy spoke his eyes got bigger & bigger His voice got louder/he relived the moment. The canoe ended up at the end of the bay. Dad found a life jacket, searched for a paddle & swam over to the canoe. The expectations were that it would be damaged beyond repair since it had been bounced around on trees/rocks before getting blown to the far shore. Not to be... w/ a few well placed kicks, the wrinkled old Grumman was sea worthy again. They were feeling very much alive and headed out this day thru Winchell/Wanihigan/Grassy/Mulligan/Lily/Brule and on time for their expected pickup. These folks were very fortunate to be on the SW shore of the island campsite, since the wind came from that direction & blew down every tree on the entire island. We searched for 15 minutes just to find the box toilet which had been crushed by a large birch tree. The only area w/out total ground debris coverage was the rock point @ the campsite. Whew - a trip to remember!

Derek & I went out Omega to Kiskadinna where we picked up additional outfitter food. The beaver brought it in. Derek was a BIG eater & we had been re-upped for some additional days. (upon our approval) We traveled the length of Kiskadinna, observing the 2 sites on the north shore/no standing trees here/heavy damage. Our mission this day (after making the contact on Omega) was to attempt to tie in w/ Cathy Quinn & her crew coming from the south out of Davis. A 305 rod really ripped up. Derek/I got a little over 100 rods (Quinn about the same)

& realized we'd not finish by dark.. . so back to base @ Henson. We figured on going back the next day to complete the work/were informed by Quinn that she was bringing in a hotshot crew for the remaining saw work. As I monitored the radio traffic, this plan didn't materialize. We were informed our pickup point had changed to Poplar Lake so planned to head north.

7/11- Broke Henson camp- Cleared portage into Pillsbury- paddled east to Allen portage. The worst of the ugly was this 95 rodder. Big black spruce - stacked ten feet high in places. Black spruce limbs are dead on the bottom of the bole & hard as bone. You can honestly see sparks fly off the chain. The canopy is so dense near the top ya can't see where your cuttin. Climbing on top of stacked spruce tops - 6-8 feet off the ground - chunkin' out a hole is mighty hairy business. Both sawyer and swamper gotta slow down & put safety first. Bumped back to Pillsbury/ Swallow & on to Meeds. Cleared all portages/ checked sites. As soon as we hit Meeds more activity was evident. People pad-

Ensign Lake narrows blowdown

USFS

dling/ camps occupied. Fortunate to get the camp we wanted on the eastern most island. A beauty site very well used. A breezy site to dry gear & keep the bugs down.

7/12 - Got another resupply of grub- getting sick of "Green Cuisine" The dried food keeps the furnace fueled w/out much flavor. My partner (& by now good friend) had a major hankerin' for a big juicy beef steak. (He's a farm boy - who knows how to work). I am in agreement a large piece of red meat (preferably wild) is at the top of

the list. We do two more days out of the Meeds camp - 1) checking portages/sites into Caribou. Many people in Caribou & the contacts made were all 100% positive. I expected some negative reaction to the power saw work we were doing, but quite the contrary held true. Many groups offered to help by carrying our gear (swamper's pack/saw gas/axe) All w/ no exceptions thanked us for the work we were doing and some wanted to throw down-fall chunks for us. Due to safety concerns - "No but Thanks" We felt good that the politics had not been brought into the bush.

2) We walked the 320 rod to Poplar & found it to have been done. Mike Schelmeski, whom I had worked with on the Sag Corridor fire had beat us to this portage. Good to scout it tho, since we planned on coming out that way. One other lake we got was Lizz between Caribou & Poplar.

Derek & I came out the NW end of Poplar Lake on 7/14- Went to Grand Marias and ate a big Steak and of course all the Sven & Oles' we could hold. All six went back to Voyageurs on the 1 5th I came back w/ 3 other on the 1 7th for another 6 days saw feast. Only a 2 day paddle out of Sawbill - the other 4 days on the South Lake Trail off the Gunflint north.

Jim, I wrote this as much for me as for you. I hope it is of some use. A documented positive memory for me. If (and God forbid) this area burns, I will be back.

Bruce Barrett

Cook County Sheriff Dave Wirt

The following letter from Sheriff David Wirt appeared in the July 26 issue of the *Cook County News-Herald*:

Wirt is Concerned
To the editor:

I am writing to express my concerns about the fuel loading that has occurred along the northern edge of the BWCAW as a result of the recent storm that passed through. My concerns obviously extend well into the future as those fuels dry out and pose a fire threat to the entire upper portion of the Gunflint Trail.

My best experience in this field comes from the 'Sag Corridor Fire' of 1995 where the smoldering campfire on Romance Lake sparked to life and turned into a major fire that triggered life threatening rescues and evacuations. That fire became a significant threat after traveling a mere

---

Cook County News-Herald, Grand Marais, Minn
July 12, 1999   Page 3 A

Wirt deals with storm

Dave Wirt was thinking about heading to the beach with about a dozen friends to celebrate the Fourth of July when he noticed a change in the weather. As Cook County Sheriff, Wirt is on guard even when he is off-duty.

Within an hour, he was at the law enforcement center in Grand Marais, all four lines and the 911 line ringing constantly. A terrible wind had toppled trees like bowling pins all across the top of Cook County, including the Gunflint Trail.

It was one of the busiest weekends of summer for cabin folk, resorters and backpack canoe campers. People were trapped and hurt. Most phones and all electricity were down. And the county Emergency Management Director, Nancy Koss, was recovering from surgery.

Where does a guy start?

"Our priorities boiled down to three: to clear roads, fly the forest and deal with the victims," Wirt said. "I kept trying to make it more complicated than that, but it really boiled down to these three things."

Wirt said that the biggest challenge he faced was the aerial

search. True, the Gunflint Trail and virtually every road leading to it fifteen miles above Grand Marais were blocked with fallen trees. "But here is where you turn to the highway department and tell them 'Deal with this' and go to the next job," Wirt said.

"We had some stumbling with the flyovers, however," Wirt said. Wirt said he flew the storm path in a State Patrol plane on July 4. "I got a feel for the damage then, but we didn't go low enough to see people," he said.

The "stumbling" sent the Sheriff all the way to Ely on Monday night where he met with US Forest Service Supervisor James Sanders, as well as others involved in the emergency efforts. Wirt said he went because he had not been able to get air search going. "I got back around 1:00 a.m. Tuesday and found out that the aerial search was already done before I went to Ely," Wirt said.

Despite the missed communications, Wirt said the fly-over Monday started the process. The Tuesday fly-over was more thorough. "We circled the lakes to see who might present themselves," Wirt said. "The next fly-over would be even pickier."

"We now want to see who may not be able to present themselves," Wirt said. "If we see a tent and canoe wrapped around a tree, for instance, that's pretty scary," he said.

Local float plane pilots Stan Pelto and Russ Smith were involved in those low-flying search efforts. In addition, by Wednesday there were three Civil Air Patrol planes and two helicopters based in Cook County dedicated to the search for victims.

But for Wirt, amidst all the crisis management of the biggest natural disaster to hit Cook County in recorded history, it was business as usual. There was the successful midnight-to-dawn rescue of a young man wrapped around a rock in the Temperance River, his heel stuck in his capsized canoe thwart. And the fireworks went off in Grand Marais as planned, despite the fog, rain or anything that might be happening over the ridgeline.

"People called that night asking me for yellow (police) ribbon for the fireworks," Wirt told the commissioners at a Wednesday meeting of the county board. "Nobody knew what was going on up the hill."

Cook County News-Herald

3/4 mile through a living forest. We both know what it ultimately took to contain and control that fire.

The situation now facing us is one where we have a 60 to 70 mile long swath of dead, dying and drying timber waiting for that one future day when all conditions will be right for ignition. According to some, and depending on the species in a particular area, that future day could yet happen this year or will happen sometime during the next decade.

What is extremely dangerous for us is that the prevailing winds during the fire season are from the west. Those winds will cross a 30 to 40 mile long swath of damaged or destroyed forest, and that forest itself nudges up against the end of the Gunflint Trail. The Gunflint Trail then continues to the east for another 30 to 40 miles and is itself in damaged and/or destroyed forest.

continued on next page

Cook County News-Herald, Grand Marais, Minn.
July 12, 1999   Page 9 B

Sheriff's log: the first three days

The following is the Sheriff's synopsis/log from the start of the July 4 windstorm until July 6.

July 4, 1999

13:07 Received (advisory) from Nat'l Weather Service advising of large storm system with strong winds for our area.

13:11 Began receiving calls that power is out/lines down & No phone service, Roads blocked county wide from falling trees.

13:23 Began getting calls for road washouts; county and Highway 61. County personnel and Minnesota Department of Transportation (MNDOT) notified.

Medical Injuries (6):

14:40 Hungry Jack area. Male in 40's with broken leg/chest injury. Ambulance transported to Duluth.

15:00 10- yr- old needed medical evacuation from Blankenberg landing at Seagull. Airlift arranged by Dr. Stover.

15:56 Greenwood Lk area-broken bone

16:14 Lake Polly-referred to Lake County

16:52 Brule Lake-person with head injury-transported by private vehicle to hospital

18:42 Medical Evacuation from Alpine Lake-transported to hospital in Ely

Attempts to Locate (ATL's): (5)

14:25 Eric Mink & Mark Anderson from Glen Lake-located @

16:11

14:31 Fifteen trapped at Eagle Mountain-cleared by S&R

15:44 People from Wilderness Canoe Base (Seagull Lk) Located-all okay 22:54

18:52 Two male hikers hiking on Borderland Trl from Clearwater Lk to Partridge Lk (Conservation Officer) looked for them, but couldn't get through trail.

23:42 People from McFarland Lake area are overdue in Getting back to Mpls.

Emergency Housing:

Bethlehem Church set up by Pastor Hogenson. Cook County Community Center set up by Arvis Thompson and Lois Johnson. Community Center closed at 00:55 as lack of people arriving.

July 5, 1999

02:23 Roads continue to be impassable. County Hwy Dept & MNDOT is clearing county roads and fixing culverts. Hwy 61 is closed to emergency traffic only. Gunflint Trail is closed to all but emergency traffic.

13:00 Overhead team in place for St Louis, Lake & Cook County.

17:10 Hwy 61 is open to all traffic with note that there are no shoulders. Gunflint Trail is open to property owners and people who have confirmed reservations at lodges.

Medical Injuries (1):

12:27 Two injured from party of 5 on the east end of Tuscarora Lake off of Owl Lake portage.

USFS notified & they arranged Medivac. Both treated & released from hospital.

ATL's (9):

8:57 Camp Menogyn has group of 6 out. 4 @ Round Lk area, 1 @ Gunflint Area, 1 @ Brule Lk area. Referred to USFS.

11:26 Jenny McCormack- Located and all okay. Roz McCormack notified that daughter is okay.

11:43 Rita Trumbauer phoned to request we locate Jean Trumbauer. Jean located and Rita notified all okay.

13:24 Dawn Jensen phoned to request info on daughter who was on Pine Lake. Officer checked for vehicle in the McFarland area.

18:06 ATL overdue camper on Gull Lake-located all okay

18:34 ATL overdue camper on Seagull Lake Rd-located, all Okay.

19:22 Overdue canoeists from Tuscarora. Contacted-all okay.

19:29 Boyscout troop went into Seagull, Alpine & Jasper Lk. Civil Air Patrol spotted group and signaled all okay.

20:11 Campers @ Gull pt. Located. All okay.

July 6, 1999

Road block was in place for Gunflint Trail. All property owners, people with confirmed reservations and BWCA permits are allowed to go up the Gunflint Trail. Lodges closed were: Borderland (Moose Horn), Gunflint Pines, Gunflint Lodge, Bearskin, Hungry Jack, Golden Eagle and Loon. Civil Air patrol planes flew over area to look for campers that may be stranded or injured.

Medical Injuries (zero):

No injuries today. We spoke with Pat (Angelos, Director of Nursing) at the Cook County North Shore Hospital who relayed that they have treated 26 trauma patients over the last 2 days due to the storm. Most had lacerations, broken bones and concussions. One has been air lifted to

Duluth and one transported to Duluth by ambulance. All others have been treated and released.

ATL's (4):

8:34 Wendy Whitney checking for relatives at Voyageur's Point. Residence checked. No one there.

8:35 Check for Peter Dupay on Greenwood Lk Rd. Officer Checked and all have left.

9:39 Welfare check for relative on Hungry Jack Rd. Spoke with party. All okay.

13:05 Welfare check for people on Voyageur's Point. Officer checked-people had already left.

Cook County News-Herald

"To the Editor"continued

If it was difficult to control the fire of 4 years ago, is it possible to defend the Gunflint Trail from what is looming to the west?

As the one who was elected to oversee the public safety concerns of the people of Cook County, I am concerned both about the ability of the U.S. Forest Service to contain any fire that would threaten the Gunflint Trail community and about my ability to evacuate the community if containment efforts fail....

And from the July 19 issue of the News-Herald:

As of Tuesday, July 13, a road block remained on the Gunflint Trail and only people with destinations were allowed to pass, because sightseers hampered efforts of utility and road crews.

Wirt, who has worked long days since the storm, said the entire operation went smoothly. Cooperating in the effort was the U.S. Forest Service, Minnesota DNR, the Civil Air Patrol, Cook County Search and Rescue, and the Minnesota State Patrol.

"Picture this," Wirt said. "A couple of state troopers actually got their uniforms dirty. They really helped out."

Sheriff Wirt was applauded by Gunflint Fire Chief Dan Baumann. "Wirt is the best sheriff in my memory. He works so well with people."

Office Of The
Cook County Board of Commissioners

COURT HOUSE • P.O. BOX 1150 • GRAND MARAIS, MINNESOTA 55604-1150 • (218) 387-3000 • FAX (218) 387-3043

MEMO

DATE: Tuesday, July 6, 1999, 12:30 p.m.

TO: The General Public

FROM: Walter Mianowski, Cook County Board of Commissioners;
           David Wirt, Cook County Sheriff

SUBJECT: GUNFLINT TRAIL STORM DAMAGE REPORT

Cook County is in the process of setting up a roadblock on the Gunflint Trail to regulate traffic going into that area. People will only be allowed to travel up the Trail if they are property owners, if they have confirmed reservations at lodges that are in operation, or if they have BWCAW permits for approved entry points. (Call the U.S. Forest Service at 218/365-7600 to find out if your entry point is open). Canoeists must display their BWCAW Permit to be allowed to proceed.

To the best of our knowledge, the following lodges are temporarily closed to the public at this time: Gunflint Pines, Gunflint Lodge, Golden Eagle Lodge, Bearskin Lodge, Hungry Jack Lodge, Loon Lake Lodge, and Moose Horn Resort. Nor'wester Lodge is open as they have their own generator.

There is no electrical power on the Gunflint Trail and there is no phone contact with the very end of the trail. All county roads have been opened up, though some can only accommodate single lane traffic at this time.

Visitors to the Gunflint Trail are advised to contact their destination <u>before</u> starting out to see if they are open for business.

The following interview with Sheriff Wirt was conducted on January 25, 2000.

Q: Where were you and how did you find out about the storm?

A: I was at home, expecting bad weather - it had an ominous look to it. I checked the radar on the Internet and saw the big red blob. I got a call from a man in Twig, a village in St. Louis County, saying there was a hell of a storm heading my way. Then we began getting calls from the Gunflint Trail.

Q: What was the purpose of the Gunflint roadblock?

A: We had to allow the electric co-op and others space to make repairs. Some resorts called saying they couldn't take people. The people we allowed through were property owners, and those with reservations. It benefited Trail businesses to let them through.

Q: Will the new fire warning system be available this summer for all Superior National Forest residents?

A: We are trying hard to get the warning system out to all residents. There is a remote possibility that receivers could be available at outfitters for the campers as well.

Salvaging the Blowdown Timber

Jim Cordes

Hedstrom Lumber Road Sign

The Hedstrom Lumber Company of Grand Marais is playing a key role in harvesting and processing the downed timber on 14,000 acres outside the wilderness in the Superior National Forest. If not cleared, this acreage would pose a severe fire threat to the area.

Established in 1914, the Hedstrom Mill employs 85 workers and produces 40 million board feet of lumber per year, ranking it as one of the largest sawmills in the state and the biggest non-government employer in Cook County. Another 45 people work at their other facility in Two Harbors. **C63**

Through the 1970's Hedstroms processed almost entirely old growth white pine, but as specialty markets developed, increased amounts of other pines, birch and aspen were utilized. They now buy logs from about 120 different loggers.

As is typical in the sawmill industry, Hedstroms has

Hedstrom Lumber

Hedstrom's Sawmill 1980's

suffered from fires. The mill burned to the ground in 1929 and 1981, and their retail lumber and hardware store in Grand Marais burned in 1997 - this fire was thought by Howard Hedstrom and others to be caused by arson.

The following is an interview with Hedstrom Lumber Company President Howard Hedstrom:

Q: How many loggers supply your mill?

A: We buy logs from about 120 different loggers.

Hedstrom Lumber

**Howard Hedstrom
President of Hedstrom Lumber**

Q: Where are the logs from?

A: 90% comes from Federal land, 2% from state, 3% from county.

Q: How is Canada dealing with the blowdown?

A: Canada had over 100,000 acres of blowdown. They began sales and salvaging within days.

Q: What is the quality of the lumber and how long will the downed trees be marketable?

A: The enemy of quality lumber is dry out, insect infestation and blue stain discoloration. Trees that break off are susceptible to this. Those that blow over but retain their root balls may live for a few years naturally, fending off these defects.

Blowdown aspen destined for paper or waferboard could be fine for 2 years. In jack pine, typically used as 2x material, strength is the determining factor; insects can degrade it. Red and white pine can decrease in value by 40 to 50% within just a few months, due to blue stain.

Birch holds its value well and is utilized locally by the Grand Portage sawmill and the Diamond Match Company. Balsam, a softer wood, gets wormy fast. Most species will retain some market value through June or July of 2001.

Q: Due to the blowdown, will there be fewer logs available to your mill after the salvaging? **C62**

A: There are 40 years worth of blowdown timber on the ground, compressed into 2 years. It will take 40 years of growth to replace it.

Q: How productive are loggers in the blowdown? **C19**

A: Logging the blowdown is dangerous and less productive. Mills buy poplar by weight, and blowdown poplar dries out fast, bringing less money. Hedstroms has changed its policy and pays now by the cord - we're possibly the only mill doing this.

Wackos wasting timber

Dear Editor:
The Fight dinner recently drew a lot of attention from the environmental extremists or preservationists. These people are evidently misinformed hypocrites.

When they attack the wise use movement they are attacking a common-sense approach to the future of our natural resources. Wise use means to conserve -- and not waste -- natural resources.

These wackos insist on wasting the timber that has blown down in the BWCA and risking burning and wasting a lot of Northern Minnesota. Also, these hypocrites live in houses built from wood, write on paper made from wood, and I am sure use toilet paper made from wood.

Wise use and scientific-based planning can provide Minnesota with beautiful forests for recreation and a strong forest products industry for now and the future.

Ernie Lund
Gheen, Minn.

Cook County News-Herald

John Gephart, a representative of the North Shore Wood Products Company of Two Harbors, said that the clock is ticking on log quality in the blowdown. "Ernest Logging of Finland, MN typically logs 10 acres per day and is logging 6 now in the blowdown."

Harry Fisher, of the same company, said "My crew can usually cover 75 to 80 acres in a week, but last week it was only 20 acres. To remove timber tossed like matchsticks, the work is very difficult and very dangerous."

Gephart continued, "Many of the logging companies would not be on the Gunflint now except that it is too wet in areas where they had planned to be. All private landowners with significant acres of blowdown have been contacted, but many want their down timber to remain down 'as nature intended it to be.'"

Blowdown White Pine at the Hedstrom Mill

Jim Cordes

State Land in the Blowdown

Within the BWCAW and Superior National Forest the State of Minnesota owns two sections or 1680 acres per township. This totals almost 100,000 acres in and around the wilderness. Of this, about one half suffered total blowdown. The DNR Trails and Waterways office in Grand Rapids reported $600,000 damage to state trails, public accesses, fishing piers and docks.

Utilization of Logs

At Hedstrom's, nothing is wasted. Even the sawdust and bark, which amounts to a sizeable portion of each log we cut, is utilized for heating fuel.

LUMBER	40.0
CHIPS	36.0
BARK	12.0
SAWDUST	12.0

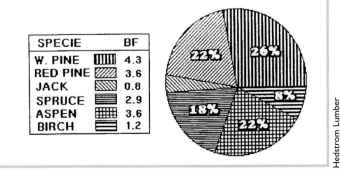

Lumber product chart

Mix of Species

Until the mid-70's, we were primarily known as a producer of white pine lumber. Since then, we have moved steadily into aspen and birch products with flexible production lines.

SPECIE	BF
W. PINE	4.3
RED PINE	3.6
JACK	0.8
SPRUCE	2.9
ASPEN	3.6
BIRCH	1.2

Hedstrom Lumber

According to Bob Maki, the area DNR Forestry Supervisor, blowdown timber was sold by September at auction for $1 to $5 per cord - mainly to cover administrative costs. Hedstrom Lumber Company bought one section (640 acres) of state blowdown jack pine near Magnetic Rock on the Gunflint Trail.

Since the sales, logging trucks have been rolling down the Gunflint and Highway 61, transporting saw logs to Hedstrom's mill near Grand Marais, and their facility at Two Harbors.

The State has been very active in the storm recovery program even though the storm damage occurred mostly on Federal land. Its operations included wilderness flights for search and rescue, clearing portage trails, and helping to organize and coordinate the overall effort.

According to Ernie Lund

"Before man was here, this country burned all the time. We're here now, and it's up to us to take care of this," said Ernie Lund, 62, a retired logger from Gheen. "The common-sense approach is to get in there this winter, go in on the ice and frozen ground, and salvage some of the record pine."

But doing that so-called salvage logging isn't realistic, and most loggers aren't calling for it, said Wayne Brandt of the Minnesota Timber Producers Association.

"Most would not be interested in doing that," Brandt said. "It's difficult. It's dangerous. And you get one-third to one-half of your normal production.

"In terms of the Boundary Waters, I think it's off the table," Brandt said. "It's officially a wilderness area. It's why we have wilderness areas. I don't see it happening at all."

Neither does Jim Sanders, supervisor of Superior National Forest.

"We've ruled that out because of the (1964) Wilderness Act," Sanders said. "It's not a tool we have available to us."

Ely Echo

Section 1

Editorial Comments

What happens to the wood?

In the aftermath of the Fourth of July storm, there are something like 300 billion board feet of timber lying flat on the forest floor or leaning against other trees in the Boundary Waters Canoe Area Wilderness. Many more of these "widow makers" will go down in the next windstorm. Predictions offered up so far by various forestry experts are to the effect that this wood will dry out and create more than 250,000 acres of highly flammable tinder waiting to explode in a massive forest fire.

Must it all burn? Must it all go airborne in a massive air pollution explosion? No one has offered any other options. While landowners, government foresters and loggers are scrambling to salvage as much wood as possible outside of the wilderness, there is the belief that since no logging is allowed in the wilderness, none of that interior timber can be salvaged.

This is puzzling to many of us who live on the edge of the BWCAW. We can understand the motive for keeping the timber stands in the canoe country intact for scenic reasons. But it is not easy to understand why timber blown down in a storm must be allowed to turn into a fire hazard.

Certainly much of the wood could never be harvested. Much of it is in remote areas which could not be reached. And the huge tangle of tree trunks in some areas inhibits use of trucks and other machinery needed for a harvest.

However, it would seem that a lot of the wood on the perimeter of the BWCAW could be readily reached, cut up and trucked out. Some areas could be reached overland immediately and others could be harvested over winter roads. It could be planned so impact to the wilderness resource itself would be minimal. Indeed, it could be of benefit. Where downed trees are harvested an intensive planting program could be initiated and the cutover area restored to white and Norway pine, similar to what the wilderness was at the turn of the century.

As it now stands, the heart of the BWCAW is virtually certain to dry out and burn, followed by a regrowth of popple, birch and balsam brush. To pay for the replanting and restoring of the accessible parts of the wind-torn area to its original pine status, money from the salvage harvests might be so earmarked.

We realize this is probably too simple and certainly not politically correct. We understand the "don't touch it... let nature take its course" theory. We don't necessarily agree with all this any more than we think somebody smashed in a car wreck should be left lying on the street.

It is doubtful that anyone in the Forest Service would be so rash as to risk the wrath of self-appointed environmental watchdogs by publicly announcing that maybe some of that storm-damaged BWCAW wood should be used to build houses, make furniture or create paper.

Indeed, the word "environment" takes on a new meaning here. Is it more environmentally sound to make use of storm-wrecked trees or is it more environmental to let them dry up and create a massive forest fire? If we get the kind of fire the foresters are predicting, it may not be possible to contain it within the blowdown area. Let's say we have a stout southwest wind like we had when the Tower fire took off a few years back. What is to stop the fire from taking out Atikokan, Ontario, or perhaps even Dryden?

There are nearly 4 million cords of timber down in the BWCAW. Even if it was all popple (the cheapest wood around and figuring none of the more valuable pine factored in), the wood value at $30 per cord, computes out very conservatively at around $11 million dollars.

That is not exactly chicken feed and could conceivably pay for a lot of replanting.

Just an environmental thought.

Public Officials & Disaster Aid

In July, senators, congressmen, Governor Jesse Ventura and other public officials toured the storm damage.

On July 8, Senator Rod Grams visited Ely, calling on the mayor and the Forest Service to discuss and assess the damage.

July 11, Congressman Oberstar was impressed after flying the blowdown. He remarked that the area looked as if "Paul Bunyan went on a rampage with his axe." The congressman helped expedite FEMA action (Federal Emergency Management Agency).

July 12, Governor Ventura flew the BWCA blowdown area. He declared that the BWCA and 8 counties were in a state of emergency. In a lighter moment the governor commented, "If there are any golf course designers - if Arnold Palmer or any of the golf course designers want to come to the area - there's a few spots cleared out for them now. They could certainly put a gorgeous golf course up there if they wanted to."

The governor made many public statements encouraging the continuation of tourism in northeast Minnesota.

July 24, Senator Wellstone visited Bearskin Lodge and the Gunflint Trail. The senator expedited FEMA action and helped coordinate efforts to clear recreational trails in the Gunflint area.

July 30, a bus load of officials toured the Gunflint. Passengers included Forest Supervisor Jim Sanders, Hedstrom Lumber Company president Howard Hedstrom, Mike Furtman of the Izaak Walton League, DNR officials and others.

Congressman Oberstar and FEMA Director Leur at Bearskin Lodge

Ventura Declares 8 Counties Disaster Areas

BWCA Included In Declaration

ST. PAUL, Posted 6:50 p.m. July 9, 1999 — Minnesota Gov. Jesse Ventura on Friday declared a state of emergency in eight northeastern Minnesota counties and the Boundary Waters Canoe Area due to storm and flooding.

The eight counties are Aitkin, Cass, Clay, Cook, Crow Wing, Itasca, Lake and St. Louis.

Initial damage estimates by the Minnesota Department of Public Safety were at least $8.4 million.

Ventura will travel to northern Minnesota on Monday to view storm-devastated areas.

From our archives:
• July 7: Extent of BWCA Storm Damage Detailed
• July 6: Boundary Waters Area Residents Clean Up
• July 6: Rescue Effort Under Way In Boundary Waters

Courtesy of the Associated Press

Public officials at Bearskin Lodge

Repairing electric lines

Arrowhead Electric

Broken power pole

Arrowhead Electric

Disaster declared in eight counties

President's decision provides money for July storm damage

By Chris Hamilton and Tom Wilkowske
News-Tribune staff writers

President Clinton on Wednesday declared eight storm-damaged northern Minnesota counties disaster areas.

The action frees up millions of federal emergency dollars to repair public property and fund low-interest loans in three of those counties for uninsured homeowners and businesses affected by the Independence Day weekend storms.

"That should come as a great relief for everyone who has been affected, from the Nett Lake Indian Reservation to the Gunflint Trail to the Iron Range," said U.S. Rep. Jim Oberstar, D-Chisholm.

The president's declaration comes at the request of Gov.

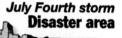

July Fourth storm Disaster area

Aitkin, Cass, Clay, Cook, Hubbard, Itasca, Lake and St. Louis counties

News-Tribune Graphics

Jesse Ventura and the Federal Emergency Management Agency, whose agents inspected damage caused by high winds, heavy rain and flash flooding in Aitkin, Cass, Cook, Clay, Hubbard, Itasca, Lake and St. Louis counties.

Duluth News-Tribune

Disaster Aid

The following article appeared in the July 12 issue of the Cook County News-Herald:

Cook County Board of Commissioners Declares State of Emergency

The county commissioners held a special meeting Wednesday, July 7 and declared a state of emergency for Cook county in the aftermath of the July 4 storm. "Now we can go to work," said board chairperson Walt Mianowski after the unanimous vote of the five commissioners.

Present at the 3:00 p.m. meeting was Judy Rue from the Minnesota Department of Emergency Management. Rue said that the declaration was a first step in getting federal dollars to those suffering storm losses. The second step is getting a rough estimate of damages, both public and private. Next, Governor Jesse Ventura asks the President for disaster aid.

One estimate was ready at the special meeting. Emergency Management Director Nancy Koss...told the commissioners that the county highway department alone was up to $24,000 in overtime expense for the three days of storm work so far. "And this is only the beginning," Koss said.

Rue told the commissioners that wind events are historically covered by insurance. Federal aid kicks in only where insurance falls short. Moreover, disaster aid is not available for vacation homes. Business losses will have to be assuaged by low-interest loans.

As for the monumental search and rescue expenses involved with locating people who might be trapped, injured or both within the boundary Waters, Rue said those costs are eligible for federal disaster aid. Repairs to roads, bridges and public buildings and facilities are as well.

The power cooperatives already estimate about $5 million in damages from the storm. Arrowhead Electric Cooperative was projecting over 232 county power poles were down or badly damaged. In a normal year, only 2 or 3 poles need to be replaced. "We need about six million in damages before we feel comfortable asking for disaster help," Rue said.

County land commissioner Ted Mershon said that most structural damage is limited. "The major costs involve cleanup of trees and restoring utilities."

1999 CARSON

If the federal government does agree to help with disaster relief, it would be just 75 percent of the total disaster cost. Rue said the state would kick in 15 percent and county 10 percent.

The county isn't the only one looking for help with storm costs. Gunflint Ranger Jo Barnier said she will be asking for additional funding as well. "We are spending money we don't have," she told the county commissioners. The Forest Service estimates that approximately 20 percent of the Boundary Waters Canoe Area Wilderness within Cook County was scarred by the storm.

Reference to "C" throughout the book indicates a color photo in mid-section.

THE DAMAGE

Arrowhead Electric Cooperative

Sketch of power lines down

On Sunday, July 4, the wind blew and essentially laid 80 to 100 miles of power line and nearly 250 poles on the ground along the Gunflint Trail from East Bearskin Lake to the end of the Trail, shutting off power to 600 customers. Calls started coming in that afternoon. The first Arrowhead worker on the site radioed in, "We aren't going to get anything done today."

Broken power pole near Gunflint Trail

The damage was awesome; the Co-op, accustomed to replacing 2 to 7 poles per year, was faced suddenly with replacement of hundreds over the worst terrain imaginable. Crews from around the state called to offer assistance and by Tuesday morning July 6, 60 workers had arrived to assist Arrowhead crews.

The logistics for this small electric co-op were daunting: acquiring material and staging it, staffing, payroll, meals, transporting people around, lodging and more.

Arrowhead linemen, helped by 70 to 80 personnel from throughout the state, worked 14 to 16 hour days restoring power. Arrowhead CEO Brad Janorschke remembers one outside crew operating an auger truck, wondering why the auger didn't go anywhere. They were from farm country, unfamiliar with bedrock.

Electrical contractors truck – Gunflint Trail

Jeanne Muntean, Arrowhead Operations Coordinator, reported that "In my view, this storm has given us many heroes - probably most of all the linemen from Arrowhead, whose lives have been put on hold for the better part of 3 weeks. They have not seen their families except to drop into bed at night and wake again at first light to do it again."

Jeanne continued, "To give you an idea of the enormity of the task - some of the poles had to be carried in by hand to be reset where the older ones stood. On one cliff the crews had to use a pulley to get the pole on top, then raise it by hand. A 40 foot, 1060 lb. pole doesn't raise easily."

Another group carrying in poles floated them across the Seagull River. According to sources the sweating, dirty crew took off their clothes to cool off in a nearby isolated bay. Their break was cut short when two lady canoeists paddled in, sending the crew "running for cover." Linemen claimed that the wind followed the roads. Some of the worst areas hit were Borderland Lodge, Golden Eagle

Local churches have been pitching in by feeding electric line workers.

Line workers aided by locals

The trucks in the parking lot of the Evangelical Free Church in Grand Marais came from all over the region. Just days after the July 4 blowdown that knocked power out all over the Arrowhead, linemen were fed and cared for during their off duty hours by many local churches and volunteers. The meal at the Free Church on July 15 was baked ham, lots of potatoes, breads and salads and countless plates of cakes and goodies.

Handing out laundry bags at the exit was Bobby Bockovich. "Mark these with your name and fill them with laundry then hand them in at breakfast," she said to each lineman as he filed out the door into the night. "Remember to put your name on the bag!" she laughed.

Bockovich would spend the next day washing, drying and sorting the clothes to give back to the men at dinner on the 16th.

The hospitality for the workers was provided by the Senior Center, Trail Center, St. Johns Catholic Church, Bethlehem Lutheran Church and other local churches. Steaks and beer were promised for Saturday night dinner.

And, yes, clean clothes were part of the bargain.

Rhonda Silence, Bockovich's daughter and spokesperson for Arrowhead Electric Cooperative, said that Trail Center was the staging area for all operations relating to the storm relief. An estimated 232 power poles were downed or damaged in the storm. Power was restored to a number of lodges and resorts on the main line on the Gunflint Trail by July 15, with other resorts on branch lines coming up last week.

Lodge, Gunflint Lodge, Tuscarora Lodge, Clearwater Road, Voyageur's Point on Poplar Lake and Hungry Jack Road.

According to Sarah and Anna, owners of at Trail Center, well-meaning summer people wanting power got in the way of Arrowhead management and crews. This could have "delayed the whole project (of restoring power) many days."

On occasion locals had close calls or caused problems by rolling up live wire and leaning it against trees, propping up sagging wires with aluminum roofing and connecting generators to house circuits, causing back-feeding into the Arrowhead lines. Some electrical workers were shocked. Overall, thankfully, there were no major injuries.

Repair crews reached Clearwater Road on the 3rd day after the storm, Tuscarora and Gunflint on the 7th. The entire main line was repaired by the 18th day. It took 4 weeks to completely restore power to the entire system. The last outside crew was sent home on October 21.

Upper Lakes Foods of Cloquet helped out by donating refrigerator trucks to several locations.

The total storm costs to Arrowhead Electric were about $2,000.000. FEMA paid 65%; the Co-op members will pay the rest.

Cook County News-Herald - July 19, 1999

Arrowhead Electric Coop

Sign of appreciation along the Gunflint

Thanks to the people who helped AECI keep going during the July 4 Gunflint Trail outage!
Our "heroes" are:

The crews who left their homes & families to help us:

ArborTec	Duluth	**MJ Electric**	Iron Mountain, MI
Connexus Energy	Anoka	**Stearns Electric**	St Cloud
East Central Electric	Braham	**Utilitrax**	Ramsey
Great River Energy	Elk River		

Trail Center

For making approximately 1,560 sandwiches! And for allowing AECI to invade Trail Center and use it as a staging area from Day 1. We couldn't have gotten the power on without their generous support and hospitality!

Gunflint Lodge

For providing breakfast, dinner, and housing for the entire crew for a week, knocking hours off driving time & helping get the power on sooner for everyone!

Johnson's Big Dollar

For donating bread, meat, cookies, Gatorade, and perhaps most important of all - water to our hard-working crews and other emergency agencies

Friends & family members who helped out in anyway they could:

Bobbie Bockovich	Office help
	Lunch deliveries
Dick Bockovich	Lunch deliveries
Jesse Cress	Meter loop construction
Karen Cress	Supply run
Darla Friest	Office help
Sara Koeneke	Office help
Clayton Koss	Refreshments
Ben & Mary Petz	Lunch deliveries
Gideon Silence	Supply delivery

The motels & resorts who juggled guests to make room for our visiting crews:

AspenLodge	Joseph Farreras
Best Western	Brad Jacobson
Hungry Jack Lodge	Jerry Parsons
Tomteboda	David Parsons
Cascade Resort	Gene Glader

Mike Lande & Chuck Soderholm
for providing aerial views
of the damage

Cobblestone Realty
Lunch Donations

The local churches who provided a dinner for over 50 hungry workers
Bethlehem Lutheran Church
Evangelical Free Church
First Baptist Church
St John's Catholic Church

Como - Eagle Mountain
Generator assistance & loan
of grills for crew lunches

Lois Johnson & the army of cookie bakers who provided treats for the crews!

Mike's Holiday
Donated totes for transporting food & ice

Nor'Wester Lodge
For Kate's pies!

In addition, a special **thank you** to all AECI members affected by the storm who were patient and understanding while crews worked to restore their electric service. If we missed anyone, we apologize - there were many, many silent contributors of food, beverages, and assistance.

Thanks to everyone!

Arrowhead Electric Cooperative, Inc.
P.O. Box 39, Lutsen MN. 55612-0039
(218) 663-7239 or (800) 864-3744

Ecological Effect of the Blowdown

What changes to the ecology of the wilderness can we expect from the windstorm? Bryan Bedrosian, an avid BWCA camper and a student at the University of Wisconsin - Stevens Point majoring in biology and ecology, summarizes the future for us.

As society takes its environment awareness into the next millennium, the need to understand nature and the way it changes keeps increasing. Though science has advanced exponentially in its knowledge of both the natural world and the interactions among its wild inhabitants, there is still much more to be learned. When a major natural catastrophe such as a blowdown occurs, speculations of species responses and knowledge of previous like incidents are best called upon to assess what the ecological effects may be and what, if anything, needs to be done to help maintain a viable environment.

Fortunately, there are few such events, like the blowdown, of this scale known in North America that had such an impact on the environment. With the exception of the glaciers and humans, Mount St. Helens and Yellowstone fire are the most comparable events. A storm with the fury as a derecho has an unfathomable effect on the ecosystem.

But when trying to ascertain the answers to questions such as what was the damage and when will the system recuperate, the terms "normality" and "damage" have to be taken into consideration. Ecosystems, such as the Boundary Waters, are constantly changing. Species interactions vary as well as many factors that influence all species, such as weather, chemical interactions, and resources available to them. The communities that were "not affected" by the windstorm indeed were affected just as much. Standing tree species are speculated to experience much greater pressure to provide resources such as cover and food for a greater number of animals because of all the fallen trees. And the animals who had previously lived in the areas that are now mostly comprised of snapped trees have to decide whether to remain in those areas or move into a non-blowdown area where they in turn might be competing with other species. By no means is an ecosystem, no matter where it is, an entity to be viewed as non-changing.

So when faced with the questions of normality and damage to an ecosystem, one has to take into account that communities are always changing. Communities are ever evolving entities, so "normal" is not an option. What many might refer to as environmental damage, is in reality a normal part of that evolution and survival of any ecosystem.

As stated earlier, only speculations about the effects of the windthrow can be made about the future of the Boundary Waters Area. This chapter will address these speculations with the aid of previous research that has been done on windthrow and like events, and interviews with experts in the field of ecology and forest management. Little is known of the ecological consequences of blowdowns, and further research in this area needs to be executed to better understand the effects of such storms (Webb, 1989).

Most likely, there are vast amounts of species affected by the blowdown. The trees are the most obvious and is the first thing most people associate the storm with because it is the first thing that can be readily seen. Other topics of discussion will include the mammals and the birds in the area.

In many stands where the blowdown had occurred, there was a large portion of mature canopy blowdown, some of which dates back as early as 1801 (Heinselman, 1996). Regeneration in these areas could happen in a variety of ways, depending on which species were present in the area and how much of the understory remains standing. A few of the possibilities of how succession may occur are as follows: (personal interview with Dr. James Cook, professor of forestry, UW-SP)

1. If the storm had downed 100% of the trees standing, the prospect of aspen and birch to thrive is great. These trees can establish within fifteen years or so and flourish for five or six decades thereafter. The aspen can produce as many as thousands of trees from a complex, connected root system. Birch saplings can sprout from the stumps of the birch trees that were snapped during the storm. Seed dispersal is very efficient for both of these species as well. These shade-intolerant trees will take advantage of the open areas and dominate for years to come.

Following the birch and aspen are the slower growing coniferous and deciduous trees. After these trees become established, they will surpass the birch and aspen, choking them of their much needed light and nutrients, therefore reducing their numbers.

2. Jack pine is another major component to the BWCAW forest community. The ability for jack pine to regenerate partially hinges on the contingency of fire because, jack pine can have one of two cone types. The first is that of an open cone, much like the other coniferous trees. Such a cone can disperse seed in the "normal" fashion at any favorable point in time. The other cone type is a closed cone, which only opens to disperse its seed when the heat from a fire opens it. Such an adaptation is advantageous in the presence of forest fires, but in the absence of a fire, it can be quite a setback for the further prosperity of the species. So, if areas of blowdown are

followed by fire in the near future, this tree species can thrive much more readily than most others. Jack pine, when germinated, is one of the species mentioned above that will follow aspen and birch, if this pine is in the vicinity.

3. In the areas where there was an extensive amount of mature canopy blown down, a significant number of the smaller or less developed trees are usually left standing. Understory trees that will usually still be standing include species such as the balsam fir and sugar maples that will now thrive because of the increase in sunlight and nutrients available to them. Generally, species left standing will have an increased chance to dominate the area than do the species that need to recolonize.

4. There is also the distinct possibility of the natural succession like that of the "unaffected" forests. In the absence of fire, jack pine is usually followed by white pine and black spruce. Both succeed jack pine naturally, but the process may be accelerated by the blowdown. If the mature canopy was comprised of mostly jack pine, it is likely that white pine and black spruce were present in the understory. When the windstorm released its fury on such an area, it is thought that most of the jack pines were downed, therefore increasing the available sunlight and nutrients for the white pines and black spruce. An increase in such vital elements will increase the potential for these trees.

5. The open areas caused by the storm also serves as a possible host for exotic species such as purple loose strife. These non-native plants are found in Voyageurs National Park and can take advantage of such disturbances. The dispersal of this plant is known to be highly effective, traveling many miles before germination. Purple loosestrife usually will invade lower, wet ground which makes much of the affected forest not be threatened by such an invasion, because it occurs on higher ground. But for the marsh areas or the lower, moist areas around the lakes, danger of this invasive plant is a possibility.

MAMMALS

The less seen and more evasive mammalian inhabitants of the BWCAW have probably been affected just as much as the forests in which they reside. For an easier glance into the animal kingdom, the mammals will be broken into the following sections: small mammals (mice, voles, shrews, squirrels, weasels, ect.), ungulates (deer, moose), and the larger carnivores (wolves, bears, coyote).

Small Mammals

The small mammal population response to the blowdown has been previously documented after a tornado

Red Squirrel in blowdown   C69

Jim Brandenburg

ripped through the Boundary Waters in 1970. The findings show that almost three times as many small mammals were found in the blowdown areas (Powell and Brooks, 1980). Speculations as to why this occurred include an increase in juvenile percentage in these areas, or that soil contents and litter moisture became more preferable for some species. A study on the red-backed vole gave insight to the fact that even though there was an increase in the number of small mammals in the affected areas, there was a higher reproductive rate in the surrounding areas (Powell, 1972).

Other studies have shown an increase in small mammal populations in burned areas, an environmental change somewhat similar to that of a blowdown. This increase was not long lasting, usually being sustained for about seven years following the burn. Such an effect is thought to happen in the tornado areas as well.

Snowshoe hares are shown to suffer from environmental degradation such as fire. In studies performed on hare response to fire, the hares retracted into areas with dense, brushy cover (Keith and Surrendi, 1971). When extrapolated to blowdowns, this could mean there will be an increase in hare population in the blowdown areas because of the increased ground cover to provide them with more nest sights and better protection from predation.

Ungulates

Other mammals effected were the ungulates, specifically the moose and whitetailed deer. The possibility of moose population increase is greater than not. The amount of palatable forage available to the moose will increase for a number of years following the blowdown. Such an increase has been documented in northern Minnesota in

1974 following a forest fire (Peek, 1974). The increase in food caused an increase in immigration numbers therefore increasing total population.

The white-tailed deer of the BWCAW will undoubtedly be negatively affected. The deer population has never been very high, considering the Boundary Waters is near the north end of their range. The deer in the area usually lie on the fringes of the wolves territories, so as not to be readily hunted by their foremost predators. Because the home ranges of the wolves has been altered (to be discussed later), the deer are an easier target for predation. Also, the stress of such a disaster will play a vital role in the survival of an animal with such small numbers because they will no longer be able to distinguish wolf territories, therefore increasing the threat of predation.

Large Predators

While the Boundary Waters is home to one of the most viable wolf populations in the continental US (Heinselman, 1996), these predators surely exhibited a decline after the storm on July 4th. Wolves are very territorial animals, having distinct boundaries between packs. And with this blowdown came the destruction of some of these divisions, causing intraspecific competition, which most often leads to the death of many wolves.

Currently, black bears response to such catastrophes is very scarcely documented. It is known that a large portion of a bears diet consists of berries. And the most important berries lie in open areas, or low-density forests, which were probably minimally changed by the storm. A common speculation is that black bear numbers will remain relatively constant through the blowdown "recovery years".

Of the mammals found in the Boundary Waters, only the species listed here are thought to be noticeably affected. Though, that does not mean that any of the other species were not affected, it implies that more research in this area is needed to understand the storm's repercussions on the mammals.

BIRDS

The next component of the ecosystem to be explored is that of the species found in flight. Bird populations will undoubtedly experience fluctuations, due to the fact that nesting sites, food availability, and niches in general have been altered due to the downed trees. Currently, there are eighteen species of birds that permanently reside and breed in the BWCAW, 110 species that are warm-season-resident breeding birds, about 60 species that pass through, but do not breed in the Boundary

Waters (Heinselman, 1996). To date, there are no studies of the effects of large scale blowdowns on bird populations, but an insight to the effects can be achieved through a few of the studies done on bird response to burns and insect increases.

It is thought that a general increase in woodpecker population will follow the blowdown in response to the insect increase around the downed trees (personal interview with Dr. Alan Haney, professor of forestry, UW-SP). As scavengers beetles will thrive in under the bark of the dead trees, creating a plethora of food for these scavengous birds.

Another bird population that will see an increase is that of the warblers in the area due to the likelihood of spruce budworm increase. The warblers should experience greater nesting success due to this increase in food and immigration into such areas will help the population numbers to swell (Wiens, 1975). Black-billed cuckoo populations have also been documented to rise because of an increase in tent caterpillar numbers (Janssen, 1987). Recent literature suggests that all of these increases should only last a few years after the blowdown has occurred and that the bird population numbers will stabilize thereafter.

Species that are thought to decrease are such species as the winter wren, red-eyed vireo, solitary vireo, ovenbird, yellow-rumped warbler, boreal chickadee, red-breasted nuthatch, bay-breasted warbler, and blackburnian warbler. These species have been documented by Apfelbaum and Haney in 1981 to experience a decline in population numbers, with a few even becoming non-existent, in burned areas.

It is thought that the bird population in general will experience the most apparent fluctuation of all the animals. With the alteration of nesting sites and food availability, the birds have no choice but to respond to this habitat change. To get a further overview on what bird responses to burns are, The Boundary Waters Wilderness Ecosystem, by Miron Heinselman, provides an excellent, more detailed, but general overview.

Raptors

The following overview on the birds of prey (raptors) of the BWCAW is primarily based on speculations of what may have happened to the different species (interview with Dr. Robert Rosenfield, UW-SP), because there is essentially no data on affects of windthrow on populations of birds of prey. More pointedly, the status for virtually all of the forest raptors of the BWCAW is unknown because there are too few counts or estimates of population abundance to establish a basis to assess status. Considering the time of year when this storm occurred, the raptors of the BWCAW can be divided into two groups: those that had finished raising their young in tree nests or cavities, and birds that still had young in their nests.

Raptors that are usually done breeding and raising nestlings by early July include Northern goshawks, red-tailed hawks, bald eagles, ospreys, boreal owls, great gray owls, and great horned owls. By this time of year the young would have already grown to an age where they could leave the nest, or fledge. So, if the nest did blow down in the storm, it probably would not have affected the reproductive success of these birds.

On the other side of the spectrum are the hawks that may have had young still residing in the nests. The species include sharp-shinned hawks, Cooper's hawks, and broad-winged hawks. If these raptors had nests among the areas that were hardest hit by the storm; it is most likely that their nesting trees had fallen, along with their nests and their contents. These hawks may have had reduced reproductive success due to the loss of young due to windthrow. However, given that most raptor species in the BWCAW are relatively long lived, breed annually, and tend to nest at relatively lower densities (i.e. number of nesting pairs per unit area) compared to other birds, it is doubtful that any long-term population effects would result from this storm. These birds of prey should have a plentiful supply of small mammals and birds to feed upon as so much habitat still is present, so it is safe to say they will be back to breed again.

Another major facet of the blowdown areas is moisture content. Considering that all living things are mainly comprised mostly of water, this a topic that cannot be overlooked. It is thought that relative humidity at ground level will rise with the increase in ground cover due to the increase in vegetation at this level of the forest. All of the downed trees will trap the moisture close to the ground, therefore increasing the humidity. Possible repercussions of this include increases in certain species populations, like insects and amphibians.

Insects have a major affinity to high humidity areas because the ratio of exposed body area to internal water contents is high. When the environment around the insects is moist, they will lose less water to evaporation, which in turn increases their activity because they then don't have to conserve energy to save their water. As seen with mosquitoes around densely covered water pools and lakes, insect populations will undoubtedly thrive with the increase in moisture.

Amphibians follow along the same suit as the insects. With their high affinity for water and moisture, if these animals are found in the areas that were hit by the storm,

they should certainly increase in numbers. The increase in insect populations also provides them with a more than adequate food source.

Of all the responses listed here, every one of them is considered to be a short term effect, lasting only up to a decade or so. All forest communities have a way of returning to a balanced state between all of its inhabitants. Whenever a disturbance occurs nature will always compensate for its losses and gains. Any population increases or declines in animal populations will only happen for a few years following the blowdown. That is unless a fire sweeps through the area, which it almost certainly will, considering the mass amounts of dried trees on the ground acting as fuel. The only question is how will it start.

No matter what disturbance effects an ecosystem, there are always responses by the forest community Though all responses may not even be detectable through our current resources, forest response is always present. The derecho that swept through the BWCAW is no exception to this. Because responses to such an event of most species has been rarely documented, it is important that we try to understand the whole ecosystem as a community to properly assess what may happen in the future, so we can further understand the integrity of the Boundary Waters Area. Management practices can not be exercised until the response of the whole community is properly grasped. And we can not fathom the community of the Boundary Waters Area, or any ecosystem, until we realize and appreciate the "raw process" of forming and shaping communities through events like the blowdowns.

But do not be deluded. It is not just the responsibility of the foresters and scientific community to help document these changes to our natural areas, but it is the responsibility of everyone. Campers and visitors to this area can also get involved in gathering information on the responses of the ecosystem. Any "regular" citizen can talk with rangers in the area to see what help might be needed in helping this ecosystem cope with this environmental catastrophe. Information of any kind can be taken to research or ranger stations of the area. If we want to see the Boundary Waters remain in its natural and "virgin" state, then all of us must take any actions within our power to preserve it.

To obtain information on the general ecosystem and its inhabitants in the Boundary Waters, Heinselman's book, The Boundary Waters Wilderness Ecosystem, is highly recommended. This book outlines origins, general forest ecosystems, and various impacts of various disturbances. The Boundary Waters Canoe Area Wilderness is an invaluable area that we all must respect and aspire to understand to help maintain and appreciate the diversity and dynamics of this ecosystem.

Reintroduction of Woodland Caribou to the BWCAW

In an ongoing effort to re-establish all the wildlife once common to the BWCA, a coordinated effort is underway to reintroduce woodland caribou to the area.

Native to Minnesota and the BWCAW woodland, caribou began to decline in the mid-19th century due to timber harvest, over hunting, and more recently, due to the presence of the meningeal worm. This worm is common in whitetail deer, and lethal to caribou.

Caribou were last seen in the Superior National Forest in the early 1940's. John Lyght, former Cook County Sheriff and longtime resident, saw his last caribou "heading north in 1942." Caribou hunting in Minnesota was prohibited beginning in 1904.

In 1988 the North Central Caribou Corporation (NCCC) was organized to explore the possibility of reintroducing the animal to northern Minnesota and southern Ontario, specifically in a 500 square mile area of the BWCAW and Quetico Park. The proposed area would be named the BWCR - the Boundary Waters Caribou Range.

The region around Little Saganaga Lake was chosen because it contains few whitetail deer which carry the meningeal worm. Also, with fewer deer come fewer wolves, which are an important caribou predator.

The proposed BWCR abounds in lakes and islands, affording these excellent swimmers safe haven from wolf and bear predation during the calving period.

The NCCC, comprised of Federal, State, Native American and private representatives, plans to release 20 mature caribou cows and 5 mature bulls over a three year period– no more than 4 - 6 animals in any given location.

Paul Burke with the U.S. fish and Wildlife Service in St. Paul claims that "The BWCA blowdown was at its worst in the proposed BWCR. The canopy was knocked down but this isn't necessarily detrimental to caribou. Trails for caribou are lakeshore; down trees won't block escape routes as may be the case with other animals. The downed trees definitely would provide more lichens, and Old Man's Beard moss– primary food for the animals. The only downside is the threat of fire, which would create an environment friendly to whitetails, the meningeal worm and more wolves."

Bears, another important predator, visit mostly areas containing campsites on lakeshores and islands, because they are conditioned to campers' food. Avoiding these campsite areas, the caribou would steer clear of areas frequented by campers and bears.

A release date for the caribou is undetermined at this time.

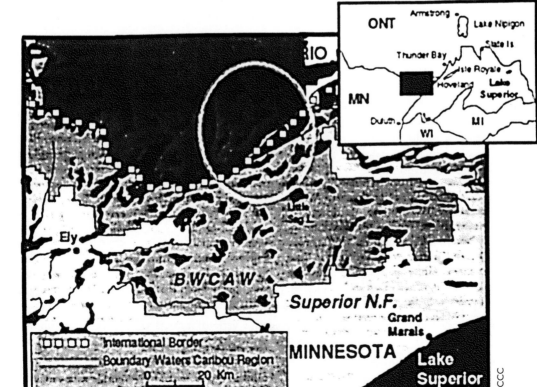

Map of Caribou release site

Wolves of the BWCAW

The presence of wolves is very important in our wilderness. The sight or sound of wolves is a highlight (or lowlight) of campers' trips. Wolf howls are one of the most moving and haunting sounds in nature, and aren't soon forgotten.

Prior to the 1970's, most people in Minnesota feared wolves. Great pains were taken to try to eradicate wolves from the state. With a bounty paid for each wolf killed, they were trapped, poisoned, shot by farmers and hunters, and blasted from airplanes to "improve deer habitat."

By the 1970's, just over 400 wolves survived in extreme northeast Minnesota, in an area constituting about 3% of their original range. Their survival in this area is attributed to special circumstances:

- Wilderness or near-wilderness National Forest land.
- A very small human population.
- Very little livestock; wolves posed less threat to property and were less likely to be hunted down as "vermin."
- Wolves from the healthy popula-

WOLVES LOOK BETTER DEAD

Control the timber wolf—menace to Alaskan big game

Tex Cobb, Alaskan sourdough

THE Northern caribou wolf rates a lot of superlatives. He is not only the largest, but also the smartest, orneriest, most vicious and bloodthirsty of his species. Further, he is the greatest single menace to the splendid big-game herds of Alaska, and probably the only predator native to the continent that habitually kills for the sheer lust of slaughter. Maybe it will help you get the full import of this if I tell you about something Larry Benson and I witnessed one winter during a hunt we made in the Watana Creek country, near the headwaters of the Big Susitna River.

We were scouting along the crest of a timber-line ridge, snowshoeing. Suddenly we heard the excited, high-pitched yelping of a running pack somewhere in the valley below us. Hoping to spot the animals, we went out on a point and got busy with our glasses. For a moment we saw nothing. There were only the hooded witch-like spruces, the ragged openings and the stark shed of the range, all a-quiver in the luminous blue haze of a snow mirage.

With dramatic suddenness, down at the foot of the slope, a band of about one hundred woodland caribou burst into view and started across a frozen pothole lake. They were fleeing desperately, a closely jammed mass of dun bodies pouring out on the wind-scoured ice, hoofs clattering, horns banging together, the fog of their breath rising on the frosty air.

Then we saw the wolves—fifteen of them—just beyond effective rifle range. They came out of a fold in the hills, floating like lean shadows through the blue glimmer of the mirage, and within a matter of seconds had closed in on the flank of the herd. The leader, a shaggy gray devil the size of a pony, began singling out stragglers, hamstringing them with swift efficiency.

One doomed animal dropped, pawing frantically at the ice, and then managed to lurch up on three legs, but had taken only two or three hobbling steps when another wolf pulled it down again. Just ahead of it a big white-maned bull went over in a spectacular somersault as one of the killers caught it by the throat

The gray caribou killer weighed 140 pounds

Field & Stream Magazine - Nov. 1944 - Wolf Hatred

tion in Ontario were able to migrate across the border, replacing wolves killed in northeast Minnesota.

Almost overnight, it seems that wolf hatred became wolf admiration– at least in the eyes of many. Bounties were discontinued in about 1970, and the Endangered Species Act was passed in 1973. As one of the first species listed, the timber wolf, Canis lupis, was given protection under the law.

Over a short period of time, a wolf hunter went from being rewarded and a hero, to a criminal who could be given a jail term and a $20,000 fine.

But the killing of wolves does continue. David Mech, a U.S. Fish and Wildlife wolf expert, estimates that up to 100 wolves are illegally killed each year – most during deer hunting season.

Mike Nelson, also with U.S. Fish and Wildlife, tracks collared wolves in the BWCA. He claims there is "no evidence of changes in wolf locations or activities since the blowdown."

"Moose, a major prey of the wolf, may benefit from the blowdown. The moose commonly fights rather than runs, using trees to protect its back while striking with its hooves. Whitetailed deer could be at a disadvantage; fleeing through the blowdown presents a problem."

The International Wolf Center in Ely is a showcase for wolves. Rich in wolf educational materials and exhibits, it opened in 1993. The Center has a resident captive wolf pack, experimental programs, field trips, and a sophisticated educational facility– and has been a howling success.

Layne Kennedy

Poachers shot three of the wolves biologist David Mech was tracking with radio collars. Mech says up to 100 wolves may be shot illegally each year.

No. *1*

WOLF BOUNTY

Claimant's Oath and Certificate of Town Clerk.

Claim of *Angus Johnson*

Town of *Grand Marais*

County of *Cook*

Minnesota.

Filed in the office of the Town Clerk of

the Town of *Grand Marais*

County of *Cook*

Minnesota, this *9th* day of

Feb , 19 *24*

Perry Nelson
Town Clerk.

State of Minnesota,

County of *Cook* } ss.

Town of Grand Marais

I, *Perry Nelson* , Town Clerk of the Town of *Grand Marais* in said County do hereby certify, that on the *9th* day of *Feb* , 19 *24* *Angus Johnson* of the Town of *Grand Marais* , in said County, exhibited to me the carcass of *1 full grown male* wolf , in the presence of *Frank Babiman* and *Henry Halorior* , two witnesses, residents of said Town, and then and there made oath that the said wolf *was* killed by him in the Town of *Grand Marais* in said County, on the *25th* day of *Jan* , 19 *24*, and that he did not spare the life of any wolf within his power to kill, which said oath is hereto attached. That the toes of both front feet of said wolf were then and there removed from said carcass in my presence and in the presence of said witnesses. And I further certify that from an examination of such carcass so exhibited to me, I did then and there find and determine that the same *was* the carcass of *said* wolf

IN TESTIMONY WHEREOF, I have hereunto set my hand this *9th* day of *Feb* , 19 *24*

Perry Nelson
Town Clerk of the Town of *Grand Mara*

Cook County, Minnesota.

The Potential for Fires in the Superior National Forest

Wildfires in the blowdown area are a major concern to everyone. The experts are sure fires will occur - the only questions are when, where and how big.

Over the past 20 years, lightning has started 57% of fires and man's carelessness the other 43%. A Forest Service employee said it well: "We are in and around a big dry brush pile and the Lord will be dropping matches on it." **C48**

The following is information gathered from the US Forest Service, MN DNR and other sources about the fire potential.

USFS

BWCA Fire

US Forest Service, November 4, 1999 - Fuels Risk Assessment of the Blowdown in the BWCAW and Adjacent Lands

Blowdown effects on fire growth

In contrast to pre-blowdown fires, blowdown fires spread much more rapidly in all directions and are more susceptible to wind change as a consequence of:

1. Increased wind exposure.

2. Faster spread in slash fuels vs. understory fuels.

3. Decreased fuel moisture due to lack of overstory shade.

Prior to the blowdown a variety of fuel types, vegetation types and canopy conditions existed which would have a marked effect on fire growth. These conditions have been largely eliminated by the flattening of the overstory, creating a slash-like fuel complex with little sheltering from overstory trees.

Wilderness fuel treatment location - types

Areas must be located which would be practical for treatment to be effective in creating disruption to fire travel:

1. Prescribed fires to create narrow strips 1/4 to 1/2 mile wide running in a north-south direction as fire breaks; these would disrupt fire coming from the west.

2. Fortify natural barriers such as small lakes and bogs as much as possible to expand their width to serve as an impediment to spot fires.

3. Treat islands to preclude spotting across lakes. The fire would then be forced to flank the lakes and treatment locations, slowing the fire to buy time for reinforcements or evacuations.

Extremely high winds probably would carry the fire off the landscape to the east, creating a large fire regardless of the treatment or suppression efforts. A change in weather would be required to control this event. Two inches of rain would end the fire and preclude the use of land forces.

The worst blowdown damage is a 4 to 12 mile wide area 30 miles long in a west-southwest to east-northeast direction generally paralleling the Canadian border.

Northern Minnesota has 2 fire seasons: May to June and July to October. Early July rains along with green-up generally precludes large fires.

Due to blowdown, lightning strikes will be more likely to cause fires, fire intensities will be higher than previously and will exceed the capabilities of hand crews. It is predicted that fire travel in the blowdown can be 10 to 20 times greater than in previous fuel. There will be a tendency toward plume dominated fires which have a more extreme fire behavior.

In fall 1999, the fuel load is 100+ tons per acre in the blowdown, 3 to 20 feet deep where the trees are stacked.

Full July leaf-out conditions exist, and (due to stacking) the leaves and needles can't be packed. Lost shading increases solar drying, decreases humidity and promotes wind induced drying.

Planning could prevent catastrophic fires that would injure people and property, and save seed stock available in the few remaining tall tree stands within the most seriously damaged area.

Frustrated, Dan Water's of Ely's Canadian Waters Outfitters remarked, "The Forest Service did an excellent job of search and rescue and opening portages. But with all that research and meetings on fire potential, they're saying now that the plan can't be implemented until late in 2000 or 2001 after the critical fire season has passed."

Gunflint District Ranger Jo Barnier commented in 1999, "During my last trip into the Boundary Waters to check the blowdown, I stopped by three recently used campsites. All three had fires or coals alive in the fire grates."

Safe Campfire Tips:

- Clear all flammable material away from your campfire location.
- Only build your fire in approved steel firegates.
- Don't build a fire on a windy day.
- Put your fire dead out before leaving it, add water, stir, add water, stir and feel with your hand until it is cool.

Fire Restrictions:

Fire restrictions may exist at various times of the year. Check with local authorities, outfitters, or forest Service information offices.

GITCHE GITCHE GUMME

© 2000 carson

The future of wilderness area fires

by Vicki Biggs

The blown down trees look like pick-up sticks in the aerial photographs plastered on front pages after the July 4 storm. The wilderness and thousands of acres of private property was a mess.

Power outages and fear of lost income obsessed most people in the first days and weeks. Then, the inconvenience and budgetary bite faded as a bigger menace began to take shape in the forests around the Gunflint Trail community.

Those trees look more like match sticks than a giants' toys. In fact, that is exactly what they are.

"There are 30 to 40 miles of wood piled up against the end of the Gunflint Trail," said Cook County Sheriff David Wirt last week. "With our prevailing (west) winds, this could be a problem."

Wirt knows what he is talking about. In 1995, he saw the "Sag Corridor Fire" burn furiously for days in a living forest. Wirt remembers well the hellish battle waged on land and from the air to contain that fire. Had the forest borne the fuel load it does today, Wirt wonders how much worse the outcome would have been.

The Sheriff wrote a letter on July 14 to US Forest Service District Ranger Jo Barnier, outlining his fears for the future based on the Sag Corridor Fire experience. (see box)

Wirt also talked to the News-Herald on July 19 prior to meeting with the US Forest Service and other agencies in Ely. Wirt went there to officially take back some of the authority he granted to the federal team called in to deal with the search and rescue efforts in the Cook County portion of the Boundary Waters Canoe Area Wilderness (BWCAW).

Wirt also wanted to discuss the points he made in his letter to Barnier-the potential for a wilderness wildfire that has no boundaries and how to avoid a conflagration in the near future.

"We first need to assess what the problem is or the potential remedies might be," Wirt told the News-Herald. The problem, fire, was the easy part. Of the three remedies, only one was realistic.

First, Wirt said the federal government might try to prevent the wood downed in the wilderness-now counted in the millions of trees-from burning. "That's impossible," Wirt said.

The second remedy, to remove all the trees, is so long a shot it is virtually impossible as well. Although on July 14, the US Forest Service authorized limited use of motorized and mechanized equipment to clean up storm damage on portages and campsites within the BWCAW, the fuel load of downed trees extends well beyond the skinny trails and postage stamp size camp clearings. Even if all prohibitions against motor use on every inch of the affected wilderness were lifted, time is running short or out. "No one is going to go in and do any logging," Wirt said. "Nor would it last long

Fire future   Continued

enough to do any logging.

The third remedy is possible, but politically dicey and more than a little scary. "We could create a defendable buffer so that whatever happens within the BW doesn't spill out onto the Gunflint Trail," Wirt said. "The ideal would be a one or two-mile buffer all around the Gunflint Trail."

In fact, before the July 4 storm, the US Forest Service scheduled a controlled burn to begin outside the wilderness and burn a bit over the boundary into the BWCAW. The forests were already compromised by standing dead spruce killed by budworm infestations. The potential for wilderness wildfire spillover onto private lands is not new. However, private landowners close to the boundaries have been understandably nervous about how controllable those controlled burns really are.

"It's a quandary," Wirt said, agreeing that the risk of a controlled burn is worthwhile but

its tenders is always there. "That community (on the Gunflint Trail) is threatened by fire and the only way to protect it is by fire."

The Sheriff, elected officials and even environmental supporters that have traditionally taken a hands off stance toward the wilderness appear to be facing the certainty of fire in the wilderness. A buffer burned around the wilderness would not prevent fire inside, but it would protect life and property outside. Plus, it would regenerate the conifers that depend on fire for reseeding.

Wirt clearly favors doing a burn buffer. "The fuels are going to exist until they burn off," he said.

Wirt also forwarded a copy of his letter to Barnier to Congressman Jim Oberstar, who planned to visit the Gunflint Trail community and meet with all interested parties at Gunflint Lodge on July 24. Senator Paul Wellstone also planned a visit to

Hedstrom's Lumber mill and visiting Bearskin Lodge.

The appearance of Wellstone and Oberstar, often at odds over management of the wilderness in recent years, could be attributed to the request from Governor Jesse Ventura for federal disaster aid that is expected but not yet announced at presstime. However, the fire danger inherent in the fuel buildup around the Gunflint Trail community is certain to be discussed.

Oberstar, the champion of the county officials and the business interests on the trail and Wellstone, the environmentalist friend, could marshal their constituents in support of Wirt's plea for a burn buffer around the edge of the wilderness

Forest Service Wilderness Fire Risk

The windstorm that tore through the Boundary Waters Canoe Area Wilderness on July 4, 1999 blew trees down over a vast area covering 350,000 acres. In some locations the majority of the trees were blown down, and in many areas there is nearly no evidence of the severe wind storm. The areas where moderate to heavy blowdown has occurred will be present for many years to come and will add an additional risk to wilderness users. Along with a new risk the wilderness users will have an opportunity to experience a new and different phase of the wilderness.

Fire Hazards:

From a fire standpoint, there will be a significant increase in the likelihood of large fires. These fires will burn more intensely, and will be more difficult to control. This is a result of the large areas of blowdown with a high volume of fuels now available to burn. This will result in:

1. Fires that can ignite and spread even one or two days after rain.

2. Fires that ignite can spread 3-4 times more quickly in blowdown areas.

3. Fires may easily jump across some lakes.

4. Fires will be much more difficult to control and exceed suppression capabilities.

5. There will be a much higher risk to firefighters and wilderness visitors of being trapped, with more difficult escape routes.

To reduce the risk of fires, you can limit your use of campfires and use camp stove during periods of high fire danger or windy conditions.

If you do build a campfire in the approved facilities be sure to completely extinguish your fire before leaving your site. Pour water on the campfire, stir vigorously, pour more water on the fire until it feels cold to the touch.

If you see or smell smoke don't panic. The fire may be many miles from your location and be no threat. If it is nearby or burning in your direction you may need to choose a different route of travel. You can also stay on or near the largest body of water and wait for the fire to pass by your location. You may also be able to use large open areas of marsh or meadow to wait in until the fire passes. Fire is a natural part of the wilderness ecosystem but it should always be respected, don't get too close to a fire, you will be able to see nature at work from a safe distance and your wilderness experience will be more complete.

Other Hazards:

In areas where there is blowdown visitors need to be extra careful because of weakened or leaning trees. These trees may continue to fall down for years to come. Don't choose a tent site under or linger in areas where these hazards exist. Use extreme caution if you choose to cut small downed trees or remove branches. Fallen or leaning trees may be under tension and may snap up or jump backward unexpectedly if cut. Be careful not to walk or let children play in or around uprooted trees as they may spring back into the cavity where the roots were before the storm.

Fire Restrictions:

There may be fire restrictions in all or part of the BWCAW. These restrictions are for your safety and to reduce the threat of large damaging wildfires. Before entering the Boundary Waters Canoe Area Wilderness, please ask for current information about fire restrictions. This information is available from local outfitters or any Forest Service office or call the Superior National Forest Supervisor's Office, Duluth.

Fire potential

Paul Tine, fuel and fire specialist for the U.S. Forest Service, said he's confident that a major fire is likely in the Boundary Waters within the next few years. The area has an average of 20 lightning-caused fires each year, ranging from almost none in wet years to hundreds in dry periods, such as 1976, he said.

"We're going to be living with a considerable change in the fire system up there for at least the next 10 to 20 years," he said. The amount of available fuel for fires has increased dramatically, and the risk of fire will remain for several years. "Normally, once trees make contact with the ground, things rot fairly quickly," Tine said. "But with a blow-down, trees tend to be jackstrawed, and they're not in contact with the ground."

In addition to providing more fuel, Tine said the flattened areas will receive substantially more wind at ground level. Standing trees diminish breezes. The combination of greater wind, more fuel and plenty of air could mean that fires will burn faster and hotter, he said, and the density of underbrush will make it much more difficult for firefighters if they need to respond.

In some cases, wilderness fires caused by lightning are allowed to burn themselves out if they don't threaten private property, said Tine, but that policy may need additional discussion if overall fire risks are higher. The Forest Service already is concerned about the amount of dead material in the Boundary Waters, he said, and it recently discussed whether to conduct controlled burns to reduce the slash in wilderness areas that are located within 5 miles of the Gunflint Trail and other nonwilderness property.

The idea of controlled burns has taken on new urgency with the storm damage, Tine said. Controlled burns may be considered for areas between lakes and other natural barriers to make it less likely that a huge fire could develop and roar across the landscape.

Cook County News-Herald

Fire potential

Ely and Northern Lake County

Compared to the Gunflint Trail area, the city of Ely was only lightly damaged. Trees were down and power was out for a time but the real damage was not far away:

Luverne Murphy, a contractor working for Lake Country Power, suspected more damage than was reported on the 4th. He hired a plane. Flying northeast toward the Moose Lake area he saw the damage and reported it to the sheriff's office. Luverne realized why the damage hadn't been reported - the phone lines were down. Roads were blocked and cell phone communication was disabled. "Ely slept" as the chain saws roared at Moose Lake. **C68**

Lake County Power Thank You

Joe Baltich Jr. at Northwind Lodge on the Fernberg road near the damaged area described the situation on July 6: "A swath of destruction 5 miles wide from Big Lake to Snowbank Lake is now where serenity used to be. The Forest Service called me yesterday and said that every campsite on Basswood is destroyed. According to Bob Latourell, Twin Islands on Moose are no longer twins. One of the islands has been erased. Half of Horseshoe Island is destroyed.

We are the only resort with phone and power. Everyone beyond us was hit. Transformers, high lines, poles, and insulators are on the ground in knots. On the Moose Lake road ALL of the trees are snapped off and you can now see the lake in areas as though you were driving along Lake Superior. It looks like ground zero at the landing. The Forest Service is asking for chainsaw capable volunteers. Loggers are coming in to pick up the pieces. I don't think you can avoid the swath of destruction from Moose but I haven't been up the lake so I can't give you more details other than what I've been told."

The following is from a story in the Ely Echo:

" 'We're incredibly lucky,' said Joe Baltich, Jr. ..."We've got some minor damage but it missed us by about 3/4 of a mile. Down at Moose Lake public landing road it looks like ground zero of a nuclear blast. Things don't look familiar at all.'

"Baltich said the scene out over Jasper Lake as the storm hit was like a blizzard.

" 'Water piled up off the lake and turned to vapor,' Baltich said. 'I've never seen anything like it.' "

Clearing trees from Ely Home   **C61**

You have to see it to believe it

by Nick Wognum

The July 4 storm that blew through the Ely area will leave a lasting impression for years to come. But you have to see it for yourself to judge the impact.

On Monday we headed up the Fernberg expecting to see immediate destruction, except there wasn't any. All the way up to the Moose Lake Road you would never know a major storm had caused so much damage. Even the first mile or so off the Fernberg was fairly routine - until you came to Hibbard's Creek. That was the first sign of what many would term "a war zone."

The last stretch of the Moose Lake Road was demolished by straight line winds estimated to be as high as 90 to 100 miles per hour. What it looked like to us was that the jetstream that flows at high speeds in the atmosphere had taken a dip down and crushed anything in its path.

I read later that the weather people called it a bow echo, or something that looked like a backward letter C on their radar screens. I do remember it was a hot morning in church and that it cooled down in a hurry after the storm went through. Hot met cold and millions of trees paid the price.

But in order for your mind to put it all in perspective, you have to go see a place you have been to and get a before and after impression. The Secret and Blackstone lakes parking lot did it for me. Wow. It looked like somebody moved the sign and put it in front of a clear cut. The sign basically looked out of place.

By Monday the Moose Lake Road was cleared enough to get through fairly easily - single lane at spots - but drivable. Thanks to whoever spent some time out there with a chainsaw.

We drove down to the landing and met Paul Myers coming in by motorboat from Basswood Lake. Camped across from Norway Point, Myers and his group had been taking the morning easy when the train arrived.

"It sounded like a freight train," said Myers. "Then I thought there can't be any trains - that must be the wind."

Hanging on for dear life, Myers and his crew rode out the storm in a screen tent and had their other two tents shredded in the process.

We decided to go up the lake and get a first-hand look.

It didn't take long to see the damage. From the Scout Base to the east, the entire ridge was basically levelled. Trees were either snapped off 10 to 15 feet up, bent over or laying on the ground.

The two small islands up the lake were also hit hard, but it was at about that point we could see the hopping and skipping of the damage. There would be a section that just got drilled and right next to it - nothing happened. That scenario would play out through Newfound, Sucker and Basswood Lake.

We also saw canoeists - lots of them. In fact, although we didn't keep count, I'm willing to bet it was close to an equal number going in as their were going out.

That's when I remembered the impact study done by the Forest Service a few years back. Of the 1.1 million acres in the BWCA, it was estimated that only around two percent of the land is actually impacted by man. The other 98 percent is either scenery from the water or woods nobody ever sees. And the water - well, the water was basically not impacted at all by the storm. We saw two trees floating in the lake - but the canoeists and motor boats seemed to be able to steer around them fairly easily. Once the portages were cleared, travel would be unrestricted again - the lack of roads as transportation was a plus in this case.

We did take the road from Sucker to Basswood courtesy of Mindy and Missy LaTourell and a $20 bill for a round trip. Prairie Portage had also sustained damage but it was well cleared and the trip across was a short one (thankfully) in the stifling heat.

Basswood was a real eye opener for us. I can't imagine how many trees lay on the ground in various sections of the lake. But, again, much of the shoreline is untouched. For instance, we drove down to where Basswood Lodge and a tent camp set up there looked untouched while 100 yards away you could see where every tree was levelled.

Hubachek's forest looked like broken toothpicks from where the wind had levelled the pines. Other popular spots were in similar shape - Wind Bay portage looked really bad. But the campsites we stopped at, although admittedly they had changed in character, were largely still functional. You definitely wouldn't have to go far to cut firewood.

As another storm brewed in the west, we headed for home but made a final stop to check on the most important tree on Basswood. Rest assured the 1,100 year-old cedar tree is doing just fine.

Moose Lake blowdown

Crew member on Basswood

The Great Escape

STORM SURVIVORS
BWCA WEST

Vermillion Lake and LaCroix Ranger District

Although it didn't experience the severe blowdown found in other areas, this region lost its share of timber and the storm took its toll on campers.

Narrow Escape for St. Cloud Couple

This story is reprinted from the July 6 edition of the St. Cloud Times.

A St. Cloud couple was among those grateful to escape injury in the storm that hit around midday Sunday.

Roger and Mary Spoden were fishing with their daughter and son-in-law on Trout Lake, near Lake Vermillion in the BWCA, when the wind and 5-foot waves pushed their motorboat onto a rocky shore. They took refuge in a wooded area where they had planned to eat lunch.

"It was very scary," Roger Spoden said. "The tops of trees were crashing down all around us. I was holding my glasses because it was raining so hard you couldn't see with

them on. A tree came down and the branches knocked the glasses right out of my hand."

Spoden estimated the storm lasted 20 minutes. "It seemed like forever."

Later, a worker from the motorized portage service that brought the Spodens into Trout Lake came with a Tower Fire Department volunteer to check on campers and anglers. The Spodens finished their day of fishing, but encountered detours Monday after they left their daughter's Embarrass home, where seven inches of rain flooded some roads.

A couple on Bass Lake near Vermilion held onto trees to avoid being blown away. Richard Johnson and Jenny Weims watched from their cabin on Lake Vermillion's Wakem-Up Bay as trees snapped off and blew over. They lost 15% of the trees on their 40 acres.

Even at the edge of the storm people never forget the trees coming down.

Jul-08-99 09:45

Lakes and Portages Status - July 4th Event
LaCroix Ranger District
Updated July 7, 1999
IBM: nr/wilderness/lacroix/July4/Events_status

Indian Sioux River North - scattered trees down (visitor report)
Moose River North - clear
Lac LaCroix - clear
Norway Trail (2 miles to North Arm of Trout Lake) -
scattered trees down (visitor report)
Trout Lake - extensive blowdown, most sites useable
    Vermillion to Trout portage open
    Trout to Oriniak portage open
    short and long portages Vermillion to Pine open
Pine Lake - sites are ok
Crab lake - sites are ok
    Burntside to Crab portage open
Cummings Lake - site on east half are ok
Pine Creek to Chad portage - totally blown down
Chad to Buck lake portage - lots of blowdown

Note: Echo Lake and Lake Jeanette Campgrounds are open
all our roads are open

USFS

Lake Vermillion Lakes and Portage Status

Camp Widjiwagan

The mission of YMCA Camp Widjiwagan is to develop, in young people, respect for self, community, and the environment, through wilderness adventure and environmental education.

Seeing the wooden canoe, the guide and the boys, I knew immediately then that they were from Camp Widjiwagan outside Ely...I had been impressed with most of the groups we had seen this summer from Widjiwagan. They almost always traveled in two canoes in groups of no more than five people, like this one...Parties from Widjiwagan came and went quietly, almost as if they had never been there, leaving no sign of their passing....I have heard the guides from Widjiwagan express this ethic as the 'Widji Way.' –*Michael Furtman, A Season for Wilderness: the Journal of a Summer in Canoe Country.*

Camp Widjiwagan and Close Calls

The following story appeared in the *Ely Echo:*

North Arm Camps Have Power Returned
by Anne Swenson

By the time evening arrived on Sunday, July 4, the parade had been delayed for only one hour, roads had been opened and the annual fireworks display went on as usual.

When seen from the north shore of Shagawa Lake with an almost full expanse of sky, the fireworks being shot up into the dark sky had found a rival in the random pockets of lightning which also lit the sky to the west and the south.

For persons living on the North Arm of Burntside and

several other areas around Ely, there was little to celebrate without electrical power. Without power, rural toilets won't flush, showers cannot be taken, and the lure of television to end a day is lost.

According to Karin Hokkanen, "The entrance to Camp Widjiwagen had trees down which looked like they had been pushed over by a giant hand." The camp was without power until 6 p.m. Thursday and its sister camp, Camp DuNord was out of power until a little later.

"We had a contest here to guess the time power would come on. Kind of like "Ice Out" in the Echo. And I think it was 8:21 when the power came on," said Brian Rupe, executive director of the family YMCA facility. "We have a lot of trees down, and the chainsaws are working. We were very blessed that no one was hurt."

Karl Tingelstad survived the storm at Camp DuNord **C47**

Camp Widjiwagan provides wilderness adventures trips of 7 to 45 days for 12 to 18 year olds, environmental education for school groups and a retreat location for organizations. Located on the shores of Burntside Lake about 14 miles from Ely, Minnesota, the camp began offering wilderness trips in 1929.

Logs salvaged from Widjiwagan

From the camp brochure:

Widjiwagen is a branch of the YMCA of Greater Saint Paul. Our mission is simple, but profound - "to develop, in young people, respect for self, community and the environment, through wilderness adventure and environmental education." Whether first time campers or seasoned wilderness travelers, our goal is for teens to learn something new about the ethic of respect which is so important, and sometimes lacking, today.

All Widjiwagan sessions and trips have a number of things in common:

Respect for Self Respect begins by believing in yourself, in your own capabilities. At Widji kids are encouraged to test their limits, to take responsibility for their behavior and actions, and to lead healthy lifestyles.

Respect for Others We place a high value on teamwork, helpfulness, and sharing. With coordinated action and a commitment to a goal, a group can accomplish many things which would be impossible alone.

Respect for the Environment The natural world is a sacred gift that must be care for and nurtured. Travel through the wilderness is conducted using "Leave No Trace" ethics and standards.

Respect for Equipment We stress the importance of taking care of the tools and equipment we use in wilderness travel. This begins with the special care required of our famous wood canoes but extends to care for nature and for other people, too.

Widjiwagan was caught in the middle of the July 4th storm. The entry road to the camp was thoroughly blocked. It looked like "a giant hand had swept the trees down." Power was off for the better part of a week.

According to the camp's Program Director Karen Pick, "Widji had about 15 groups in the BWCA that day, but 4 groups in particular were in the storm's path. Fortunately, because of some good judgement and luck, none of our groups sustained any injuries. They do have some good stories though."

It Took Us 8 Hours to Portage 80 Rods
by Patty Brodeen

On July fourth of 1999, I was leading a trip for YMCA Camp Widjiwagan. This was a very exciting trip fro me, it was my first trip that I had led by myself and we were to be traveling around the Boundary Waters Canoe Wilderness for 13 days. The group was made up of five girls that ranged in age from 12 to 14 years old and they were all excited about being in the wilderness.

The trip started out very uneventful. It had rained quite a bit and the six of us were looking forward to our day of rest that we had scheduled to be on the holiday of our nation. We had plans to swim and relax. We got to our campsite on an island in Kekekabic Lake early, on the third of July, and set up camp. Two of my campers set up the tent in one of the three spots at the campsite (this spot ended up saving our lives). The next morning my five campers slept in late as I prepared breakfast.

The air was very warm and humid that morning. The storm came in fast. We watched as it rolled across the sky towards us. We went into our tent as we had done for

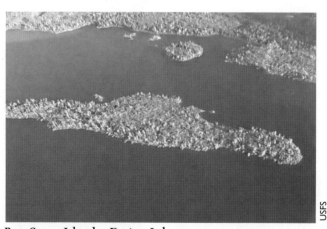

Boy Scout Island - Ensign Lake

USFS

previous storms. We begun to play cards when the wind and rain began to pick up. The wind was coming so fast. Our tent started to roll over with us inside. We used our bodies as weights on the corners and sides of the tent. The force of the wind on the tent was too much and one of the seams gave out and the rain was able to enter the tent. As the water rushed into our tent, we grouped together in the middle of our pile of wet sleeping bags and we began to sing camp songs. I continuously kept an eye out of the tent at the trees. They had all fallen down. The large red pines fell all around us, there was one along each side of the tent.

When the storm had subsided I briefed the group for what was outside the tent. Any amount of preparation could not prepare them for the shock outside of the tent. We climbed our way over the tree that landed in front of the tent. We looked around at the mess and were amazed. Every tree at our campsite and in the surrounding woods had fallen down. Looking across the lake where once there was a huge canopy of trees, you could now see the dirt. We spent the rest of the afternoon climbing around the down trees trying to get our campsite in order. A tree had fallen on our aluminum canoe but had, luckily, left our wood-canvas canoe untouched. A fair amount of our food had been wrecked, waterlogged. But it did not matter much in the long run because most of our appetites had diminished. All of our belongings were soaked and we were emotionally drained. We had a very restless night of sleep that night. We awoke with every clap of thunder and flash of lightening.

The greatest adventure of our trip was trying to get to our pick-up spot in only a few days. The portage out of Kekekabic Lake was awful. It took us sixteen times as long as usual to cross the eighty rods. (It took us eight hours to cross the eighty rods.) The trees covered the portage and we had to go under, over, and around them with our canoes and packs. Another group came along behind us and helped in our efforts. Without their help we would have never been able to get our wood-canvas canoe across in one piece. We had to lift the heavy canoe far above our heads to clear it from the trees, all while standing on another tree.

After one day, we had traveled only a few miles. This left us with many more miles to travel before our pick-up site. The next days were full of traveling. We paddled and portaged from sunrise to sunset. It was very difficult for all of us. The fierce winds pushed us back and the unclear portages slowed us down. We finally made it to our final lake, the night before our scheduled pickup. We had made it! Our nerves finally calmed and our appetites returned that night and we ate like kings.

The storm had an incredible effect on all of our lives. We were able to conquer our fears and do things none of us thought were possible. The growth that occurred in each of us strengthened our bond together. Through it all we supported each other and by singing, laughing, and joking, we made the best of every situation, what else can you do when Mother Nature decides to get tough. The best part of our story is all of the girls plan to go back to camp next summer for another great, but hopefully not as eventful a trip.

Big Waves on Snowbank Lake
by Kate Starns

I was leading five 14 year-olds on a 13 day trip in the Boundary Waters for Camp Widjiwagan. Due to a stressful first half of our trip and a float plane evacuation of one member of our group, we were on Snowbank lake during the July 4th storm. We had met our injured member and were all recovering from our adventures. Here is what I wrote in my journal about the storm:

We sat through a HUGE thunderstorm with immense straight-line winds. I'm talking BIG and POWERFUL! Tons of trees fell down and our aluminum canoe flipped over, sending my paddle flying. I've never seen a storm like that before.

We were fortunate enough to be camped in an open campsite, with few trees. Our tent was near the edge of a 10 to 15 foot cliff over the water. During the storm, to keep everyone calm, we were all sitting on our life jackets in our four person tent. Our tents were faced the wrong way for the wind, and as a result, one of my campers had to hold out her arms so the tent wall wouldn't collapse. I remember the wind shifted direction several times. I also remember thinking that 'these are the strongest winds I have ever seen up here.'

The lake was in an uproar, with whitecaps everywhere. At one point, a wave hit the bottom of the cliff and the splash went all the way into the tent! That was a big wave to splash all that way! It was just like the ocean. It was incredible.

After the storm had passed (it seemed to take forever), we all crawled out of the tent to survey the damage. The top of a nearby tree had fallen and just barely missed our two-person tent. There were several uprooted trees and halves of trees on the ground in the nearby forested area. Our aluminum canoe was now upright. Fortunately it had only flipped over and not gone further.

We were very lucky.
Kate Starns

Ted Starn's Story

Our group from Camp Widjiwagan was camped on the western end of Saganaga Lake, and had just gotten up late because it was our layover day. We made our pancake mix, started a fire, and got about two pancakes made before it started to storm, so we put the lid over the pancakes and climbed into the tent to wait out the storm.

Soon the rain started to pick up a lot, and once the rain was as hard as it would get, the wind started to pick up too. One end of the tent was blown down, and I stood up to hold it up. My left arm was toward the lake, and I could feel sticks, branches and pinecones hitting my forearm. My counselor then told me to get down and to duck and cover with the rest of the group. We stayed like that for a little while, and then Joel, the counselor, looked out again. I heard him mutter, "Holy *$!?" and then he came back in and told us all to get as close as we could into one corner. We stayed like that for about twenty minutes until the storm started to calm down.

Once the storm was gone, he said to us, "Okay, here's the deal— there are three trees fallen right near our tent. There is one about three feet away from the door, one giant cedar that fell about three feet to the other side, and the tree that we tied our rain sheet ropes to fell across the corner of the tent." We were all in shock because of the severity of the storm, and when we got out of the tent we realized the extent of the storm. Trees had fallen on all sides of our tent, and every tree near the lake was blown toward the land.

When we ventured into the woods to find the biffy, we found the once open forest a tangle of trunks and branches. When we finally found the biffy, it was buried beneath a large tangle of trees.

Here is a diagram of our campsite after the storm:

After we had gone outside and taken some snapshots, we emptied the tent, hung up our sleeping bags and then put the tent up in a dry place by the fire pit, because that was the only place that was clear. Luckily, neither of our canoes were damaged during the storm. But just when we had the tent up, we could feel the wind start to pick up all of a sudden. Joel looked up at the sky and said, "Guys, as much as we'd all like to have this over with, I think we're in for some more." But luckily it wasn't anything big and it just drizzled for a few minutes.

It was not until we started moving the next day that I realized the severity and size of the storm. We would pass through lakes where a whole ridge had been covered by giant aspens— now, just the lower halves of the trees were standing. And on our portages, we could see how the wind gusts had blown a whole group of trees all in the same direction, across the portage. To get the packs across we had to either crawl with them on, or slide them through the mud. With the canoes it was a different process. We would put one person between each of the trees, and the group would hold it until another person got set

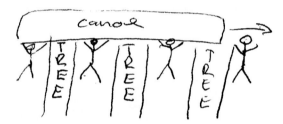

in the section ahead. *It looked like this:*

Doing portages this way took us about ten times as long and was very tiring. But luckily our group had mostly paddling left and we didn't have to do so many portages that we fell behind. Overall, I think that being in the storm was a good experience because it was a lot of fun and gave me a challenge.

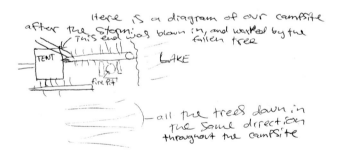

Doreen and Chick Palermo on Gabbro
by Anne Swenson

–From the Ely Echo

No matter where one went around town during the past week, there were people with stories to tell. As the word spread around the country, people with connections to Ely, whether friends or visitors, began to call seeking details.

But if there was any thought that the storm was a major news story elsewhere, CNN television put it all in perspective: "There was flooding in Hibbing, Minnesota Sunday," the announcer said, "and a nearby wilderness area was damaged by winds."

For people like Doreen and Chick Palermo of Durham, North Carolina, though, it was an experience to remember. They had saved the BWCAW portion of their several month long trip, celebrating their retirement at the end of their journey.

Already they had crossed the southern states, camping along the way; met with snow while camping at Crater Lake in California, drove up the California coastal highway and gravitated toward Ely. Their pickup truck towed their 24 foot trailer.

For Doreen this was the trip she had longed to take, canoeing and camping in the Boundary Waters, ever since she had seen an advertisement in a travel magazine about four years ago.

Early in the morning of July 4 the couple had been driven down the Spruce Road to start their trip into Gabbro Lake. They planned to camp for four nights on an island there. They paddled to the island just as the storm hit, only to find that four children and their two dads were camped there. The two men were out in a boat when the storm hit, and rode out the storm by getting out of the boat and hanging onto its sides while the storm raged.

"Water was coming across the lake like a curtain," Doreen said. "The wind picked up our canoe so we sat on it like it was a horse." On the campsite 12-14 trees crashed to the ground.

The families departed and the couple managed to put up their tent and cook supper. "The rainstorm lasted all night long or at least until four in the morning," Doreen said. She noted that her husband had been hoping for the experience of rain on the tent roof, but this was more than he expected. By the end of their stay it appeared that the level of the lake had risen four feet.

"The comfort level was lake water, Tang and food," they agreed, as they sat enjoying coffee after dinner at the Ely Mantel House. They hadn't been prepared for the taste of packaged food from the outfitter's stock, and now they were enjoying the culinary reward from their trip. Their 27-year marriage had survived intact, and they looked strengthened by this new experience. Computer software developers, they said, "We can now survive the Y2K problem."

Red Pines down on campsite

USFS

Reference to "C" throughout the book indicates a color photo in mid-section.

The Portage Was Now a Raging River
by Andreas & Tracy Whitley

We were in the storm on the 4th of July, however we were not in the location of the severest winds, however we were on the edge of the storm. Our story may be of interest to you as we were experiencing the BWCAW for the first time and also on honeymoon having celebrated our wedding on the 26th of June.

We arrived in Ely on the 30th of June and met up with our outfitters John and Kathy Schiefelbein at North Country Canoe Outfitters who greeted us and made us feel very welcome. We planned our route and overnighted at Ely. Bright and early on the 1st of July we headed off to our entry point at Little Isabella River. Our itinerary was for a 9 day trip in quiet areas to enjoy the scenery and wildlife whilst relaxing after the stresses of the wedding.

Our choice of entry point, recommended for its quietness and chances of spotting wildlife, was quickly rewarded with almost literally bumping into a moose on rounding one of the river bends within half an hour of starting our paddle.

Our first three nights camp were uneventful apart from the usual experiences of people camping in BWCAW for the first time, where can we hang our food bags, what was that noise outside our tent and why didn't anyone tell us that after dark the outside belongs to the mosquitoes!

Our third night was spent at a wonderful camp on an island in Gabro Lake. We watched the sun set over calm waters, with the sky only showing some sign of cloud. The following morning was calm again but the sky was dark and cloudy but didn't look threatening.

As we paddled towards our next camp the skies became more and more threatening as what appeared to be two or three sets of storm clouds drew closer together. We reached the 120 rod portage between Gabro Lake and South Kawishiwi River, we portaged half our kit to the far end without any problems and headed back to the start to pick up our canoe and remaining bags.

On the way down the portage we had passed another group who were heading in the reverse direction, when we reached the start of the portage we stoped and had a chat with them remarking on the weather and other

Tracy Whitley - Calm before the storm

general BWCAW chit-chat. The conversation was cut short by a clap of thunder, they started to shelter from the rain and we decided to complete the last stage of the portage so that all of our bags and we were in the same place. Tracy gathered the bags and I lifted the canoe and we set off down the portage.

Before we had taken our first steps the wind had started to pick up and the heavens had opened. Apparently the rain was like walking through a power shower it was so intense, I did not realize this as I was under a BWCAW umbrella, otherwise known as a canoe, so my top half was bone dry but my legs were soaked. Within just a few minutes the portage, we had easily walked down not 10 minutes previously, was now a raging river reaching over our ankles in depth.

As well as the torrential rain we also had to contend with the wind. Every now and again the canoe would try to change my walking direction, as a gust of wind would catch it. This combined with the thunder and lightning made walking with the canoe and interesting experience. As we progressed down the portage our path was blocked with fallen trees, luckily they were 'small' enough to allow us to clamber over them this occurred at a number of points along the portage.

We eventually reached the end of the portage and the rest of our kit. Our tarpaulin was retrieved and a quick shelter constructed to protect us and our belongings from the rain that was still torrential. We waited under the shelter for what seemed an eternity as the wind and the rain continued their incessant barrage. Eventually the barrage started to decline and we emerged from the shelter. The lake was still covered in white tipped waves and we managed to dry ourselves off and warm ourselves up by stomping back and forth along the portage.

Once the rain finally abated we gathered our gear ready to head on to our next campsite. We couldn't head off immediately as the wind was still causing big waves on the lake. Once these had died down we set off in search of our next home. We passed a group fishing from near their camp and across the river a tree had fallen; they told us that they had seen it go over while they were sheltering from the storm. As time went on the day became brighter and warmer; it also became a lot hotter as we were paddling in full waterproofs!

We arrived at our next camp on South Kawishiwi River at mid afternoon just as the previous occupants were finishing breaking camp. They had just spoken to a ranger who had warned them that another weather system was coming and so they had decided to cut their fishing trip short and head out that afternoon. We set up camp quickly whilst it was dry, this gave us time to get a fire going and improvise a washing line to dry our kit; some of which had become wet during the storm.

As the afternoon drew on the weather improved and our kit dried without any real need for the fire. As afternoon became a very pleasant evening we cooked dinner and ate it in wonderful conditions. The lake was like glass and the sun kept breaking through the clouds that threatened one minute and then diffused the next. I have a

wonderful picture (on slide) of the sunset that evening and it shows quite clearly the calm before the storm!

We went to bed as usual once the sun went down and as we were close to Farm Lake and Ely we thought we could here fireworks that we assumed were for the 4th of July celebrations. As the celebrations faded we drifted off to sleep but then at around midnight we were woken by what I must say was the most spectacular pyrotechnic display that I have ever seen. From midnight until about 3 a.m. the heaven was ablaze with lightning flashes and thunder claps every 1-30 seconds (at worst) and this display was constant. The sound of the rain landing on the tent was the nearest we could imagine to putting your head inside a snare drum.

Luckily our site was not affected by the storm that evening and our canoe and bear bag were where we had left them the night before. As we made our way from Clear Lake back to Ely we came across more storm damage in the form of felled trees around the lakes and

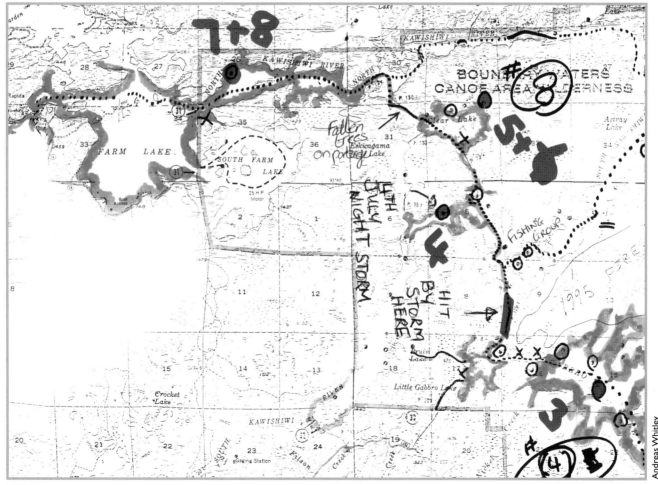

Whitley trip map

Andreas Whitley

also across some of the portages. Some of the trees were right down across the portages and were too thick to step over so we literally had to clamber over the branches and trunks. Others were leaning across the path so you had to duck under them to pass. One tree was across the path at a height that meant you couldn't duck under it with a canoe, so when we got to this obstacle the canoe was slid over the top while I ducked under the bough and collected it at the other side to continue the portage.

After completing our final portage we thought we had left the problems of the storm behind us, however the storm had one final obstacle for us to negotiate. Whilst planning our route the final 200 yards were shown to us, 'as you leave Farm Lake simply paddle under the bridge into White Iron Lake and right up to our docks' (back at NCCO) was how it was described.

As we turned the corner on the approach to the bridge we noticed that the current was quite strong. We headed over to the docks on the far side of the flow and assessed the situation. Being canoeing veterans now we foolishly decided to see whether we could attempt the final 200 yards to the docks. As soon as the nose of the canoe hit the flow we were instantly pointed away from the docks and back down the way we had come. As we reached the docks again we were told that people had seen motorized boats on full throttle fail to negotiate the 200 yards under the bridge, so we decided to concede defeat

Aerial view of blowdown

and set ashore at the dock. We emptied our kit out and wandered over to NCCO, the storm had managed to hamper our trip but luckily for us, only the last 200 yards.

As we arrived at NCCO John came out to greet us and hugged Tracy and said how relieved he was to see us. We said it was good to be back and explained about the storm we had been caught in, it was at this point we were told about the real storm damage that had been caused just a few miles northwest of where we had been. We then realized just how lucky we had been.

We chatted with John and the NCCO staff who were all genuinely interested in our experiences during the storm. We all agreed that whilst out in the BWCAW you have to respect mother nature and work with her on her terms because she is not only beautiful but can also be very dangerous and even deadly (but luckily not in this instance).

The storm did not spoil our honeymoon in any way. It showed us another side of the BWCAW which was beautiful and interesting as the calm and sunny side, in a strange sort of way. We both agree that we would love to return to the BWCAW and experience its wonders again, perhaps with some friends or our children - who knows.

Sincerely,

Andreas and Tracy Whitley (BWCAW Survivors!)

BUCKS - U.K.

The Storm May Not Be Natures Work

Jim Brandenburg, a well known nature photographer, seems to have lost more than just trees on his property near Ely.

Jim was in the woods near his home by Moose Lake when the wind came up. He made it to the house just as the trees began to crash around him - many of them huge pines.

When I spoke to him four months after the storm he still had difficulty talking about the event that changed his landscape so dramatically. He compares his feelings to "Vietnam syndrome, an extremely traumatic experience." Jim claims that the storm "may not be nature's work but a product of Man's carelessness with the environment." Lee Frelich, an ecologist for the University of Minnesota Department of Forest Resources, subscribes to that theory.

Asked about the fire potential near his home, Jim replied, "To say that our family is deathly afraid of fire here is an understatement." The Brandenburg family is planning to move some valuables to a safer location.

Jim has flown over the BW since the storm, and notes that the Kekekabic Lake area sustained the worst damage. The Forest Service cabin there which was previously well hidden from water routes now is as obvious as "the little house on the prairie."

The following are comments by Mr. Brandenburg aired July 8 on Minnesota Public Radio:

It's a loss. It's a great loss that does feel like we've lost some sort of family member. There's kind of a mourning. Knowing it's a natural process helps it a little bit. All death and birth is, of course, natural but this one is (on) a gargantuan and very humbling scale that I have never seen in my own personal life.

I have traveled the world for (National) Geographic and photographed and documented some great natural events and catastrophes, and always found that I could deal with it and shoot it and come back with the information. In this case having flown over the Boundary Waters yesterday, it was difficult for me to shoot, for two reasons: emotionally it was a little bit startling - I just was simply awestruck at the sheer size and breadth of the destruction.

On the other hand, it was so big that it was almost

Letters to the Editor

Are we to blame?

To the editor,

Some of us have said, "At least we humans were not to blame for this latest disaster in the BWCAW." But is this entirely true? Are we totally innocent of the devastating extremeness of the straight-line winds that brought down some of the last great white pines in the Minnesota Arrowhead?

Or, are we somehow implicated in the unusually extreme and unmoderated weather patterns (extreme winds and temperature, excesses of rain and snow) that we have experienced in this last decade of this century of technological devastation of nature, as well as the end of an entire millennium of burgeoning science devoid of respect for nature's systems?

In this century, among other drastic changes we have made, we have reduced the ozone layer and cut down half of the great rain forests. Both of those huge, old, and once stable systems may have previously had weather moderating effects. Our recent violent unmoderated weather may be a result of those serious changes and losses.

The weather we now have seems to reflect our own violent culture more than the nature which produced the magnificent and awesome "Bois Fort," which our recent ancestors tore down as soon as they saw it.

Now we've lost even more of those great trees-and it happened on July 4th. July 4th is a man-made date celebrating independence-ironically it is our blind attitude of independence from nature which may have resulted in the extremeness of the wind force that destroyed so much of our nature "preserve"-thus showing us that we cannot just set aside some precious things and make them safe from our damaging actions elsewhere. All is connected.

Dianne Wachs,
Loon Lake

Cook County News-Herald

frustrating - I couldn't capture it on film. I knew that the camera would not pick up the feel. I've seen the Twin Cities newspapers and their coverage - and they had some of the finest photographers working in the Midwest up here - and it didn't even come close to capturing it, and my photographs didn't even come close to it. So those of you who have seen it on television and news media, you just can not comprehend the scope. **C66 & 67**

...I had a book that came out a year or two ago, "Chased By The Light," where probably my favorite image was of a small island with two loons in front of it, up in the Boundary Waters. And that island is a landmark up here, and it's a favorite of mine. It's....called Twin Island on Moose Lake. That island is virtually gone, and it's extremely traumatic to see that it'll take two, three generations for it to come back to something like it was. So in our own self-centered way, we'll never see it like we like to see it in our hopelessly romantic view of looking at nature, where everything has to be pretty and well-ordered.

L̲ast fall, *National Geographic* nature photographer Jim Brandenburg released his award-winning new book, *Chased By The Light*. The book, which spent nearly a month on the bestseller lists at the *Minneapolis Star Tribune* and *St. Paul Pioneer Press*, chronicles Brandenburg's personal challenge to make just one photo each day during the 90 days between the autumnal equinox and winter solstice.

The majority of the photographs were made in Brandenburg's favorite setting: the Boundary Waters Canoe Area. As a *National Geographic* photographer for more than 20 years, Brandenburg's typical assignments often required in excess of 300 rolls of film; for this assignment he used the equivalent of three rolls.

Wilderness Ranger Nancy Pius

Nancy Pius, an outspoken 11 year veteran of the BWCA, works as a USFS Wilderness Ranger in the Kawishiwi (Ely) District. She was very involved in dealing with the aftermath of the storm.

Nancy and two others were eating lunch on the 140 rod Billygoat Portage between Jackfish and Mudro lakes when the wind hit. Huge aspen were blowing in 360 degree circles. They heard Ranger Pete Weckman on the radio at Moose Lake saying, "I'm all right but all the trees are gone!"

According to Nancy, "The wind completely blocked the portage. With much effort, we did the portage, coming out at the Chainsaw Sisters place. The Echo Trail was a mess. Dave McGlauphlin of the Forest Service cleared the trail, opening one lane. Four other groups wanted to help but had no safety gear. They applauded Dave as he finished up."

Nancy wants chainsaws used through the year 2000 in the BW. "There is much more potential for accidents using hand saws in the tangled blowdown."

Nancy worked on search and rescue and with the Hotshots on portage and campsite clearing. "I led a Hotshot crew; we had five very skilled sawyers. They enjoyed clearing portages - the tougher the better. At night they would boast

Beaver with Hotshots and Nancy Pius

Sawyer Clearing Portage

about who cut the most dangerous trees. They cut from canoes at the landing and in hip deep water at times." **C52**

"When a tree with a root ball is cut, the upper part of the tree can pop back up– the roots going back into the hole. Sawing those booby-trapped trees is very stressful. You always have to be aware of all the circumstances. I remember sitting on a poplar while the other end was being cut 50 feet away. The tree jumped when it was cut.

"We cleared the Wood to Hula Lake portage, and the next day there were fresh moose tracks on it. It made all this work seem worthwhile. When their tour ended, the "Shots" didn't want to leave the woods - they loved the work."

Nancy explained that there are three classes of sawyers, depending on what diameter of tree they are qualified to cut. Class A can cut 1-12 inch trees; Class B can cut up to 24 inch trees; and Class C can cut all sizes including "killer trees." Killer trees are exceptionally dangerous and their disposal requires extraordinary skill. If no Class C sawyers are on hand these trees are marked with a special tape and taken care of when a "C level" is available.

Very familiar with the major blowdown area, Nancy sketched its southern boundary for

Sawyer working on "Killer Tree"   **C55**

Trapped Canoe   **C15**

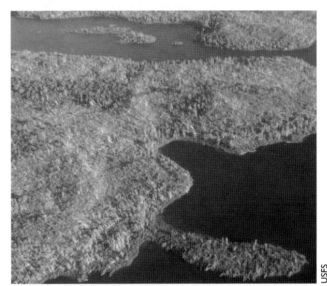

Ensign Lake Blowdown   **C16**

"Killer Tree" tape   **C55**

us: "The lakes comprising the southern boundary of the blowdown are Kek, Knife, Ensign, Missionary, Eddy, Ogish, Seagull and Jasper. There were no useable sites left on the first three."

The Kek, Sioux Hustler and other trails may not be reopened, largely because of fire danger. Nancy commented about fire and visitors: "The situation here is comparable to Yellowstone. People will come and gawk;

overall numbers will stay up there. Eventually campers will gravitate out of the blowdown areas to the 90% not seriously damaged."

"There has always been a risk of fire here. Unless there are super critical fire conditions I wouldn't be afraid of going anywhere in the wilderness.

"After all is said and done we don't manage the wilderness - it manages us!

Perich flies blowdown

by Shawn Perich

Author's note: Last Saturday, U.S. Forest Service enforcement supervisor Pancho Smith and pilot Pat Loe invited this writer to join them on an enforcement flight over the Boundary Waters Canoe Area Wilderness (BWCAW). Smith was on the lookout for motorboaters in nonmotorized areas, but it gave me a chance to look at areas where the forest was blown down during the July 4 windstorm.

We didn't cover all of the storm-damaged area, but I took notes along a flight path that took us north along the Gunflint Trail from Devil Track Lake, west to Basswood Lake near Ely, and then east to Pine Lake on the eastern end of the BWCAW. If you are planning a canoe trip or just know the country, this may help give you some idea of what you may expect.

Going north from Devil Track Lake, we began seeing damage near Little Trout Lake. There was a patchwork of blowdown trees and Loe showed us the path left by a forest fire that occurred on a windy day last spring. Continuing north, we continued to see wind damage as we neared Poplar Lake, midway up the Gunflint Trail.

"If it wasn't for the swath of blowdown in the BWCAW, this would be considered major damage," said Smith.

We followed the Gunflint Trail northward. The damage became more evident. Aspen trees were twisted and bent. West of Loon Lake, we could see where some salvage logging was occurring to help create a fire break. Despite all of the damage in this area, there were still numerous places where trees were standing.

Leaving the Trail, we turned westward into the BWCAW. Reaching the vicinity of Little Saganaga and Gabimichigami lakes, we entered the main swath of the storm. Damage here is incomprehensible. As far as you could see, nearly all the trees were down or bent by the storm. The only places that escaped damage were low areas, such as spruce swamps, the lee side of steep hills and the spruce and cedars growing along the edge of lakes.

The damage continued like this past Ogishkemuncie Lake and Kekekabic Lake. The ranger's cabin on Kek, once hidden in a stand of pines, now stood alone in a sea of downed trees.

"It looks like the little house on the prairie," said Loe.

As we neared Knife Lake, you could see that most of the storm damage occurred on the Minnesota side of the border. We also saw canoes and occupied campsites on many lakes. Smith said about the same number of canoers have entered the wilderness since the storm, although travel patterns have changed. Some parties opt to stay in one location rather than touring through the lakes.

The amount of traffic in the BWCAW is surprising. Smith said that in a four-day patrol with two other officers the previous weekend, they contacted 500 people, primarily canoers, as well as a few motorboaters on the motorized portions of Saganaga and Sea Gull lakes.

"Most of the people we talked to wanted to know about the condition of the campsites," Smith said.

Most of the campsites and portages in the BWCAW are now open. In fact, for canoers and anglers, the biggest change will be the scenery — the blowdown doesn't affect lake and portage travel. However, if you plan to enter the area east of Ely and west of the Gunflint Trail, it will look very different than it did the last time you were there. Also, the Forest Service has now instituted a fire ban for the blow down area.

As we neared Basswood Lake, the swath of damage narrowed. The main damage seemed to have occurred south of Basswood, although there were patches of blowdown on the lake. Some campsites were pulverized, others missed. Even in areas where there appeared to be no damage from the air, you could see an occasional tree broken off at mid height. On one little island, all the white pine were destroyed. The Four Mile Portage was blocked with downed trees.

Turning to begin our eastward return, we passed over an area where white pines were planted as part of a blister rust study that began 70 years ago. Most of the pines there were destroyed. The island where Root Beer Lady Dorothy Molter lived sustained damage, too.

We followed the Canadian border as we went eastward. I saw an eagle perched in a pine. On the west end of Saganaga there wasn't much damage, but nearing Ameri-can Point we could see the blackened landscape left by the Sag Corridor Fire in 1995. We passed over another area where a large fire burned in 1976. Young, undamaged jackpine was as thick as dog hair.

Passing south to Sea Gull Lake, we again entered an area where the windstorm blitzed the forest. Three Mile Island was heavily damaged. The lower end of Sea Gull and the country around Alpine Lake was devastated.

"When you look at this from the air, it becomes mind-numbing after awhile," Smith remarked. "It's not until you get on the ground that you realize the blowdown is so thick you can't even wiggle."

Although some folks who have driven the Gunflint Trail remark that much of the blow down seems to be mature aspen and that a surprising number of white pines survived the storm, from the air you can see this is not the case. Flattened jackpine stands appear as dark areas, the trunks of downed paper birch look like snow. You can see the huge trunks of toppled white pines, too.

We crossed the Gunflint Trail and continued eastward. Approaching Gunflint Lake, we saw a monstrous pile of debris from cleanup operations piled in a gravel pit. The south side of Gunflint Lake looks like a clear cut. On the north side, you could see a swath of blowdown extending into Canada.

On the east end of Loon Lake, most of the damage was on the windward side of the hills and along ridge tops. From here east, the topography of the Gunflint Trail is more rugged. There was considerable damage south of Duncan Lake and south of West Bearskin.

Continuing east, there were pockets of blowdown. At Pine Lake, most of the blowdown was on the south side of the lake. One large white pine on the north shore was twisted and toppled into the water. We turned south when we reached McFarland Lake, at the eastern end of the BWCAW and headed back to Devil Track.

And, although we looked on Sag, Sea Gull, Basswood, and Pine, we found no illegal motorboaters. Last Saturday, everyone in the wilderness appeared to be obeying the rules.

Cook County News-Herald

Outdoor writer, Shawn Perich - flies the blowdown

Courtney James, EMT

The Forest Service recruited qualified people from throughout the U.S. to help with search and rescue and campsite/portage clearing.

Courtney James of Grand Marais served as an Emergency Medical Technician, accompanying search and rescue crews. Later he worked with chainsaw crews during portage and campsite clearing.

Courtney worked on two 1-day and two 8-day operations. The following personnel made up the crew on one of his 8-day trips:

*4 chain saw operators - 3 DNR workers from the Twin Cities and 1 DNR "desk person" from Duluth.

Chain Saw Crew on Portage

*2 swampers (workers who throw aside cut wood) - 1 local Forest Service employee familiar with the area and 1 EMT (Courtney).

According to Courtney, several of the chain saw operators were chainsaw instructors who displayed phenomenal woodcutting skill. Some of the EMT's on the crews didn't help with the clearing; others like Courtney helped with swamping.

A one day trip would typically last 12 hours, beginning at 6:30 AM in Grand Marais. Eight-day trips were comprised of 12 hour days, each beginning early at 5:30 AM.

The Forest Service furnished all materials, saws, food, tents, packs, canoes or motorboats; but some of the medical items included were strange. Courtney was issued freeze packs requiring ice, and large amounts of vitamin C.

Brule to Juno Portage

One of Courtney's crews cleared the badly blocked Stairway Portage - it took two sawyers and two swampers 6 hours. On that trip, they viewed the Canadian side from Rose Lake and saw total devastation. The Canadians had their chainsaws running immediately after the storm.

On one trip, Courtney worked with three Native American men - one from Fond Du Lac and two from the White Earth Reservation. All were good workers. He heard one of them remark, "Gosh, look what we've got - a white man carrying our canoe."

Another group consisted of two students from Northland College in Ashland, Wisconsin; two from Carlton College in Northfield, MN; Jason Morse, a teacher; and Ellen Hawkins, a local Wilderness Ranger. This group "really clicked," working together. One day they received an emergency call that a dangerous storm was closing in. They made it off the lake just as the wind picked up and lightning crackled. –Most of the workers were edgy, expecting another major storm at any time.

On another trip, Courtney joined the Flathead Hotshots (from Montana). Just before they pushed off, a call came requesting that no gas or saw be carried in the Hotshots' canoes, which tended to be tippy. Firefighters who worked on the large, recent Saganaga Lake fire remembered pumps, gas and other equipment "going into the drink."

Some of the Hotshots had fishing licenses, hoping to find time to try their luck.

Courtney's group cleared Flour, Burnt, Smoke, Brule, Horseshoe, Winchell, Wonder and Sunhigh lakes. A swath was ripped through Wonder and Sunhigh lakes; it took hours to find the latrine on Wonder Lake, and 6 hours with hand saws to clear the campsite and latrine trail. A damaged canoe was found abandoned on the Wonder Lake portage.

Courtney had little opportunity to use his medical skills - he himself was the only casualty, badly spraining his ankle. He carried his pack while hobbling along, using a canoe paddle as a crutch.

However, workers in the crew were more relaxed, having an EMT along.

History of Duluth Pack
by Sparky Stensaas

The Duluth Pack has its humble roots in a poor French-Canadian named Camille Poirer, who made his way west and north to Duluth. Arriving here in 1870 with his "little stock of leather and tools", he began a small store and quickly made a go of it in this booming frontier town on the shores of Gitchi Gummi.

On December 12, 1882, Camille filed for a patent on a new type of packsack. It was a canvas sack that closed with a buckled flap, had new-fangled shoulder straps in addition to the traditional tumpline, a revolutionary sternum strap, and an umbrella holder (for portable shade in this newly cutover country). Known then as the Poirer pack, this northwoods classic is today referred to as the original Duluth Pack.

In 1911, Camille sold off the pack business to the new Duluth Tent and Awning Company. We opened shop on 1610 West Superior Street in then bustling Wend End. (You can still find us at this address, sewing and hand-riveting the finest, most durable canvas canoe packs made.) In addition to the packs, we made countless awnings for booming Duluth businesses. Remember, during the early 1900's there were more millionaires per capita in Duluth than in any other town in America. Duluth had lumber barons, shipping magnates, railroad tycoons, and big shots in the iron ore business. In our early catalogs you'll find hay wagon covers, cots, wall tents and heavy canvas aprons for working blacksmiths.

America was changing. The Roaring 20's found the common man with more money and more leisure time. Auto-camping became the rage and hoards of adventure-hungry sportsman and fun-loving families headed for the hinterlands. Duluth Tent & Awning responded by creating the "auto-pack" that clamped on to the running boards of a touring car to carry extra gear. We also made canvas tents that attached to a car to create the first "mobile home".

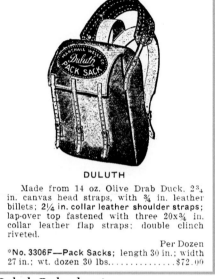

PACK SACKS

DULUTH

Made from 14 oz. Olive Drab Duck, 2¾ in. canvas head straps, with ¾ in. leather billets; 2¼ in. collar leather shoulder straps; lap-over top fastened with three 20x¾ in. collar leather flap straps; double clinch riveted.

Per Dozen
*No. 3306F—Pack Sacks; length 30 in.; width 27 in.; wt. dozen 30 lbs..............$72.00

Marshall Wells Catalogue 1930

Duluth Pack advertisement

Duluth Pack has always made rugged packs for working people. This certainly the case in the 1940's with our Cruiser series packs. They were the perfect field pack for the timber cruisers who snowshoed countless miles through the great North Woods grading lumber for the logging companies. Built narrow and in the box style, the cruiser pack could haul a load yet allow the men to slip between thick brush easily. We still make the cruiser series which are popular with hunters. The #4 Timber Cruiser is the top of the line.

The 1960's and 70's brought us into the age of jet travel and even more leisure time. Durable luggage was once again a necessity. Though we had been manufacturing bags for big companies like Gokey's and Orvis since the 50's, Duluth Tent & Awning decided to introduce its own line of heavy duty canvas and leather Sportsman's Luggage. It was an instant hit. If the airline ticket in your pocket says New York City, but your heart says "woods and waters", then we have the luggage for you.

In June of 1991 we opened a tiny 900 square-foot "hole-in-the-wall" retail store in Duluth's Canal Park...a revitalized warehouse district on the waterfront. We quickly expanded three times and finally built our 5000 square-foot flagship store a few doors down...opening in April of 1998. At Duluth Pack we carry our full line of luggage, packs and bags. In addition Duluth Pack can be your source for canoe camping gear, winter recreation, outdoor clothing, northern books and cabin furnishings. We specialize in quality goods made in America of traditional materials. . . Filson and Woolrich clothing, Hudson Bay and Pendleton Blankets, Iverson Snowshoes, Bell Canoes, Amish furniture, and much much more. Stop in and see us when you visit the Head of the Lakes in Duluth, Minnesota!

Sparky Stensaas

Duluth Tent and Awning wall tent

Marshall Wells Catalogue 1930

Troop 56 and the Scout Spirit
by Bruce B. Harper, Assistant Scoutmaster, Troop 56, Blacksburg, VA

Troop 56 was one of many Scout troops in the BW on that day. Luckier than some, they left Minnesota without injuries, only scary stories to tell their friends and families back home.

Well, Troop 56 from Blacksburg, Virginia had a wonderful time on our 10 day trek. As for the storm, you had to be there. It hit us on our second day out and I believe it will leave a lasting impression on everyone, Scout and adult, who rode out the wind and waves and rain. After surviving the storm, it was a little easier to understand why entire hillsides were covered with flattened trees, why campsites were obliterated by fallen branches, and why portages were clogged with matchstick piles of lumber.

All three of our crews had an adventure and were none the worse for wear for the event (although the thunder and lightning storm that Sunday night didn't help anyone sleep easy). The aftermath of the storm showed how Scout spirit works, as crews pitched in with camp saws (and the dull hatchet our crew was issued) to clear the portage trails.

My crew was on Amoeber Lake when the storm struck. Anyone who would fault anyone for not getting off the water would be wise to keep his mouth shut. We hurried lunch when we saw the dark clouds approaching and headed across the lake to the campsite. The wind picked up quickly and the lightning started to flash. At the time, it only looked like a typical afternoon thunderstorm.

Person in severe blowdown

Firegate under trees

In a matter of minutes, it went from a normal thunderstorm to a storm from hell. The wind picked up speed and force in an instant and the rain came down in sheets. Large waves were kicked up across the lake. Visibility was nil. Those who were trying to do the right thing and get off the water suddenly went from being in a somewhat controllable situation to being in serious danger. The storm arrived that quickly with that much intensity; there were no signs or warnings that this was a potentially deadly blast. The miracle is that there weren't any more serious injuries than there were.

In the first several days after the 4th, the effort went into clearing branches and brush to make it easier to get to the large trees, so one could climb over or under with the packs and canoes. There were lots of multiple-trip portages and many two-man carries to get canoes from one side to the other. Many folks were grateful to the Forest Service folks who showed up with chain saws to take on the bigger trees. One crew working on one of the trails into the eastern end of Kekekabic Lake had been at it for five hours, clearing a path through trees at least a foot in diameter.

While it will be months before all the trails and campsites are reasonably clear, any trip this summer will still be an experience– just not a unique experience like those of us had who were in "The Storm of the Millennium."

We arrived back on base on Sunday, July 11 and got back to Blacksburg after midnight on Monday, July 12. It will be a few days before we are caught up and collected, but expect some trip reports real soon now. The advice from this list helped all three of our crews to prepare quite well for our adventure (except for the storm!).

The troop was outfitted at the Sommers Scout Base at Moose Lake. Bruce Harper had nothing but praise for the Sommers guides: "We actually had a great time. The Base guides had everything under control. We'll be back again."

Charles L. Sommers Scout Base

BOY SCOUTS OF AMERICA
NORTHERN TIER NATIONAL HIGH ADVENTURE
5891 Moose Lake Road, P.O. Box 509
Ely, MN 55731-0509
Phone: (218) 365-4811 • Fax: (218) 365-3112
E-Mail: info@ntier.org

The Charles L. Sommers base of the Northern Tier National High Adventure Program is situated high on a hill overlooking Moose Lake near Ely. The base took a hit on July 4, as did a Scout troop that won't soon forget their wild experience and evacuation from Eddy Lake.

Sommers is one of three prestigious Boy Scouts High Adventure bases in the U.S. The others are Philmont in New Mexico and Florida's Sea Base. Serving scouting since 1923, the Sommers base rests on a scenic 120 acre site and includes about 50 rustic buildings. Many are beautiful log or cedar buildings on stone foundations.

The Sommers complex operates satellite bases near Atikokan, Ontario and Bissett, Manitoba. In 1999 it outfitted 5283 Scouts from all over the nation. Sommers has 115 seasonal and 6 full time employees.

Doug Ramsey, base General Manager, told me about the storm. "The wind blew for 20 minutes, toppling trees throughout the complex - giant white pines, birches and poplars - with many landing on the buildings. Five vehicles were totally destroyed.

**Sommers
Road Sign**

area of total blowdown. Strangely, of their 600 - 700 canoes only one was destroyed: a $4500 24 ft. voyageurs-type canoe stored on sawhorses. It took a direct hit.

The staff was worried about fire, with dead trees everywhere and no buffer between the base and some of the worst BWCA blowdown.

On July 4, 56 Scout troops - 454 Scouts and their leaders - were in the wilderness. Incredibly, there was only one serious injury, on Eddy Lake - evidence that the Sommers guides and troop leaders had the situation under control even in the most trying times.

Sommers Staff

Totalled voyageur canoe - note the beautiful log and stone building - Sommers Scout Base C14

Picture Eddy Lake: an isolated, beautiful spot in the central BW. Typically it takes two days to reach it from the nearest entry point. Until just after 1 PM on Sunday, it was an idyllic spot. It was here that a troop from Fremont, Ohio, on their first trip to the wilderness, chose to set up camp.

The Scouts were having lunch when the rain started. Tony Stull, a 16 year old, said "The first thing we did was to get under the dining fly to get out of the rain. The wind came up and it was looking worse, so we piled into the tent. We were all laughing, thinking it would blow over, until we heard the crack."

A jackpine 60 to 80 feet tall smashed through the tent, hitting 16 year old Tyler Stierwalt and pinning him to the ground. A branch caught Tony Stull's ankle and 15 year old Matt Shearn was knocked to the ground. Those who could ran into the lake to avoid falling trees.

"We're not religious but we were all praying hard. We all thought we were going to die," said Stull.

Sommers Staff

Totalled sailboat - Sommers Scout Base

"The staff did some immediate clearing to keep the camp operating, but a logger pulled out much of the downed material."

When I visited the camp in August it still looked rough, with lots of trees still lying where they fell among the buildings, and with slash piles from the cleanup throughout the area. The base was damaged more heavily than other Moose Lake outfitters because it is closer to the

When the rain stopped, Sommers guide Pete Esposito lifted the tree off Stierwalt, an action he described as "pure adrenaline." Stierwalt's injuries were the most serious: a severe bruise on his side and a broken collarbone.

There was no radio contact with the base because the tower at Sommers had blown down. The Scouts started a big bonfire and waved their paddles, successfully attracting a Forest Service aircraft which evacuated Tyler to the Ely hospital. Stull could have gone too, but remained to finish the trip with his troop.

The group left Eddy Lake with only the clothes on their backs and some food they retrieved. The tents and packs smashed by the trees were left behind.

The troop worked through the fallen trees to Knife Lake, where all campsites were demolished. They paddled the length of Knife and then camped in the open in the heavy rain that fell late that night.

Had they experienced anything like this before? Scout leader Denny Setzler shook his head, then replied, We had a tornado in Fremont in 1978 but it didn't compare with this.!

Doug Ramsey, Sommers General Manager, knows Eddy Lake well. His heart sank when he saw it after the storm; he didn't recognize it.

Would they be back? "Yes," said 15 year old Jeff Young. Give us a couple years to recover - we'll be back.!

A Wall of Wind and Water Picked Up From the Lake!

This story is reprinted from the *Ely Echo*.
by Shannon Craig and Paul Jester,
Arlington Hts., IL

Hi there.

We just wanted to share our experience of the July 4th Storm. We started out the day at Smitty's on Snowbank about 11 a.m. to just paddle around the lake and explore. We brought some emergency supplies and food in case it were going to rain, as it had Saturday. We wanted to be prepared- but we weren't prepared for what came!

We were paddling toward Fishook Island when we saw the lightning striking the north ridge and the black sky coming quick. We headed for the campsite and got unloaded. I said to Paul,

Snowbank Lake - blowdown begins on North Shore of Snowbank

who loves thunderstorms, "Looks like you're going to get your dream of being out in a wilderness thunderstorm." (Paul: "Did I ever!")

The thunder and lightning were getting louder and closer. Paul got a little fire going so we could dry out later and cook some Bison dogs. Then a pair of loons in the bay across from us called what turned out to be an alarm, and

then in it came. First some wind and rain, then all at once a wall of wind and water picked up from the lake. Trees were blowing and bending and debris from the forest was flying everywhere.

Paul ran to put our things under the canoe to keep dry, and we stood next to two cedars and watched. Then a cracking, popping sound and the first tree went, just in front of us onto our canoe. Then another tree right next to it and a couple behind us. I kept saying, "Oh my God, what are we going to do?" to Paul. We ran down a path, but then Paul saw that the first tree had fallen partially into the fire, so he grabbed his axe and quickly hacked some of the branches away; the rain did the rest.

The lake looked like a stormy ocean with huge swells. That's when you know you've got nowhere to go and have to deal with this event right here! We ran back the way we came only to run back again as a couple more trees gave way, and fell behind us as we fled- one Paul pushed away as it was heading right for me.

We spent the rest of the time in a small grove of small balsams and cedars holding hands, praying and keeping our eyes on the trees! Then we saw a break in the sky to the west and knew we'd have a chance to get back.

Paul was somehow able to wriggle our old Grumman out from under the tree, which didn't even get a dent! And we managed to make it through without so much as a scratch. And as soon as it looked calm enough, we headed back to Smitty's. They said they knew we were out there, and if we weren't back soon, they would have come searching for us– which was very good to hear.

We know some people had it MUCH worse than us. We were lucky, and kept our wits about us and tried to do the right things. Later, finding out and seeing the scope of the storm, makes you realize what you made it through. When we got back to our home for now in Illinois, after dealing with traffic and the pollution, etc. of this area, Paul commented, "I'd rather have gone through that storm than live in this masquerade people around here think is life."

A part of us stayed on that island, and a part of that island stayed with us. That was living– that was life.

Abandoned Tent on Snowbank Lake
by Dan and Lisa Thornberg

Snowbank Lake near Ely, July 1999–After listening to weather reports and deciding that we would be OK going in (we figured we could handle scattered thunderstorms –the "some severe" part must have gone over our heads!), we entered the Boundary Waters on Saturday, July 3rd, after waiting for the rain to quit in the early afternoon. Got off even though it was windy and gray. The day cleared but continued windy and as we were a little low in the water, we soaked a few things en route to our campsite.

We had trouble finding an open campsite so we saw a lot of the lake. (It helps to have a motor on your canoe!) We finally wound up on the opposite end of the lake (northeast) in a nice secluded bay. I remember thinking to myself that if we got any weather we'd be protected on almost all four sides. We set up camp and originally pitched our tent a few yards from the water in an exposed area. It was pretty hot and humid and I talked my wife into switching to a spot that had trees around it in order to keep the sun off us when we wanted.

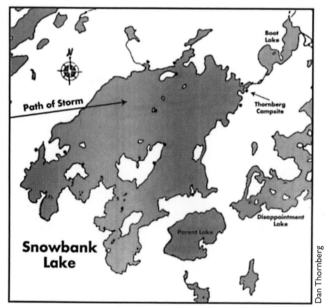

Map of Snowbank Lake

The spot was a little tight and we wound up putting the tent near two good-sized pines so that the left side of the tent was directly behind them. I was a little nervous about being so close to trees but they looked pretty solid so I decided not to worry about it. We cooked some steaks and then headed out to fish walleyes near a couple islands.

Caught one right away and then not much. It was getting dark, so we headed back, trolling for lake trout on the way. To our surprise, instead of a laker, we caught a small walleye suspended over 70 feet of water. We turned in and slept well.

Sunday, July 4 dawned dead calm, sunny and warm. We had breakfast and then headed out to fish lake trout over by the big island. No luck. Around 11:00 we noticed that it was beginning to get dark and stormy over on the northwest side of the lake so we kept an eye on it while we went to fish walleyes again by the smaller islands. The storm appeared to be heading slightly away from us. There were lots of lightning flashes and distant thunder but it still didn't seem like it was going to come our way.

Around noon, we decided it was not looking as good so we headed back. Arriving at camp, it started to look more like it would miss us after all, so we went out and fished the small bay right in front of our campsite. The opposite side of the bay was tree-lined and thus blocked our view of the main part of the lake.

About a half hour later, we felt a few big raindrops and looked up to see a fairly angry sky right above the trees so we decided to head in quick. We were just seconds away from our camp so we were back very quickly. However, as we neared the landing we looked out on the lake and saw a wall of water and wind with white foam at the bottom heading straight toward us. Oh oh, we'd better hustle! Now we had no time to get ready at all so we flew to the tent and got the fly zipped the instant the wind hit.

We held the tent and wondered if it was going to stay up. My wife was on my left side and, remembering the trees, I told her to make sure she stayed in the middle. After about two minutes, the wind suddenly switched directions and started blowing the tent from behind. Totally surprised, I was trying to figure out how that could happen. Then Lisa reached to her left about a foot and a half and said, "There's a tree here!" I said, "It's probably a branch that broke off. Make sure you stay in the middle!" Then she looked up and said, "The tent's broken!" and showed me the support rod bending inward.

I was still not figuring out what was going on. The wind was still blowing hard, but we weren't experiencing anything more than the tent being fluffed around on the back and sides. So I decided to open the fly and take a look. When I did, all I saw was dirt in front of us. "There's a wall here!" I told Lisa. So I poked my head out and finally saw what had happened.

Rootball blocking tent entrance

The two trees nearest the tent plus another one close by, had all come up by the roots and had fallen on and above our tent! The first one was pinning it to the ground and the next one was six feet in the air. We never heard a thing other than the wind.

Looking toward the little bay to our right we saw waves three to four feet high. Well, the wind finally died down and we stepped out to take a look. Talk about a war zone! Fourteen trees down on our campsite. Canoe full of water. Motor full of water. Equipment blown around. One fishing pole and the starter key for the motor completely disappeared.

Trees over tent

What to do? We tried to get the tent out but could not budge it. We thought briefly about staying but then, although it had cleared and gotten sunny for awhile, we saw what looked like another storm coming so we decided to hightail it for the entry point. We packed feverishly and loaded the canoe, leaving the poles and stakes for the tent in case anyone found it and could get it out. I tried to start the motor with a needle-nose pliers replacing the starter clip but broke the ignition on the third pull. (I found out later that the motor was soaked and so wouldn't have started anyway.)

At this point I was becoming a bit worried. It was about a three mile paddle and the skies were not looking good. We paddled as hard as we ever had and fortunately the weather held. When we got to the landing, we found one canoe and three cars smashed by trees. Our SUV was parked in a fairly open area so it suffered no damage.

While loading our gear in the parking lot, we met a couple named Scott and Karen just going in. They were traveling in an old bus and had come in from Utah. Scott's parents live in Richfield, Minnesota, so they had been visiting or were on their way there. We shared our experience and told them we had left our tent at the campsite. So Scott said, "If we can get your tent out, can we have it?" I said, "Sure! It's no good to us." Apparently, they were going in just for a day and then decided to spend the night and had not been able to rent a tent. We exchanged addresses and they launched while we headed home after staying the night in Ely. We decided to regroup and try camping later in the summer or early fall.

A couple days after we got back, we got a phone call from Scott's parents saying they had our tent and we could come and pick it up. Scott had worked for over two hours sawing apart the tree that had the tent pinned. They just got it free minutes before dark and moments before being eaten alive by mosquitoes! Amazingly, it could still be set up and they spent the night nice and dry even though it rained again.

Venture Scouts on Moose Lake

The following is the story of an all-female Sommers Base outfitted Scout crew caught on Moose Lake during the storm. It was posted to the CanoeCountry.com mailing list. Their website is ‹www.canoecountry.com›.

July 16, 1999–We just returned from our 10 day trip out of Sommers. We had two crews of female Venture Scouts and each did very well. One crew did 78 miles and the other did 72 miles in the western section of the Boundary Waters. The interpreters were great young men who really enabled the girls to make it their own trip. They were always there when needed but knew when to stand back.

The highest part of the adventure was coming back to Base on day 9 and getting caught in a

Moose Lake blowdown

USFS

freak storm of 80 mph winds that leveled many of the trees at Base and along the lakes. We sat out the 28 minute storm huddled up in a low spot on the steep slope on the south side of Moose Lake a mile from Base. Our interpreter was great in helping me keep the girls calm. It was very scary and dangerous and we had no where else to go.

We managed to salvage all our gear and the canoes from under the large spruce tree that fell on them as they floated tied together in the lake. We had gotten off the water before the (main) cell hit, because of a passing thunderstorm. God was with us.

Damage in the form of downed trees was very heavy. I imagine that the portage trails will be a lot of work getting through for quite a while (years) to come. Sommers suffered no serious losses. Buildings were intact; canoe racks were missed by the trees, etc. But it is a mess. Crews that were out were all

okay. Some needed equipment ferried out to them. There were some damaged canoes on the trail.

One of the funniest moments came on day 8. We made a portage and came ashore even though another group was there—thunder again. (Did I mention that we were rained on every day for 9 days?) The Boy Scout crew there were on their first day and were privately outfitted. As the girls worked together to off-load the canoes and start the portage some of the boys began giving advice, like: "You need to drain the water out of the canoe before you flip it." Our crew leader was about 5'3' and 115 pounds. She smiled sweetly and said, (This is day 8 of 9– I think we can handle this." She and two others (same size) then proceeded to buck the second canoe onto their thighs, swing it up and settle it onto the carrier's shoulders. Our interpreter smiled and said, (They do that well, don't they?" He then lifted his canoe and followed the others down the trail. The two girls and I lifted our packs and followed.

Their (Boy Scout) leader complemented our crew leader on our teamwork. The girls were so proud of what they had come to be able to do. You should have seen us our first day. Those 75 pound canoes are awkward to handle when you are small.

We will be back in two years. (Already have another trip in the planning stages for next summer.) We will never do less than the 10 day trip. You need it all to really get into the program and the routine. It was the best trip we have ever taken in our six years as a Post/Crew.

I can't say enough about the Base and the staff. They were great!

BWCA CENTRAL

If Not for My Friends I Wouldn't Have Survived
by Lisa Naas, Minneapolis

I planned a canoe and camping trip with four friends to go to the BWCA over the 4th of July. I entered on Saturday, went six or seven miles into the BWCA, through four portages to our base camp on Lake Polly. The weather was hot, so time was allocated between swimming and hanging out in the hammock.

Sunday was a nice morning - we spent most of it fishing, although not a thing was biting. When thunder started rumbling we headed back to camp. We were ready for the rain and had tarps over everything. We were pretty relaxed when the storm started - rain in the Boundary Waters was not new to us. The storm kept getting stronger, and I went to pull my canoe further up on shore.

USFS Beaver Aircraft at campsite

That's when it happened. What happened I'm not exactly sure; I have no recollection of it, and only one person saw anything. But this we know - the top half of a tree snapped off and hit me on the left side of my head. That knocked me back into another canoe and eventually deposited me on the rocks at the water's edge, unconscious.

The next thing I remember, I was being moved onto a tarp and had trouble breathing. I could hear my friends talking about moving me and that

Beaver Aircraft lifting off with Lisa

I was going into shock. I remember them carrying me on the tarp while holding my head to get me into my tent. There they got me into my sleeping bag. They got my breathing regulated and were working to keep me out of shock. I kept hearing them refer to their emergency first aid manual. What prepared friends I have!

Two of my friends headed back to the point of entry to get help. The other two stayed with me, having me wiggle toes and fingers, asking me questions to keep me

conscious. I still didn't understand what happened to me, but I knew it was a bad situation and felt sorry about putting my friends through it.

After a while I could hear the roar of a plane's engine. This relieved me. It meant that my friends were O.K. and were able to send help. Once the EMT saw me, she realized she didn't have enough equipment to move me and she sent the plane back for more. The plane returned with the equipment and the sheriff and a deputy on board. (I didn't realize until later that it was actually a different plane that was sent back.)

Suddenly there were a lot of people around me in my little two man tent. They placed me on a backboard and somehow maneuvered me out of that small tent. I kept my eyes closed but could hear them talking about the steep rocks they had to go down to get to the plane. They were making the best of their situation too, and appreciated that it wasn't a 300 pound person that they had to take down those rocks. The got me loaded on the plane and took off for Ely.

By the time we arrived at the hospital in Ely I was spending less and less time conscious. The staff was wonderful, but the prognosis wasn't. They were sure that I had a broken neck. The doctor called my parents himself, and it was the first time during this ordeal that I felt scared. They had to send me to Duluth by ambulance because the weather had turned bad again and we couldn't fly.

I remember arriving in Duluth. The only thing I remember clearly was right before they put me under for surgery. I fought a little because I thought (This has to be a dream- it couldn't possibly be real."

The next thing I remember was waking up after surgery in the intensive care unit. My nurse filled me in on everything: fractured skull with surgery to remove a blood clot from the brain– they were doing more tests, but did not believe that my neck was broken, and it was Monday morning.

My first concern was for my friends. They wouldn't know that I had been taken to Duluth or that my condition was stable and I was going to recover just fine. I also felt really bad that they would have to carry out all of my camping gear on top of everything they had of their own.

Monday and Tuesday are pretty blurry. I remember my parents arriving from Arkansas. My brother came from Colorado. My friends got out of the Boundary Waters and finally found me. They were relieved,

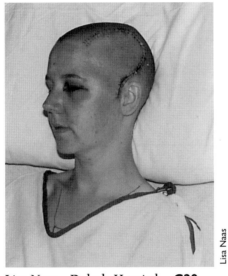

Lisa Naas - Duluth Hospital **C29**

but were still in crisis mode. They didn't realize until they got back to normal life what heroic things they had done. If not for their actions, I would not have survived.

The rest of the week was full of mile markers. Wednesday I went for my first walk and looked in the mirror for the first time. I bore an eerie resemblance to (Uncle Fester" from the Addams family!! (Yep, they shaved my head for the surgery.) Thursday I was totally (cordless," no IV's or anything and I got to eat chocolate ice cream. Friday I had a bunch of visitors which made me feel great. The last visitors of the evening were my friends that saved

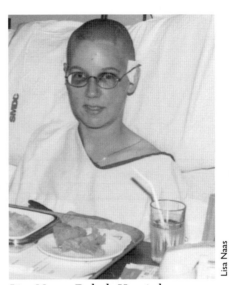

Lisa Naas - Duluth Hospital

me. I was so excited to see them I almost jumped out of bed. They were amazed to see me up and walking. It was pretty gratifying to them. Needless to say, there were lots of hugs.

Lake Polly Evacuation
by Michelle Orieux - July 9,1999

This story is reprinted from an online forum hosted by the Minneapolis Star-Tribune:

I'm using this forum to share our experience in the BWCA on July 4th and to be able to thank the many people who helped us out. I challenge anyone to read (and fully comprehend) our story and still say No to carrying a phone in the BWCA!"

We could still hear the hum of the engine in the distance. It was the loudest noise we had heard all weekend. Ordinarily this kind of noise would be unwelcome in the BWCA as it is the silence we cherish. Today, however, was not ordinary. The noise was from the floatplane carrying our friend to safety. We were comforted by the fact she was finally going to get the medical attention she needed. Later we learned she was in critical condition and was in need of surgery to remove the blood clot within her

fractured skull. Still later, we learned she will recover, but it will be a long process. Right then, we were relieved we made the choices we did and were waiting for our friends who had alerted help to make it safely back to camp. What had happened during the last five hours began to sink in.

We could see the sky turning dark and hear the rumble of thunder in the distance. The five of us set up additional tarps and took cover to wait out the storm. Within 15 minutes the rain started and the winds picked up. Our friend saw her canoe needed to be secured. She ran down to grab it. Trees started snapping. There was no place to run for shelter as the brunt of the storm came too quickly. Too many trees to count came down within a matter of minutes. Our tarps were ripped in half. A large white pine split in half fifteen feet above the ground. It came down, throwing our friend to the ground. Someone shouted, (She's down..." the four of us looked towards the water to see our friend was not moving. We admitted later that at that moment we thought she was dead. We happily discovered she was still breathing, but unconscious.

We are experienced campers. We have made countless trips to the BWCA over the years, both together and separately. We know and respect the wilderness. However, we are not experienced in saving lives. We did know the rule - (never move a victim with a head or neck injury." But, we were deep in the woods, many hours from help. The rain was coming down hard, streaming all around her and she was going into shock. We gently rolled her onto a tarp and broke the cardinal rule. The driest place was her tent. We carried her there and tried to keep her warm with the few dry items we had. She was bleeding and her face was badly bashed. Her left eye was purple and severely swollen. She was in and out of consciousness, and vomiting blood. We needed to get her help. Two of us stayed with her and the other couple made the long journey back to our entry point.

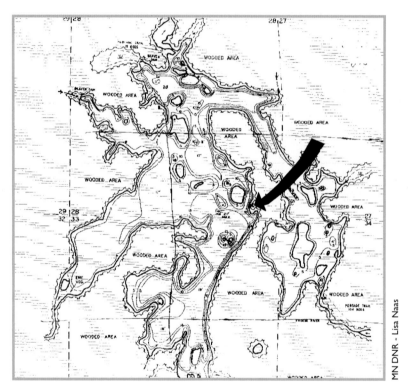

Lisa Naas campsite on Lake Polly

A few days earlier the trip in took five hours to canoe and portage. The couple made the trip back in less than two hours. No cellular service was available at their car. They drove as far as they could dodging the downed trees. They were finally able to get cell service and reach a 911 operator. They had to keep calling back to make sure help was on the way. We are very aware now that if they had not had a cell phone, our friend would have died. The roads back to Tofte were impassable and she would not have made it through the night without medical assistance. Once they knew help was on the way, they reluctantly started the trip back to the campsite in order to reach it before nightfall.

The campsite looked much different than the day before. Trees were lying everywhere. Pine, birch and cedar came down on both sides of two tents, but miraculously only one tent was slightly damaged. The rumble of thunder and the cracking of trees continued long after the

storm had passed, reminding us we were still in danger. We had to saw branches off huge downed trees to move around the campsite; even the latrine was now unreachable. We had joked the day before about having to search for firewood at this campsite - that had all changed.

Our friend was in excruciating pain. We knew we needed to keep her awake; asking her 1001 questions and trying to monitor her state by her answers. We thought about how deeply she has touched our lives as a co-worker, roommate, bridesmaid and friend and prayed for the chance to make sure she is fully aware of how important she is to us. We felt completely helpless. The isolation from civilization that we all were seeking in this trip was now our biggest obstacle.

Finally after five hours, we heard the floatplane.

We want to sincerely THANK the following people for their assistance in getting our friend to safety and to acknowledge that the kindness of strangers has had a significant impact on us:

• Floyd with Lake County.

• The 911 operator.

• Chip the plane dispatcher.

• Barb Garrison the EMT out of Ely.

• Both pilots of the floatplanes whose skill located our campsite by the color of our tents and approximate location.

• The Sheriff and Deputy of Lake County who gently carried our friend down a 90 degree embankment to the floatplane.

• The group from Chanhassen/Western Suburbs who helped us carry our packs over the 189 rod portage when they realized why we were towing an extra canoe and tripling back to get our packs.

• The man at Sawtooth Outfitters who said he would not charge for an act of God, when he saw the badly damaged canoe and learned of our friend's condition.

We are forever grateful for your kindness!!!!

USFS Beaver Aircraft Pilots

THE ELY ECHO
Section 2

FOURTH OF JULY SPECTACULAR
STORM SPECIAL
MONDAY, JULY 12, 1999

Where credit is due

Few visitors to the Boundary Waters have any idea of the mechanics of the wilderness. That is, how outfitters, guides, youth camps and government agencies manage the people who come and go, particularly in emergency situations. They got a first hand look last week.

The final screech of the fierce storm which ripped across the border lakes had scarcely begun to quiet when the Forest Service was on the go. In short order, federal, state and county personnel were being mustered into an integrated rescue force.

Most of the hundreds of canoe and boat campers scattered across the 250,000-acre devastated area, had no idea what to expect. Many who were in remote areas, found their tents destroyed, canoes smashed or blown down the shore or into the lakes. Those who had canoes intact and were attempting to get out found portages blocked by a jackstraw jumble of fallen trees. Injured campers and those with them dealt with their problems as best they could, wondering frantically what was their next move.

The first thing most of them saw were Forest Service float planes, initial response from the air, which eventually became a fleet of U.S. and private float planes and Minnesota state helicopters. Many campers had ridden out the storm without significant damage, but other camps were demolished. Circling low, the float plane pilots assessed each case, dropping down to land where signalling campers indicated major problems. Injured were quickly evacuated to the Ely hospital or beyond, as required, for medical attention. Campers with tents and canoes gone were brought out as quickly as possible. By the second day, search and rescue teams could no longer find any injured or truly desperate people.

At the time planes were overhead, teams by boat and canoe, some 80 people in all, were penetrating the area to check campsites first hand. Wednesday, 18 trail crews were flown in to various access points with the aim of "chainsawing their way out," to open up many of the main portages. Other crews were being readied to go in and clean up campsites with hand saws and axes.

A considerable part of the infrastructure outside of the Boundary Waters was also hit hard. Outfitters and resorts on the perimeter had roads and driveways blocked, power and phone lines down.

Lake Country Power, Minnesota Power, GTE and other repair crews were on the job restoring electricity and phones on nearly a round-the-clock work basis. By Wednesday, most phone lines were operating. Power in some areas was established, but the storm had snapped a number of electric power poles which had to be replaced and new transformers installed along with hundreds of yards of electrical lines replaced or repaired.

Road crews with chain saws and heavy equipment were busy clearing blocked roads. Resorters, outfitters and private landowners were out with chainsaws clearing out places of business, home sites and everything nearby.

A Lake County road crew were reported working to clear a massive log jam on Highway 1 between Ely and Isabella. County staff and volunteer loggers were sawing their way through a maze of pine trunks. Auto traffic began piling up on the road. One grizzled logger, tired of hearing drivers ask when the road would be clear, went to the lineup and yelled that if they wanted to get through in the near future, autoists had better get out of their cars and pitch in. Within minutes a mob of autoists were on the highway carting off chunks of tree trunks as fast as the county crew could saw them up. In short order, traffic was restored.

Unfortunately, media reports from sources outside the area described this part of NE Minnesota as a total disaster. The Ely Chamber of Commerce said dozens of would-be vacationers cancelled reservations. They didn't have to. Three days after the storm, roads were all clear, power and phone lines largely restored and most of the Boundary Waters was again passable for canoes and boats. Good news reports have been few.

Except this one.

The Forest Service airbase is located on Shagawa Lake not far from Ely. The three Dehavilland Beaver DHC-2's are highly versatile aircraft used for ferrying personnel and cargo, fire detection and suppression, fish planting, wildlife surveys, law enforcement work and much more.

These aircraft can carry seven passengers, or three passengers and their gear (with one canoe on the pontoons). The pontoons make them amphibious; they can also be winterized with skis or outfitted with wheels.

Wayne, a veteran USFS pilot, says that "Beaver aircraft have replaced towers in the Superior National Forest. From a tower, vision can be limited to a mile; while in a Beaver it is generally 20 to 30 miles.

"Helicopters are often used for fires but the Beaver is more efficient and economical to operate, scooping 150 gallons from lakes versus 110 gallons for the copters. The Cost of operating a Beaver is $90 per hour, compared to $700 for the helicopter. The flying range is much longer - 6 hours versus 1 1/2 hours. Helicopters can be more accurate with water drops but are more prone to accidents than fixed wing craft. **C51**

"Our three aircraft were built between 1957 and 1963 and have seen thousands of hours of service. We are

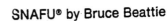

SNAFU® by Bruce Beattie

Beaver Pilot Wayne Erickson and Hotshot Crew

limited to 4,000 feet over the BWCA except for emergencies."

The day I visited the pilots I was lucky. It was too foggy to fly so Wayne Erickson, Dean Lee and Pat Loe had some time to visit and answer questions.

On July 4th, Pat was watching the Independence Day parade in Ely. "It got really dark about noon. At 12:30 the wind picked up. When the lights in town went out I knew something was up. Then my beeper went off." This signaled the start of a very busy summer.

On July 4th and 5th Wayne and Pat evacuated about 20 people from the wilderness. At least 12 other persons were evacuated by motorboat and other means. Helicopters and ambulances were kept busy transporting the injured once roads were cleared - to hospitals in Ely, Grand Marais, Two Harbors, Duluth, Virginia and other towns.

Hospital treats dozens

Pat Angelos, director of nursing at North Shore Hospital has become a veteran in answering reporters questions in the past week. "Yes, we saw about 27 people with storm related injuries," Angelos said, almost before she was asked. Only a handful of that number were airlifted out of the Boundary Waters.

Angelos said the injured began to arrive around 5:00 p.m. on July 4. Four extra nurses and three doctors were there to attend to the patients. One doctor and one nurse actually went with a severely injured man in an ambulance all the way to a Duluth hospital. The man, who sustained chest and leg injuries was in stable condition by Tuesday, July 6.

"The rest were lacerations, frac-tures and contusions from trees hitting them," Angelos said. She said that two patients were admitted for overnight observation and released.

One patient, a young boy, was to be flown to the county hospital by helicopter but went to Duluth directly.

By late Tuesday morning the US Forest Service claimed that 19 people had been air-lifted out of the Boundary Waters. Angelos stressed that only a few of those 19 people were injured. Angelos said that the rest were the camping companions of the injured.

"I'm surprised that there were not more people critically injured-the injuries certainly did not reflect the devastation," Angelos said.

Cook County News-Herald

The wilderness Beaver evacuations included (location and type of injury):

Insula Lake - Broken leg and ribs.

Poly Lake - Head and neck injuries. A woman was hit by a tree and then a canoe.

Hansen Lake - Back injury.

Alpine Lake - Two broken legs.

Knife Lake - Broken back.

Eddy Lake - Broken collar bone. The scouts built a huge fire and waved their paddles to attract the pilot.

Tuscarora Lake - Two people with possible back injuries and broken ribs.

According to Wayne, "All the calls that came in on July 4 were from cell phones. There are typically 8 to 10 evacuations per year. The reasons include drownings, heart attacks, bee sting reactions, broken bones from falls, lightning hits and many other emergencies."

On the airbase office wall hangs a big map of the Superior National Forest, with pins and flags showing where the evacuations took place and what caused them. Most flags are white with a red cross; others are black with a skull and crossbones.

I was working early Sunday at the Tofte District office. "The radios are always on." At about 0630 I heard a very faint distress call from a Wilderness Ranger. The ranger had found a woman in her 12th hour of epileptic seizures. She was on a lake too small for the Beaver so she was portaged to Mesaba Lake and then evacuated. The aircraft requires a mile of lake surface to land and take off. The evacuee's insurance usually pays for the flight."

During the storm's search and rescue phase, Beaver aircraft were joined by a DNR helicopter, Minnesota State Patrol aircraft and 5 planes of the Civil Air Patrol from St. Cloud that flew grids over the wilderness searching for campers.

Captain Richard Josephson, emergency service coordinator for the St. Cloud squad said, "Covering such a large area looking for campers can be quite a challenge. It's awfully difficult to spot an individual in such a vast area so we had to make sure we looked over the entire area carefully."

USFS Pilot Pat Loe loading canoe on pontoon

The pilots were afraid that campers could be under trees on remote portages or dead-end lakes.

Wayne flew over one suspicious site on Ashigan lake. "When we landed we found a crushed canoe and large trees down on the tent. We moved to the tent and felt anxiously around the trees for a body, but found nothing."

Typical members of a search and rescue flight are the pilot, a deputy sheriff and an emergency medical technician (EMT).

Sarah and Anna, owners of Trail Center resort on the Gunflint Trail, told me that "Two Federal Emergency Management Agency (FEMA) workers brought in to deal with deaths caused by the storm told us that after 40 years of experience doing this, they thought it incredible that there weren't lots of fatalities."

The pilots were shocked when they first flew over the damage, and continue to be amazed today. Their numerous passengers included politicians, Forest Service officials and others who were equally amazed. According to Pat, "You no longer need a compass - all the trees are pointing east! You can walk from Jackfish Bay near Ely to the Gunflint Trail on trees without touching the ground."

The conversation turned to fire suppression. The Forest Service may add one more pilot and possibly a Canadian CL - 215 to its inventory to hold down fires in the 40 mile long slash pile.

Suddenly word came in that the fog had lifted sufficiently. All three Beaver pilots ran out of the building and within minutes were airborne.

Nancy Pius

USFS Beaver Aircraft clipping White Pine snag during fire suppression

USFS

Hotshot Crew on break

Thousands of Birch and Pine Ripped From the Ground

By Scott Augustus

I was with two other guys from the Twin Cities. On Sunday afternoon we had just finished paddling across Ensign Lake and we were taking the portage to Vera Lake when the clouds started rolling in. By the time we had crossed the 180 rod portage (about 20 minutes), we saw lightning and decided to wait for it to stop before paddling.

The violent storm clouds came in from the west real quickly, and within about 10 minutes the rain was coming down in sheets so hard that the other side of the lake was not visible. Our canoe almost blew into the lake at one point, but we managed to secure it. We darted off into the woods for shelter from the winds and stayed there for almost an hour, listening to all the trees cracking around us. We were lucky enough to be on low ground; there weren't many large trees nearby, and we weren't hurt.

After the storm passed, we were collecting our gear when a couple of canoeists paddled by, looking for a second canoe that the storm had blown into the lake, which they eventually found. As it turned out, they were part of a Boy Scout troop from Atlanta staying at a campsite about 100 yards from where we had stood during the storm. Almost every tree on their campsite was down, and they told us that three of the Scouts had been hit by fallen trees, and all three were OK. (Two of them were in a tent when a tree came down crashing onto the tent).

We saw campsites that had no trees left standing. The site that we had camped at the night before was completely devastated. There were areas where hundreds of birch trees in a cluster were all snapped in half, and there were thousands of pine and birch trees that had been ripped out of the ground by their roots. The next morning, we tried to exit Vera Lake via a portage to Knife Lake, which was completely impassable for all the downed trees. We ended up leaving the same way we arrived, through the 180 rod portage back to Ensign Lake, and the only reason that portage was passable was because the Boy Scout troop had passed through earlier in the morning, and they had partially cleared their own path.

Fraser / Vera Lakes blowdown

USFS

Voyageur Outward Bound
by *Velma McDonald*

I interviewed Velma McDonald on a dark stormy October evening in Finland, Minnesota.

The young woman, a veteran Outward Bound guide, gave me the background of events leading to the evacuation of members of her party from Insula Lake. Velma told me about Voyageurs Outward Bound: (It's a part of International Outward Bound and the leading outdoor education organization in the world."

The base consists of buildings on 40 acres on the banks of the Kawishiwi River near state highway 1, just south of Ely, Minnesota. Voyageurs has challenged more than 30,000 young people since 1964 to push and surpass their limits while exploring some of the most picturesque wilderness in the world.

Voyageurs' 100 to 110 person staff teaches wilderness courses emphasizing survival skills. About 1000 students were enrolled in 1999. All canoes used are 75 lb. Grummans. All packs are Duluth Packs.

Voyageur Outward Bound Guide Velma McDonald
C44

During their activities students travel in groups of 5 to 10 with two instructors. Expeditions last from 4 to 84 days, traveling the most uninhabited wilderness areas in Minnesota, Montana, Texas, New Mexico, Manitoba and Mexico.

Some of Voyageurs' curriculum includes: canoeing, backpacking, rock climbing, sea kayaking, cross country skiing and dogsledding.

The school works closely with the Forest Service, and "leave no trace" ethics are emphasized. Students do volunteer work with the Forest Service, and other public service. They help

Outward Bound canoes   C45

with the John Beargrease Dogsled Race and with other events.

On July 4, Velma, another guide and 7 students were at a campsite on Insula Lake.

According to Velma, "The day began sunny but by noon it was overcast, with thunder from the southwest. Suddenly, the grey turned to dusk."

Velma continued, "Our group went into our practiced lightning drill - looking for shelter in low places. The wind hit us at 2 PM, breaking off large trees all around us. My biggest fear was that we might be impaled by broken branches."

Trees did fall on two youngsters, crushing a boy's right knee and bruising a girl's ribs. Luckily, a Forest Service person and volunteer were on the lake; they radioed for help and within 30 minutes a float plane was at their campsite. The instructors helped load the injured into the aircraft. This was probably the first evacuation of the storm.

Insula Lake wasn't in the main path of the storm but suffered a micro-burst of about two minutes.

Voyageurs had 20 groups out on that day. Some fought blocked portages with trees stacked 15 to 20 feet high, but there were no other injuries.

As we were leaving the restaurant after the interview, Velma, who is black, got some looks and comments from customers. She was disgusted to see how really "backwoods" some people are. She said that she was raised in the south, so she had heard it all before.

With Velma as a guide I'd feel very comfortable under any circumstances in the wilderness.

Molter Island
by U.S. Forest Service

Marianne and I were portaging into Knife Lake, where we were surprised to meet an older lady picking flowers and salvaging nails out of some old logging timbers. She invited us to her island home for

Dorothy Molter Resort on Knife Lake

Bill Trygg

a cup of tea. The lady must have had friends who played practical jokes on her, because she had a fire hydrant on the path to her house, and several telephones in her living room.

The following is a brief history of Molter Island, from some USFS files.

KNIFE LAKE RESORT _ Dorothy Molter (Formerly called Pine Island Camp)

This resort property is located upon two islands (one large and one small) in the western end of Knife Lake. The two islands are connected by a catwalk. The islands are located directly on the historic Voyageurs route and because of their beautiful and scenic nature I have no doubt they were much used by Indians and Voyageurs as camping places (See attached photograph).

According to Charley Ott, a retired State of Minnesota warden, in a personal letter to me of 1/10/1973 the original owner of this property was William Berglund, a retired game warden and a good one. Charles' comments to me are quoted as follows:

The partner of Bill Berglund was Gunder Graves, and they bought the island in the west end of Knife Lake. I

150 Snowmobilers Make Ely Trip

The 11th annual snowmobile trip to Ely, which is the highlight of the Cook County Snowmobile Club activities for the year, took place over the weekend. About 150 snowmobilers took part, coming from as far away as the Twin Cities.

The club members left at 9:00 a.m. Saturday morning from Saganaga Lake for the 70 mile jaunt over frozen lakes.

Club president Gene Nelson reported good lake conditions, although a little slushy on the trip going over. The cooler weather on Sunday provided perfect snowmobiling for the return trip. The club also noted that practically no litter was noticed along the trails, which was a marked improvement.

A stop-over was held at Dorothy Moulder's cabin on Big Knife Lake, where she had her usual pot of soup prepared for the group.

The local club was entertained by the Ely Snowmobile Club at a cocktail party and dance on Saturday evening to climax a very enjoyable trip.

Cook County News-Herald

Snowmobile trip to Dorothy Molter Knife Lake Resort - March 8, 1973

camped on that island in September, 1927 while on a trip from Gunflint Lake, to Kettle Falls on Rainy Lake. There was no one living along the border until we got to Basswood Lake. There were trapper cabins, if one knew where they were located."

"I knew Bill Berglund, Jack Linklater, Bill Hanson - Winton Wardens. These old time game wardens were woodsmen, and were dedicated to their work."

Doc. J. F. Wolff says that Berglund's partner was Charley Singer, who left when Bill took up with Dorothy, and became caretaker at Kiwadinippi (sp) on the Stoney River. Doc published Joe Brickners Diaries several years ago and he says the above information came from Brickner, who was the chief warden. Maybe both statements could be true with Gunder Graves coming first, followed by Charley Singer. Maybe it isn't too important - anyway we know about Bill Berglund's constant role. His so-called Pine Island camp was located on Lot 5, Section 31, T65N R7W. It was built in 1931 and gradually developed over a period of years. Mr. Berglund presumably used winter sleigh hauling for transporting building materials and supplies, and motor boat during the summer. It was only from 1945-46 that he used aircraft for transporting supplies and guests. This resort was originally considered more or less of an outpost as the guests usually came from resorts on Moose Lake and canoe parties in addition to some direct reservations.

Mr. Berglund owned this place up until the time of his death in March, 1948. After proceedings were completed in probate court - Dorothy Molter took over as owner. There are various stories as to how Dorothy acquired title but I prefer the one which says that Dorothy, a professional nurse from Chicago, nursed and took care of Bill Berglund until he passed away, and in gratitude he gave the property to her, and his relatives did not contest the gift.

While the planes were flying most all guests and supplies were handled by planes. After the planes ceased flying they used boats and motors, canoes, snowmobiles or what have you. Dorothy was well known by everyone who travelled in the area and even the deeply committed wilderness people had kind words for her.

One time when I called at her place she had a very black, black-inflamed eye. After I asked her how the other fellow looked, I found out that a little boy (a relative) was staying with her. He had a pet chipmunk and it got out of a box and ran behind the stove. Dorothy leaned over the stove to see where the pet was and ran a spoon handle (in pot on stove) in her eye. She finally had to go outside and have it treated.

We were never able to deal with Dorothy for the property, so it was acquired thru a proceedings in condemnation. Brief details of the transaction follows:

Case Name and No.   Dorothy L. Molter t3884 (5-66 Civil 6)

Descriptions -

   T65N R7W - Sec 31 - Lot 5

   T64N R8W _ Sec 30 - Lot 4

   T64N R9W _ Sec 25 - Lot 2

Acres - 11.13

Consideration - $39,000.00

Reservation - Reservation for personal use to Dec. 31, 1975

               Removal of personal property to 6/30/76

               Use of Boathouse only to 9/1/67

Declaration of taking filed - 1/20/1966

Final Judgement dated - 8/30/1966

Improvements -

Cabin 19 x 27	Fish cleaning house 6 x 10
Residence 19 x 33	Storage houses (2)
Cabin 13 x 25	Toilets (4)
Cabin 13 x 24	Tent frames (2)
Boat & supply 15 x 30	Catwalks 2 - 50' long
Oil house 9 x 11	Root cellar 10 x 12
Ice house 12 x 13	Water pump
Docks - Site improvement etc.	

The buildings are still in place and will remain so until the reservation either expires or is released. When the time finally comes for building disposal I plead again for discretion with fire. Disposal should be carefully planned and be carried out with reason and the aim of making the area look more like a wilderness without the buildings.

Reference to "C" throughout the book indicates a color photo in mid-section.

My Son Turned to Me from the Bow of the Canoe with Terror in his Face

by John Jeanneret

Dear Jim,

Thanks for your letter asking about the July 4th storm in the Boundary Waters. My son and I were indeed in the path of the storm and we would be happy to help you with your book.

I was on Ogishkamuncie Lake with my 15-year-old son, Derek, when the July 4th storm hit. We had just put in at Sea Gull Lake on Saturday, July 3rd. It was our first trip to the Boundary Waters, and Derek and I had hoped to spend about seven days leisurely paddling a loop from Sea Gull Lake west to Lower Knife Lake, then northeast along the Canadian border through Monument Portage and back down to Sea Gull.

We spent our first night on Alpine lake and then set out early on Sunday morning for Ogishkamuncie Lake. Our plan was to find a campsite in the morning and then spend the rest of the day fishing. As we made our way west on Ogishkamuncie lake, we were a bit disappointed to find that all the campsites were already occupied. Right after lunch, the sky to the north grew very dark and we started to see lightning in the distance. But the wind was steady from the west and it looked like the brunt of the storm would pass to the north, so we paddled along looking for a campsite. All the campsites we passed were taken, we were almost to the west end of the lake, and the weather was getting worse. There was one more camp site left, on the

John and Derek Jeanneret · July 3, 1999

John Jeanneret

western tip of the last island on the lake. We paddled there quickly only to discover that the dot on our map was wrong—there was no campsite. At this point, the weather was starting to look very threatening indeed, so we circled around the island looking for a campsite in earnest. We did find a campsite on the eastern end of the island, but it too was already occupied.

As we rounded the island, a heavy rain began to fall, so we started paddling for the safety of the portage at the west end of the lake. We had almost cleared the island, when the rain began to fall in sheets. We were still on the water, pulling due west for the portage, when the first blast of wind came through. We heard a roar from ahead of us and looked up to see a white "wall" of wind and water coming over the trees from the west. My son turned to me from the bow of the canoe with a look of terror on his face. I had just a couple of seconds to get the bow pointed up directly into the wind. We were still about 50 yards from shore when the white wall of wind slammed into us hard and nearly lifted us out of the water. Fortunately, our canoe was fully-laden and riding low. I barely managed to keep the canoe pointed into the wind. I had to scream to Derek to be heard over the roar, "Paddle! Paddle! Dig! Dig!".

It took everything we had to make any headway at all against the wind. After the longest thirty seconds of my life, we finally paddled into the lee of the shoreline where the force of the wind was not so great. We angled off the wind slightly and paddled straight for the relative safety of the portage between Ogishkamuncie and Annie lakes.

When we got to the portage, we leapt into the water and started pulling the canoe onto land. In the mouth of the portage, we were somewhat sheltered from the tremendous wind. But our relief was short-lived, and we began to hear the sickening CRACK! of trees snapping all around us. We pulled our canoe, filled with our gear and about two inches of rainwater, up as far into the portage as we could, dodging falling trees as we went. We grabbed our ponchos, left the canoe in the mouth of the portage, and headed upwind further into the portage, seeking shelter where the trees were already down. We took refuge under the trunk of a large birch tree that was suspended about three feet off the ground by its own sturdy branches and waited out the storm.

The terror had lasted only a few minutes, but Derek and I were exhausted, wet, and shivering. Once we found our "hole" to hide in, we curled up under our ponchos and tried to make ourselves very small. At first, I thought we had been hit by a microburst, but the wind kept howling. Then I thought it might have been a tornado, but it lasted far too long for that as well. Finally, about twenty minutes later, the wind slackened and we went back to the mouth of the portage to see whether our canoe had been destroyed. To our relief, the canoe was still there, completely surrounded by fallen trees, but remarkably undamaged. We were amazed to see that the canoe was completely filled with water. By that crude rain gauge, the storm must have dropped about 12 inches of rain on us in only 20 minutes!

After the storm passed, and we warmed up again, Derek and I considered continuing our journey west through the portage and into Annie Lake, but the portage was completely destroyed. We had no idea of the extent of the damage, and we were unfamiliar with the territory to the west so we decided to head back the way we had come. We retraced our route on Ogishkamuncie Lake, going from campsite to campsite, making sure everyone was OK. Every campsite we visited was destroyed, and almost every tent had been flattened by falling trees but, fortunately, no one on Ogishkamuncie Lake had been injured.

Derek and I made camp on Ogishkamuncie Lake that afternoon. We were awestruck by the extent of the damage. Large trees with deep root systems were simply snapped in half. Trees with shallow roots at the shoreline and on islands were ripped out, taking huge hunks of topsoil and small boulders with them, and leaving clean, smooth rock behind. In every direction, as far as we could see, it looked as if an immense herd of dinosaurs had just stampeded through the wilderness. In areas where the trees had been thick, all the trunks leaned against one another at drunken angles. Open spaces, such as campsites and portages had become wood piles where trees were stacked up four, five, even six trunks high.

Derek and I made ourselves an enormous feast that evening to celebrate our good fortune. We even managed to get a fire started. But we soon realized that other folks had not been as fortunate. From our campsite, we watched sea planes landing and taking off to the north for the rest of the day, apparently evacuating seriously injured campers from the South Arm of Knife Lake.

But our adventure was not yet over. The night of July 4th, we were treated to another big storm. The rains came again, the wind blew, and an intense electrical storm lit up the sky all night long. The trees that were left standing had been weakened and there was no telling how much more wind they could take. I had tried to pitch our tent where we would not be squashed in our sleep by another falling tree. I spent a long, sleepless night monitoring shifts in the wind, listening for the cracking of trees, and ready to abandon the tent at a moments notice.

On monday morning, Derek and I started clawing our way out of the wilderness, retracing our route back to Sea Gull Lake. The very first portage between Ogishkamuncie and Kingfisher lakes was the worst. With the help of another pair of campers who were also at that portage, Derek and I managed to find the trail, even though it had been completely obliterated by fallen trees. The Ogishkamuncie/Kingfisher portage is 38 rods long (about 200 yards). It had taken us only five minutes to walk that portage on the way into Ogishkamuncie Lake, but it took about two hours to get all our gear and the canoe through the tangled mass of fallen trees on the way out.

The Ogishkamuncie/Kingfisher portage did prove to be humorous in one respect. Barb Koth, Glenn Kreag, and their dog had arrived at the portage ahead of us. (We did not know them at the time, but their story was covered on the front page of the Pioneer Press on Wednesday, July 7). Barb and Glenn could not find the portage and chose instead to line their canoe through the rapids. Glenn was very calm through the ordeal, but we could hear Barb screaming at him hysterically for the entire two hours. Fortunately, they all came out okay. I wonder if Barb and Glenn are still dating?

As we made our way back to Sea Gull Lake, the portages gradually became easier as the debris got a little thinner and Derek and I got into the rhythm of slowly moving our canoe and gear over, under, and through the fallen trees. We chose to walk our canoe through the rapids between Alpine Lake and Sea Gull Lake rather than tackle the 105 rod (600 yards) overland portage, which were told was virtually impassable. At the end of a long, hot day, we camped at a beautiful site at the west end of Sea Gull Lake. The weather finally began to clear, the sun came out for the first time on the trip, and we finally started to get our gear dried out.

On Tuesday morning, the weather was turning bad once again. Derek and I agreed that we were not enjoying this trip very much, and we decided to make a quick dash across Sea Gull Lake to the take-out with the wind at our backs. When we first set out, the waves did not look too bad and we neglected to put on our life jackets. Once we got out onto the lake, we quickly realized our mistake. The wind and waves were so severe that we did not dare to stop paddling long enough to grab our life jackets. Our "dash" turned into four hours of intense and frightening paddling as we fought shifting 30-knot winds, three-foot waves, and whitecaps on Sea Gull Lake. When we finally arrived at Blankenburg Landing, we felt very lucky to be alive.

We soon discovered that the telephones were out and we could not call Gunflint Northwoods Outfitters to pick us up at the landing. We finally flagged down a couple of good-hearted local folks who agreed to give Derek a ride about ten miles down the road to Gunflint Outfitters, while I stayed with the gear. About an hour and a half later, Derek returned with Sheryl from Gunflint to pick me up.

The ride back to Gunflint was amazing. There were downed trees all over the road and trees on top of almost every building along the way. I had thought that we had been in the epicenter of the storm out on Ogishkamuncie Lake, but there was plenty of damage around Gunflint Lake as well. Fortunately, our car was undamaged. We loaded up our gear and headed down the Gunflint Trail toward Grand Marais. All along the forty miles of Gunflint Trail, the level of devastation continued to amaze me. There were literally hundreds of large trees covering the road. We were told that, after the storm, it had taken a small army of firefighters about six hours to chain-saw their way through the mess on that road to evacuate the injured.

John Jeanneret

Making camp on an island in Ogishkamuncie Lake right after the storm 7/4/99

This was my first trip to the Boundary Waters. I have been looking forward to visiting this wilderness area since I first learned to paddle a canoe in the Boy Scouts. Now that my son, Derek, is grown, we were looking forward to making the trip every year. Early news stories reported that the July 4th windstorm left some 20 million fallen trees in its wake. When all that fallen wood dries out, the fire hazard will be enormous. My guess is that the entire 250,000 affected acres will be consumed in huge conflagration next summer. Although I realize that this is just part of nature's cycle of renewal, I can't help but feel saddened by the loss of this beautiful forest.

I have since read that the decision to clean up the affected area of the Boundary Waters was very controversial. My understanding is that the Forest Service normally bans the use of motors and chain saws in wilderness areas. In this case, they bowed to intense pressure from local business and property owners and agreed to allow chain saws into the area to clear fallen timber from portages and campsites. I fear that this cleanup effort, though well-intentioned, will ultimately prove to be a mistake. Clearing the portages allows easy access to the area. Easy access means that many more people will be camping in the affected area when it does burn. And when it burns, it is going to be one hell of a fire storm.

Sincerely,
John Jeanneret

John Rose

Angie McParland

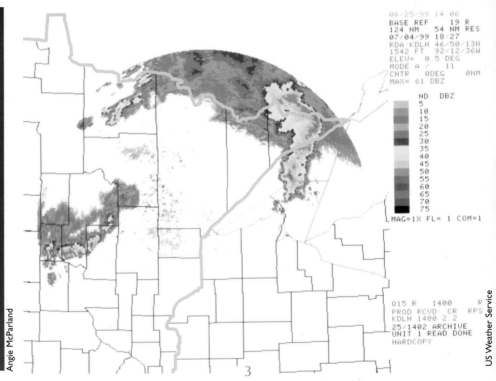

08/25/99 14:06
BASE REF   19 R
124 NM   54 NM RES
07/04/99 18:27
RDA:KDLH 46/50/13N
1542 FT   92/12/36W
ELEV= 0.5 DEG
MODE A /   11
CNTR 0DEG   0NM
MAX= 61 DBZ

    ND DBZ
        5
        10
        15
        20
        25
        30
        35
        40
        45
        50
        55
        60
        65
        70
        75
LMAG=1X FL= 1 COM=1

015 R   1400   R
PROD RCVD: CR   RPS
KDLH 1400 2.2
25/1402 ARCHIVE
UNIT 1 READ DONE
HARDCOPY

US Weather Service

1) *Storm cloud over Saganaga Lake*

2) *Wall cloud in Thunder Bay, Ontario*

3) *Storm radar image - July 4 - 1:27 PM*

4) *Gooseberry Falls going gangbusters -*
    July 5

Jan Fiola

Irving Hansen

5

Cascade Lodge

7

Cascade Lodge

8

6

Cascade Lodge

9

5) *Irving, Brett Hansen and others clearing the Caribou Trail*

6) *Rainstorm polluting Lake Superior*

7) *Cascade Creek over Hwy. 61 Cascade Lodge near Lutsen, MN*

8) *Turquogis sky, green glow, mid-storm wind and waves - Winchell Lake*

9) *Rainstorm damage & debris over Hwy. 61 near the Cascade Lodge, Lutsen, MN*

Richard Hill

Dave and Nancy Seaton

Dan Baumann

Sommers Staff

10) *Giving water to injured eaglet on Ogishkemuncie Lake*

11) *Storm damage at Golden Eagle Lodge - Gunflint Trail*

12) *Storm damage at Bearskin Lodge Cabin Gunflint Trail*

Bearskin Lodge

13) *Damaged Hungry Jack Outfitters sign - Gunflint Trail*

14) *Voyageur Canoe crushed - Sommers Scout Base Moose Lake near Ely*

15) *Abandoned canoe in blowdown*

16

17

19

16) *Blowdown near Ensign Lake Narrows*

17) *Laurentian Divide at Gunflint Trail*

18) *Frank Stewart, Arrow Lake Resident - Ontario*

19) *Snapped hanging Poplar*

18

Cook County News-Herald

USFS

USFS

20) *USFS latrine in tree -*
    Alpine Lake

21) *Damaged latrine*

22) *USFS blowdown*
    area map

23) *Tree on home at*
    Hungry Jack Lodge

20

21

23

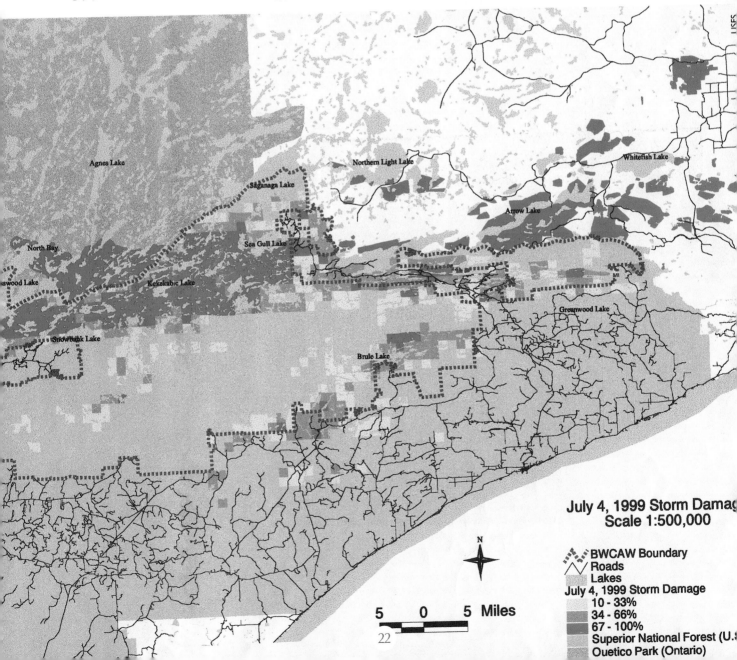

USFS

Agnes Lake

Northern Light Lake

Whitefish Lake

Saganaga Lake

Arrow Lake

North Bay

Sea Gull Lake

sswood Lake

Kekekabic Lake

Greenwood Lake

Snowbank Lake

Brule Lake

July 4, 1999 Storm Damag
Scale 1:500,000

N

5   0   5   Miles

22

BWCAW Boundary
Roads
Lakes
July 4, 1999 Storm Damage
  10 - 33%
  34 - 66%
  67 - 100%
Superior National Forest (U.S
Ouetico Park (Ontario)

24) *Tourists and others clearing the gunflint trail*

25) *Long line of vehicles waiting as Gunflint Trail is cleared*

26) *Campsite proposed to close BWCAW*

24

25

Bearskin Lodge

27

27) *Clearing the Gunflint Trail*

28) *Vehicle totalled in Bearskin Lodge parking lot*

26

USFS

28

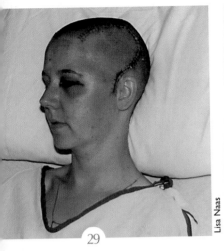

Lisa Naas

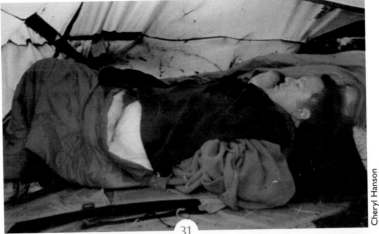

Cheryl Hanson

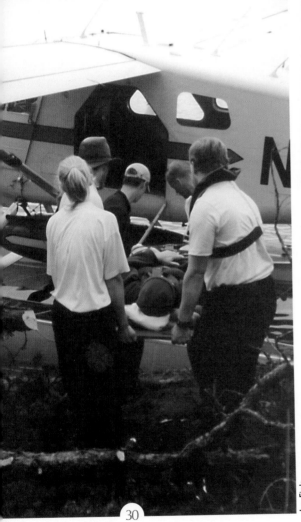

Jan Fiola

29) *Lisa Naas, storm victim - Polly Lake*

30) *Evacuation of Vicky Brockman - Alpine Lake*

31) *Mark Mattison after being struck by a tree*

32) *Aircraft evacuation of Vicky Brockman*

33) *Vicky Brockman under the tree*

34

35

34) *Twin Cities television station helicopter at Golden Eagle Lodge*

35) *Beaver Aircraft with Hotshots and gear*

36) *Beaver Aircraft with Hotshots and gear*

36

37) *Campers working their way out near Seagull Lake*

38) *Tree over tent supported by the bear rope - Winchell Lake*

39) *Patti Pollock at campsite before storm*

40) *Bob Pollock with trees over tent after storm*

41) Karen MacDonald,
Scout and Jem near
the Stairway Portage

42) Damaged canoes -
Wilderness Canoe
Base - Seagull Lake

43) Torkelson Trip Map

Jaye Martin

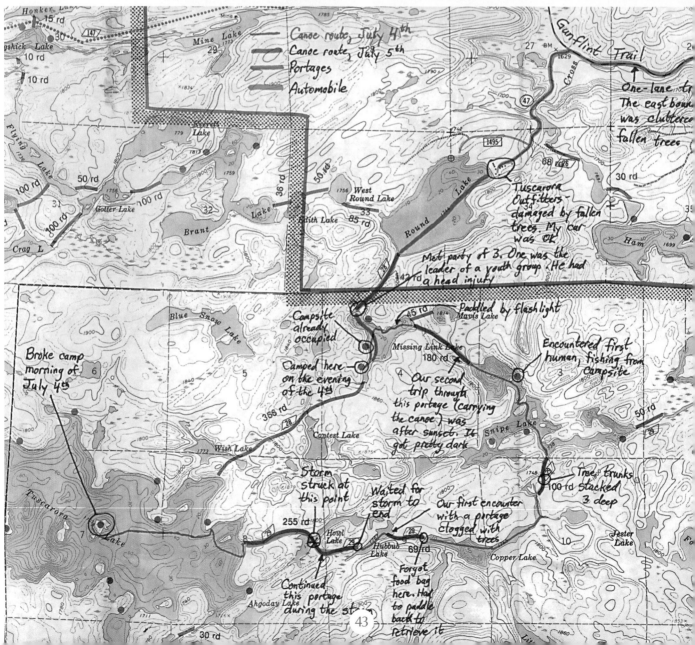

Canoe route, July 4th
Canoe route, July 5th
Portages
Automobile

One-lane ro...
The east boun...
was cluttere...
fallen trees

Tuscarora
Outfitters -
damaged by fallen
trees. My car
was OK

Met party of 3. One was the
leader of a youth group. He had
a head injury

Paddled by flashlight
Mavis Lake

Encountered first
human, fishing from
campsite

Campsite
already
occupied

Missing Link Lake
180 rd

Camped here
on the evening
of the 4th

Our second
trip through
this portage (carrying
the canoe) was
after sunset. It
got pretty dark

Broke camp
morning of
July 4th

Trees trunks
stacked
3 deep

Our first encounter
with a portage
clogged with
trees

Storm
struck at
this point

Waited for
storm to
end

Continued
this portage
during the st...

Forgot
food bag
here. Had
to paddle
back to
retrieve it

44) *Outward Bound Guide Velma McDonald*

45) *Outward Bound Canoes*

46) *Hotshot trying his luck fishing while waiting for a Beaver Aircraft*

47) *Karl Tingelstad survived the storm at Camp DuNord*

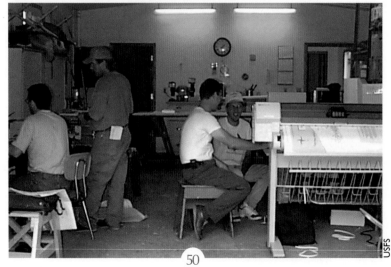

48) *Lightning strike fires - BWCAW*

49) *Senator Wellstone, Forest Supervisor Jim Sanders and Gunflint District Ranger Jo Barnier at Bearskin Lodge*

50) *USFS Storm Recovery Office - Ely, MN*

51) *Helicopter dropping water on wildfire*

52

53

Nancy Pius

Vince Ekroot

54

55

USFS

USFS

KILLER TREE

Hotshot clearing a campsite landing by standing in the water

Major blowdown area

54) Guide Vince Ekroot with four pound rainbow trout

55) Killer "Dangerous" tree being removed by Sawyer

56

56) *Ontario hydro worker removing tree from power lines*

57

58

59

57) *Sawyer and swamper clearing portage*

58) *Sawyer viewing beauty and devastation*

59) *USFS road clearing crew near the Gunflint Trail*

Cook County News-Herald

Jim Cordes

Ely Echo

Images of Nature - Larry Waddell

Jim Cordes

Roger Hahn

60) *Logger, Doug Popham, clearing roads of windstorm debris*

61) *Clearing trees from a home - Ely, MN*

62) *Blowdown in snow*

63) *Ed Hedstrom with blowdown White Pine logs at Hedstroms Sawmill - Grand Marais*

64) *Portaging out of Wonder Lake*

65) *USFS Wilderness Ranger Brandee Wenzell with damaged canoe and slice of 1686 blown down Red Pine*

66) *Twin Island in Moose Lake before storm*

67) *Twin Island after storm*

68) *Dogsled on Four Mile Portage*
Northwoods Guiding Service, Bill Slaughter

69) *Red squirrel in blowdown*

John Lofstedt

Storm clouds on Gunflint Lake

Trail Center

Crushed vehicle at Loon Lake

THE
HUNGRY BEAVER

The Journal of the Kekekabic Trail Club

SPECIAL COMBINED ISSUE
July/August 1999   *50 cents per copy*   Vol. 10, No. 7-8

Storms remodel BWCAW — more than ever, volunteers are needed

by Neal Chapman

The July 4th storms that struck the BWCAW area left behind more work than the usual Hungry Beavers can handle.

The KTC is assuming its usual leadership role in the recruitment and training of volunteers, and in organizing work trips to begin the process of reclaiming the damaged trails. The Eagle Mt. Trail, although not in "the" damage area, received 250 treefalls. A path through the treefalls is probably already cleared by the time you read this. The Lima Mt. Trail, which had just been cleared two weeks prior to the storm, will also be reopened shortly.

Volunteers of all skill levels and of all disciplines are urgently needed to help with all the work that lies ahead. Not only do we need people willing to "go up" and clear trails, but also needed are those willing to make phone calls, write letters, and perform other "behind the scenes" tasks. We have set up a section of the club's Internet site (http://www.kek.org) to make signing up easy. We will discuss this at the regular monthly meeting at Midwest Mountaineering on August 3.

We will also be holding additional public informational meetings at REI in Bloomington on Wednesday, August 4 at 7 p.m. and REI in Roseville on Thursday, August 5 at 7 p.m. Additional meetings and locations will be announced as they are set up.

REI has already pledged $1,000 to assist the club in this effort.

We are working closely with the Superior National Forest to identify areas that we can safely begin to work. There will be some trips this summer and fall, but undoubtedly most of the activity will be in the spring after winter storms have made the area safer in which to work.

The year 2000 will indeed be a special year for us, our 10th anniversary, AND the biggest challenge yet. With ALL of your help, we can and will do it. ✱

Kekekabic Trail Club

The Kekekabic Trail

History

The following section includes an edited and summarized version of the history provided in the Kekekabic Trail Guide, authored by Angela Anderson, Martin Kubik and others; copyright Kekekabic Trail Club, 1996:

In 1949 Whitney Evans wrote, "The Kekekabic Trail is one of the toughest, meanest rabbit tracks in North America. The trail struggles its way through swamps, around cliffs, up the sides of bluffs, and across rocky ridges.

...In other areas it is a peaceful path loping through open stands of timber with a soft mossy carpet underfoot. It is the kind of trail that would break the heart of a man who didn't have what it takes to go into the wilderness and try to 'smooth' it."

That "rabbit track" is in the heart of the BWCAW July 4th blowdown area. It is a trail that has tested the heart of many volunteer men and women over the past decade that have worked to keep it clear. And more recently tested the best of the US Forest Service trail crews as they worked to remove the very heavy downfall from the July 4th storm. It is a trail that is loved for its history, its solitude, and its wilderness challenges.

The 38 mile long Kek Trail cuts across the BWCAW with eastern access off the Gunflint Trail, 47 miles from Grand Marais. The western access is off the Fernberg and Snowbank Roads, about 18 miles east of Ely.

The trail received its name from the Kekekabic Lake, located on the central portion of the trail. Kekekabic is derived from the Ojibwa word "kekequabic" meaning "Hawk-cliff Lake". The main line of the Kek was originally established for fire protection through access to fire towers and forest management. It was constructed in the mid 1930's, with completion in 1938. The airplane displaced its use for fire protection in the 1940's. It experienced a revival during the 1960's, as backpacking became popular, and the trail was cleared and maintained for hiking by the US Forest Service.

After the Forest Service ceased maintenance in 1982, trail use dwindled. In the spring of 1990, the newly formed Kekekabic Trail Club (KTC), a volunteer group, cleared the trail with support and cooperation from the U.S. Forest Service. Every year since 1990, the KTC has organized clearing trips. Additional trails have been added to the roster of KTC responsibilities. In 1999, nearly 200 volunteers put in some 6000-person hours, clearing over 120 miles of trail.

Storm on the Kek by Mark Stange

While the Kekekabic Trail Club normally confines its trail clearing to the ninth of May, the fact that a late Spring storm had created a significant blockage of the club's namesake trail, prompted club leaders to plan a special clearing effort. One four-person crew, led by John Koffski, set off on the 30th of June. I joined them four days later with a second crew of four.

My crew consisted of three 25 year-olds from the Czech Republic. A fellow Czech, Martin Kubik and a founder of the KTC, had convinced the young people that they would enjoy a working trip in the BWCAW. One had been in the U.S. for only a week. We canoed across Snowbank, portaged the 140 rods to Disappointment, and canoed to the eastern shore. There we met Koffski's crew, who were exhausted from the heat and insects and eager to return home. Koffski had brushed out the treefalls, leaving only the logging of tree trunks for us.

The damaged area was just east of Meas-Moiyaka lakes, 90 minutes' hike from Disappointment. As a preview of the coming July 4th storm, hardly a single tree was left standing in that area. It also previewed the danger, as the tangle of trees left many logs in a state of great tension – called "killer trees" by loggers.

Indeed, just before noon on the Fourth of July, one such log, only four inches thick, snapped open when sawed and struck one of the Czechs in the face with great force. We repaired to our Medas campsite and were relieved to find the injury to be only a small cut and a black eye. However, the weather seemed to be taking a turn for the worse, as ominous dark clouds rolled in.

Suddenly the wind picked up to gale force. It took two people to hold down each tent. The tarp over the cooking area broke free on one corner and snapped furiously in the wind. In a little over a half-hour the wind abated and soon the rain stopped. The high winds had made the rain seem insignificant, but there were two inches in the bottom of the cook pot – quite a lot for a half-hour storm!

The sun came out and the day turned beautiful, free of the oppressive heat and humidity of the morning.

Directly over the tents a tripod had formed as two large trees had fallen onto a third. After our delayed lunch, we went back to work. There were several treefalls between camp and the trail, but all the trees were already down in the work area, so the extent of the storm was not readily apparent.

Leaving the next day, however, we were immediately stopped by a pile of downed trees. We dropped our packs, engaged our saws, and soon we were back on our way – for 50 meters. Another impossible tangle. Another sawing exercise. And so it went. At times the Kekekabic Trail appeared to be the "Kekekabic River," as the rains – another three-plus inches had fallen during the night – left a great deal of water looking for a place to go. The usual hour and a half hike turned into a five-hour hike back to Disappointment.

The busy Snowbank portage was cluttered with treefalls. Time to break out the two-person crosscut saws again. (The KTC can thus lay claim to having cleared the first portage after the storm.) After a long headwind paddle across Snowbank, I found my car – actually my wife's car – squashed by a 90-foot pine. Fortunately, the USFS had been worried and was checking the lot periodically. They rescued us with a ride back to Ely. Several phone calls later, Kubik and club members from Cloquet shuttled us back to the Twin Cities.

Recovery: Response to the Storm
by Derrick Passe

When the Kekekabic Trail Club learned the extent of the damage to the Trail by the Windstorm, we immediately began to plan a reconnaissance trip. On August 6th six KTC Members headed up to Ely with two canoes to get on the Trail to determine the work we had ahead of us. Our plans were for two people to hike the Old Pines Loop to see if the magnificent trees had survived the storm. The other four would hike and canoe along the trail from Thomas Lake to the East Trailhead. We stopped at the USFS Office to pick up radios and to get additional firsthand information on the Trail. After discussions with the USFS, it was determined that hiking the Trail from Thomas Lake to the East Trailhead would be impossible in the time frame that we had available. We prevailed upon Smitty's on Snowbank to provide us with a third canoe and headed out across Disappointment Lake on August 8th, two canoes going to the North and the other canoe heading South to intersect the Trail at the South end of Disappointment Lake. Heading North, limited damage was apparent along the way until we arrived at the Jordan Lake Portage. Here the damage from the blowdown became apparent by the number of trees that had been cleared from the portage by USFS crews.

We didn't get into the midst of downed trees until we arrived at the Kekekabic Trail where it crosses the Thomas

River. We set up camp on Thomas Lake and returned to the trail to flag it either direction from the portage. Splitting into groups of two, we managed to flag less than 1/2 mile of trail in two hours. This was but the first of many trail crossings that we made. Paddling parallel to the trail we repeated this procedure at Strup, Agamok, Seahorse, Warclub and Faye Lakes. It wasn't until we arrived at the trail along Bingschick that the trail became passable again. As luck would have it, the portages out of Bingschick had not been cleared by the USFS and we had to slide the canoes over trees to traverse the portages and canoe out.

Recovery: Clearing the Kek
by Steve Schug, USFS, Superior National Forest

"Jubilation" was the word of the day when the 14 USFS crews finally completed clearing the Kekekabic Trail on September 27, 2000. "A life experience," was how one described it.

Some 35 crews from across the nation had applied for the job; those selected had the most certified sawyers and an EMT. They also had a commitment to the principles of "minimum tool," in that fully nine of the crews used NO mechanized tools (chain saws). Three crews used chain saws for less than 30 minutes each. Of the 8750 hours of actual trail clearing, only 32.4 hours were spent using mechanized saws, approximately one-third of one percent!

The members of the Kekekabic Trail Club, one of our primary partners on the Superior National Forest trails, deserve special recognition for their efforts. They were instrumental in completing follow-up recovery work left over from the fall of 1999 and for their diligence in getting to the most remote section of the Kekekabic Trail and laying out ribbon line along the trail tread. Crawling over areas of 90+% blow down was extremely difficult and arduous work.

The bill came to 400 thousand dollars, which represents a very strong commitment to maintaining trails in the BWCAW. For their efforts, the Superior Forest won the Primitive Skills Award for the Eastern Region of the U.S.

The Kek now has a different set of vistas. Brush will be the biggest challenge to trail clearing in the near future. Fire will be introduced over the next several years in 4000-6000 acre blocks, with lakes generally defining the lines. Any hand line work will be done with "minimum tool" rules. In times of high fire danger, use of the trails may be suspended, as hikers certainly could not outrun a fire.

Recovery and Future:
It's a Hell of a Mess Out There
by Bruce T. Anderson

The Kekekabic Trail lives! In spite of fires, storms, rerouting, bureaucratic neglect and hostility, and most recently, the Storm of the Century, people still hike the trail. From October 29 to November 1, 2000 I hiked the recently restored Kek from the Gunflint Trail to Snowbank Lake. The most important observation I can make is that the Forest Service has done an **outstanding** job of clearing this trail. Secondly, the beaver are having an impact on the trail on the east side, and thirdly, the most difficult section of the trail to hike was the 17 km west of Moiyaka Lake, the section unaffected by the Storm. I began hiking from the

eastern trailhead in the mid-afternoon of Sunday, October 29. The Wilderness boundary sign is still in place. The damage intensifies closer to Bingshick Lake. The campsite on the east side of Bingshick Lake has many downed trees including some cut by beaver. I camped here on Sunday night in the frost.

The next morning the adventure began. The log bridges were very slippery. Where there was any elevation, I crawled on my hands and feet to avoid slipping off. Just east of Howard Lake, the trail ran into a beaver pond that I had to bushwhack around. The high ground between Howard and Gabimichigami Lake looks like Paul Bunyan did a flamenco dance there. The beaver have taken to the small marsh at the foot of the hill east of the campsite at Gabi Lake. Once again I was on a trail that ran into a pond.

The high ground between Gabi Lake and the Bridge is demolished. I recognized nothing. The larger campsite west of the Bridge is fine, although there is not much shade any more. That night I had to set up camp in the woods about halfway between the Bridge and Harness Lake. The campsite at Harness Lake was a mess. Most of the large pines that used to surround that relatively small campsite were down root balls and all. Pieces of these trees were all over the campsite.

Heading westward I came to an area where the only standing trees of any size were the white pine. Many of these were tipped. The "Golden Arches" marking the spur trail to the "Little House on the Prairie" were still there, although they too were topped. The large white pine just to the west, where so many of us have taken pictures, were broken off about three meters from the ground. The area south of Kekekabic Lake was the most thoroughly damaged area I saw. I had a clear view of Bakekana Lake to the south, which I had never seen before.

I could not find even a hint of the spur trail to the campsite on Strup Lake. I was shocked to come on the Kekekabic-Strup portage. I had seen photos of this portage since the Storm but I was completely surprised. The aspen forest to the west was completely flattened. No more Beartrap. It was like hiking through a brush pile. There were a couple of broken aspen wrapped in "Killer Tree" tape. I was able to outwit them and proceed.

Now I came across some downed trees that required me to crawl under them on my hands and knees, or in some cases on my belly. The marsh near Thomas Lake, where I have gotten off track a couple of times, was easy to traverse. Also, Thomas River, where I usually have to wade, could be crossed on rocks. The beaver dam at Bushwhack Lake was a mess. I buried my boots in over the top on about a third of my steps. I was very pleased to arrive at Moiyaka Lake campsite with quite a bit of daylight to spare. However, there is such a beautiful view from the campsite over the Lake that I spent too much time admiring the lake and ended up fixing dinner and setting up my tent in the dark anyhow.

There were a lot of tree falls between the two Disappointment Trail junctions. Once again, I was on my hands and knees and belly a lot more than I wanted to be. The density of treefalls intensified between the Boardwalk and the summit of the large hill overlooking Snowbank Lake. I used my walking staff to feel my way over the Lulu

Lake beaver dam with little trouble. Also, the western-most beaver dam was crossed easily, although the connection to the trail on the west side of the beaver dam is not obvious. Manlove Meadow is starting to look like a real forest again. There is even a scenic overlook.

This is the fifth time I have hiked the Kekekabic Trail in the ten years of the Club's existence. Since I have an audience, I would like to thank the people who made this possible – Martin Kubik for continuing to focus attention on this trail, Wayne Hensched for putting the trail on the map, Ed Woolverton for showing me the behind the scenes of the Kek, Steve Schug for overseeing the resurrection of the Kek, and Judy for bringing me to the Other Side.

Future: The Kekekabic Trail – its finest hour is yet to be! by Folke Arbin

Yes, the up-keep of the Kek IS one helluva big job, but here it still is, two whole generations after its inception. Yes, as had happened in the past, we humans can always call it quits on the Kek, and it will disappear among the downfalls and the legends and the ignorance, leaving just a few more square miles of INACCESSIBLE north woods. There is enough of that already. Even the wolves and moose think so. If not, why would they hang out so much on the trails?

Yes, hiking the Kek across God's Great Clear Cut in the BWCAW, with mile after mile of downed aspen, 3 ft. white pines and tinder-dry jack pines, it quickly becomes obvious: **the Kek's finest hour is yet to be!"**

How so? Because the blowdown was not the end of the forest! It was just the start of a dynamic new phase! Sunlight will be the new boss who will decide everything. And, there will be fire, both natural and prescribed.

After 50 years of slow stagnation into a forest of pine, birch, balsam, and aspen mix, suddenly it's a fresh start for everything. Whatever it will be. A bi-culture of balsam and aspen for sure, but there were a lot of standing maple, too. Species long suppressed, will now explode, while other species fade or disappear completely until microclimates readjust.

How can these events be studied? Satellite mapping and flyovers? Nah...you have to get in there and walk around, count plants, measure erosion, examine the details. Except you can't get in there without the trail.

So, for the next decade, the Kek will provide unique access for scientists. The value of their findings will far out-weigh the value of all the unburned forests of the '40s and recreational hiking of the 50s-70s. (Well, the value of keeping the CCC boys busy in the 30's may have been beyond measure. Too bad we don't have a CCC today.)

Long live the Kekekabic Trail!

Future Response to the July 4th Storm by the KTC by Derrick Passe

Each May, the Kekekabic Trail Club sends volunteers to the BWCA to prepare the hiking trails for visitors. In the past these trips have consisted of sawing blowdowns from the trail and nipping brush that grows in alongside the trail. Future trips will be oriented more to managing the rapid growth of underbrush that will thrive with the increased sunlight on the trail. Questions remain as to how controlled burns in the blowdown areas will affect the trail and what measures the KTC will have to take to preserve this trail for the backpackers of the BWCA. Those interested in helping can contact the KTC at info@kek.org or by calling 1-800-818-HIKE or writing to the KTC, 309 Cedar Avenue S., Minneapolis, MN 55454.

Location of Kek Trail

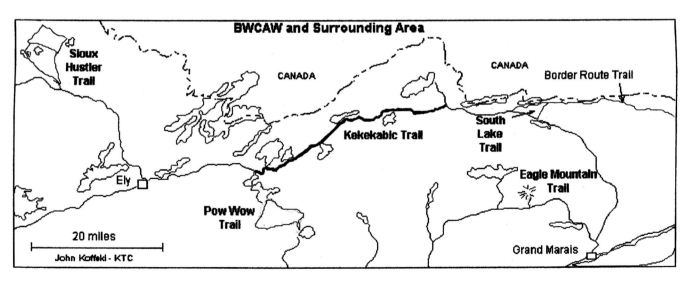

Almost Buried Alive on Bonnie Lake
by Kevin and Matthew Brelie

July 4th dawned muggy and warm. It was one of those mornings that your windshield fogs up as you drive, and the air feels sort of "juicy" as you breathe it. In an effort to beat the day's heat, my 17-year-old son Matthew and I rose early to get a jumpstart on the day. We had finally been able to squeeze 5 days out of our busy schedules to take a quick trip to some of our favorite spots in the BWCA. We drove up from Two Harbors, reached Moose Lake landing, had everything packed, and were shoving off by 6:30 AM.

We could feel the heat build as we paddled. There was no breeze, and the lakes were flat calm paddling, which helped us make excellent time as we clipped off the lakes behind us. Moose, Newfound, Sucker, Birch, Carp, Melonseed, and on to Knife Lake. As we paddled down Knife, we could hear thunder in the west, and figured we were in for an afternoon storm. We started looking for a campsite where we could have some lunch and maybe sit out a thunderboomer, and then afterwards push on to Kekekabic Lake – our destination for this day. We paddled past site after site; all filled with campers sitting near the waters edge, enjoying the beautiful day. We were almost to the portage to Bonnie Lake, and since we had found no unoccupied campsites, we decided to cross and have lunch on the other end of the portage. By the time we reached the other end of the portage, we could see lightning in the west and knew we would soon have a thunderstorm. We decided not to go out on the lake with the storm imminent, so we sat and had lunch on the shore, watching the display in the sky across the lake. It was then that Matthew turned to me and said, "The sky looks kind of green, doesn't it?" I chuckled and told him that's when the worst storms usually come. Little did we dream what was to befall us! It started to rain a little bit so we decided to move back up the portage a ways and put our rain gear on. We propped the canoe up between 2 poplar trees and stood underneath it while we donned our rain gear. The wind started to pick up, and the trees that the canoe was propped between began to sway. We figured that we better get the canoe down so it wouldn't pinch. Just at the moment that I lifted the canoe and turned to set it down, the "for real" wind slammed into us. Immediately a large jack pine fell within feet of us. We both had the same idea – run for the lake! With Matthew in the lead, we headed for the shore, which was only about 30 yards away. (The following events play through my mind in ultra slow motion and I am amazed that they took so little time.)

Before we went even a few steps, a large poplar about 12 inches in diameter snapped about 10 feet up from the ground and started to fall toward us. Matthew turned to get out of the way, and I saw a large branch come down across his back. He kept running toward me, so it seemed he was okay. As I turned to get out of the way, the ground beneath me started to rise. This was truly a strange feeling, and I think a few crazy thoughts ran through my head. I remember thinking this is Minnesota – we don't have earthquakes! By the time I realized that I was on a root pad and the trees in front of me were going over, I had ridden the root pad up about 6-7 feet. The roots beneath my feet began to pop. A hole opened up underneath me, and I fell through into the space below the root pad. Rocks and dirt were falling on me and I thought I was going to be buried alive. I remember thinking that it wasn't supposed to be like this...that I was supposed to go when I was sitting under a tree with a smile on my face. Then a new thought popped into my head – I can't die! Who will help Matthew get out of here? As these thoughts ran through my head, the root pad finally tore loose and the whole pad stood up in the air. Matthew had run over to me and was just kneeling down to help me out of the hole when 3 more large poplars fell directly onto us, but landed on top of the root pad. We looked up and it was like being in a cage. In retrospect, that was probably the safest place to be at the time, but we had had enough of the forest for now. We climbed out between the trees and ran to the shore of the lake where we took refuge over the edge of the bank at the waters edge. We could not look across the lake because the wind was shredding the top of the lake so badly and blowing it at us that it was like needles in your face, so we huddled with our backs to the lake and prayed.

After about 6-8 minutes of wind (which seemed like hours) the wind died and all was peaceful again. We couldn't believe we were alive, much less uninjured! We headed back up the portage but were immediately met by downed trees stacked 8-12 feet high. Our canoe was upside down underneath a large poplar with the stern end crushed to the gunwale. We found our packs and were able to retrieve them from under various trees with a little digging and branch snapping. Since the tree on the canoe was too large for our saw to cut through, we began the laborious task of chopping through it with our hatchet. This took approximately an hour and a half or so with rest breaks. Once we got the canoe out, we righted it and started to punch out the stern end to give it some semblance of shape back. We then got out our duct tape and proceeded to repair what we could. When we set it in the water – it floated!

At this point we were still under the impression that we had been struck by a tornado and did not realize how widespread the damage was. We looked at the maps to plan an alternate route out through Spoon Lake and west and then headed across the lake to the next portage. When we neared the portage to Spoon, we realized that there was no going easily in that direction either. We figured that if we were going to have to cut our way out, going back to Knife Lake would be easier, so we headed back again towards the Knife Lake portage. By then it was about 4:40 PM, and we were both pretty exhausted. We decided to make camp and to get an early start in the morning.

That night when we went to bed, we could hear thunder rumbling in the distance again. A while later we were wakened to another crashing thunderstorm and thought that this wasn't very fair. We stayed awake for a long time as the rain poured, the lightning flashed, and the wind blew. Eventually we drifted to sleep again and rose at 5:00 AM. There were float planes circling all over the area and we gave a "thumbs up" to one that buzzed our campsite. We could hear planes landing and taking off on Knife Lake. After a quick breakfast we were packed and ready to go at 6:00 and shoved off. Once we got to the portage, we started picking our way through the maze, cutting branches where we needed to and crawling under or climbing over downed trees. In some places we had to detour far off the portage trail because the trees were just piled too high. We did a lot of "2-manning" of the canoe over and under the trees. Occasionally we would take one pack and I would crawl up, stop, Matthew would hand it to me and climb past me and I'd hand it to him, and repeat that procedure until we got over a particularly large pile. While we were on the portage, a group from Sommers Canoe Base caught up to us. We traded a few stories and finally made our way to Knife Lake. It took 3-1/2 hours to go thirty rods. We figured at this rate, we should be home in time for school to start in the fall! It wasn't that bad, however, once we hit Knife Lake. We paddled past the same campsites as we had the day before, and an eerie feeling came over us. We saw

campsites that were totally devoid of people, but still had tents set up (with quite a few that had trees lying on them) and gear strewn about. As we paddled and talked quietly together, we figured that there must have been some bad casualties from this storm and silently sent our prayers to them. As we worked our way back towards Moose Lake, each portage became a little easier. People were cutting routes as they went, and it seemed everyone we ran into had a story to tell.

We finally reached Moose Lake landing at about 8:30 PM that evening and were met with one last insult. One of the huge beautiful white pines at the landing was down across the trail to the parking lot. By now we were old hands at climbing, crawling, and sawing so we made short work of passing the tree and getting to our truck. The parking lot was a disaster, and many vehicles had trees lying across them. Fortunately, ours was okay. We packed quickly and loaded our trusty flattened canoe and headed home!

To say this was a unique father/son bonding experience is an understatement! Matthew and I both feel blessed to be alive. We are also glad we were there for the "show". Never have we seen anything like the awesome destructive power we witnessed that day. We have sat through many a thunderstorm together in the forest, but we both agree that in the future impending storms will have much different thoughts crossing our minds.

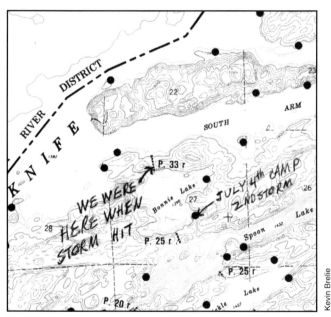

Map of Campsite

Kevin and Matthew Brelie at "burial" spot, June 2000

Terror on Seagull Lake
by Steve Loper and Cathy Groth, Minneapolis

My girlfriend and I decided to go camping in Grand Marais for the 4th of July weekend with reservations that a friend couldn't use. We had no real plans other than site-seeing and to possibly do a day trip canoeing somewhere along the Gunflint Trail. We originally wanted to go canoeing on Saturday, but the weather was cloudy and it looked like rain. We decided to try for Sunday. The next morning the sun was out, the fog was burning off Lake Superior, it looked like we made the right decision.

We took our time driving up the Trail since it was our first time so we stopped to take in many of the beautiful sites. We then came across an outfitter that had canoes for rent on Seagull Lake – a lake that was recommended from a website that I looked at last week. Fifteen minutes after walking in the door we had a canoe, paddles and life jackets. As we loaded our lunch and extra clothes, one of the outfitters mentioned that a thunderstorm was coming. My first thought was wait it out, but since he didn't seem too concerned and if a storm was coming it was surely going to the northeast and we were heading straight west. Being tied up in all of the excitement of being in the wilderness like this for the first time I guess I lost my concern as well.

As we paddled out from the dock, the lake was as smooth as glass and there wasn't a breath of wind in the air. We were at the northeast corner of the lake and to our southeast the sky was turning blue. We heard a low rumble of thunder. We ignored that since we were going west where the sky was cloudy but not blue or gray like typical rain clouds. After 45 minutes of canoeing we noticed that the weather conditions were slowly getting worse, lightning could be seen off in the distance. I now realized that we probably made a mistake in setting out. There were plenty of islands along our route so we decided to get to one and just plan on getting wet. As we pulled the canoe up the rocky shore a light, cool breeze had started coming from the southwest – the same side of the island as we landed on. With rain a few minutes away, we quickly made some sandwiches and put on our jackets. It wasn't more than 2 or 3 minutes later when the sky seemed like it was on a dimmer switch and it became dark instantly. I have never noticed an instantaneous change in brightness before and that is when the eerie feelings started that we were in for more than what we thought.

I maybe had two bites of my sandwich when I saw the canoe bounce on the rocks and decided to pull it up closer to us. Before I could scale the 5 foot cliff that we were on a gust of wind came up and blew the canoe like a paper bag down the shoreline. I threw my sandwich and jumped in the lake only to see it airborne and sailing 20-30' away from us.

Cathy was yelling for me not to go after it since the once calm lake was turbulent and the winds were getting stronger with time. I watched the canoe go to the northeast part of the island near a shallow rock point. I thought that if I could run through the trees to that spot, I could retrieve it without too much risk. I yelled to Cathy in the now fierce wind and rain, "stay there, I'll be right back." I ran through the boggy island, jumping over dead trees and large rocks. As I got to the other side of the island, I could barely see the canoe. It was filled with water 50 or so feet away and bouncing with the whitecaps.

Now the rain was so intense with the wind behind it that it was like horizontal hail. I stood and looked at the canoe one last time in sheer disbelief that we were stranded on this island and were also in the middle of a bad storm. Then I saw a small Alumacraft buzzing by, set for a collision course with the partially submerged canoe. He apparently missed it and didn't spot us either.

As I stood in shock, I heard the wind now become louder and stronger than I had ever heard in my life. An island, 200 yards to the east, had many tall pines that all bent sideways and each of them started making what would be loud cracks that were dampened by the huge winds.

At the same time, I realized that the trees around me were also snapping 20' off the ground, sending large projectiles flying randomly. I turned into the wind and rain trying to look at what was falling and where to run to next as if it were a video game. As I got halfway into the island, I heard a blood curdling scream from Cathy, I instantly went into a panic mode. The thoughts of being stranded on an island and having to replace a canoe just took a turn for the worse. I ran through the rest of the woods as fast as I could yelling to her that I was coming. As I came to her she was hysterical and jumped into my arms; we nearly squeezed each other to death. Cathy was shaking violently and was difficult to understand. She thought that I went after the canoe into the lake and with the storm getting worse, she panicked. Also, the tree that we set our belongings next to uprooted right behind her back without making a sound. When she turned around she lost it. We cuddled together for the next 30 minutes, just thankful that we were alive and that the storm was winding down.

All of a sudden I could hear the faint sound of a boat motor. We both jumped up to see the fellow with the Alumacraft. He said that he saw our canoe and figured that he would come back to look for us. Thank God! Mark is a fishing guide on the lake. His parents own the lake's only resort. We motored 1/4 mile or so and saw the two tips of the canoe barely out of the water, pulled it out, and headed back to the outfitter. I can imagine what a sight it was for them, as 3 of the employees ran to the dock to see a canoe on top of a small fishing boat with two pale paddlers who had just left for a day of fun an hour or so before. I tried to give Mark some money for gas but he wouldn't take anything. Whatever I could have given him wouldn't have been enough for the ride that stormy 4th of July.

It was now 2:30 in the afternoon. The people we rented the canoe from offered us a place to change clothes and to stay for the evening. We thanked them but decided to just drive back to Grand Marais to see if our tent was standing. They looked at us and said that the Trail could be blocked by trees since the phone and power lines were down. We decided to check it out for ourselves. Six hours later we arrived in Grand Marais.

Our trip to Grand Marais was made possible by people in about 20 cars helping 2 men with chainsaws leading our caravan. It was a welcome site to meet a bulldozer at the Laurentian Divide which had helped clear the road from Grand Marais.

This was definitely a 4th of July that we will never forget.

Trees Flying in Every Direction
by Richard Hill

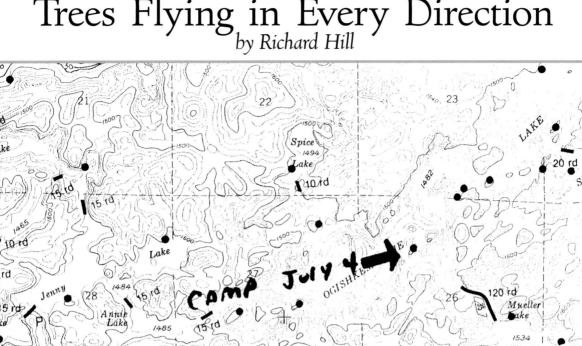

Hill trip map

Dear Jim,

My fifteen year old son and I were a few days into our annual BWCA canoe trip when the unbelievable storm hit us. I am no stranger to the BWCA and have made many ventures in this area. Some of our trips were in the spring soon after ice out and others were in June or July. Summer weather was always perfect, generally warm and comfortable. We always took precautions and were always prepared for most emergencies.

We arrived at Sea Gull Lake a few days before the 4th of July. We leisurely paddled toward Ogishkee muncie Lake enjoying the summer weather and the solitude of the BWCA Light winds made paddling effortless, thus adding to our enjoyment.

We arrived at Ogishkee the day before the 4th and set up camp on an island camp site. We had been here many times before, so this place held a lot of memories as it was very special. The weather was perfect, calm, warm and no rain. It was great to set up camp in the warm sunshine. We caught a couple of walleye for supper and relaxed in the evening sun.

I guess I had a feeling that something was wrong on the 4th of July. The stillness and extremely high humidity woke us early, it was just too hot to sleep. We ate breakfast and headed out to Spice Lake for canoeing and fishing, it was getting hotter by the minute. Distant rumbles of thunder sent us heading back to our camp site. We stopped to catch a couple of Bass for supper for I had a feeling we might not get a chance to fish later on as the weather was deteriorating rapidly. I secured our canoe on the shore under a group of small cedars. We gathered our gear and put it under our tarp to stay dry. We were going to have a light lunch and wait out the storm under the protection of our rain tarp. I suddenly noticed the stillness and glanced at the western sky. I noticed a broad band of emerald green, I told my Son to get his rain gear on as I knew we were in for something really bad. I had seen a similar sky many years ago that spawned a tornado so I was very concerned.

Before we could fasten our rain gear the first blast of the storm hit us. It was exactly 12:50, I remember looking at my watch. We couldn't believe what was happening. The blast of wind and rain uprooted and sheared off all the weaker trees on the island, they were flying in every direction and we had no where to go for protection. We were dodging falling trees when a group of Jack pine fell on us knocking us to the ground, luckily we weren't injured. We quickly dove under a group of criss-crossed jack pine and hung onto one another while the wind roared.

The second blast of the storm came at 1:00 and it was incredible. The wind was as loud as if you were standing next to an F-16. Standing up would have been impossible. The storm leveled our island campsite. Nothing was left standing with the exception of a few small birch and cedar. All the beautiful Jack Pine were gone. The lake was a froth of ugly brown water swirling in every direction. No waves, just swirling dirty water. It seemed that the storm actually lifted the lake water up. We laid under those Jack Pine until the storm let up at 1:20 it was 30 minutes of pure Hell. We crawled from beneath the trees and began to look around, everything was a shambles, the beautiful forest was gone. I believe we were actually in shock as we looked around.

Jack Pine over tent

Our gear was scattered everywhere. The first thing I looked for was our canoe, it was buried under fallen trees but was only slightly damaged, glad it was the aluminum canoe and not Kevlar. Our tent was crushed flat by two large jack pines and all our gear was soaked. We knew we had to do something by night fall because we weren't out of the rain yet. We gathered up all of our gear and moved it to the last piece of flat and clear ground on the island.

Beginning the portage

We made new poles for the tent and duct taped the holes, and tried to dry out our gear and settle in for the night. A series of heavy thunder storms kept us up most of the night. I guess we were still a little gun shy after the days events.

We decided to stay an extra day as we needed to completely dry out our gear and pack it up. We surveyed the area from our canoe and we couldn't believe the total destruction. It almost looked like a war zone. The tall white pines at the south end of the lake were gone. In one of them was an active Bald Eagles nest. We had observed the two young Bald Eagles from our camp site. We hiked up through the tangled mess and located the massive pine and what was left of the nest. And wouldn't you believe it, we found an injured eaglet. It was badly injured and wasn't far from death. We gave it some water and left it alone as there was nothing else we could do. One of the many casualties of this powerful storm. **C10**

We left early in the morning and headed for our first portage. It was hard to believe how different everything looked, as all the familiar landmarks were gone. The first portage was a disaster. It was nothing but a twisted tangled mess of jack pine, poplar and cedar. We knew we had our work cut out for us. All I could think of was, " thank goodness for a good strong partner". We dragged and carried our gear over and under and around the twisted mess of trees.

What we couldn't get over, under or around we had to saw our way through. Our next two portages were in the same condition, virtually closed off. We thought the damage would be less as we went further north, but the path of the storm was immense.

We made our way to Sea Gull lake that evening and made camp for the night. The damage there was less, which brought us some relief. I only hoped that our pick-up truck that was parked in the Trails End lot was not damaged.

We paddled our way across Sea Gull, early the next morning. We arrived at the boat landing and much to our relief the truck was not damaged. We made the rest of the trip home without incident. This was one camping trip that my Son and I will never forget. And will we ever go back? You can count on it.

Richard J. Hill and Mark J. Hill

Wilderness Canoe Base
by the Wilderness Staff

It was good timing for Wilderness Canoe Base. On Friday, July 2nd, 14 groups of campers left for home, leaving only one group of seven in the wilderness on July 4th. Guide Matt Bliefernich was in charge of this group; his party was just completing the Little Sag Lake to Elton Lake portage. The campers, fresh from high school graduation, had said they were ready for high adventure. They didn't have long to wait.

While setting down their gear, they were startled to see the storm wall moving across Elton Lake. There was no time to get away or take cover. The group formed two circles, holding hands and looking outward in all directions for falling trees. They dodged the first one, but the second, a huge birch, crashed down on the circle of four, knocking them to the ground. A branch struck Matt on the head and the other three sustained back, hip and rib injuries. Matt doesn't remember a thing from two hours before the storm to two hours after.

Wilderness Canoe Base is located on Fishhook and Dominion islands - two of the 250 Seagull Lake islands. Regarded by many as a very special BWCAW lake, it is/was the home of thousands of old growth white and Norway pines. The storm took most of them, including probably the oldest red pine in the BWCAW, dating from 1492.

Damaged canoes at Wilderness Canoe Base **C42**

Wilderness Staff

The wind had its way with the area, not sparing shorelines or low areas as it did in some locations. The south end of Seagull was totaled. The north end experienced fingers of wind that devastated isolated areas. The Base was hammered; in 20 minutes they lost 85,000 trees on their two islands. There were trees on 40 buildings, with many roofs caved in.

Immediately after the wind, Canoe Base staff, including EMT's, began searching by motorboat for casualties, and found them. A camper found just south of the palisades with an injured back was brought out on a backboard via motorboat and transferred to an ambulance on the Gunflint. A woman on Alpine Lake with a broken pelvis was stabilized by Wilderness EMT's and then flown out.

Later, the staff was bringing out the remaining Alpine Lake campers and gear by motorboat. A second storm with heavy lightning closed in on them from two directions as it chased them across the lake. Expecting another major storm, they went full throttle. Seeing that they were losing the race, they ditched all the gear on a small island to lighten the load; then barely made it home ahead of the wind and rain.

Wilderness Canoe Base caters to Lutheran church groups from all over the Midwest, and inner city youth from the Twin Cities. The summer staff is 50 to 60, with about 10 volunteers. The base outfits up to 20 groups of campers at a time. It boasts of more than 50 buildings, and a 150 foot suspension bridge connecting the two islands. Some of the buildings were removed from the BWCA wilderness - moved many miles over frozen lakes or taken apart and floated and portaged to the Base, where they were reconstructed. But that is a whole other story.

Sitting comfortably around the lodge fireplace late one January evening, we talked about the future of the Canoe Base, the BWCA, its wildlife and forests. Since the Base is fully within the blowdown area, some were apprehensive about the future. We all agreed that the year 2000 would be an interesting one.

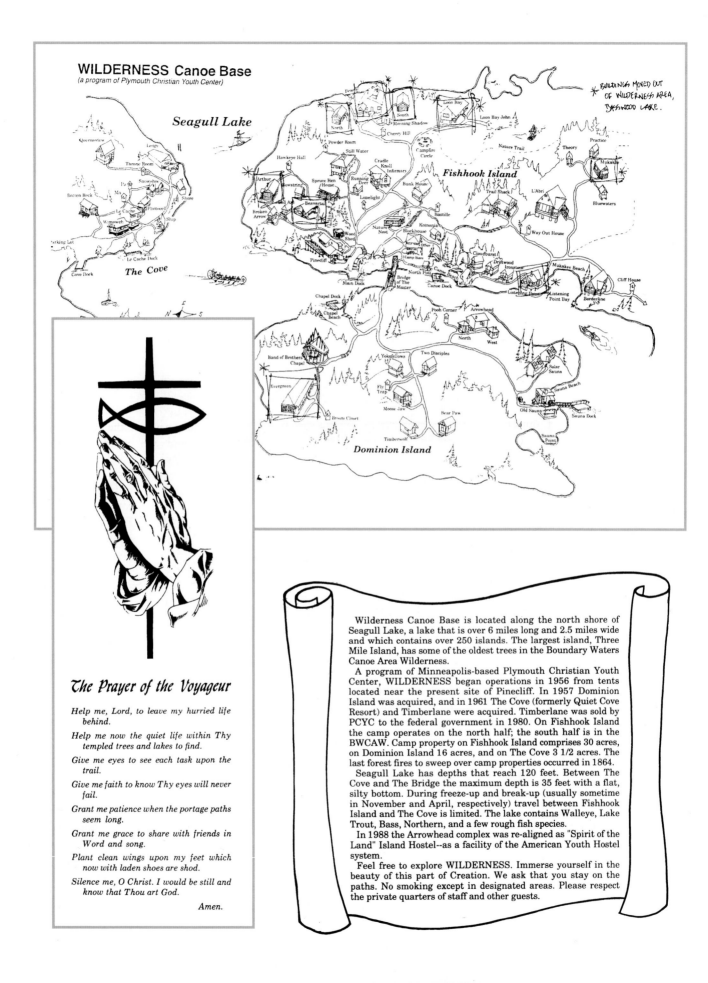

WILDERNESS Canoe Base
(a program of Plymouth Christian Youth Center)

Seagull Lake

The Cove

Fishhook Island

Dominion Island

* BUILDINGS MOVED OUT OF WILDERNESS AREA, BASSWOOD LAKE.

The Prayer of the Voyageur

Help me, Lord, to leave my hurried life behind.

Help me now the quiet life within Thy templed trees and lakes to find.

Give me eyes to see each task upon the trail.

Give me faith to know Thy eyes will never fail.

Grant me patience when the portage paths seem long.

Grant me grace to share with friends in Word and song.

Plant clean wings upon my feet which now with laden shoes are shod.

Silence me, O Christ. I would be still and know that Thou art God.

Amen.

Wilderness Canoe Base is located along the north shore of Seagull Lake, a lake that is over 6 miles long and 2.5 miles wide and which contains over 250 islands. The largest island, Three Mile Island, has some of the oldest trees in the Boundary Waters Canoe Area Wilderness.

A program of Minneapolis-based Plymouth Christian Youth Center, WILDERNESS began operations in 1956 from tents located near the present site of Pinecliff. In 1957 Dominion Island was acquired, and in 1961 The Cove (formerly Quiet Cove Resort) and Timberlane were acquired. Timberlane was sold by PCYC to the federal government in 1980. On Fishhook Island the camp operates on the north half; the south half is in the BWCAW. Camp property on Fishhook Island comprises 30 acres, on Dominion Island 16 acres, and on The Cove 3 1/2 acres. The last forest fires to sweep over camp properties occurred in 1864.

Seagull Lake has depths that reach 120 feet. Between The Cove and The Bridge the maximum depth is 35 feet with a flat, silty bottom. During freeze-up and break-up (usually sometime in November and April, respectively) travel between Fishhook Island and The Cove is limited. The lake contains Walleye, Lake Trout, Bass, Northern, and a few rough fish species.

In 1988 the Arrowhead complex was re-aligned as "Spirit of the Land" Island Hostel--as a facility of the American Youth Hostel system.

Feel free to explore WILDERNESS. Immerse yourself in the beauty of this part of Creation. We ask that you stay on the paths. No smoking except in designated areas. Please respect the private quarters of staff and other guests.

Evacuation from Alpine Lake
by Jan Fiola

Trees down over landing

Vicky under tree   **C33**

Latrine on Alpine Lake

Jan Fiola, Vicky Brockman and Ann Martinson were preparing for rain on Alpine Lake but were not prepared for what was about to happen. The rain began to fall in sheets. "We just thought that we would protect ourselves by going into the tent."

The wind buffeted their tent as the three worked to keep it from blowing away. "I felt like I was in a blender," said Fiola. Trees started snapping all around them; a 25 foot pine crashed through the tent, landing on Martinson's chest and Brockman's hips. Jan tried to free her friends but couldn't budge the tree.

After the storm was over, her calls brought three men, who managed to move the tree. Martinson had only minor injuries, but Brockman's injuries were much worse. The men went for help at about 7:30 PM. Wilderness Canoe Base EMT's Maren Olson, Joel Rogness and others arrived and stabilized Vicky; then helped carry her to a waiting Forest Service float plane.   **C30**

For Martinson and Fiola, the adventure wasn't over. As night fell, the "Wilderness" crew helped them navigate the 20 rod portage around the rapids, using head lamps to light the way. "This was the scariest part of the entire drama," said Fiola. Then they crossed Sea Gull Lake as another storm closed in. When they reached Wilderness Canoe Base, they found buildings without electricity or running water.

They spent the night with 50 people, all of them sleeping in one large room. "It felt like heaven," Martinson said. "It was dry and we were safe."

Vicky had been evacuated to St. Mary's Hospital in Duluth, where she was treated for lacerations and a broken pelvis.

Evacuation from Alpine Lake

Evacuation from Alpine Lake   **C32**

Sea Gull Lake Survivors

The following story was carried in the July 17, 1999 Bayside Cook County Mosquito. Editor Tom Fiero's cousin, Cheryl Hanson, was caught in the storm on a Sea Gull Lake island, along with her husband Chuck and four friends.

by Cheryl Hanson

Hi Tom! Delighted to hear from you. I understand there are a lot of stories floating around! Enjoyed reading "The Walking Wounded," though I'd call it the Sunday School Picnic version. In case you haven't gone to print yet, a few details you missed while diligently flipping pancakes...

The 3 women had all gone to their respective tents. EVERY ONE of the tents had trees fall on them, although Joyce was the only one hit by a tree. The 3 men had gone to the free standing tarp to wait out and watch the storm. The wind was immediately so strong that they ended up enshrouded by flapping nylon and giving all their attention to keeping the tarp from blowing away. They were facing each other a few feet apart.

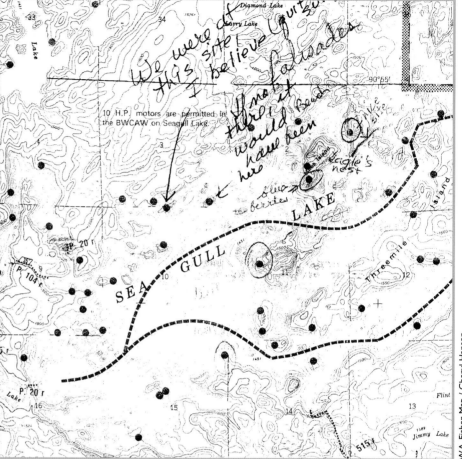

Seagull Lake Map

W.A. Fisher Map / Cheryl Hanson

When the "crack!" sounded, Mark's eyes crossed as he was propelled to the ground and out from under the tarp. The tree had fallen on his back. He staggered to his knees and began vomiting. After the rest of us got out of our

Joyce Arthur suffering from shock

Cheryl Hanson

Tarp where Mark was "downed"

Cheryl Hanson

tents (Wendy and Joyce having had to chew or cut their way through the netting because in the wind they couldn't even operate the zippers), we realized how potentially serious Mark's injury was. His 7th vertebrae was where the pain was. Wendy, being a physical therapist, knew that if there was a fracture and anything slipped out of place, this would likely mean paralysis.

We rolled up a fleece blanket to carefully support his neck in a stationary position and packed dry clothing around him, because he had gone into shock and was shaking. It was determined Chuck and I would canoe for help. We planned to go back to our outfitters at Way of the Wilderness and call for help.

Because of heavy crosswinds, we decided to head east-ish into the wind instead of across the lake as originally planned. After 45 minutes paddling, we saw another canoe

Wendy's tent that she "bit" her way out of

in the distance and headed toward it. In the canoe was Fred Risser (sp?), an old timer with 30 years experience in the BWCA. He advised us to go to Wilderness Canoe Base instead. After another 30 minutes or so we spotted another canoe coming right toward us. We said we had an emergency and had to get to Wilderness. It turned out the two paddlers were both staff members from Wilderness, and they said they'd take us there.

Then off in the distance we saw a motor boat checking out camp sites. We waved them down and said we had to find an EMT. You can't imagine our relief when we found out that the woman in the boat, Maren, was an EMT (and had a backboard with her)! So we showed them where Mark was on the map; they left and we continued on to Wilderness with the goal of getting a helicopter, sea plane or whatever. (Keep in mind, we were operating on

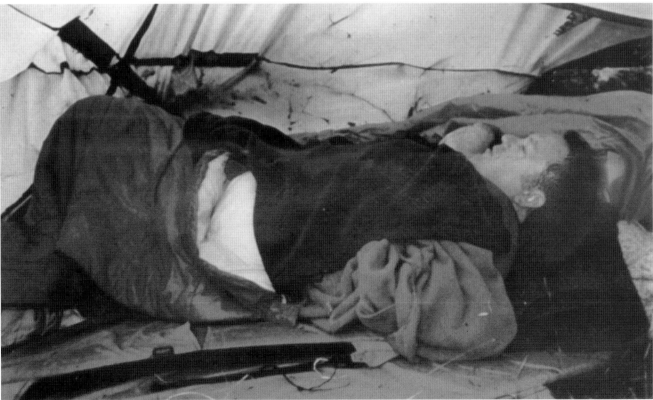

Mark Mattison after injury **C31**

Trees over trail

The morning after, L-R: Joyce Arthur, Bob Arthur, Mark Mattison, Wendy Mattison and Chuck Hanson

the assumption that we had a serious cervical neck injury on our hands.)

Of course, when we got to Wilderness, there was no power, phones, radios or anything. I have to say, the staff at Wilderness were WONDERFUL, and dispatched people to clear the roads to the landing, find a radio and radio for help, etc., etc. About an hour and a half later the boat appeared with Mark strapped into it. He and Joyce and Wendy left for Grand Marais (many times having to sit and wait while trees were removed from the road). The other amazing thing was that word had been quickly passed along about the injury, and the owner of Sea Island Resort and a guest by the name of David Brown, who was a doctor, also had gone out to help bring Mark in.

Meanwhile, Kathy Lande from Sea Island Resort kindly loaned us a motorboat so that Chuck, Bob and I could go back and clear the site. We left at about 4:30 or 5:00 p.m. She said she would try to free up someone with a chainsaw to come and cut up the trees that were on top of our gear and canoes.

We got to the site and it was a disaster area! Fairly soon, David Brown and a young man with a chainsaw

showed up. (David remarked, "It's unbelievable no one was killed.") They cut the trees off and agreed to take a load of gear and one canoe with them. We cleared the rest of the site and by dusk were heading back with the last canoe in tow. We had a couple more adventures on the way and continued to have visions of spending the night on the lake.

We got back by dark, as more rain and wind were threatening, got a ride to pick up the vehicles, loaded our soggy stuff in the vans, got a quick bowl of soup offered by Kathy Lande, and set off down the Gunflint. It was quite a ride–3 hours instead of 1, HEAVY rains at times, incredible devastation. So we got to the hospital at 1:30 a.m., not knowing whether Mark had been flown to Duluth, or what. It was an incredible relief to find there had been no fracture! We had been told there was an emergency shelter at the Community Center, but in the driving rain, only found locked doors. We went back to the hospital where they said Bethlehem Lutheran Church had been opened up, so we spent the night there, courtesy of Pastor John.

A once in a lifetime (I hope!) adventure, all in all!

Mother Nature Took it Up a Notch and Broke them Like Matchsticks
by Bob Pollock

Hi Jim,

My wife Patti and I were right in the path of the storm on July 4, 1999. Here is our story:

Looking back now, we were extremely lucky. Rarely do Patti and I go to the BWCA/Quetico without making at least a few portages. We like to get away from the crowds. Once, for a three day trip we left work in Superior at noon, arrived at Round Lake entry point at 4:00 PM and made Little Sag just after dark. All this just to see if the lake trout were as dark as we had heard. They were. We've had many weather-related experiences. I've been tripping up there for 24 years, Patti for 12. We have been in some nasty storms. We once took a lightning hit on a Phoebe Lake camp. The bolt had hit the rock we were camped on and still had enough zip to travel up the tent poles and burn the plastic connector that held them together. My leg and Patti's arm got a good jolt, as they were the only body parts not on

Bob Pollock and crushed tent   C40

Bob Pollock

our thermarest pads when the bolt hit. That was the first time I've ever smelt burnt ozone.

Anyway, this storm was different. Boy was it. We had four days off for the fourth of July holiday and decided to take an easy trip. I got us a paddle permit for Seagull Lake entering on July third. No portaging, lots of extra gear, chairs, coolers, and steaks - even ice for the drinks. It promised to be a great trip. And it was at first. We found a beautiful camp on an island on the south end of the lake. We are very careful where we set up our tent. (I should mention that once on a trip we had a tree fall on our tent and flatten it. it was unoccupied luckily.) While investigating this camp we found what looked to be a recent lightning strike near the only good spot to pitch a tent. A bolt appeared to have struck a large red pine and split it all the way to the ground. Strangely enough another large pine and a big cedar close by had also been severely damaged

by lightning, almost certainly during the same strike. The damage was bad enough that chunks of wood flew 20 feet from the damaged trees. It made great firewood. We were joking that pitching the tent near the strike would be fine because lightning never strikes twice in the same place. We set up camp, had a great dinner and watched a perfect sunset. I caught a dandy walleye near camp at dark - a good fish for the BW. We hit the hay and planned to get up early and try for some more walleyes.

The morning was calm, clear and warm. You could tell it was going to be a hot day. Fishing was slow so we went in for breakfast. Around 10:00 AM we decided to try some trolling for lake trout. There was a deep hole about a half-mile south of camp that looked promising. It was dead calm, hot and muggy. No-shirt weather already. We trolled for about an hour and I noticed some dark clouds moving in from the southwest and with them a slight breeze. We didn't get a weather forecast before we left because we prepare for the worst and don't worry about it. We do Keep our eyes open to changing conditions however, and when the first lightning strikes started off in the distance we decided to get closer to shore. At that time it looked like the storm was going to miss us, but the middle of the lake with lightning in the area was no place to be. When we were near camp we switched to walleye gear and started jigging the shoreline with one eye to the storm. The clouds were still quite some distance away but now producing some impressive lightning flashes. After fifteen minutes of fishing it was becoming quite obvious that more dark clouds were building to the south of us and would be heading our way. We decided to get off the water and get ready for some rain. At this time there was no indication it would be anything other than a good thunderstorm, but I've been around enough to know that the conditions were right for a potentially powerful storm. Besides, I didn't like the looks of the eerie greenish tint the sky had taken on. I had no idea it was a sign of what we were about to encounter.

When we reached shore I told Patti I would secure the canoe and fix us a drink. I asked if she would get the headlamps and reading material from the tent. We always set up a lean-to shelter so if it rains we don't have to ride out a rainstorm in the tent. By this time it was getting dark enough to need the headlamps if we were to do any reading. Securing the canoe was easy. Usually I tip it over and tie the front to a tree in case of windy conditions. This camp however had two small cedar trees spaced perfectly for wedging our Wenonah Odyssey upside down in between them. All the fishing gear went underneath (fishing rods hung in trees), and I was up in the lean-to making drinks within three minutes. Patti was still at the tent when I finished my chores and took a look across the lake. I could see about a mile across the water to the south shore. It was obvious it was raining hard over there and it was moving our way. What happened next was a lesson in just how powerful mother nature can be. In less than thirty seconds the first gust hit our camp. (We were camped on the south end of the island). That first blast tore all the stakes out of the ground and left the lean-to flapping in a sustained wind that was at least 60 mph. I still had my drink in my hand and was so surprised that all I could think to do was put down the drink and grab the rope that was still attached to the wildly flapping lean-to. At about the same time I noticed two small spruce trees (3 to 4" dia.) blow over next to me and thought, "boy that's strange, this wind must be stronger than it looks." Just then Patti came running down the hill from the tent saying that two good-

Patti and tent before the storm **C40**

Bob Pollock

Tent after storm - Cedar in foreground

Bob Pollock

sized trees had blown down on either side of the tent while she had been in it. I guess we didn't realize it at the time but we were yelling at each other to be heard over the wind. At this point things started happening fast. Trees were blowing down and breaking off all around us. We knew we were in a life-threatening situation. Patti asked me what are we going to do? All I could think of was to get down to the shore so we could get upwind of the falling trees. So we headed for the water which was about 150' away, dodging falling trees all the way. We got there safely, but a new dilemma arose. You couldn't look south into the wind because rain and water coming off the lake would pelt your eyes so hard it was impossible to keep them open. I was concerned about an oncoming tornado, and we were in a very bad spot if this happened. Common sense should tell me that there is little chance of a tornado in the BWCA, but man, what was going on right now was anything but common. Faced with a choice of dodging falling trees or standing where we were with an oncoming whirl-wind, I was ready to head inland. Anyway it didn't matter because there was no way to look into that wind with all the debris and water flying the way it was. So we had to take our chances and remain where we stood. **C37**

Now things were starting to get interesting. When we first reached the water just minutes ago, we were on dry land, about 10 feet from the waters' edge. The standing waves at this time were about three feet and building. The wind was also building. It was becoming tough to stand up without aid so we had to head for the nearest tree for support. It was a cedar tree approximately 12" in diameter that had grown out from the ground horizontally before turning upward. I grabbed that with my left arm and Patti hung on to me with both arms. I could feel the cedar pulling up with each gust, but it was holding. Now all we could do was wait it out. I had forgotten about our two black labs Bucko and Cedar. Just then Cedar jumped up on me, something she rarely does. She was nervous, so I gave her a pat and she sat down. She must have been able to tell that we were scared, either that or the storm was making her uneasy. But where was Bucko? After scanning the immediate area I could see him curled up under a freshly uprooted tree about 10 feet away. He wasn't moving so I let go of the tree and gave him a shake. Still no movement. Another shake. Nothing. At this point I thought he had likely been hit by a falling tree, made it down with us and had died of internal injuries. He'd been my best pal for 11 years, but I didn't have any feelings one way or another about him dying. I wonder if a bit of shock was setting in. I gave him one last hard shake and he lifted his head slowly to look at me. He had to look right into the howling wind and rain and was squinting. He was okay and the look he gave me said "Hey bud, leave me alone, can't you see I'm trying to stay comfortable here?" I did and that was the last time we gave any thought to the dogs until the storm was over.

All we could do now was stand with our backs to the lake and watch the show that was taking place in front of us. Smaller trees were falling at a regular pace. It was hard to say what the sustained wind speed was. Somewhere between 60 and 80 mph would be my guess. The largest pines were holding their own. They were bent and holding at an angle that you would have had to see to believe. All we could hear were the trees cracking and the wind howling. Then it happened. A huge gust came through that nearly knocked us over. You could hear it, feel it and watch the devastation. That gust took down about 10 of the largest red and white pines within 150' of us. It didn't uproot them - they snapped off. These trees were anywhere from two to three feet in diameter. Most broke off at the bottom and went down all at the same time in the same direction. Some broke near the top, I suppose where they had a weak spot. It was the most incredible thing I'd ever seen, watching those old soldiers hold their own only to have mother nature take it up a notch and break them like matchsticks. The wind at this point was.no longer howling, it was screaming, but the sound of those big trees cracking and crashing to the ground could still be heard. It was very eerie, very surreal. I don't remember being scared at that point, just awestruck. It's hard to say how long that gust lasted. The wind then settled back into a steady howl. Some of the big pines still stood, a credit to their superior strength. But it wasn't to remain so. Not long after that, (10,20 minutes?), another gust came through and leveled the remaining largest trees. That second gust had to be stronger

than the first as it left no large trees standing, except for the ones that had broken off partway up.

The island now looked like a bomb had hit it. Four-foot waves were hitting the shore behind us bringing the water up well over our ankles where we were standing. We had been wearing only shorts and T-shirts and were completely soaked. The temperature had dropped quite a bit our shivering had become constant. My wife asked, "When is it going to stop?" in a tone I had never heard her use before. That must have jarred me awake because I started thinking we had better get some extra clothes because we don't know how long this thing is going to last and I didn't want to have to worry about hypothermia on top of everything else. Our extra clothes were up in the tent about 60 yards away and our raingear was in the lean-to about 30 yards away. Trees were still coming down. Thirty's better than sixty, so I headed for the lean-to moving through a maze of downed trees and keeping an eye out for falling ones. The wind is still howling and it's raining like crazy. When I reached the lean-to site I found our gear had been scattered everywhere. After some searching I found both sets of raingear and headed back to the water. I got back to the water without incident and we put on the wet raingear. We immediately felt warmer. The storm was showing no signs of letting up. But it wasn't getting any worse and there were no more of those hellacious gusts. Finally, the wind started to die down some. Then as quickly as it came on, it is over. The sky brightened and it was very quiet. Looking out over the lake we saw that the waves were quickly subsiding. Branches, small trees and unidentifiable flotsam littered the surface. I thought, "Man if anyone was out on the lake when the winds hit there is no way they would have been able to keep a canoe upright". But we didn't see anyone in obvious trouble, so we went up to assess the damage done to our camp. It's creepy how quiet it is now.

My number one concern next to our well-being was the canoe. If this break in the weather holds I want out of here. I don't need to take a walk to know that our camp has been completely destroyed and I'm not interested in going through another blow. A quick check shows that the canoe is miraculously okay. A three-foot diameter red pine uprooted and fell on the front of it but caught it too far forward to do any damage. When the tree landed the canoe skidded backwards unharmed. The two small cedars that held the canoe were no worse for wear. In fact, of all the trees that suffered fatal damage, none were cedar trees. The cedars took the full force of the storm, being the closest to the water, amazing. They must have one heck of a root system.

So now we need dry clothes. They are up in the tent. When we reached the tent we found that two huge red pines had fallen criss-cross fashion across it and flattened it to the ground. (See pictures). If we had been in it during the storm we certainly would have been badly injured - or worse. It took us nearly 15 minutes down on our knees under the trees to reach our clothes. They were in water-proof bags so they were dry. It felt good to be warm again.

Now we discuss what we are going to do. It doesn't take long to reach an agreement. The tent is destroyed, the lean-to is in bad shape, and there isn't a place that doesn't have trees down at this camp. Since we don't know what the weather is going to do and currently the lake looks calm enough to paddle, we opt for the "lets get the hell out of here while we can" option. It takes us over an hour to break camp - usually a fifteen minute job. I sawed trees and cut ropes to get at our gear while Patti stuffed it into our packs. We worked as fast as we could because we could see that there were still storms in the area. I think all we lost was a dog collar and a dog bumper. (A bumper is a dog "dummy" used for retrieve training. We had several along.) At one point during the packing Cedar had jumped in the water and was swimming down the shoreline after who knows what. She returned with one of her bumpers that apparently had blown into the water and was drifting away. How she saw it I'll never know.

Somewhere during the time we were packing up a couple of guys canoed up to our camp and asked if every-thing was alright. They were scout leaders and had been camped nearby with their troops. We said we were okay and we talked some about the storm. They mentioned they had just seen someone in the water hanging on to their canoe and swimming with it toward shore. They couldn't tell if the person had swamped during the storm or had swum out to retrieve a blown away canoe. As far as they could tell he/she was okay. They said they were going to check out a couple of more camps so we said goodbye and continued breaking camp.

A pretty good breeze was blowing from the southwest by the time we got the canoe loaded. We didn't have much freeboard available with the wet payload we were carrying, but since we were heading north with the wind that shouldn't be much of a problem. One last look at the camp-site as we shoved off gave us a glimpse of a very different camp than just the day before. Not in our lifetime would anyone be enjoying the company of those towering pines again.

Down the lake we paddled as fast as we could. We had about a ninety-minute paddle to get to the parking lot where the truck was parked. I had already been wonder-ing how the truck had fared. The sky was dark to the north but strangely enough some of the clouds were going south while some were still moving north. It was gusty weird weather and I was very uneasy about being out on the lake in these conditions. Seagull Lake isn't a big lake but after watching that wind come up just an hour ago I knew we'd never make shore if it happened again. We stayed as close as we could to shorelines as we island hopped our way up the lake.

The wind was steadily building as we reached the largest open stretch of water we would have to cross. At that point we were forced to stop on the west shore of the nearest point because we were taking on water. The damn wind came up so fast that we didn't even have time to paddle fifty yards around the point to relative safety. Luckily we beached on a large flat rock and quickly tied both front and back of the canoe off. The waves were start-ing to break over the canoe but there was just no way to drag the fully loaded canoe up any farther and there was no time to get around the point out of the high winds. There we stood at Mother Nature's mercy once again wondering just how strong this blast was going to get. I took a quick run down the point to look for a good spot for us to hole up if the winds got too bad. There wasn't much cover and by the time I got back another problem presented itself. A large 100-foot white pine, branches and all, was coming down the lake with the wind and it looked like it just might end up on land right where our canoe was tied. If it beached itself the canoe would be sandwiched between land and tree. There would be no getting over the tree without first unloading the canoe, dragging it over and loading up again, a very difficult proposition. The other choice was to untie immediately, jump in the canoe and head around the point high waves or not. That's what we did. We took on some water but made it around the point to relative safety. I looked back as we were rounding the point and saw that the big pine did make land right where the canoe had been tied. What the hell were the chances of that? I was beginning to feel that maybe it wasn't our lucky day. We pulled up out of the wind and took a look to see how much water we had taken on. There was a good amount but the dogs were acting like sponges and had soaked up a substantial amount, making it unnecessary to unload and dump the canoe. They had been instructed to lie down and stay during the paddle and didn't look too happy about their situation, but hey, neither were we.

We were now looking out across the largest part of the lake we had to cross - maybe a half mile. The wind had switched and was coming from the east at a good clip. The waves from the east were crashing into the waves from the southwest making for an interesting lake surface. We've paddled in conditions like this before so off we went before things got any worse. The canoe rocked side to side as we cut through the waves and water came right up to the gunwales, but we weren't taking on any water. Once we made that last big stretch we were home free. The next few miles contained lots of tightly grouped islands providing plenty of shelter from the winds. The sky started to look a lot less cloudy with plenty of sunshine and the winds were subsiding. The paddle became enjoyable, and I was having my usual regrets whenever I come to the end of a northwoods trip.

It was only a half-hour to the parking lot now. I looked up into the sky at a couple of crows that were drifting around overhead and had to laugh. I pointed them out to Patti and she laughed also. Both crows had a lot of primary feathers missing. We could see the sun shining through big gaps in their wings. Their flight was rather shaky, but considering what they must have been through I suppose they were lucky to be flying at all.

Blowdown White Pine afloat

When we reached the landing we encountered a group of teenagers that had just landed. They were from Racine, Wl. Except for the group leaders it was their first trip into the BWCA. They had only been on the water about a half-hour when the storm hit. The group made it to shore but falling trees destroyed a couple of their canoes before it was over. The group left everything where it was (they were outfitted), doubled up in the remaining canoes, and beat it back to the landing. Having had enough wilderness experience, they were headed back home. They planned on telling the outfitter where he could find what was left of his gear. (I wonder how that went?) It turns out our truck was fine. Most of the parking lot was under about six inches of water. I hadn't noticed that it had been built in a tag alder swamp and that couldn't have been better.

There were no big trees to blow over. I saw only one downed tree and it was across someone's boat trailer. I didn't see any damaged vehicles and there were probably forty parked in the lot. At this point we thought we were home free. We thought wrong. We headed back down the Gunflint Trail about 5:00 PM. We stopped at the resort at the end of Seagull for something to drink and found it was locked up. We figured they were out checking on campers because on our way out we saw motor boats in the no motor areas. We checked out the pop machines and found they couldn't be used because the power was out. This was no big surprise, but the condition of the Gunflint Trail was.

We dodged trees for about a mile before we reached a line of vehicles stopped in the road perhaps ten trucks and cars. We must have been among the first ones on the way out because the road ahead was impassable. People were out of their cars and milling around. We could hear chain saws and found out there was a crew just ahead cutting a lane so cars and emergency vehicles could get through. Apparently there had been no vehicles able to travel the Gunflint Trail since the storm hit. That included emergency vehicles and from the looks of things plenty of help was going to be needed.

It took us three hours to make the forty-five minute drive. It was stop and go all the way. Traffic was stopped for periods of up to 30 minutes. The line of vehicles continued to grow until we could no longer see the end. It did give us a chance to talk to others that had weathered the storm and we heard some interesting stories. It was also interesting to note that even though there was no place to go people were still cutting in line with their vehicles whenever they got the chance. The cutting crews did one hell of a job clearing the road because the number of trees down was incredible. The damage stretched for nearly forty miles. Trees and power lines across the road. Trees down on cabins, resorts and driveways. The shoulder of the road had been washed out in many places. By the time we reached Grand Marais it was dark and we realized the extent of the storm. We stopped for gas and headed for Superior. It stormed hard all the way down Highway 61 and made for extremely treacherous driving. By the time we pulled into home we were exhausted but one group of very happy campers.

So there's our story. I'm including some pictures. Believe me when I say we didn't spend a lot of time on photo ops. Use what you can. It was one absolutely incredible experience. The sight and sound of those big pines coming down are etched in my memory forever. My wife said that's it, she's done with the boundary waters. After two strikes, (the lightning experience and this storm), she doesn't want to be around for the third. I can't call it quits. Wilderness tripping is in my blood, always has been and I suppose it always will be. Let's just hope when that third strike comes, I'm as lucky dodging it as I did the first two. *Sincerely, Bob and Patti Pollock*

A Forest Service Feat Almost as Amazing as the Storm Itself
by Ken Hubert

The July 4th BWCA windstorm is a nightmare that my wife and I will treasure for the rest of our lives. It's hard to explain exactly why we would value so highly such an experience. It's not like being a gawker at some car accident where a morbid curiosity forces you to slow down in the event that you might see something. Instead, it's just a feeling that as deeply invested as our recreational lives have become around the Boundary Waters, we would rather have experienced the event ourselves than have to be told about it. And yet, that's exactly what we're trying to accomplish by writing this, tell you about a storm so amazing that you really had to be there to appreciate its intensity and the emotions that it conjured within us.

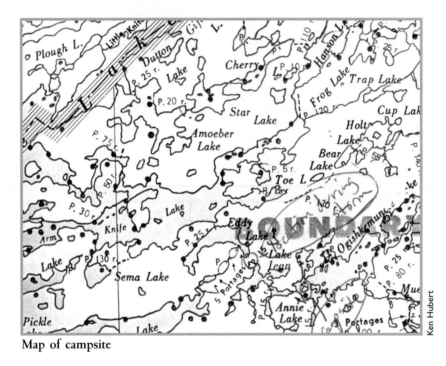

Map of campsite

We have been traveling to the BWCA since early in our marriage in the '70's. Not the type to stick to one route each year, we have varied our entry points and lakes on most of our travels. All of our trips together had also included other couples and/or our kids. So this trip, with the kids taken care of by others, was to be our first to the wilderness just as husband and wife. Kind of a pre "empty nest syndrome" type of thing. Having never gone in through the Seagull Lake entry point, primarily because of a fear of the number of larger groups allowed to enter in this direction, we decided to ignore the possibility of those bigger groups and see what the area had to offer.

We pushed off into the Seagull River on the morning of the 3rd in the midst of a light sprinkle. By the time we reached the middle of Seagull Lake the sprinkle was a downpour, but our attitude was still incredibly upbeat. Amazing what good rain gear can do for you. As we worked our way across Alpine and the other lakes leading to Ogishkemuncie, the rain came and went in spurts. The sound of thunder occasionally made us wonder if we should get off the lake, but since no lightning was ever observed we kept paddling until we reached the campsite on the far western island of Ogish. As we set up camp the clouds broke up and we spent a tremendous evening fishing, swimming, and enjoying the wonders of the wilderness.

The next morning dawned hot and heavy. The air felt thick enough to cut with a knife. After a brief morning swim, we decided to take a day trip to the South Arm of Knife Lake, playing at Eddy Falls along the way. Wearing just swimsuits, t-shirts, and sandals, we packed a lunch with our first aid kit, hung our food pack, and headed out. By 11:30 or 12:00 we had taken the requisite pictures at Eddy Falls and decided to have lunch on the shore of Knife Lake before we went exploring its waters. But that's when our plans changed.

Standing on the end of the portage, we looked west across Knife, our eyes attracted by the dance of lightning and the tremendous thunderhead moving in our direction. Instinctively knowing this wasn't going to be good, together we decided to try to outrace the storm back to our campsite. A quick run up the portage to Eddy Lake, we jumped in the canoe and paddled straight across the narrow width of it. We then raced east to the next portage all the while staying under the overhanging trees as close to shore as possible. Reaching the Eddy/Jean Lake portage we sprinted across as the rain started to fall. Looking out over Jean Lake we decided that we'd gone as far as we dared. The risk now outweighed the benefits.

As I'd done on previous trips when we'd been stopped

because of lightning, I stuck the bow end of the canoe between two small trees and balanced it as a shelter. Figuring that the storm might take a while, we decided to make lunch while we waited. As I held the canoe in place and the rain fell Vicky started to cut summer sausage to go with our crackers. And then the wind came up. Lunch was forgotten as Vicky helped me hold the canoe in place. We took the bow out of the trees and laid the belly to the wind, crouching underneath it.

As the wind speed increased, the rain and trees both went horizontal. Looking back down the portage, all you could see was a wall of water flying along as if being sprayed from a fire hose and trees that were bent over much farther than they were ever made to bend. The first gunshot sound of a tree snapping caught our attention instantly. But, as more and more trees bowed to the will of the wind, the sound kept repeating itself as if we were on the edge of a busy trap shooting range. At this time I began to wonder if we were on the very edge of a tornado and I hoped that it wouldn't turn in our direction.

New backrest for the latrine

Ken Hubert

More trees fell including one that landed right by us. We decided that we needed to move again. Just beyond the end of the portage, about five feet out in the lake lay a large flat rock. Since we were back in a little bay and the wind was roaring down the length of the lake we were able to slide the canoe, with us still crouched under it, out to the rock and away from the trees. For the next half hour or so we sat watching trees snap off twenty feet from the ground, other trees pushed over by the wind pulling up the complete root system, and the water of Jean Lake gradually come up to almost completely cover the rock we were sitting on. With the devastation continuing for such a long time period, it became evident that this was not a tornado.

Eventually, with the storm subsiding, we began to realize that the shivering of our bodies might be more than just the fear we had experienced. Dressed in just our suits and t-shirts, the wind, rain, and drop in air temperature of something like twenty degrees had created a definite chill. Vicky had another shirt for herself in the backpack that we'd dropped when we aborted our lunch making endeavors. Planning to go get it, she slid from under the canoe only to let out a surprised yelp as, in the water not more than twenty feet away, there was a calf moose. The calf,

just as surprised, bolted for the woods with no mother moose in sight.

With the storm done, we assessed our situation. The gear we had with us was fine, but we had no idea how our campsite had survived. Looking across Jean Lake we could see all the trees laying in one direction, as if Paul Bunyan had come through and just pushed everything down. It was then that Vicky looked at me and said, "It must have been straight line winds." Even so, we didn't know the extent to which they'd damaged the wilderness. We had commented on the beauty of the portage we were on during our first trip across it. Now we went part way down it and marveled instead at the magnitude of the damage not realizing that this was now the norm for a large portion of the BWCA. **C38**

With two portages to be crossed to get back to Ogishkemuncie, we pushed off and paddled in a hushed awe at what had taken place. The first portage was traversed easily with only a few trees to slide the canoe over or under. Without packs the portaging didn't seem too bad. The portage into Ogishkemuncie, however, was almost impossible. Only with the help of a man and his son who had taken refuge on that portage were we able to get through. With no saws in our daypack it was a real challenge. After getting across the portage we thanked them and then, not knowing if or how any campsites were affected, we offered to share ours with the father and son team. They declined, however, saying that they had just come in that day and they were going to turn right around and head back out. They did stay long enough to make sure that our campsite was okay.

Paddling around to the landing site of our camp, we saw that access to our tent was completely blocked by downed trees. In fact, almost every tree on the island was down. One of the few left standing still proudly displayed our food pack. Clambering over downed timber I retrieved my handsaw and proceeded to clear a path from the lake to the tent area The tent had a tree on top of it, but luckily the tree was a black spruce and after we cut away a few branches we were able to slide the tent out from under it. No holes and the poles still intact, the only problem we faced was the water that got in when the tent door ended up facing skyward during the storm. We spent the rest of the afternoon clearing brush, drying sleeping bags, and wandering around, I believe, a little in shock. Probably the most unique aspect of our campsite ended up being the two good-sized trees that fell on top of each other just behind the latrine forming a nice backrest.

Still not realizing the extent of the storm, we began to hear planes fly into the lakes around us. Very unusual, but it was easy enough to deduce that they had probably been called in to evacuate people who were hurt. Every so often we heard one throughout the rest of the evening. A couple who we'd met before the storm had waited it out on Kekakabic and got back to Ogish about five hours after us. When they'd come from Eddy to Jean they'd seen the same calf moose alone in the water. With mom probably under a tree somewhere I'm sure the little one eventually ended up as wolf food. We also listened to screams in the woods during the evening that sounded like an animal in pain. Just to keep things interesting that night it poured, thundered, and lightninged the entire time we were in the tent. After the storm we'd been through it was not very conducive to sleeping.

Trying to get back to our campsite

Monday was spent drying things out from the all night rain. It was also spent listening to plane after plane land and take off, each time increasing our concerns. We had originally planned to be in the woods until Wednesday, but decided to cut it short and head out on Tuesday instead as we worried about what our families were thinking. With us and our campsite okay, we took a tour of the western half of the lake.

Only one other campsite was still occupied. A father and son from Saginaw, Michigan had a tree fall on their tent, and couldn't find their latrine anymore because almost all of the trees were down on their island. Before the storm they had been observing a baby eagle in a nest across the narrows. With the nest knocked down by the wind, they had gone into the woods to see if the baby was still alive. They found it lying on the ground, barely surviving. They propped it up at the base of what used to be its nest in hopes that the parents could still keep it alive. Truly a slim chance and besides, you have to wonder if the parents survived the storm.

The next morning we packed up and headed out observing campsites along the way. None of them were occupied. Reaching the 38 rod portage to Kingfisher Lake, the landing site was made difficult by the trees that were uprooted. Our friends from Michigan had gotten there a

little earlier than us and, with saws in hand, we slowly worked our way across. Cutting branches and small trees where we needed and shoving canoes and gear over and under downed trees, a portage that should have taken 15 minutes took over an hour. The next portage from Kingfisher to Jasper was a little shorter but certainly no better. It was like trying to fight through a giant game of pick up sticks. As difficult as these were I didn't look forward to trying the 100 rod from Alpine to Seagull.

The portage from Jasper to Alpine was very nearly clear, only a few trees creating small problems, but nothing major. It was here that we met our first group that was trying to head into the woods. Such is the nature of the BWCA traveler. Paddling across Alpine we stopped at a campsite near the portage and asked the group if they knew anything about it. Turned out they were a group of scouts from North Carolina and asked if we could call the group leader's wife when we got out to let her know that they were all just fine. They told us the portage was impassable, but being worked on from the other side. Around the point they said the short portage was open and as it turned out, easily passable.

That night we stayed in Grand Marais and made phone calls to our kids. Our daughter, staying with some friends, had been very worried and was relieved when we called. Our son, staying with his grandparents, told his grandmother not to worry because his dad knew what to do in the woods. Perhaps he has a little too much onfidence in his dad's abilities.

A little over a month later I went back into the BWCA by way of Brule Lake. Although it was not hit as hard as the area that we had been in there were still areas of severe damage. All portages and campsites in the area were cleared by that time, a Forest Service feat almost as amazing as the storm itself. The question that most people ask after hearing about the trip and the storm is; do you plan to return? The only answer we can give is an emphatic yes. An area that has been such a large part of our lives is not one that you give up easily. We plan to continue traveling the lakes and streams, enjoying what nature has to offer whether it's a moose in the shallows or 100 mile per hour straight-line winds, although we vastly prefer the former.

Totally Lost on Sag Lake
by Scottie Hoffman and Marston Peterson

"The Storm Cloud" on Saganaga Lake   **C1**

Another Sag (Saganaga) Lake close call turned a dream fishing trip into a nightmare for Marston Peterson and Scottie Hoffman of the Twin Cities.

Marston's mother Paulene Peterson knew without being told that her son was in serious trouble – as a psychic, she's been through it before. During a dream that Sunday night, she saw a boat full of ladies in brown shirts and shorts attending to the two boys.

Paulene claims that when you think you're going to die, your energy passes to your mother. She claims she was with the boys during the BW storm.

Marston and Scott hadn't realized the complexity of Sag Lake, with its uneven shoreline and incredible number of islands. They were totally lost – somewhere southwest of Horseshoe Island, they found out later.

According to Marston, "We saw the storm coming at us across the lake. We gunned the motor and headed for the nearest island, but the storm caught us, closing in from three directions. We were in 10 foot rollers. We thought we were going to die, but our extra wide boat helped keep us on top."

Somehow they reached shore – they were incredibly lucky. Marston said, "There were boy scouts on the island, which was stripped of trees. A number were injured. One boy had a broken leg, and a troop leader had suffered a moderate heart attack. The whole troop didn't look too good. Several ladies from the Forest Service (in brown clothes) were helping them out."

Reference to "C" throughout the book indicates a color photo in mid-section.

A Storm Survivor's Story
by H. Sue Manzo, Tacoma, Washington,
daughter of Art and Dinna Madsen of Saganaga Lake

(Reprinted from the Cook County News-Herald, July 26)

Many have stories to relate of the disastrous windstorm of July 4. Mine is to tell of the tremendous effort in clearing hundreds of trees for over seven hours along a 20 mile span making the road passable for the ambulance to evacuate injured storm victims, plus freeing others marooned who had attempted to drive down the Gunflint Trail. The godsend who accomplished this was a man and his 17 year old son working with their chainsaws.

Each summer my family visits and helps my parents at their wilderness resort on the Canadian side of Saganaga Lake. My objective July 4 was to meet my husband at the Duluth airport early that evening as he was returning to the lake. My father, Art Madsen (age 94) drove me the six miles down Saganaga to the public landing.

The sky was filling with fast moving black clouds while underneath there was an unusual turquoise green color. Due to the disturbed atmosphere a large number of eagles and birds had left their perches and were soaring above the tree tops.

My father pulled quickly into the landing and told me to unload fast. He said, "I've got to wheel. When you see black clouds forming like that, it could mean a twister." I threw my two bags on shore and jumped out pushing the boat free. It was just beginning to sprinkle as I got into my car.

I left the landing at 12:55 p.m. Five minutes later it was extremely windy and the trees were bending over the road. Thinking that the storm would probably be localized to a small area, I continued on hoping to drive out of it. Due to the intensity of the wind, the gusts began rocking my car. Rethinking what my father had said about a twister, I rolled down my window slightly to listen for the sounds that I've heard accompanies tornados. I could only hear the raging wind and rain, but it was definitely something more than just a bad storm.

About half a mile past Seagull Outfitters a tree blocking the road brought me to a standstill at 1:10 p.m.

Damaged Hungry Jack Outfitters sign - Gunflint Trail C13

Dave and Nancy Seaton

A few minutes later two trucks passed by me.

Glancing up I recognized Becky Kayser (formerly Johnson of Grand Marais, whom I'd known since I was a young girl) peering out their passenger window.

With their pick-ups they simply drove over the downed tree and made it only 15 feet farther until a heavy poplar (10" in diameter) hit their first truck from the left landing on the road.

In spite of the storm's force, Dick Kayser (Becky's husband) jumped out and quickly sawed the poplar free from his truck. I could only make out a few feet beyond that, but saw that he continued down the road.

Two other vehicles pulled beside me and I backed up considering that I might drive back to Seagull Outfitters. The first vehicle, a car, pulled over to the right near a rock embankment. The second, a minivan, pulled up to the downed tree. Attempting to find the most sheltered area, I pulled adjacent to the car.

The trees were bent across the road from the right at a near 45 degree angle. About ten minutes later a fellow jumped out and ran to the back of his vehicle yelling through the raging wind for me to "Back up! All the trees in front are coming down!" I could only move back about 20 feet until I was again blocked behind by downed trees. He then backed into my spot. Right away every tree on our right, as far as we could see, began to crash across the road. The trees closest to the road gave way from their roots, and those farther back snapped off 10 to 20 feet up from the ground. My station wagon swayed in the wind, and I was pelted with all types of debris, dirt, bark and branches. It sounded like rocks hitting my car. I kept watching on the right side to see if there was any danger of any other trees falling near me.

Since the wind was blowing from the southwest, I only expected trees to fall from the right. I groaned as a jackpine unexpectedly came from the left and struck across the roof of my car.

But at this point, my main concern was how my father had fared. I prayed that he had somehow made it safely up the lake, but by judging the time frame, I knew his traveling time was at least 20 minutes, and the storm began a mere five minutes after he left the landing.

When the wind had abated somewhat a fellow from the minivan walked up the road climbing over and around the mass of trees. He came back to report that he had seen a man up ahead cutting his way out with a chain saw.

I said, "That's Dick Kayser, a professional forester from Wisconsin. I'm going to ask him to help us." I hurried, as I thought there may be very little down in front of him and he'd soon be on his way. It was still raining and I only had sandals and shorts on and a light windbreaker which wasn't waterproof. I had a large trash bag which I donned making a headhole.

Trees bending over Gunflint Trail 1 PM 7/4/99

I ran ahead climbing over trees. The ones that were too large I had to walk around. Dick Kayser was about a block ahead, but there wasn't even a two foot space which didn't have a downed tree. I could see no end to the downed trees barring our way.

Path through Gunflint Trail

I told Dick that we were a block behind and that I thought we could pull the tops diagonally out of the way, but there were larger ones that we'd never move. I asked if he could cut us free, there would then be other men who could help him clear ahead. He began to backtrack and it took him about 45 minutes to cut back to us.

I ran ahead so we could get busy clearing the smaller trees. As I approached the minivan, one woman was near hysterics. I told them that Dick would help cut us out, but I didn't know how much gas he had for his chain saw, so we needed to move all the smaller trees we could.

There were two couples in their early thirties in the minivan. One lady was eight months pregnant, but also helped with the lighter branches. I asked the other lady who had been so frightened to also come and help; she rallied and joined us.

In the car was an older gentleman, his wife and his mother. This gentleman also came to help us. The "little" trees that I thought we could have dragged to the side were much heavier than I realized and even teamed up we could barely budge them. the two fellows in the minivan unloaded their canoe and attached a strap to their bumper to drag a couple of trees to the side.

We realized that Dick was cutting and clearing much faster with the chain saw, so we went to assist by dragging away his cut logs. Once he freed us, he cut and we cleared 3 1/2 miles down the Gunflint Trail until he was nearly out of oil. Fortunately, I found some that my husband had stored in the car.

We then cleared another three miles or so with Dick's son Mark (age 17) cutting with a second chain saw. Becky cautioned him to be careful for if he became injured there was no way we could get him to the hospital, but it was obvious that they were both very skilled in the use of a chain saw and cut at a remarkable rate.

We came upon two men from the forestry who were cutting from the other side who had cut their way up from the Seagull ranger station. They were greatly appreciative of the seven miles or so that Dick and Mark had cleared. They advised us that another storm was coming and that we should wait at the ranger station. Our little caravan of five vehicles decided it was better to help all we could, as the ambulance was cutting their way up from Gunflint to rescue two injured youth at the End of the Trail. They told us that they were also cutting from the Grand Marais side from Greenwood on up.

For the first time we heard the extent of the damage along the Trail. They said the ambulance was headed our way, but it was blocked solid beyond Gunflint down the Trail.

Dick and Mark had been cutting at an unbelievable pace, and Mark's sister Katherine (age 14) cleared as much as anyone, then would run for water, pop and food about every 15 minutes to sustain the energy level of her father and brother.

We would all be forward helping to clear and then dash back to our vehicles to pull the 20 to 50 feet ahead. Becky Kayser would pull their first pick-up forward, and then jog back to their second truck to move it ahead. Later another lady took over the driving of the second pick-up.

We met the ambulance about two miles north of Gunflint. There were two men with chain saws cutting for the ambulance. We now had a caravan of 16 cars. The ambulance driver said we were to pull over and park wherever we could as the road was now closed.

We explained what had already been accomplished, convincing him that once he had picked up the injured storm victims that he would get down the Trail faster only if we continued to clear. We guaranteed that our procession would keep a path for the ambulance to pass. He relented.

At this point we had plenty of men to help and we were clearing quite a bit faster. Many used hand saws and axes. Now, all I had to do was drive, park and chat with others in line.

The grader from Grand Marais met us just on the other side of Laurentian Divide lookout. It had been seven hours to this point and it took another hour and a half to reach Grand Marais. I left Grand Marais at 9:20 p.m. and drove through lightning and pouring rain to Duluth, arriving at the airport just before midnight. My husband had been waiting since 2:30 p.m. We made it back to Grand Marais about 2:30 a.m.

My father had planned to meet us at the End of the Trail on July 5 at 2:30 p.m. I still had no word as to how he had fared. We had no way to contact him to cancel, and the sheriff's department was not able to make radio contact with anyone up there. We were granted special permission to proceed up the Trail at 2:30 p.m., as it had been open only to those evacuating down the Trail.

Upon rejoining my parents on the lake, my father related his own hairy story of traveling up the lake July 4th. As I had suspected, he was in the midst of the storm five minutes after I left. The winds were so fierce that he had to keep full speed on, or the winds would have whipped his boat around. He was traveling close to shore where there was rock wall, as he knew lightning would strike the highest point.

About 15 feet from his boat on the rock wall, lightning struck a tree with a deafening crash. With the wind that strong it was driving the rain horizontally, and it was picking up the top of the waves and whipping the water northeast. As he finally neared the front dock there was a wall of rain just three to four feet behind him closing in fast. My daughter ran down to the dock to catch his boat, or he would have been driven into shore. Just after he had arrived safely, Dick Powell reported that the waves became five feet high. Dick said, "Your dad just barely made it in time."

Top of the Gunflint Trail
by Pete Lindgren

Pete Lindgren is a four year veteran fire leader for the Forest Service, working at the Seagull Lake Guard Station near the end of the Gunflint Trail. Pete described how the Seagull Lake area fared.

"That Sunday I was suspicious of the weather and called my family in Cook, MN, which is generally in the direction from which a storm would come. They had a few trees down but nothing major. But within minutes of my call, 90% of the surrounding forest was on the ground."

Trail's End Campground - probably 50% - but no serious injuries. There were still a lot of big pines left."

Pete continued, "The only communication out was my handheld radio. Luckily the county's tower near Gunflint Lake withstood the wind; otherwise there would have been no communication and no evacuation.

"Clearing the Gunflint Trail was a tough job. At the beginning there were only two of us sawing, but by the

---

Facilities and Administrative Sites:
The Seagull Guard Station house, warehouse, and radio tower received substantial damage during the storm.. The damage includes loss and damaged shingles, gutters, and facia, as well as several holes in the roof, and possible truss damage on the house and warehouse. Additionally, a corner of the roof and building on the warehouse was crushed by falling trees. The radio tower was flattened by trees and damaged by high winds.

USFS

Status of the Guard Station

At the guard station a mass of trees were down and buildings were severely damaged. The branch of a red pine tore a hole in the station's roof. Pete thought of the campers at Trail's End Campground.

"We sawed our way out of the yard and got as far as the Blankenburg landing where we were flagged down by a party with an injured boy. The boy's family was at the landing during the wind. The 8 year old was crouched down when the tree hit him, driving his knees into his chest. We radioed for a Life Flight and the helicopter was there in 45 minutes. His parents went out the next day after the Trail was cleared.

"Continuing up the Trail, we found lots of big pines down at

time we got to Loon Lake we had 1 1/2 miles of cars trying to get out and so many people helping that we were actually getting in each other's way."

There were 17 parties trapped at Iron Lake Campground - hundreds of trees blocked the access road, which took two days to clear.

Pete believes that the Gunflint Lake area sustained the most damage outside of the wilderness. He, along with others noticed lots of wildlife "hanging out" on the Trail over the next few days, especially just before dark. Pete worked 16 or 17 days doing search and rescue around Gabbro Lake with Melissa Carlson and John Melang - fellow Forest

USFS

Damage at the USFS Seagull Guard Station - Note Communication Tower down

Service employees. One portage of 90 rods took 5 hours of sawing.

Pete doesn't believe that a huge fire will occur; more likely it will be fires the size of the 1995 Sag fire (Saganaga Lake). He feels that the storm changed the way the Forest Service will operate: there will be lots

One lane Gunflint

of extra training, brushing up on skills and knowledge, and hopefully more fire-ready people at the guard station.

The July 26 Cook County News-Herald told about Trail's End campground and the volunteer spirit of the campers.

Anon

Page 10 A   Cook County News-Herald, Grand Marais, Minn.   July 26, 1999

Campground hosts are grateful

Susan and Bob Theune, campground hosts at Trails End, sent anecdotal accounts of how twenty campers dealt with the debris left by the July 4 storm that smashed through the forest. As was the case in many camps and resorts, enormous trees fell like a giant's box of toothpicks. The sheer volume of wood, not to mention the surprise of being forced to hack one's way out with little or no modern equipment, makes these stories representative of many heard around the county and state of late.

No last names and addresses were supplied by the Theunes as the campers are long returned home and have not given permission to share their sagas. In addition, the News-Herald does not recommend that anyone save

trained loggers try the kind of timber handling that is described. Downed trees are dangerous.

The Theunes wrote of four sets of campers who did more than their share in literally digging out from under the blown down trees on July 4. Raymond, Denise and Kane used hand saws and axes to clear thirteen sites.

The willingness of all the other campers was illustrated to Ray when he put his saw down for one minute while moving a piece of wood. "When he went to pick up the saw, someone else was already using it," Susan Theune said.

John, his wife and two daughters used their tow truck with a tow belt to pull some huge Norway pines off a road in the campground. They also removed the

branches. "Without the use of the 4-wheel drive vehicle, the roads would not have been cleared," Bob Theune said.

Another family-Bob, Carla and a brother in law-brought a chain saw with them and fellow campers were glad they did. Bob (the camper) sawed his way out of a totally blockaded campsite, eventually joining up with those using hand saws to work towards him. "Never have campers been happier to hear the noise of a chain saw as on that 4th of July!" said Susan Theune.

One camping party "rode" out the storm sitting in a car. Kerry, Sue and two of their friends took to the car for safety. A giant birch dropped right next to the car but missed it. The campers put their small hand saws and triangle saw

to work immediately after the storm passed. "When not sawing, they were pulling branches, which others had sawn, off to the side of the road-they worked until the roads were clear," said Bob Theune.

At last the 2.3 miles of roads in the campground were cleared well enough for campers to leave their sites, the Theunes reported. The hosts were amazed and full of praise for their guests and all that had been accomplished with no more than hand saws, axes, one chain saw and one truck with tow belt.

Trails End Campground

Survival at Maraboeuf

by Ralph Pribble - July 8, 1999

Just returned from the BWCA Monday night, after a 4-day trip on the Granite River route. Having done six or seven trips up there over the 4th, I expect thunderstorms this time of year up there, but not the kind of storm that hit on Sunday.

Our group of six had already had one storm the day before with lightning, thunder and drenching rain, but it wasn't too big a deal; afterward the sun came out and it was gorgeous through Sunday morning. But by midday on Sunday more storms were building.

As we canoed north up Maraboeuf Lake there were ominous dark-gray and purple clouds lumbering in slowly from the west, along with flickers of lightning and that heavy grumble of distant thunder that makes you feel uneasy. It got dead still on the water, the air warm and very humid. We ate lunch floating on the water together - thought we might as well eat before the rain. As we approached the portage around Horsetail Rapids we started picking up the pace to get there and off the water before the storm hit, as the lightning was coming uncomfortably close.

We landed okay, and before unloading walked the 24-rod portage to see if we could avoid it by running the rapids. We decided no, and had just returned and were unloading the canoes to start the carry when suddenly it got very dark and the wind began kicking up. I looked down the lake behind us and saw a wall of white froth about a quarter-mile away, coming right at us. It was the rain beating the surface of the lake, with a dark, violet, angry sky behind it. I yelled "Here it comes!" and most of us dropped what we were doing and dived for cover, some under the canoes, others to the base of trees.

Dale had just flipped his canoe onto his shoulders to move it to a safer place, and a sudden blast blew him staggering with the canoe up the portage path into the brush. Jill and I huddled at the water's edge between our canoe and a tree and held on, and then the rain hit like a giant garden hose with one of those spray thingies aimed at us. A good sized tree went down right in front of us, its branches just missing me and the trunk stopping short of squashing Randy and Malinda a few feet away.

By some great luck we happened to be in an area that had burned badly about five years ago, so there weren't many trees left standing to go down around us. But most of those that were left did go over. I kept swiveling my head all around looking for what might be coming next, so we could at least try to jump out of the way. The winds seemed to be gusting from everywhere, driving big waves down into the narrow end of the lake next to us, and the rain slashed us in great wind-driven sheets. As we huddled there I thought, "I sure hope this doesn't turn into a tornado."

There was nothing you could do but hold tight and take it. The thunder and lightning was continuous. We were all soaked right through under our rain gear. If you looked upwind to try to see what was coming, you got bucketfuls of water in the face which ran right down your collar.

After ten minutes of this we started to hear, in the pauses between thunder crashes, great ripping and cracking noises from the opposite shore, maybe 100 feet away. There were more trees over there and they were thrashing like weeds, and were going down continuously. You could see tall dark spruce tops in the flying gray rain whip around and then go all the way over. This went on for what seemed like ten minutes.

I was sitting on the roots of a cedar tree maybe 12 feet tall, and I could feel them lifting under me as the tree bent in the gusts. At least if it went over it didn't seem large enough to hurt us much, but I was afraid that flying branches or even whole tree tops might start coming at us from the other shore.

After awhile it seemed like everything around us that was going to come down probably had done so. The wind and rain started to ease and we began to relax a little. I grabbed my pack, which was starting to float in the two feet of water which had run down to the back of our canoe onshore, and we flipped the canoe over. After about 25 minutes the storm was over.

Trees now blocked the portage as far down the path as we could see, making it all but impossible to carry. We scrambled through it to check things out - there were maybe 15 trees down in the 24 rods, including a big red pine right across the other end. We were laughing and energized by our lucky escape. The rapids were now considerably higher, so we thought we could walk the canoes down a smaller, fast moving channel beside the portage path which luckily didn't have any trees across it. And that's what we did.

Lucky us. Not only were we lucky that we were in the burned area (with fewer trees to fall over) and that we hadn't yet begun the portage, but it also was our last remaining portage in the trip, save one small liftover at a falls. So after we'd gotten through that we had clear sailing until take-out the next day.

That night we had more thunderstorms and heavy rains, with a fantastic lightning show to the south and west after dark. Everything was wet, wet, wet. But luckily no more high winds. (Thank God - there were big tall pines all around us in our campsite which had somehow escaped that afternoon's destruction.)

We didn't even realize how bad the storm had been until the next day when we started encountering other people who told us of the extent of the damage. Though the whole area around us on Sunday had obviously been hammered, our route was probably mostly in the more peripheral area, at least compared to ground zero jut a little to our west. Cars were smashed in parking lots; the Gunflint Road had hundreds of trees down across it. In some places every tree beside the road for a hundred yards was snapped clean off half way up the trunk.

We were coming out most of a day after the storm, and chainsawers had cut at least one lane back to Grand Marais. That's about 50 miles, with the worst damage along perhaps 20 miles of the north end of the road. Mary's car, at our put-in 12 miles down the road from the take-out, was saved from being smacked by a van next to us which took most of the hit from a big aspen. She backed out through its branches. Another guy in the same lot was pulling out with a boat and trailer. His windshield was smashed, a football-sized hole in the glass right in front of his face. I hope he didn't have far to go.

Unbelievable storm. Several other parties I knew who were also up there the same weekend escaped without major harm. Dave's 19 year-old daughter was in a canoe camp with a friend, where she got hit in the head and had a mild concussion. Their canoe and tent were smashed but they weren't far from the road and so could get out. Another friend was in a tent and got hit across the back by a falling pine. It was kept from flattening him by their bear rope which ran from that tree to another. He had used a super-strong climbing rope and later had to untie the knot with a pliers.

Some people may yet be trying to make it out over clogged portages. I heard today the injury count was up to 58, with two critical but no fatalities yet.

Perhaps the worst thing about the storm is that so many old-growth pines were lost. Aerial photos I've seen look like the aftermath of Mount St. Helens in some places. It's almost like a quarter of the wilderness was suddenly clear-cut. It isn't going to look the same at all in many places, at least not in our lifetimes. But right now, I'm just glad we all got through it safely. It was, of course, sort of cool - now that we're home.

– This message was posted to the CanoeCountry.com Mailing List. The Canoe Country web site is found at ‹www.canoecountry.com›.

CanoeCountry.com

This BWCA-oriented web site played an important role in alerting the public to the severity of the storm.

The general media were silent about the storm for nearly two days. Chad Jones, webmaster for CanoeCountry.com, remembers the day of the storm. "At that time my business was located on the Trail. Just after the wind, I received an e-mail from Sue McDonnell, head of the Gunflint Trail Association, telling me the extent of the damage. Within two hours of the storm I had the first e-mail broadcast of the event going out to thousands of people through all of our data bases and bulletin boards."

The following messages were posted to the CanoeCountry.com Mailing List just after the storm:

Anyone knowing of coordinated volunteer efforts, please post to news.

Partial washout at the bottom of the Sawbill. Under-cut pavement. BE CAREFUL!

Last night Bethlehem Lutheran in Grand Marais provided shelter for eight campers from two different sites who were displaced by the wind storm. One group of campers had been on Sea Gull and another on Iron Lake. Both parties described the damage as "devastating."

Sounds like things up the Trail are pretty bad. Many many trees down all over. Power out and many people with trees on houses, cars, cabins, etc. Haven't been up there myself but from talking to some people up around Poplar Lake it sounds like anyone that wants to spend part of their holiday weekend lending a helping hand would be much appreciated up there. Anyone with a chainsaw is especially welcome.

Chad Jones

If Anyone Hadn't Jumped They Would Have Suffered Death

by Jeanne Sharp

Dear Jim,

I was in the BWCA during the storm. I went with three other women (Mary, Kara, Jennifer). None of us had been to the Boundary Waters before. *We were four women that just wanted to see the Boundary Waters.* We read a book, bought some maps, and took a class in preparation. We were good campers and good canoeists and began our trip with excitement and antici-pation. I honestly imagined our 5 day trip into the BWCA to be slow-paced and peaceful.

When the storm approached just after lunch we pulled our canoes off the water and set up a lean-to at a vacant campsite. We opened one sleeping bag and laid it flat to serve as a blanket. We sat waiting for the weather to pass, giving hand massages, reading passages from our book on wilder-ness, telling stories. While I was standing telling a story the wind was picking up. At one point the tarp caught the oddest breath of wind and violently pulled up about four feet and came right back down. The natural flapping wind played the tarp before and after this odd gust but it was this odd gust that sparked conversation.

"This isn't a regular storm."

"What if this tree that's leaning falls?"

"That tree is seventy-five years old. It has seen storms before."

"What if a tornado comes?"

After we jumped out from under our tarp a tree fell through the middle of it.

Jeanne Sharp

"We'll know a tornado by that train sound it makes."

Suddenly, there was silence and a ready stance as we heard a train approaching from the North. I listened and heard a wave of trees falling at us from the distance. Then I heard an even louder sound. I turned to the South and saw two huge (about one hundred years old) pine trees falling straight toward us. I heard someone yell "Watch out!" or "Jump!". Was it me? I jumped to the East. I saw Jen jump with me. It must have been a hell of a jump because we jumped over a pile of deadwood that we were unable to manipulate around while we put up the tarp. I jumped up and grabbed Jen. We were all right. I held her two hands with my two hands and yelled my loudest in the wind and rain, "Where are Kara and Mary?". She screamed back, "I don't know". We crawled across the newly fallen tree. As my eyes searched the messy edges of the giant, crashed tree I thought two thoughts, "Please God let me have strength to see whatever I'm about to see." (I wasn't sure that someone hadn't been crushed.), and "I'm not leaving short of the number four." (I wasn't sure that someone hadn't been killed.) We found Kara, helped her to her feet. She was okay. "Where's Mary?" She didn't know. We found her under several branches. When we tried to help her up she said, "No, leave me.". "Why, are you hurt?" Then Mary sat up and then she stood up. Later she explained that she didn't know the trees had fallen yet and was waiting for them to miss her.

We were all okay. We were half laughing, half crying, certainly shaking. The winds stayed fierce for thirty minutes after that. More trees fell around us. We were scared stiff the entire time. I remember looking out at the gray swells of Lake Saganaga and thinking how the lake looked unrecognizable. Every time a tree cracked or creaked or fell one of us would yell out an idea, "Let's huddle under the biggest fallen tree for safety.", "Let's hike in-land and find a clearing to stand in.". In general we simply stood in the middle of the woods in 100 mile an hour winds with the rain coming down hard and kept our eyes looking up for trees falling. I remember being very frightened as I knew there was nothing I could do to ensure our safety. At one point I yelled out, "Everyone, pray to your God!". I said prayers asking God to keep us safe. When the winds finally calmed we began to feel the emotions. The biggest recurring emotion was sheer joy that we were alive.

One of the pine trees that fell toward the camp fell right in the middle of our tarp. The tarp is still there today as the four of us couldn't budge the tree. It's pretty amazing we are all alive. Two of us jumped East and two jumped North. If anyone didn't jump or jumped South we would have suffered death.

The tree that nailed our tarp

Jeanne Sharp

Aside from feeling happy to survive we had other thoughts and feelings. There was sadness of the loss of so many mature trees. There was curiosity about who experienced the storm and who would believe what we experienced (we didn't know at the time that the storm affected more than our area). There was anxiety about any more inclement weather. We were unsure about our finishing our trip and reaching the outfitters by nightfall as we were exhausted and we lost a lot of time. There was spiritual wondering as we dabbled in why it happened and why we survived. But, there was elation that we were alive.

After putting on dry clothes and taking some pictures we left the camp. We canoed only twenty minutes when we saw a man alone in a canoe that was bent a bit (U shaped). His name was Michael. He was by the falls when the storm hit. A tree fell on his canoe as he lay under it. He had to use a saw to get out. He was near a man, a woman, and their baby at the falls. The family took cover under a rock ledge and were unharmed. He planned on camping out on the fourth and exiting to an outfitters on the fifth

By the time we reached the outfitters that evening (about 7 pm) we realized that the storm was large, flattening everything in it's path. We canoed passed Camper's Island and saw 3 tents and canoes and no people. About 90% of the trees were down on that island and the outfitters said that the campers hitched rides out with motor boats that passed. Everything had changed. As far as we could see in all directions canoeing the rest of the day the forest was flattened. There were trees floating in lakes and rivers but very few trees left standing. Once back on the Gunflint Trail we saw and heard everything that we later read in the papers, saw on the news, heard on the radio.

Since our trip I've heard that the land of the Boundary Waters lay vulnerable. I realize that we were lucky. We were four women that just wanted to see the Boundary Waters.

We saw the BWCA in her maturity and we saw her reborn. When people try to imagine what the BWCA will look like in one, five, ten, or one hundred years I just remember that on July 3 we didn't know what the BWCA would look like "tomorrow".

Thanks, Jeanne Sharp

Reference to "C" throughout the book indicates a color photo in mid-section.

The Sound of a Forest Falling
by Mary Winston Marrow

Dear Jim,

Hi, my friend, Jeanne Sharp, has been in touch with you about our experiences in the Boundary Waters last summer during the July 4 storm. She sent me a copy of your correspondence and suggested that I write you about my experiences.

As Jeanne told you, we were on a 4 day camping/canoeing trip in the Boundary

Survivors Jeanne Sharp, Jennifer Sly, Kara Malmgren and Mary Marrow

Waters and were on our final day heading out when the storm hit. None of us had been in the Boundary Waters before, and overall we had a great trip.

That Sunday - July 4 when the storm hit, we got off to a rather slow start to our trip. As we knew it was our last day in the Boundary Waters, none of us were too eager to leave. We packed up camp, had breakfast and gathered our things to leave. We also weren't too excited about canoeing on Lake Saganaga as we'd heard that the winds could get quite strong and it could be a difficult and tiring day. In addition, as it was July 4 and motorized vehicles could be on the lake, I was worried about having a lot of boats to deal with. I do remember commenting on how it was odd that there weren't more boats out that day. In retrospect, I imagine people had heard the weather forecast and decided not to chance the storm.

The day was partly cloudy and there was no indication of stormy weather ahead. We paddled out and started what we thought would be an uneventful trip to our final destination.

After maybe 45 minutes - 1 hour, the sky started clouding over and it was looking a bit stormy. As we had weathered out a couple other passing storms during our trip we weren't too worried. Soon after the clouds rolled in, we noticed some lightning and thunder and pulled into shore to wait out the storm. We pulled into a nearby camp, tied our canoes up and pulled out our tarp, books, sleeping bag, food, etc. to wait for the storm to pass. We pitched the tarp in a camp site area and were getting settled.

It started raining some, but nothing unusual. I remember going back to our canoes to get something and noticing a tree that had started falling towards the clearing where we had the tarp (this happened long before we arrived). Another tree had stopped it's fall. As I crawled back under the tarp, I made some sort of comment/joke about this tree and laughing about the chances of a tree

falling on us. (in retrospect there is some interesting foreshadowing in that conversation!!).

A bit later (I don't have any good sense of time at this point), one of us was reading a book, we took photos, and I was starting to fall asleep. Just as we were getting comfortable, the wind really picked up and it started raining a lot harder. At this point, the tarp was doing us no good, and I stood up feeling a bit disoriented and not quite sure what was going on. The tarp was flapping wildly at this point. We were all standing trying to get some idea of what to do.

At one point, we started talking about tornadoes and the sound of trains. There was a brief and surreal moment when we were actually discussing whether or not what we heard was a train or not. At that point, I remember thinking - who the hell cares anyway, nothing remotely resembling a train should be anywhere near us! Another thought I remember having was all of the times I had practiced tornado drills in school and that if there was any time when it was time to jump, now was the time!!! All of this happened in a matter of split seconds.

I don't quite remember all that happened next. I do remember looking off (I think towards the north) and seeing what seemed to be a wave coming down a nearby hill of wind, water, and trees. The sound of trees falling was incredible. Imagine the sound of one tree falling and then magnify that to the sound of a forest falling. Really amazing. At that point, I dove into some nearby shrubs in an area that must have looked safer and more protected. I really don't remember why I decided to jump then, or why I chose that area to jump into. This all happened so fast - a matter of seconds.

I landed face first in a soft area of pine needles under some smaller trees and just lay there face down for awhile. It all happened so fast that I didn't even realize what had happened. Kara had jumped behind me, while Jeanne and Jen had jumped off in another direction.

After the trees stopped falling, Jeanne, Jen, and Kara came up to me moments after the wind passed to see if I was ok. It took me a minute as I thought it was still coming. It took a while for me to get oriented and realize what had happened. The funny things is that I was waiting for a storm in front of me to hit when the trees that fell on our tarp were behind me.

After a few moments, I stood up with Jeanne, Jen, and Kara. We tried to find a safe place to be. We kept finding one place, and then someone would feel unsafe, and we would move to another. I think we finally stayed under some big trees that had fallen and created some sort of a shelter. I remember thinking that there really was no safe place at that moment. While the worst of the storm had past, the wind and rain was still coming down very strong. I remember looking out at Lake Saganaga. When the storm had first started, there were a few small white caps. At this point, the lake looked more like an ocean with huge swells rolling and twisting in the water. Branches of trees and debris were dancing and swirling in the water After maybe 20-30 minutes, the winds and rain calmed down and we could finally take stock of where we were.

Trees were lying all around us. It was the most amazing sight - trees twisted and tossed on the ground like huge splinters and kindling. The tarp that we had put up for shelter lay under one of the big pine trees that had fallen. We tried to lift it but couldn't move it. I think we got most of our things out from under the tree.

We then hiked inland some to see the destruction. I will never forget the sight of these huge trees. I had a sense of being in a "Land of the Lost" episode with all of these huge trees and debris all around. The extent of the destruction was beyond anything I've ever seen. While a few of the smaller trees were still standing, the forest as we'd known it just an hour earlier was gone. Trees, broken about 6 feet from the ground lay twisted and splintered all around us. I remember looking into the "guts" of the trees around us and touching the inner pieces of the tree. I was surprised at the malleability of the wood, and - I took a couple souvenirs to remember.

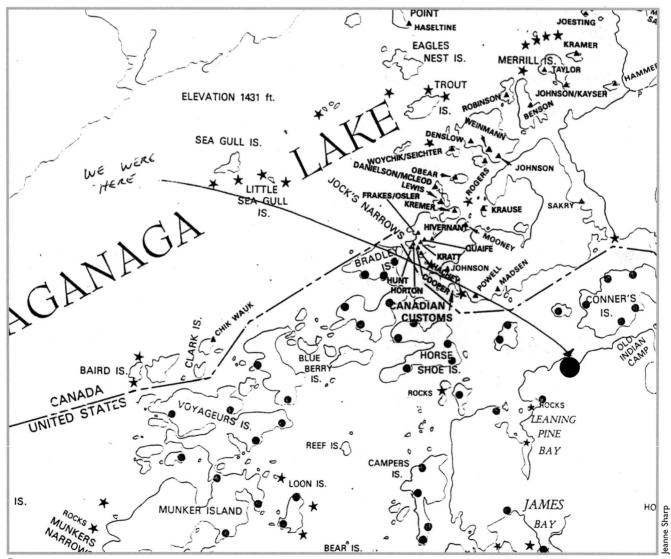

Campsite map

Jeanne Sharp

As we were looking around, I remember us talking about whether or not anyone would believe what had happened. We took several pictures to document our adventure, and then started planning how to get out. As this was our first trip into the Boundary Waters, I remember wondering if this was "normal" - I knew that there were a lot of strong storms in the area, and maybe this was to be expected?

When the lake and winds had calmed down, we loaded up our canoes and started paddling out. Thankfully our canoes were high and dry. Bless Jeanne as she had the foresight before the worst of the storm hit to pull our canoes up and secure them more tightly. On the way out, we came across a lone canoer - Michael. His canoe was twisted at the it bow. We learned that he had been hiding under his canoe when the storm hit and a tree fell on it. He was quiet and surprisingly calm after his experience.

After we'd been paddling for a bit, another storm rolled in and we headed for land. At this point, I remember getting worried, thinking that we couldn't go through that again. Thankfully, this storm passed quickly and relatively uneventfully.

As we were paddling out, the destruction around us was unbelievable. We met a few more people along the way who told similar stories of trees falling around them. We canoed past islands of complete destruction - with hardly a tree standing. After another 3-4 hours of canoeing, we made it to our take out point. All of the power was out and phones were down, so a man at the takeout place (I forget the name of the outfitters, but they were so helpful) agreed to drive us back to our cars.

The road was almost impassable. It looked like a big hand had come and just knocked all of the trees along the road down. The man driving us told us that locals in the area had been working to clear a path for an ambulance to get through and pick up someone who had a serious spinal injury.

As we were driving, we heard more stories of how many near misses there were - people driving along the road when the trees started falling, trees just missing their cars, trees falling on people's houses, etc.

It was hard to digest everything that had happened. I still don't think I fully appreciate how close we were to having a big pine tree fall on us. We left the tarp we were standing under where it was trapped under the tree. We have photos and things to document it all - which makes it more real.

Overall, I had a great time in the Boundary Waters and hope to go back again sometime. We were incredibly lucky to get out of the storm without any injuries. To me the storm added excitement and adventure to an otherwise great trip. However, I realize that others weren't as lucky as we were and am truly thankful that we survived with no injuries or major losses.

I wonder how things are now. I've read about the risk of fire in the Boundary Waters in the coming years. While I would like to go back to the Boundary Waters again sometime, I think I will wait until after some fires have gone through. I can't imagine what it would it be like to be there in the midst of a huge forest fire!!!

Sincerely,
Mary Winston Marrow

July 4, 1999: "Not the Greatest Weather"
by Mary Gunderson, Yankton, S.D.

This story is reprinted from *Hut! Magazine*, published by the Minnesota Canoe Association.

The last Independence Day of the millennium dawned hot and sunny. Every exertion made the thick, damp air seem heavier on my skin. The six of us spent the morning quietly, eating breakfast, and each at his/her own speed taking down tents, stuffing sleeping bags, and gathering up gear. Whenever the oozing sweat was unbearable, we jumped or dived into the water off a six-foot high rock ledge into water 12 to 15 feet deep. We floated on PFDs in various configurations and swam. About noon, we pushed off in three canoes loaded with gear and paddled from Devil's Elbow Lake.

A 25 rod portage across a peninsula took us back to the Granite River. We straddled the U.S.-Canadian line as we paddled toward Saganaga. On the Canadian side, pine trees hugged the rocks and defined the horizon. On the U.S. side, the forest is rejuvenating from a 1995 fire, the wave of curved boulders of the landscape broken by charred tree trunks. Persistent chickadees sang out all along the way. We saw loons and the ducks with the Woody Woodpecker fringe on the back of their heads.

By 1:30 pm, the sky clouded. We stopped for lunch in the canoes near the U.S. side, eating dry Genoa salami, pita bread, and Wasa sesame crackers, along with dried apricots, dates, banana chips and handsful of GORP. The clouds darkened to deep blue gray and we heard rumbles of thunder. We kept paddling. I looked back over my shoulder from the bow of the canoe. The clouds, especially those to the south, turned a deeper shade, a purple color I recognized from a morning two years ago when friends and I canoed on the Missouri River followed by a purplish cloud.

"I felt a raindrop," I called to Randy in the stern.

"It'll probably just rain and be a great sunny day, he suggested, hopefully.

We kept paddling, staying close to the rocky shore. I gauged places where we could scramble to land easily. Each of us was an experienced paddler and camper. We had all canoed before through rain in the BWCA. We kept paddling. Finally, we sighted the Horsetail Rapids portage. The purple cloud followed behind.

Ralph and Dale went ahead to look at the 24-rod portage. The rapids looked rough and rocky for running. These rapids had an additional feature, a threaded area where trees grew out of huge rocks. These separated the main rapids from a shallow stream, too shallow for pulling canoes through. They reported: "The portage is rocky, steep. but the rapids are too fast for running. We'll portage."

Raindrops started falling.

"Are we going to portage now?" I asked, dreading the probably affirmative reply. I glanced out at the water and saw an eerie white glow, maybe 12 feet across and 8 feet high backed by gray purple clouds, all heading toward us.

"We can stand in the rain or portage in the rain," Ralph said resolutely.

As he finished his sentence a gust of wind hit us and rain began to fall in sheets. Everyone who hadn't already, pulled on rain gear. Randy and I turned over our canoe on the Duluth packs, leaving some space for crawling under. Dale picked up his borrowed, beautiful Kevlar canoe with the wood trim. "I'm going up the trail," he said, balancing the canoe on his shoulders.

As Ralph called out: "Don't do that!" a tree leaned into the space between Dale and the canoe. Another gust of wind pushed him backward. I held my breath and waited for canoe and man to be pulled upward by the wind.

Dale set the canoe down and sat, cradling it around his shoulders. Jill and Ralph huddled near their canoe. I dived under our canoe, spread- eagled in the mud and wriggled up to where there was grass and roots that formed a kind of chair. A gust of wind sprayed rain from either side of the canoe. This cozy shelter would do fine for me.

Randy called out, "There's a tree next to the canoe swaying from side to side and the earth is moving. It may go over on the canoe."

I looked around and judged the diameter of the tree. I studied the bottom of the canoe curving over my head. Hmmmm. Was that tree big enough to crush this canoe and me underneath it?

"I'm fine here."

"The tree is moving. The earth is moving," Malinda said.

"It may go over. Get out of there!" Randy said.

Reluctantly, I crawled out in what was now sheets of rain. Ralph, Jill, Randy and Malinda all sat in the rain. Even though I was already soaked through, I craved some protection from the rain. I went to sit with Dale's canoe at my back, shielding the worst of the gusts. I sat in a pool of water streaming down the incline. (I'd like to report here that the $10 pair of lavender plastic-nylon-lined rain pants I got at Hoigaards in 1987 still haven't sprung a leak.)

For a matter of minutes, small hail the size of coconut flakes pelted the ground. A tree crashed in front of Ralph and Jill. They watched trees on the opposite shore snap off, the tops blowing away. The rain poured as if a bucket's contents splashed all of us. After about half an hour, the rain stopped.

We all stood up and surveyed the area. Jill sang a few bars of "Wade on the Water," in her clear, strong soprano.

"That's appropriate," Ralph said.

At storm's end, the water level in the lake had risen about 10 inches, marked by the end of the Randy/Mary canoe that wasn't touching water when we turned it over and was well into the water at storm's end. The guys checked the portage and came back to say it was impossible. Trees were down over the portage. But the water level came up enough on the quieter part of the stream for us to walk the canoes through.

Ralph and Jill went first, stepping carefully through the rushing water. Dale and Malinda took off. "Get in and we'll get out when we have to," Dale told her. By the time Randy and I were stepping through the gushing water, Ralph came

Red pines down on campsite

back to say: Malinda and Dale just ran the rapids. The water grabbed their canoe; they both managed to duck the low-angled trees and maneuver the sharp left-hand turn at the end. Malinda looked startled and amazed at their accomplishment. Randy continued to walk our canoe, adjusting his loose teva's with every fourth or fifth step.

Near the end of the rapids, a 70-foot red pine had fallen over from its roots. It blocked the portage path and jutted into the stream. pine pitch steamed as it poured into

the water. If we'd portaged before the storm hit, we would likely have chosen to wait out the storm near that tree. Whew. I was shaking. And, very thankful.

Shortly ahead, we made the five-rod portage around Horseshoe Falls at the entrance to Lake Saganaga. Ralph had planned an afternoon swim at the foot of the falls. But the water, now brown with soil and roiling with pine needles, leaves and other debris, didn't entice us. The weather wasn't clearing either.

We paddled into Saganaga, one of the largest in the BWCA. On the shoreline, we called out sighting split or downed trees. We discussed the need to inform the Forest Service that the portage at Horsetail Rapids needed immediate attention.

We made camp on an unnamed, small island. There were a few downed trees on the island. Saganaga is a motorized lake, unlike the lakes within the designated Boundary Waters Canoe Area. Fishing boats came and went. Canadian Customs station sat across the water from us.

We prepared and made dinner. Malinda and Dale presented an American flag made of craisins, dried blueberries, and jordan almonds.

After dinner, Randy and Dale somehow started a campfire from the wet kindling at hand. Natural fireworks provided a show to the south. The lightning was far enough away so that we didn't hear it. Some lit the sky like fluorescent bulbs. Others cracked in single dramatic lines. Later, we learned that was the storm that dumped water to flood levels on Hibbing.

The next morning we headed for the take-out point. We saw more and more trees down as we paddled south.

A couple of boaters stopped to tell us that the storm was extensive and that the Gunflint Trail, the road to Grand Marais, was still closed due to fallen trees. We heard that campers had been rescued from campsites. Another guy, a young man in a fishing boat fitted with canoe racks, called out to ask if we were all okay. The magnitude of the storm was beginning to sink in.

At the first take-out point, several cars and vans were smashed by trees. A man from Ontario described the same whitish glowing cloud I'd seen during the storm. He said: "It was like something from (the movie) Independence Day."

Both of our vehicles were safe. My car, at our put-in 12 miles down the road from the take-out, was saved when a medium-sized aspen fell on the van beside it. Leaves and branches grazed my car from windshield to back fender. Randy and Dale pulled the branches aside and I backed the car out. It didn't have a scratch on it. A man in the same lot pulled out ahead of us. His windshield had a football-sized hole in the glass right in front of his face. I hope he didn't have far to go.

Trees over Gunflint Trail 7PM 7/4/99

Jeanne Sharp

We loaded canoes and ourselves. We drove the Gunflint Trail and saw miles and miles of destroyed trees and many smashed cars in driveways. In some places every tree beside the road for a hundred yards had snapped half way up the trunk. The storm was 24

Power pole down near Gunflint Trail

Arrowhead Electric Co-op

hours past and people with chainsaws had cleared at least one lane throughout the 40-some miles back to Grand Marais. We saw the worst damage along the north 20 miles of the road.

In many places, the Rural Electric Cooperative had propped up downed power lines with storm-fallen trees. We stopped a couple of times to take photos. for a bonus,

we picked wild strawberries growing in abundance along the road.

The scenes of destruction didn't stop until we reached the top of the hill that descends into Grand Marais.

A few afterthoughts:

*The straight-line winds gusted from 70 to 80 mph. This kind of storm isn't so unusual on the prairie. But on the prairie, there aren't millions of trees. In addition, the trees in Northeastern Minnesota were sitting in sodden soil from a wet June.

*I've always relished the wonderful peace and calm I experience canoeing and camping in the BWCA. It's easy to imagine the lives of the voyageurs, Ojibway and Lakota before them living there. The storm reminded me that portages are regularly groomed by the Forest Service, at least to the degree that downed trees are removed and paths are reinforced by logs and sand. The hand of humans is very active in the BWCA. Nature took charge on that Sunday afternoon.

*I learned early in life that when there was a thunder/lightning storm, NEVER stand under a tree. On the prairie, trees are the tallest item and attractive to lightning. In the forest, trees give a semblance of safety. Having a canoe overhead gives a semblance of safety. None is a guarantee.

*There are an estimated 17 to 25 million trees down in the BWCA. The storm devastated about 1/4 of the BWCA, the most-visited wilderness in the United States. In some places piles of fallen trees are reported to be chest high. The BWCA is open and canoers are arriving. Officials are grappling with whether or not to use chainsaws or handsaws for the clean-up. All of us will find an altered BWCA in months and years to come.

The Canadian Side

After devastating parts of northern Minnesota, the winds continued their destructive ways through southern Quetico Park and the areas of Northern Light, Arrow and Whitefish lakes. They damaged the town of Nolalu and then Thunder Bay, throwing trees on thousands of vehicles and many homes, according to Doug Guinn of Thunder Bay Appraisal Service. Major roads in and around Thunder Bay were blocked; airplanes were tossed around at the airport. Funnel clouds were reported and photographed at several locations. **C2**

Thunder Bay and areas west lost power for four days. 100 linemen were brought in from other areas to help repair the damage. Farmers lost barn roofs, hay and barley crops were blown down in the worst wind storm seen since the 1970's.

John McClure of Grand Marais was at a fishing camp in Ontario when the storm came through. "The area that I was in was leveled," he said. "Most roads were blocked and campers were stranded for several days." John continued, "The storm followed the Boreal Road, which was at the center of the

Demolished Trailer - Thunder Bay

Thunder Bay Chronicle Journal

Winds of 90 km-h take out trees, power and boats

BY DAVE LAMMERS
THE CHRONICLE-JOURNAL

As if the lights were turned off and on over top of the city, a series of severe thunderstorms swept through Thunder Bay on Sunday, accompanied by high winds, lightning and heavy rain.

"These were very fast moving storms," said Ron Morrow, a forecaster with Environment Canada in Thunder Bay.

The dark set in around 3 p.m. in Thunder Bay, with the first storm mowing down trees and knocking out power across the city and in the surrounding area.

The storm hit first west of the city in Quetico Park around 1:45 p.m. It moved east at a rate of about 80 km-h, hitting Nolalu at 2:45 p.m.

About 50 tubers were caught out on the Kaministiquia River west of Thunder Bay.

"I was scared to death," said Tamara Tyler, who was tubing with River Rat Rentals, along with her three young children.

"My heart is still pounding."

Michelle Hamilton, of Stanley, helped tubers to safety, giving several people a ride back from the river.

"There was a good 25 or 30 people stuck on Whitefish Island," said Hamilton.

"I yelled to the people to stay there. There were four kids and two women who were freaking."

Winds reached 90 km-h and more, knocking down trees including at Whitefish Lake and Arrow Lake.

"They produce wind — that's the big characteristic of them," said Morrow about the weather system which originated in Northern Minnesota.

Ministry of Natural Resources fire crews used chain saws to clear a passage into Arrow Lake Provincial Park where fallen trees blocked roads for campers, 70 kilometers southwest of Thunder Bay.

Morrow said the worst part of the storm clipped the southern part of Northwestern Ontario from Quetico Park through Thunder Bay to Pass Lake.

An Environment Canada lightning detector recorded several strikes around the region.

There were heavy downpours in some areas, but only 17.6 millimeters of rain was recorded at Thunder Bay International Airport.

Storm clipping

storm. This main road wasn't blocked because it ran parallel to the winds.

"Quetico Park wasn't hit too badly - only a strip in the south. Arrow Lake was real bad, as well as Whitefish. Northern Light Lake was at the northern border of the storm." **C18**

After the storm, John tried to walk a one mile long logging road to fish in a brook trout lake. After two hours of fighting the blowdown, he gave up.

The Canadians began logging immediately after the wind. They rely heavily on their timber industry. On the U.S. side, loggers weren't given the green light to begin work until September. According to the Ministry of Natural Resources, the storm affected 25,000 hectares or about 62,000 acres of forest in Ontario. They said that "It is a small amount compared to Minnesota."

Due to the fire hazard caused by the blowdown, the Ministry of Natural Resources restricted campfires beginning July 30.

Thunder Bay Chronicle Journal

Storm damage map - Southern Ontario

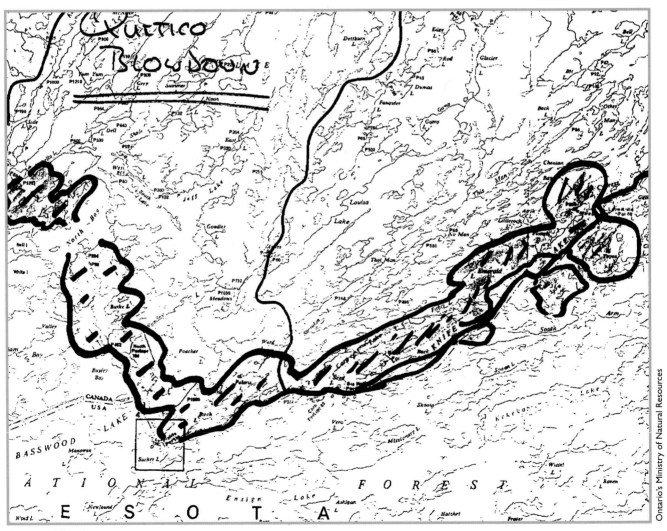

Quetico blowdown map

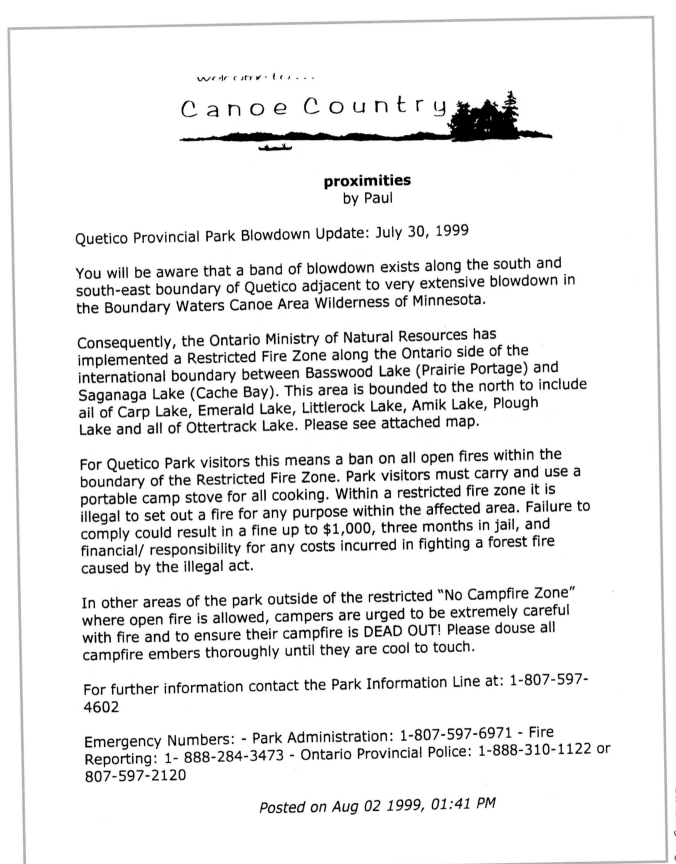

welcome to...

Canoe Country

proximities
by Paul

Quetico Provincial Park Blowdown Update: July 30, 1999

You will be aware that a band of blowdown exists along the south and south-east boundary of Quetico adjacent to very extensive blowdown in the Boundary Waters Canoe Area Wilderness of Minnesota.

Consequently, the Ontario Ministry of Natural Resources has implemented a Restricted Fire Zone along the Ontario side of the international boundary between Basswood Lake (Prairie Portage) and Saganaga Lake (Cache Bay). This area is bounded to the north to include ail of Carp Lake, Emerald Lake, Littlerock Lake, Amik Lake, Plough Lake and all of Ottertrack Lake. Please see attached map.

For Quetico Park visitors this means a ban on all open fires within the boundary of the Restricted Fire Zone. Park visitors must carry and use a portable camp stove for all cooking. Within a restricted fire zone it is illegal to set out a fire for any purpose within the affected area. Failure to comply could result in a fine up to $1,000, three months in jail, and financial/ responsibility for any costs incurred in fighting a forest fire caused by the illegal act.

In other areas of the park outside of the restricted "No Campfire Zone" where open fire is allowed, campers are urged to be extremely careful with fire and to ensure their campfire is DEAD OUT! Please douse all campfire embers thoroughly until they are cool to touch.

For further information contact the Park Information Line at: 1-807-597-4602

Emergency Numbers: - Park Administration: 1-807-597-6971 - Fire Reporting: 1- 888-284-3473 - Ontario Provincial Police: 1-888-310-1122 or 807-597-2120

Posted on Aug 02 1999, 01:41 PM

CanoeCountry.com

Quetico Park blowdown update

Sawbill Outfitters

Sawbill Canoe Outfitters, located 24 miles north of Tofte at the end of the Sawbill Trail, was relatively untouched by the storm. However, the 50 site National Forest campground at Sawbill Lake had large trees go down throughout. Tents were crushed but there were no serious injuries. 75 campers were stranded at Sawbill waiting for roads to reopen.

Hundreds of trees blocked the Sawbill Trail, the only road access. It took about 5 hours for Mike and Ken McMillan, who own a local tree service, to clear the last 5 miles of the Sawbill Trail. Dave Monson, the county road grader driver, worked with the McMillans, pushing the trees to the side as they were cut. County Road 3, going toward Kawishiwi Lake and campground, wasn't opened for several days. Three cars were crushed in the Kawishiwi Lake parking lot, but again, no injuries.

One canoeing party was caught on the Kawishiwi Lake road during the storm. They were pulling a utility trailer with two aluminum canoes tied to it. As the storm struck, large trees fell in front and behind them. As they sat trapped between the two trees, a large tree fell directly across their trailer, crushing the two canoes as flat as pancakes.

Sawbill Canoe Outfitters, owned by Cindy and Bill Hansen, is a popular outfitter for the BWCAW. It is located at the Sawbill Lake wilderness entry point at the end of the Sawbill Trail. The business was founded by Bill's parents, Mary Alice and Frank Hansen, in 1957. Their neighbor, Sawbill Lodge, was founded in 1930 and went out of business in 1981. Sawbill Lodge was sold out to the Forest Service under a provision of the 1978 BWCA Wilderness Act. The beautiful log lodge was dismantled, moved and rebuilt by Bill and Beth Blank at Solbakken Resort in Lutsen, MN.

Frank and Mary Alice Hansen helped pioneer the canoe outfitting business. They built it from a tiny operation in 1957 to the thriving business it is today. For many years, they continued their jobs as school psychologists in the Minneapolis area,

Welcome to

Sawbill

Canoe Outfitters

Chipper clearing Sawbill Trail

Trees over County Rd. 3 between Sawbill & Isabella - late July

Fourth of July 1999 started and ended with a bang

by Nancy McReady

For the McReadys on Fall Lake, the day began by decorating the CWCS float for the parade. Nothing fancy, but enough signs and red, white and blue to show off Conservationists With Common Sense's celebration of trucks returning to Prairie and Trout Lake Portages.

Trucks returning to Prairie and Trout Lake Portages

and operated the outfitters during the summer months. In 1977, they took early retirement from their "real jobs" and moved to Sawbill full time. They retired from the outfitting business in the mid 90s, but still live at Sawbill where they visit with the many friends they have made over the years.

Bill Hansen is an outspoken wilderness advocate. He is a founding member of Northeastern Minnesotans For Wilderness (NMW), an effective regional grass roots group that is made up of people who recognize the contribution of wilderness to the quality of life in northeastern Minnesota. While relatively new, the group works closely with national groups on behalf of wilderness preservation, including the Wilderness Society, Sierra Club, and Isaac Walton League. Hansen has testified before the U.S. Congress several times, urging them not to degrade wilderness lands protection.

According to Bill, the dramatic increase in world population over the last few decades has put increasing development pressures on the few remaining wild places. In a perfect world, wilderness would not need to be designated, but would exist on its own. Unfortunately, without legal protection, our special wild places would quickly be overrun with development, destroying the very qualities that make them special. While arguments will likely persist over the management of wild places, most people now agree that there is great wisdom in their protection and preservation.

Environmental groups such as Friends of the Boundary Waters Wilderness and the Isaac Walton League have played a major role in preserving the BWCA. They wage a constant tug of war with anti-preservation groups such as Conservationists With Common Sense and some logging and recreational vehicle interests.

If some preservationists had their way, the Echo Trail would be closed. On the other hand, some anti-preservationists would like to see the Fernberg Road connected to the Gunflint Trail.

Will Forest Service walk lightly in clean-up effort?

The astonishing storm damage in the Boundary Waters wilderness and how to deal with it has highlighted some of the philosophical questions surrounding management of the country's most popular wilderness area. With campers stranded and portages choked with trees, the Forest Service had quick decisions to make about how much of a role to play in rescuing stranded canoeists and how to clear trails.

There have always been those who point to the developed campsites and maintained portage trails in the BWCAW and say it would more properly be labeled as a park, rather than a wilderness. For them, the BWCAW is simply a recreation destination, one that should be made as convenient and accessible as possible.

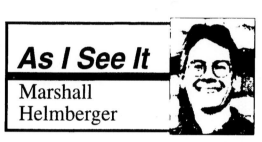

As I See It

Marshall Helmberger

For years, however, wilderness advocates have pushed for a less active management role—a position that the Forest Service has adopted at least to some degree in recent years. That means conveniences such as canoe rests and portage markers are no longer built or maintained in the BWCAW. It means people who get themselves in trouble can not always count on the Forest Service to bail them out, except for in life-threatening situations. Wilderness advocates argue that travel in the wilderness is, by its very nature, risky. Taking away that risk, they say, makes the experience less than it should be.

But what to do in the face of a cataclysmic event? The Forest Service responded to the disaster this week with its usual assortment of pragmatic compromises. As soon as the extent of the destruction became known, and as campers called in reports of severe injuries, the Forest Service began transporting injured people out of the area through airlifts and the use of motorboats where passage was possible. That decision was not unusual— the Forest Service has long allowed motorized use for rescue of people with life-threatening injuries. This time, however, the agency also allowed the use of chain saws for initial clearing of a few portage routes in order to enable canoeists trapped in the middle of the wilderness to find their own way out. That decision, while perhaps not consistent with the views of wilderness purists, was made for public safety reasons, according to spokesperson Mark Van Every.

At the same time, however, the Forest Service was not transporting people from the wilderness who had suffered only minor injuries or who were running low on food as blocked portages prevented their exiting from the wilderness on schedule.

The balancing act was typical for the Forest Service. While acknowledging that people assume risk when they venture into the wilderness, Van Every said the devestation wrought by the storm was "beyond the normal risk." "It would be inhumane to suggest that we do nothing," he said.

A more telling decision is expected to come in the next few days, when the Forest Service will decide how it will go about the massive clean-up effort in the wilderness. Many portage trails and campsites are choked with downed trees— yet the Forest Service may yet decide that the clean-up will go ahead using only hand tools.

The agency does what is called a minimum tool analysis, in which they attempt to determine the minimum tool required to do the job. It's an almost countercultural view in a society where bigger and faster is almost always seen as better, but it is an attitude that is perhaps appropriate for a wilderness area, where the impact of humans is supposed to be minimized.

In assessing how to proceed once the public safety issues are addressed, the Forest Service will no doubt consider the fact that the area will remain a heavily used wilderness despite the destruction. Those who venture out into affected areas in future weeks, likely won't want to hear the sound of chain saws anymore than most other wilderness adventurers.

Despite the natural instincts of most of us to want to fix the siutation, such natural disasters are part of nature. We have so many places on earth, where human intervention on the landscape is all too evident. A wilderness should provide the opportunity to witness the sheer immensity and power of natural processes, essentially untouched or unmanaged by humans. The Forest Service has learned that over the years and we can expect they'll take as light an approach as possible in their efforts to make the affected areas passable once again.

Ely Timber Jay

Will USFS walk lightly?

Wonder Lake

USFS Wilderness Ranger Ellen Hawkins - Wonder Lake

Wonder Lake blowdown

After the storm, the condition of the Alton to Wonder Lake portage was indescribable, its 200 rod length totally blocked. The chainsaw crew had to struggle with huge aspen, birch and pine that were stacked 10 to 15 feet high in places. While working for the Forest Service I helped clear the campsite on Wonder in six hours with four people; it took several hours just to find the latrine. Old growth pine were down everywhere and the sour smell of broken wood was strong in the air.

The portage to Sunhigh Lake was also bad. Its one campsite couldn't be found - there were no trees standing at all, no shade, no bear tree.

Dave Nelson and his girlfriend were camped on Alton Lake but fishing on Sunhigh as the storm began. John Oberholtzer, a worker at Sawbill Outfitters, narrates Nelson's survival story.

Wonder Lake portage C64

Trapped Under A Canoe!
by John Oberholtzer, Sawbill Outfitters, August 18, 1999

The mystery canoe sat for weeks on the Alton to Sawbill portage, passed by dozens of campers. Happily, not an item was touched.

For several days last week, we were mystified by a Royalex canoe abandoned on the Alton to Sawbill portage. The canoe was grotesquely indented at the stern and was equipped with fishing gear. I received a call the other day from Dave Nelson, and he was asking if the Forest Service could drop his canoe at our place for him to pick up. An odd request, and then the light bulb hit. Dave proceeded to tell me a very amazing story.

The afternoon of the storm, Dave and his girlfriend were on a day trip from their camp on Alton. They were seeking big pike on Sunhigh Lake when darkness descended at mid-day. They leaned the canoe against a big pine and crawled under it to wait out the storm. Then, Dave says, "All the trees started coming down."

They were trapped below the canoe when a pine fell across the canoe mid-beam. Dave painfully extracted himself and then carefully assisted his girlfriend whose head was pinned below the bow seat. Sans saw, Dave began to dig out the canoe but quickly ran out of soil. to extract the canoe, he pounded it out, bashing the stern with a rock. The canoe popped back into shape (amazing Royalex), and the couple headed toward Wonder Lake.

About 100 feet into the Wonder to Alton portage, elevated ten feet off the portage, in a tangle of wind blown trees stretching in all directions, Dave determined portaging was infeasible. the canoe was abandoned, and they negotiated a 200 rod maze of pine, birch and aspen. Exhausted, they rested while staring at the mile and a half of shore and woods between them and their campsite. After wading, swimming and bushwhacking, a tree hammered tent greeted them. They extracted the tent and slept uneasily on bruises and concerns of being in the BWCA without a canoe – up the river without a paddle.

Their luck continued in the morning when not a canoeist was in sight. Dave improvised a raft from his Thermarest and huffed and puffed to the Alton to Sawbill portage. In disbelief, he saw not a soul, and splashed in to continue his arduous trek to the landing. Finally, a camper in the bay spotted him pushing a Thermarest through the water, and loaned Dave a canoe. Dave immediately returned to his girlfriend and they headed home.

A few weeks later, the sawyer crew that cleared the Alton to Wonder portage retrieved the canoe and, mysteriously, left it as a conversation topic on the Sawbill side of the Alton portage. Finally, the canoe was towed to the Forest Service guard station. There's not a fish in it, but that is one hell of a fish story!

Nancy Plus

Artists depiction of trapped campers

Stunned by the Damage

Four of us - two couples - were in Perent Lake on the BWCA on Sunday when the storm went through. We had no idea what was occurring. We held our tent up by the seams with our hands to keep it from collapsing and shuddered every time we heard another tree snap or crash.

When it was over, we crawled out to go check on our friends, and we were stunned by the damage. A huge pine landed not more than four inches from our tent– had it shifted a bit more, we would have been crushed. Our friends had a huge tree stop just inches above their tent, suspended by some other trees that had gotten caught up. A massive cedar landed right in the middle of camp, and we had to cut that one down to even get to the other side of the camp. Walking around the island, we saw we had lost 35-40 trees and knew then that there would be some serious injuries to others.

Paddling back through Hog Creek on Monday took forever because we had to keep maneuvering around the trees that were down, and when we got to the parking lot four hours later, we saw our vehicles buried under trees as well. Four trees fell on our truck and trailer, and two fell on our friends'.

Once we got those sawed up and out of the way we ventured out onto the roads, only to get stopped twice. The first road we tried (the Sawbill) was closed because of so many trees being down, and the second road we tried (the 600 road) was closed because it was washed away. It took a while to find another way out, but we finally did, only to come into Tofte and see the devastation there from the rainstorm.

Shoreline damage

Ely Echo

Reference to "C" throughout the book indicates a color photo in mid-section.

Major Superior National Forest Hiking Trails: The Superior, Kekekabic & Border Route

"The magnificent Encampment River bridge was washed out."

The Superior Hiking Trail, running 220 miles between Duluth and the Canadian border, was described by Backpacker Magazine as "one of the ten best trails in the country." Built and maintained primarily by volunteers, work on the trail was begun in 1987, beginning at a point near Two Harbors. It was completed to Canada in 1996.

The envy of many trail organizations throughout the country, the Superior Hiking Trail Association (SHTA) boasts 3,000 members. Its office and store in Two Harbors has more than 4,000 visitors per year. An estimated 50,000 people hiked the trail in 1999.

The Independence Day storm decimated the trail. Executive Director Nancy Odden, reporting for the Superior Hiking Trail newsletter The Ridgeline, tells us about it.

July 4-5th Deluge Soaks Trail and Office

by Nancy Odden

Around midnight on July 4th it began to rain. There had been a short downpour earlier in the day which had passed on quickly. The rest of the day was mostly overcast with the sun trying hard to break through. During the evening as we watched the fireworks, we could see nature's fireworks in the distance. Lightning could be seen in several directions, but it seemed so far off and in a direction that led us to believe the storm would pass us by.

Around midnight it began to rain hard. But this was different - a very hard rain and absolutely no wind. It gave me an eerie feeling. I did not sleep that night. The rain continued. Usually it rains hard for a while and then passes on - not this time. It continued to rain hard for hours. At one point I got up to see what time it was. I shined the flashlight on the clock - 4:30 a.m. It had been raining hard for over four hours. I crawled back into bed and the rains continued for about another hour.

(....In the office the next day....)

As we worked in the office I was wondering what was happening on the Trail. By this time I had heard of the violent winds that devastated the BWCAW up in the Gunflint Trail area. Was our Trail demolished? The Superior Shuttle was on its rounds, so hopefully we'd get some news. A few people stopped by - most were heading up the Shore, a few were coming back - -but none had much information about our Trail. We'd received a large amount of rain. The Split Rock River bridge had washed out during spring ice breakup - was it gone again? Not knowing was frustrating.

Tuesday brought the first concrete news of the Trail. Many bridges were out. The magnificent Encampment River Bridge which had just been built by volunteers on National Trails Day was washed out - it was less than a month old. The Trail section from County Road 3 to Castle Danger had to be closed. Reports came of damage at the Cascade River. That area was hit by forceful rushing water; several bridges were gone in that area and there was a major washout on the west side of the river. Trees were down in the area around Carlton Peak and the Temperance River was now wider at the area above the interpreted Trail and our Trail was washed out.

Still, we had no knowledge of many areas of the Trail. A call for volunteers went out. Hike a section of the Trail, we asked, and report what you find. During that first week, we received reports about most of the Trail. Meanwhile, Ken and the MCC

Superior Hiking Trail Association volunteers

SHTA

crews were busy working on the Trail. Volunteers called Ken to arrange for work projects and an amazing amount of work was accomplished by the end of the week. Many of the bridges were put back in place within days of the storm. A reroute on the west side of the Cascade River was completed by July 14th. An entire new crib had to be built for the Encampment Bridge, but that was completed, the bridge put back in place, and the Trail section reopened by July 15th.

As I write this article (July 20), the Trail is completely open. There are still trees down in several areas, most notably the areas near the Cross River, Temperance River, and Carlton Peak. Occasionally downfalls will be found in other areas. The last major bridge, Trout Creek, will be put in place today. The area around Alfred's Pond is still under a few inches of water. The area around the Gooseberry River is covered with debris from the river. But when held in comparison to the heavy winds that occurred in the BWCAW during that storm and the damage received in that area, we can be thankful.

According to the Forest Service, much of the trail system within the wilderness was devastated by the winds. Entire sections became a jumble of windfalls, unrecognizable. Two important trails - the Kekekabic and most of the Border Route Trail - will not be open for hiking in 2000.

Wilson Creek bridge rainstorm washout

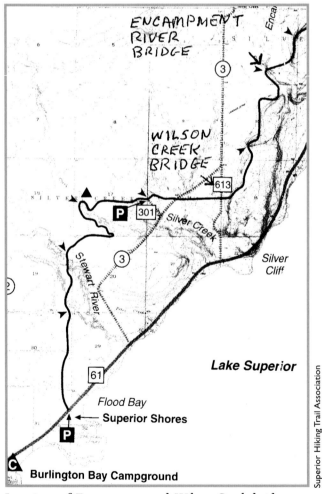

Locations of Encampment and Wilson Creek bridges

Encampment River bridge rainstorm washout

THE HUNGRY BEAVER

The Journal of the Kekekabic Trail Club

SPECIAL COMBINED ISSUE
July/August 1999   *50 cents per copy*   Vol. 10, No. 7-8

Storms remodel BWCAW — more than ever, volunteers are needed

by Neal Chapman

The July 4th storms that struck the BWCAW area left behind more work than the usual Hungry Beavers can handle.

The KTC is assuming its usual leadership role in the recruitment and training of volunteers, and in organizing work trips to begin the process of reclaiming the damaged trails. The Eagle Mt. Trail, although not in "the" damage area, received 250 treefalls. A path through the treefalls is probably already cleared by the time you read this. The Lima Mt. Trail, which had just been cleared two weeks prior to the storm, will also be reopened shortly.

Volunteers of all skill levels and of all disciplines are urgently needed to help with all the work that lies ahead. Not only do we need people willing to "go up" and clear trails, but also needed are those willing to make phone calls, write letters, and perform other "behind the scenes" tasks. We have set up a section of the club's Internet site (http://www.kek.org) to make signing up easy. We will discuss this at the regular monthly meeting at Midwest Mountaineering on August 3.

We will also be holding additional public informational meetings at REI in Bloomington on Wednesday, August 4 at 7 p.m. and REI in Roseville on Thursday, August 5 at 7 p.m. Additional meetings and locations will be announced as they are set up.

REI has already pledged $1,000 to assist the club in this effort.

We are working closely with the Superior National Forest to identify areas that we can safely begin to work. There will be some trips this summer and fall, but undoubtedly most of the activity will be in the spring after winter storms have made the area safer in which to work.

The year 2000 will indeed be a special year for us, our 10th anniversary, AND the biggest challenge yet. With ALL of your help, we can and will do it. ✱

Kekekabic Trail Club

To Hell and Back

Brent Harring, a Minneapolis man, tells us about his solo trip and being trapped in some of the worst of the BWCA blowdown. "The portages were terrible. Carrying a canoe and pack, many times I couldn't get the pack through the trees. I did a lot of sawing. Once I sawed a tree under pressure. It snapped off, burying a branch right next to my foot. I was very lucky. I can't see how sawyers could do this for weeks!"

by Brent Harring

Between 1989 and 1996, I spent most of the summer weeks of my twenties in the "backcountry" of Minnesota and Wisconsin guiding, counseling, and instructing in adventure and challenge-based learning programs for youth. During that time, I spent maybe eight or nine weeks a summer variously "on trail" canoeing, Montreal paddling, backpacking, or sea kayaking. I spent six summers working in and around the Boundary Waters Canoe Area Wilderness (BWCAW) – my first in 1990 as a guide/counselor with Wilderness Canoe Base; and '92 through '96 as a field instructor with the Voyageur Outward bound School.

Like anyone who has spent considerable time there, I've paddled and portaged through most regions of the Boundary Waters and, from time to time, shouldered a fairly high degree of personal risk. During those summers, I encountered and survived perhaps half a dozen memorable and extremely dangerous weather situations, all involving lightning, and dozens of somewhat less risky thunderstorms and other severe weather situations.

I moved to the Twin Cities in the fall of '96 and shifted to other lines of work while my trail time all but disappeared. Perhaps surprisingly, I took my first ever solo trek of any kind on a three-day solstice weekend the summer of '97, spending two nights on the Superior Hiking Trail – my only trail time for the entire year. '97 was the first in actually 11 years that I didn't take the canoe path. I finally made it back to the BWCAW for a short week in '98 with a small youth organization in North Minneapolis, and this past year determined to spend my one three-day weekend of the summer in canoe country on my first ever solo canoe trek. It just happened to be over the 4th of July.

I stayed up late and packed Friday night, then hit the road northbound Saturday morning, July 3rd. My aim was to drive straight through to the Tofte Ranger District headquarters of the Superior National Forest, then figure out a plan involving a permit from there. Depending upon where I received permission to put in, I intended to rent a solo canoe from somewhere along the way and then head out. With the trekking edge of my adventurous past requiring perhaps a little sharpening, I decided I would crank into one of the little-known Primitive Management Areas (PMA's) of the BWCAW if I could swing the logistics. Instead of simply camping at a regular designated site like most folks, I wanted the challenge of getting seriously off the beaten track and into a more stark condition of solitude and self-reliance.

It was foggy and raining when I hit Tofte. The rookie ranger on duty had never been approached with a PMA permit request, and the staff there said that I was the first person to ask for one that summer. Since I didn't have many days to get in and out, I needed to find a PMA close to the edge of the wilderness boundary that I could shoot for that night. My choices therefore narrowed at once to Fungus Lake PMA west of the Sawbill Trail, and Hairy Lake PMA up the Gunflint Trail. I had never been inside of either one. Fungus, upon closer scrutiny, didn't really have a paddle route. That left Hairy which seemed to have a couple.

A quick check of the database confirmed that I could get a #51 entry point, Missing Link Lake off of Round Lake, that afternoon to put me in range of Hairy PMA for the night. A call to the Gunflint Ranger District confirmed that another party, no doubt Outward Bound, was already present in Zone 2 of the PMA for the two nights that I was requesting. So, I settled for Zone 3, my second choice with a smaller chain of lakes, keeping a thought in the back of my mind that lake size in the PMA's is generally very small, and a "lake" on the map does not always turn out to be a lake on the ground – as August travelers off the biggest paddle routes will often discover.

My travel goal immediately became to get onto Little Copper Lake inside Zone 3 by sunset since my permit actually required me to encamp inside the PMA that night. My route covered four lakes interposed by three regular trail portages, then about a half-mile "crash" over maybe a moose trail if I were lucky– about four miles total from the Forest Service roadhead on Round Lake to get to the shore of Little Copper. I looked at my watch. It was about 2 p.m. "Nip and tuck," I thought, but it was a fine challenge and I figured I could just do it. My aim was to be on the water by 5 p.m.

I stopped at the first pay phone I encountered up Highway 61 and began calling a couple well known outfitters on the Gunflint in search of a solo rental canoe. Sawbill Outfitters had a slightly better deal for me, but Gunflint Lodge had the model I really wanted, a kevlar Mad River "Independence." It would be my first trek in a solo canoe.

At around 4 p.m. I arrive at the Lodge. "You'll never make it," said the woman behind the rental log when I explained my intended route into Little Copper by nightfall. I paused to consider my response: "Get out! 'To serve, to strive, and not to yield, ma'm! I used to be an OB instructor. I don't think you realize who you're talking to. It shouldn't be a problem for me!" Judiciously, I refrained. In fact, I made a point not to hint at any links to Outward Bound just in case I was, in fact, about to do something fairly stupid. "It'll be close. I'll just have to hustle. All I actually need to do is get inside the PMA boundary tonight. If I have to, I can get in the rest of the way tomorrow," is what I muttered. The Independence was to be back in roughly 48 hours.

At the Round Lake public access several miles away, I parked my car, floated my boat and quickly loaded up. I took a photograph of the launch moment and looked at my watch. It was 5 p.m. and I was right on schedule – four and a half hours till sunset. It was shaping up for a perfect evening paddle into the "B-Dub" including warm air, calm water, and lots of sun. With a smile on my face and a downright gleeful sense of adventure in my heart, I removed my shirt, dipped my paddle, and lit into an urgent traveling pace that I knew I would have to maintain till dark.

After about two-and-one-half miles of paddling and one-and-a-quarter of portaging, I had crossed Round, Missing Link, Snipe and half of Copper Lake, and reached the point on the shoreline of Copper where a small stream enters from Little Copper. I had made excellent time, but there was still that uncertain half mile to go in front of me, straight through the woods. It was 8 p.m.

I waded onto the bank adjacent to the stream and took my first good look at the detail on the Fisher map. There was 87 feet of gain into Little Copper that I hadn't bothered to notice before. I looked around with a slight twinge of apprehension. The west bank appeared impassable due to the density of vegetation. The east bank looked

Brent Harring

Brent Harring

pretty doubtful up the way. After five minutes of searching the vicinity, it was clear that the "moose path" I was chancing on just wasn't there, and I started having vivid flashbacks to a crash with a group of students a number of years earlier over an eerily similar piece of terrain, that had turned into a six hour odyssey ending in the dark.

I looked back at the map. An hour's worth of paddling and portaging back north the way I had come into Snipe Lake would put me at the nearest designated campsite. I had noticed a really comfortable looking site another quarter mile back again that would be catching full sunset in about an hour. It had a big granite peninsula. I was sorely tempted.

From where I stood, the sun was already down below a hill to the west and the woods were beginning to dim. The mosquitoes were suddenly out bad and, to my dismay, the blackflies also-- so late in the season. "Shit, shit!" I said out loud. I had to decide right away if I was going to bail and head back to Snipe with all its stony certainty of comfort, or plunge into the brush for Little Copper on the grounds that simple force of will could still put me

in my tent by dark somewhere on the next lake over. I pounded a couple fistfuls of trailmix and decided to press on.

I left the daypack with my food in my still-floating canoe. Though likely ineffective in the event of an actual foraging bear, it was the best hedge that I felt I could take the time to muster. I set a compass bearing to the top of the stream, and shouldered my #4 Duluth Pack that I could never seem to keep under 65 pounds. I'm 5'9" and typically 155 pounds with my boots on.

My plan was to find a tent site near the Little Copper shoreline, come back for my food, then bring the canoe up the next day if I discovered it was doable. I was acutely aware at this point that I needed to be moving as quickly as I could while maintaining a heightened level of alertness for my own safety. I set off optimistically up a relatively open gentle slope on the east bank, and plunged quickly into a dense thicket of cedar and spruce.

After about 100 struggling yards of rapidly declining optimism, I hit an ancient beaver dam at the foot of a broad sedge meadow perhaps 200 yards across. I used the dam to shift to the west side of the flowage in an effort to avoid water deeper than my knees, and set to stumbling and slogging across an incredibly uneven terrain of hummocks and sumpholes. My intention was to make as directly as I could for drier land rising from the bog along a steep hillside to my right, and thereby stay mostly out of the water. About half way across the meadow, it became easier to return to lower ground and actually wade a series of elongated "trenches" than to continue trying to work across what I found to be an awkward grass-matted, cobblestony terrain with increasingly dense patches of thicket on the lower hillside.

Having slogged the bog, I next began an ascent up a steep hillside using the sound of the now falling stream to my left as a directional guide. Passage rapidly became more difficult and I continued to fade to the right to try to get out of the rock and alder choked streambed and into more open and even ground. The ambient air was still above 80° F and the heat and waning light forced me to remove my headnet in order to vent and to see more clearly. I tied three bandannas around my ears and neck, but the mosquitoes and blackflies instantly made my face their feast.

As I sweated profusely packing up the slope, getting bitten all to hell, I could feel my body kick hard into reserves as my quads began to howl. The two thoughts in my mind were suddenly that it was a real mistake to be out here by myself having forgotten to bring a Benadryl supply - which I had just realized - and that it would be remarkably easy to go down with a lower leg injury right now if I didn't stay completely focused on my every motion and footfall.

At some point after negotiating around several areas of heavy deadfall, I realized I could no longer hear the stream. After an instant of panic, I reckoned my relative location based on the distinctive contours of the immediate area, cross-checked them against my topo map, then plotted a line-of-sight bearing at right angles to my previous line of travel. This would cause me to eventually intersect the stream and also correct my rightward drift.

About 60 yards later, I was right back in the streambed trying not to break my ankles but at least knowing exactly where I was. Finally, I topped out at a second beaver dam. I faded rightward along the dam, then ascended another forty feet or so up a steep but semi-open slope to the top of a sheer promontory rising along the western edge of what I surmised I would shortly visualize as Little Copper Lake. - -But from where I finally stood, I could see perhaps a mile down the way into a large open area. It was nothing but bog.

Words here and now don't quite describe my feelings there and then. I had known all along, of course, that this was a possibility. I proceeded wearily along several yards

of flat terrain, then dropped my pack into the first and only open spot I could see that looked large enough to accommodate my dome tent. My plan in that moment became to go back for my food, camp on the hump, tear down as soon as I awakened in the morning, and head straight back to Missing Link Lake where I had seen the campsite with the granite slab.

It was 9 p.m. I slammed what was left in my water bottle, grabbed my map and my headlamp, and headed back down the hillside. At the mouth of the stream, I stashed the canoe, filled my bottle, and paused a moment as the sun went down to focus myself for the second crash back up to Little Copper. I swore a few times and headed back into the woods, my legs trembling already from exhaustion.

With just a daypack, however, the return trip went comparatively fast. As darkness fell, I finally spotted my Duluth Pack in the brush. Physically exhausted and with clouds of mosquitoes all around, I groped in my pants pocket for the headnet that I had earlier stuffed away. It wasn't there. The frustration and panic that wracked me as I tore through my other pockets, confirmed that I was nearing the end of my internal resource rope. One of the armhole strings must have been hanging out of the pocket and snagged a branch. This had happened to me once before, on that same former PMA entry that had come so clearly to mind earlier in the evening. Since that loss, I had routinely carried a spare headnet packed way in the bottom of a stuffsack. for reasons which seemed

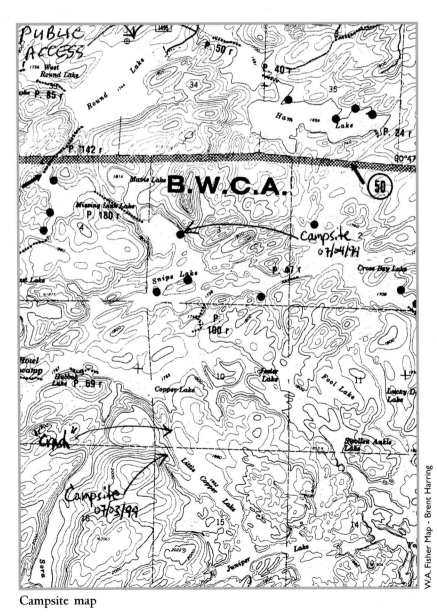

Campsite map

W.A. Fisher Map - Brent Harring

inconceivable to me in that moment, I had purposefully left my spare headnet at home.

I knew what was going to happen next. I put on my rain kagul to shield me from the slaughter, and threw my tent up as quickly as I could. It wasn't fast enough. When it was done, I quickly tossed all of my gear and food inside, something I normally never do, and threw myself in after it. For the first time since I had purchased the tent in '91, a pungee stick tore right up through the tent floor as I tumbled recklessly inside.

Cursing repeatedly out loud, I tore off all of my clothes and simply sat there naked in my tent, clawing at the welts across my upper body and bleating like a beast. When that had passed, I laid out my sleeping bag, killed all the mosquitoes inside of my tent, and was about to turn in when I realized that my water bottle was missing. I was pinned like a bug between staunching my dehydration, and avoiding the pain that I knew I was about to endure if I jumped outside in a pair of shorts.

I made the leap. It hurt. At least I could still move my legs when I returned. Topical anesthetic may, in fact, outrank small but strategic servings of chocolate as the most essential psychological aid on trail. I then spent another twenty minutes killing all the mosquitoes inside my tent again, and fell into a sweaty effort at sleep. A couple of hours later, a thunderstorm rolled in towards the south. Although far enough away to keep me from worrying about the lightning, it rained and thundered a good share of the night and the boomers prevented me from sleeping more than maybe three or four hours.

When I awoke on the 4th, I simply got up fast and got the hell out. At least the rain had stopped. I snapped a photo of myself sitting bleakly in the brush, disinclined to force a smile, then eased on down the slope with my food pack first. On my last descent with the #4 Duluth, I discovered that the terrain was rather open, and even kind of friendly, if I kept a parallel course about fifty yards west of the streambed. It's amazing what good light and a relaxed pace can reveal in the woods. I figured I probably could have even horsed the canoe up through there had there been actual waters to paddle on the other end.

Once again on Copper, I gunned the Independence, so fittingly on the Fourth, toward the first portage back the way I had come. Little did I know that the fireworks were just beginning. I was really anxious to dry things out, cook a meal, and simply relax. I knew I had just been spanked, and was reflecting upon how foolish it may have been, given my constraints, to have tried bombing so desperately into Little Copper by myself the night before. By 9 a.m. I was back at the granite slab on Snipe, and immediately began to encamp.

I have a nearly unconscious discipline that emerged through long experience with youth on the trail: the tent always goes up first regardless of just about any other factor because the rest of the factors, human and environmental, can change mighty fast, making everything else instantaneously more difficult. After scoping three available tentpads, I chose the flattest and most

root-free, declining a pad deeper in the trees because it was too lumpy. I went ahead and slung my tarp low in a third area near the front of the woods, anticipating from the cloud activity that more rain could be arriving soon.

Having knocked off the essentials, I knocked off the clothes. The sun was burning through the partial overcast and it was humid and quite warm again. I went skinny dipping for a good long while to clean off, cool down, and soothe my aching blackfly welts, then changed into what is undeniably the most comfortable fair-weather camp garb ever contrived: purple butterfly sarong slung breech clout style. It's definitely the butterflies that make all the difference.

I then cooked my first meal since I had left Minneapolis, a fabulous minimal "alpine spaghetti," and scrubbed the dishes. It was just past noon and I removed my watch. There were absolutely no bugs, and I thought to myself that this was the rich, benign state of obligation - and insect-free outdoor comfort that most folks are talking about when they discuss disappearing into the northwoods for awhile. If you spend much time there, of course, you know that it never lasts.

It had clouded over entirely while I had been cooking, and about then the breeze began to kick up. When a light rain started falling and the boomers kicked in again across the way, I closed up my tent and retired under my tarp to pass the weather with attention to a couple sewing repair projects. It was still warm enough that I was dressed comfortably in only my sandals and a pair of shorts.

It startled me to alertness when a corner of my tarp suddenly let loose and commenced to whipping fiercely in the wind. It may not seem modest, but I normally expect my knots to hold, and I started paying closer attention to what was going on. As I stepped bare-chested into the rain to reset my tarp, I looked down the slope of my granite peninsula and saw that the Independence had flipped upright in the wind and was rapidly filling with water. I ran to the canoe, kicking myself for having stowed it so sloppily, and drained the boat. I then moved it further down the lee side of the peninsula and braced the gunnel against a jackpine near the water's edge with the bottom facing the direction from which the wind was howling.

When I returned to the tarp, I immediately moved my seat to the extreme uphill end of the shelter in order to get out of the direct line of fall of a standing dead pine tree upwind. I rechecked my position for safety in case it came down, and tried to settle back into my sewing. With an increasing level of awareness, I kept noticing the wind speed notching up and, after a time, began to feel like the situation was developing outside the realm of my experience. Suddenly, I threw my kagul on over my bare skin and bolted for the canoe thinking that it was quite possibly about to simply disappear with the wind. "This is it," I thought, recalling the tale of an old OB instructor whose entire brigade of canoes had once vanished in the middle of the night during a fierce "straight line" wind storm back in the eighties. Ever since then, he had always tied his canoes down at night.

It had darkened like dusk and the rain was dumping in heavy sheets which were being punted sideways by the wind. I looked across the open lake downwind of the peninsula as I ran, and wondered how I would possibly recover the canoe if it took off in the next instant. It didn't and I quickly ducked into the lee of the boat and lay down on the ground. The root mass of the jackpine was heaving gently as its trunk swayed, and I reached up and wrapped my arm around a thwart thinking that I could just sort of lie there and hold the boat down. Discovering a much more believable option, I reached up and unbuckled the webbing straps from a map case above the inverted seat, and buckled them back together around a log running lengthwise underneath the boat.

A minute later, I was tying the bow end painter line to a protruding root. The wind was making a huge roaring sound like I had never heard before and I realized that my situation was now seriously sketchy. My mind scampered about trying to decide where to go that was safest. An area back by the latrine had seemed kind of sheltered alongside a hill. I looked up in that direction to the tent area, just in time to see a fifteen foot top section of one of the adjacent dead pines loft silently skyward in the wind rush for a second, then drop slantwise to the ground. It appeared to fall right onto my tent, although I couldn't see for sure. "I'm not going back to the woods," I said to myself as I finished my knot, and jumped back into the lee of the canoe.

I repeated, "This can kill me, this can kill me" as I struggled to understand what was happening. It occurred to me that I was about to be in a tornado and I started to panic. I wondered if I should maybe jump into the lake, but my PFD was up under my tarp where I had begun to stand on it as protection from ground current due to lightning. I tried to look in the direction of the wind to see what was coming, but the rain drops were actually flying straight at my face and I could only see what was going on

Jack Pines over Brents tent

Broken Jack Pine over Brents tarp

by looking sideways to the wind. No, I decided it was simply a big straight-line windstorm. There had been no sign of a funnel cloud, nothing was moving sideways, and the wind was obviously driving in one clear direction across the peninsula.

There was one standing dead tree upwind of me, but I was just outside of its line of all in the direction of the wind. I reasoned that, even if it came my way, I was distant enough that perhaps only the very tip of the tree might connect with the hull of the boat. I lay down on my side and was able to tuck my head up under the gunnels. From my knees down I was actually in the lake. Once I had decided that it was not a tornado, I became quite calm with the thought that I was probably in the safest position I could find.

While I was lying there, I could hear what sounded like branches snapping underneath the enormous roar of the wind. I never once looked up. The root mass underneath me continued heaving and sighing about four inches up and down in almost a rocking fashion. Without my watch, I completely lost any sense of time after awhile. Partially immersed in the lake as I was, already wet from resetting the tarp in the rain and wearing only a nylon shell, shorts and sandals, I focused on staying aware of my level of warmth which was declining somewhat, though not yet to the point of shivering. I worried about what would happen if the root mass underneath me let loose and the tree fell over. I was concerned that my head and neck might get pinched between the weighted canoe gunnel and the rising roots in that situation, but decided I would be able to sense if that were about to happen and could quickly pull my head out from underneath the boat.

Gradually, the heaviness of the rain and the strength of the wind began to die down and, at some point, the rain just suddenly quit. Although I had not fallen asleep, it was a lot like waking up. Stiffly, I climbed to my feet and took a look around it was weirdly dark with not a hint of the sun, and I realized that I had no clue as to the time of day, or how long I had lain there. I looked at the sky and honestly thought, "Is it 3 or is it 9?" I looked up towards the woods as I walked around the end of the canoe, and could see neither tent nor tarp. I was certain that both had just been crushed by falling branches or perhaps had simply blown away, and it occurred to me that, without shelter, I would have to start packing up now and go. "People died just now," I thought. "Somebody's dead out there."

I passed my somewhat scattered aluminum cookset, and was astonished to find everything still there. Upon closer inspection of the tent area, I was actually shocked to find my Eureka! dome still standing. It wasn't crushed, just obscured by several trees that had fallen in front of it. In fact, trees had fallen in front of, behind, and remarkably, above my tent. That is, two large jack pines, probably two hundred year-old trees, had let go by their roots and eased on over so that their trunks were suspended about eight or ten feet directly above the tent. I shoved on them for awhile near their bases to get a sense for how stable they were, and they seemed completely anchored as they were, wedged against some other trees. the only damage to the tent, unbelievably, was a small rip in the rainfly near the windward guy line which was obviously a stress tear from the wind forces. I immediately decided that I would spend the night, and continued to look around.

My tarp, on the other hand, was gone. Sure enough, the dead pine I had moved out of line with had crashed across its center, exactly where I had been sitting earlier in the storm before I had moved from the middle to the end. I congratulated myself for seeing that one coming, and figured my parents would be proud. Even had I remained under the tarp, I would have been fine in the seat that I had moved to. I picked up my watch and checked the time. It was 2:10 p.m. and the whole storm episode had lasted less than two hours.

Perusal of the remainder of my campsite revealed that two trees were now blocking the path back to the "government latrine," which itself was now sealed with a seven-inch diameter spruce that had fallen across its top. I broke out my collapsible Sven Saw and cleared the "slammer," then cut the branches from the two trunks across the trail. Out of curiosity, I checked the third tent pad that I had decided not to use. Two white pines, easily two hundred years old as well, had fallen over and were leaning directly across the pad maybe a foot off the ground. My dome tent would have been completely crushed in that location, although it appeared that I would have survived there too if, for some reason, I had been inside of it – at least if I had been lying down.

With my tent intact and my tarp not necessary, I decided to chill out and go fishing for northerns. That is what I did for the rest of the day, accompanied by the unusual repeated presence of floatplanes and, extraordinarily, helicopters. In fact, the only time I had ever seen a helicopter in the Boundary Waters was during the summer of '95 when the region around the nearby "Sag Channel" and numerous smaller areas throughout the wilderness

had burned. I waved at all the aircraft. At some point, I counted three Beaver floatplanes, by sound, throttling to takeoff over on Tuscarora Lake about a mile-and-a-half away. It's a completely singular sound associated, in my experience, with only one thing, and I knew that there was a major multiple medical evacuation going on.

Around 6 p.m., a couple paddled by as I was casting from shore, and asked if I had been over the portage in from Missing Link Lake. I replied that I had come in that way yesterday and would be heading out that way again in the morning. Without breaking cadence, they told me that it had been taking them about five times the normal amount of time to get across the portages, and advised me to get an early start. That statement was the first suggestion to me that the storm may have been fairly widespread.

I had been timing my progress the previous afternoon on the way in, and knew it had taken me about two hours to get onto Snipe Lake from the put-in on Round. Allowing for the fact that roughly ninety percent of all the unsolicited travel advice I had received from passing paddlers over the seasons had been utter bunk, I reckoned that I would, nonetheless, triple my exit time and plan on taking six hours to get back to the roadhead. I figured I would leave my campsite by 9 a.m. and shoot for the parking area by 3:00. This would give me enough time to get loaded up, return my boat to Gunflint Outfitters, and still be in Duluth in time for supper with friends before heading back down to Minneapolis that night.

Later in the evening, I switched to trolling and made several passes along the north rim of the lake and around a couple islands. There were noticeable numbers of freshly downed trees along the shoreline, but nothing to me that seemed extraordinary. Some had snapped midway up their trunks but most had simply been pushed over after their root systems had failed.

When I neared the foot of the "one-eighty" portage into Missing Link, however, I began to wonder what I might find in the woods the next morning. Two fully grown quaking aspens, their trunks probably two feet in diameter at breast height, had snapped at about fifteen feet leaving a pair of enormous white-fleshed splintered stumps that had been visible a half mile away from my campsite. The debris and trunk remnants had variously fallen or been driven directly into the portage path so that the trail appeared completely blocked within the first two rods. The couple's Grumman sat there at the landing. When I paddled by on my final trolling pass, it was still there three hours later at 10 p.m. I decided I would leave as soon as I could the next day and headed back to camp in order to sleep.

Because of having spent so much time in the backcountry being responsible for others' safety, counting the seconds between the lightning flash and the thunder crash in order to reckon the risk of ground strikes is a subconscious automatic discipline for me. Sometime after midnight, the boomers began and a thunderstorm eventually rolled in right over me and occupied what seemed like the greater share of the night. As the rain poured, I decided that where I lay was in a theoretically "safer" location from direct strike and ground current than most places in my vicinity, and chose to remain lying on my foam ground pad inside my tent throughout the storm. It's the kind of choice that never presents a great deal of certainty, and I knew that my sense of safety was quite highly calculated. For the second night in two, I had almost no sleep.

At some point after several hours, I rolled over onto my back and, in the dim awareness of partial sleep, became aware of the silence and thought to myself, "Oh, it's over." Instantly, and I do not exaggerate, the lightning strobe-flashed directly above me and, before my mind could name the first syllable of the second count, the thunder broke in the tooth-rattling concussion of a "zero-count." In as many thunderstorms as I've endured in "lightning drill" position, squatting or standing silent and alone in the downpour on my foam "PFD" vest for ground strike insulation, I have experienced actually very few zero-counts. It's an entirely singular experience that has always caused my whole body to jerk in the most visceral involuntary fear response that I have ever known. The routine impression that has flashed through my consciousness in the wake of a zero count has always been that I will die in the next moment, and I recall that it has made me want to weep. I have always felt like I have "survived" those moments.

After the zero count, there was inexplicably, not another lightning flash. It was silent. I took the experience personally, and decided that the closing boomer at the edge of dreamland was a warning for the hubris of thinking that I could get into Little Copper Lake by myself the night before. I had now been spanked twice. In the morning, I inspected my camp area for what I was convinced had to have been a ground strike within twenty-five yards of my tent, but could find no evidence of such. It bothered me. I had a clear impression that I had witnessed the supernatural in the night.

Before I left the campsite on Monday, July 5th, I watched a downed luna moth quivering its saturated wings in a tiny, emerald effort to dry them, and pondered the straight-line storm that its tremblings were doubtless setting in motion on the opposite side of the earth. I sipped my coffee while I considered the path ahead and then was on my way.

Back at the foot of the "one-eighty," the one hundred eighty rod portage into Missing Link Lake, I was relieved to find the

Lightning bolt

Ely Echo

Grumman gone. My solo portage method was to bring my paddle and my #4 Duluth forward first and scout the way, then return for the food pack and the canoe for a total of three crossings including two carries. In this case, I grabbed my Sven Saw and water bottle, and started up trail. Fifteen feet later, it was clear that, regardless of how the couple had mysteriously rammed their tandem aluminum boat through the rubble with obvious but extremely minimal saw work, I would have to cut a bit more of it away in order to horse my kevlar solo canoe through the blowdown on my own.

The path was heavily impeded, and I spent over half my exit time on that first portage alone. I decided to not even try to take pictures to capture what the blowdown looked like on the portage, and to just focus on getting through. My plan was to walk the entire trail, sawing appropriate openings as I went, then bring my pack over next, sawing again as the necessity became clear while carrying a load and, finally, bring the boat over last with hopefully no need for additional saw work at that point - a total of five crossings for a distance of nearly three miles.

My third spanking occurred almost immediately. I set to cutting away a sizable branch that was horizontally blocking the trail. It was too high to go over and too low to go under with a canoe, like dozens I would encounter that day. It was attached to the downed trunk of one of the toppled quaking aspens. What I didn't see was an additional downed tree resting across the trunk of the first. Basically, I was about to unleash a dynamic logjam situation of which I was completely oblivious.

As I finished the cut, instead of the distal limb falling away as I had imagined, the stump I had just created along the trunk slammed straight into the trail mud as the weight of the two trunks shifted with their unapparent brace removed. I didn't even have time to flinch. The stump buried itself two inches from my left toe. A queer rush traveled through my body as I looked down and imagined what would have happened if the stump had come down a few inches over on top of my foot.

"Idiot, idiot, idiot!" I repeated and sat down to reconsider my situation. I realized that now it was particularly risky. I was anxious to leave and trying to ram my way through the debris by myself with the help of my little Sven Saw and rather incomplete knowledge of static and dynamic blowdown theory. I had just enough tools, aptitude, and enthusiasm to be really dangerous to myself, and decided to slow down.

Suffice to say, it took me over three hours to get off that portage that I had covered in about forty-five minutes on my way in.   About two thirds of the way across, I encountered an encumbered party of four from Camp Widjiwagen coming in with enormous, freshly laden blue canoe packs, a Grumman, and one of their classic but "Jurassic" (in size and weight), wood and canvas canoes. I watched three of them eventually wrangle it through a hole I had recently cut for the relatively tiny Independence, and asked them where they were headed. "Lake Superior," they said, "The Grand Portage."   At this point they were on the early section of their route and heading westward. They didn't seem to have a Sven Saw. I had been over the Grand Portage. "Good luck, you guys, it will be a big deal if you even get there under these conditions. I hope you make it." They were sort of silent and I wondered how far they might get before they would probably have to abort.

On Missing Link, I ate lunch on a cliff site, swam for awhile, and watched the aircraft that continued to pass overhead. I had the "one-forty" left into Round and then a one mile paddle to my car, and was beginning to note the time. As it turned out, the trail was relatively clear and fast, and I took the opportunity to saw away at several sections of lighter blowdown, mostly as a service for others coming along the way.

About midway over, I met two men coming in with only a canoe. We stopped and traded stories, and it turned out they had evacuated a guide from Wilderness Canoe Base, my old scene, to the communication point at Tuscarora Outfitters on Round Lake the day before, in order to call in a medical evac to Tuscarora Lake. Four people had sustained serious injuries from a single falling tree they said – confirming my hunch about the floatplanes earlier. I thought about the wilderness guide, and wondered what I would have done in those same shoes, in that situation, at age twenty-two back then.

When I returned to the Missing Link side of the portage to grab my canoe, a family had come up behind me and parked themselves in the middle of the trailhead to eat lunch, about the most irritating thing you can do around others in the Boundary Waters. I declined their offer of carrot sticks, and instead stood around to listen to their version of events on Tuscarora the day before. When the boomers lit in again off in the distance, I said my instant farewells and took off at a steady jog with the Independence, bemoaning my tendency to chat and cursing the possibility of a potentially lengthy delay from a lightning drill with only a mile of open water to my car.

At Round Lake, I loaded my boat for the last time and studied the sky. It was an unreadable uniform grey. The wind was up, but it was at my back from the south, and thunder was rolling in behind it, pretty far out still and to the east, about twenty five miles distant by the sound. I had to decide if I could risk the twenty minute open crossing before the lightning became proxi-

mal. A "what the hell" attitude is not normally part of my approach to the backcountry, but I figured I could do it in fifteen minutes with the tailwind.

About two thirds of the way across, I suddenly caught what I call a "crispy crackler," a thunderstrike which, by the sound, puts it in the general category of a "ten count." By the time the delay reaches ten seconds, you're in a situation, particularly on open water, that could theoretically place the next arc, if it is "cloud to ground," on top of your head. The challenge here was that there was no way to reckon the delay since the flashes were invisible. I turned my boat about forty degrees left to strike as direct a route as I could to the shoreline, and yet maximize the ferrying force of the wind behind me. The storm stayed off to the east but I finished the paddle as close to shore as I could, weaving in and out of the strainers in about two feet of water and getting kicked around by two-foot swells.

When I reached the put-in, I was moving really fast. It was about three o'clock, but I still had to load up. The first thing I noticed as I came around the end of the gravel cul-de-sac and into the parking area, was that my car, indeed, had not been crushed. The second thing was that there was a tent set up on the parking bed, something I had never seen before at a Forest Service landing. I had just finished tying my canoe to the roof and the wind was dying down, and was about to jump into my Tempo and ride, when I heard the clinking of bottles coming from near the tent and wondered if a bear was ransacking what was clearly some kind of bizarre novice encampment.

I figured I would investigate and try to help out and chase it away if I could, and began walking over to the tent. As I approached, there were voices inside and I wondered why people would be hanging out in their tent in midafternoon in dry weather. Several interesting possibilities then lept to mind and I turned on my heel and headed back to my car. As I was opening the door, a man popped up from behind the tent and, in an accent which later proved to be Italian, asked if I had just come off the lake. I said I had and he replied, "You can't get out. The road is blocked." I asked what was blocking it and he said "Trees." I said, "How many?" and thought about my Sven Saw and that maybe the two of us could pull them off to the side. He said, "We tried to walk out to the lodge on the other side of the lake, but there were too many. We had to come back." I asked him what he meant. He said that I should just go take a look for myself.

I was entirely unprepared for what I saw when I rounded the corner to round Lake Road #139. There was a solid wall of leafy vegetation and several whitish tree trunks slantwise above the grade like a giant "Do Not Enter" sign. I climbed on top of one of the first trunks and, from about fifteen feet off the ground looked down the way. I thought, "There could be fifty trees down here, maybe five hundred." The entire roadbed was buried under mature quaking aspens, huge ones like the two that had stymied my way off of Snipe. They had all blown over in an endless, neat line of parallel aspen corpses.

Back at the parking lot, my new companions in entrapment turned out to be a couple European employees, he Italian, she French, of a pasta company in Des Moines. Go figure. It was their first trip to the Boundary Waters at the suggestion of a co-worker. They had bailed off of Brant Lake west of Round immediately following the storm, and had been stuck at the Round Lake access since July 4th afternoon. They told me that at Tuscarora Outfitters, about a quarter mile to the east on Round, staff had told them not to expect the Forest Service to clear the road until possibly Wednesday morning. I considered the believability, from my St. Paul co-workers' perspective, of having to miss two days of work because I was "trapped" at a lake in northern Minnesota, and decided I had better take lots of pictures.

Round Lake Access

Brent Harring

Since the sun was out again, I hung my wet gear and clothing on a derelict canoe trailer nearby, and began making plans to camp out for a couple days in the lot. We could hear chainsaws whining away across the lake, and I wondered if I would have been on the road by then if I had gone ahead and rented a Sundowner canoe from Tuscarora Outfitters instead. The Italian reported that they had opened their own road all the way out to the Gunflint. He had, however, also seen three cars smashed by a single tree in their parking lot, so I felt fortunate enough in the situation as I was. A float plane came over low and we all waved, and I wondered what it looked like from the air to see people trapped in a parking lot behind miles of downed trees, and if they were reporting to others from the cockpit that we were there.

At about five o'clock, right about the time some things were dry enough to begin taking down, we started hearing chainsaws from the direction of up Round Lake Road. It was unclear at first but, after about twenty minutes, was obvious that there was more than one saw, accompanied by some rumbling heavy equipment as well, and that they were definitely coming our way and coming on fast.

About that time, a family of four, including two small children, trudged up from the landing and began to quickly load their Oldsmobile. I walked over, anxious to explain the dramatic news that we were all trapped but that we were also, apparently, just about to be rescued. The father, especially, seemed weirdly unresponsive to my report and kept loading the car while he

explained that, after the storm, all they wanted to do was simply get out and get home.

Although he seemed disinclined to talk, I had to ask him how they had managed during the storm with their young kids who must have been terrified. He explained that the kids had just kept playing a game on the floor in the middle of the tent with their mom while he "sort of held up the sides," and that they never really knew there was a storm on. I couldn't imagine that anyone could have stayed inside a tent during the storm without being able to see if anything was going to fall on them. I asked him about that, and he said that their tent had been next to sort of a cliff and that he hadn't really worried, in that position, about anything dropping on their heads. I felt that the "Cleavers" from Iowa had just scratched by on dumb luck, as they say, and thought he should know it, but decided not to add to his level of stress.

By the time I finished speaking with the new arrivals, it was clear that the chainsaw cavalry was at hand, and I began grabbing all my stuff and just jamming it loose into the back seat and trunk. The pasta people grabbed their camcorder, and I my camera, and we assembled in front of the blockage to witness our rescuers break through. I marveled out loud that, even though the chainsaws sounded like they were at our very feet, we still couldn't see a thing. As if on cue, a sawblade suddenly poked through the foliage and slowly ripped a couple vertical cuts, the sawmaster invisible behind it. **C59**.

It was like a scene from the "Magnificent Seven" or something. A veritable chainsaw hero suddenly stepped through the brush, his big rifle chainsaw in his big gloved hands, his big pistol radio harnessed across his chest, and his big orange helmet with his big blue earmuffs on his head. He strode directly up to us in his big brown boots and a big yellow shirt, with a big Forest Service belt buckle and big canvass chaps over his big green pants. He smiled widely, set down his saw, announced his name was "Bill," I think, and asked us how we were. I said, "Man, that was cool, this is just like a scene from the Magnificent Seven or something," and we both actually laughed at the drama of it all.

Another uniformed cutter stepped through the debris, followed a couple minutes later by a huge yellow skidder and a crew cab Forest Service pickup truck. We walked back into the parking area, and the skidder geared to a halt as a helmeted shot-gun rider, with forearms larger than my thighs, jumped down from the dozer blade. Two more guys got out of the truck and, without a word, all six of them formed up in a circle in front of the skidder, their immediate mission complete. I thought this was the funniest, most fabulous thing and was actually laughing out loud, but was too embarrassed to get a photo of the moment. A couple of them eventually posed for me; then they wrote down all the vehicle license plate numbers in the lot and went upon their way.

The trek back down to Grand Marais was the strangest ever. I jumpstarted the Iowegian Olds a couple times, which stalled if it was placed in park, and then the three of us civilian cars cara-vanned out of Round Lake behind the skidder. It seemed like it was nothing but cut trees on both sides of the road for the entire mile-plus stretch back out to the Gunflint. I turned east on the asphalt, back down the Trail, weaving slowly in and out of sections of blowdown that head been cleared to just one lane. It looked like the region inland from the "Third Coast" had finally been smacked by a freshwater hurricane, and I knew that even the old-timers would shake their heads and say that they had never seen anything like it. This was like the '97 flood in the Red River Valley-- a "five hundred year" storm.

At Gunflint Lodge, it was managed chaos. The power was down and dozens of pieces of heavy equipment were moving everywhere. I was astonished that there were actually that many dumptrucks, for instance, on the Gunflint Trail period, and marveled at the political and economic clout that must exist to have drawn all of them at once to this particular business only twenty-four hours after the storm. The outfitters building was deserted, so I wandered around trying to find a staff person so I could pay for and check in my canoe. Several people pointed me down to the main lodge where I eventually spoke with a woman at the front desk of the restaurant. She was conducting business by candle light and paper receipt. I gave her my credit card info, to be dealt with at some point much later, and was instructed to simply leave the canoe up by others like it.

It was nearly six-thirty by this time, and I was already three hours behind getting back to the Cities. What would normally be about a fifty minute drive to Grand Marais was taking two hours I had been told. That meant I had roughly seven hours of road time back to Minneapolis. I decided to stay overnight with friends in Duluth instead of trying to drive home past midnight with as little sleep as I was going on. I figured I had better leave a voice-mail at work right away, so it would sound believable, to let them know I would be in the next day around noon. The pay phone in the darkened gift shop was still up and, while I was waiting, I listened to what I took to be the owner talking insurance and disaster aid with, I guess, lawyers and presidents on the other end. I figured I'd look for an open phone farther on down the Trail.

Back at the outfitters, I left the Independence where I figured they would find it. Some of the staff were unpiling crushed heaps of boats in the canoe yard where mine had been stacked earlier, but nobody seemed to notice me. I wondered, if I had been trapped or injured up in the PMA with my tent under the canopy and my canoe hidden in the brush, how long it would have taken for anyone at the Lodge to have eventually noticed my late return and finally recall, say a week later, that crazy guy who was trying to get up into Little Copper by himself over the Fourth.

Later in September, I happened to call Outward Bound near Ely, and was told by an old colleague that the Tofte Ranger District had phoned them after the storm asking if I was with the school and whether they knew who I was, so I figured someone would have found me eventually. My roommate had been in Chicago at the time and, although a few friends and co-workers knew I was going to the Boundary Waters for the weekend, only the ranger who wrote my permit and two of the staff at Gunflint Lodge who heard me describe my route had any idea of where I actually was.

Half way down the Trail at Windigo Lodge, the bar was still serving even though the power was down. I quaffed a brew while waiting for the tourists to get off the phone, and had a chance to tell my story to some locals who seemed pretty unfazed by it all. Back on the Trail, the damage quit about fifteen miles from town and the road was then open continuously in both directions.

Down on Highway 61, the scene at the river crossings and along the shoulders and in the ditches was downright astonishing. Huge volumes of water were still pouring out of the woods and, in many places all the way to Duluth, the shoulders had been blasted and undercut to the now crumbling and jagged asphalt edges of the roadbed. I stopped for a minute at the bridge over the Cascade River, not quite believing it was still there given how high the water was over a day after the storm. The massive brown torrent was flushing a huge load of sylvan debris into Lake Superior that was visible in a thick trail of flotsam and discol-oration about a hundred yards offshore. I followed it for at least a mile and a half before I lost sight of it from my car, and wondered if they might yet find a body or two in it, maybe washed off the Superior Hiking Trail upstream.

As I pen this final paragraph, the day is February 4th, exactly six months after the storm. I've still got my shredded tarp, even though it's unusable, and my well-worn tent is probably now due for an early retirement. I know from accounts of friends still at Outward Bound and Wilderness Canoe Base, that many parts of the land that I've become the most familiar with over the seasons have been completely and permanently altered in the wake of this storm, and I expect much of it to burn over hard in the next few years. There are four-hundred-fifty year old pineries that I've walked which are now gone, and I'll be back up there as soon as I can to witness and probably mourn some of the changes on the land for myself. Maybe I'll give Gunflint Lodge a call to see if they've got any damaged Independences around yet for cheap. Or maybe next time I'll go in my tandem with a friend who can remind me to bring along an extra headnet.

Ordeal in the BWCA
by Peter Torkelson with Jean Hanson

Jean wanted a camp saw. I already owned one, but it was old and dull and the blade wobbled a bit and it wasn't really the best design to begin with, so I looked over the camp saws while at a United Store. My model was still available, selling for about twenty dollars, but I could pay about five dollars more and get one of better quality. I splurged, spent the twenty-five dollars, and presented the folding bow saw to Jean as a gift.

That twenty-five dollar purchase turned out to be a wise move. It was the most valuable thing that we brought along on our 4th of July weekend trip to the BWCA, 1999.

We rented a canoe from an outfitter on Round Lake, made two portages of 140 rods and 366 rods, and entered Lake Tuscarora, located about seven miles south of the end of the Gunflint Trail. Jean and I canoed to a vacant island

campsite (a popular one that is usually occupied, so we felt lucky), stayed for two nights, and broke camp at 10:30 Sunday morning, July 4, to head back to the outfitters. We could have returned through the same series of portages, but Jean and I were up for a change of scenery and opted to take a longer and little-used 5-portage route instead. We had a leisurely morning in the canoe, watching loons and exploring a campsite, and we began our 255-rod portage out of Lake Tuscarora around noon. The skies were darkening and the clouds rumbling, but rain had come and gone all weekend long and this seemed to be just another routine rainfall heading our way.

Mid-way through this particular portage is a swampy area where the path became a series of planks, sort of a causeway, running for about 200 yards. We planned to

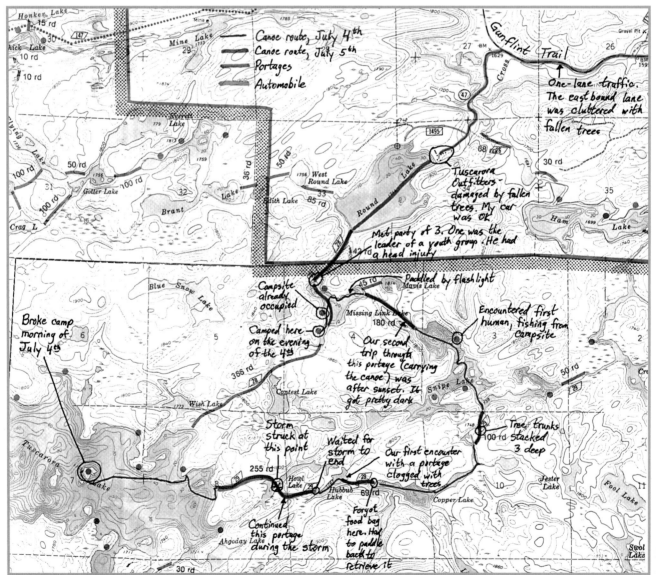

W.A. Fisher - Torkelson Trip Map **C43**

Peter Torkelson

walk the portage twice, carrying our packs on the first trip and then returning for the canoe and food bag. On the second trip, with the canoe on my shoulders, I was about three-quarters across the causeway when the winds and rain began. At first it was a challenge to keep my footing on the planks while the canoe acted as a giant kite, but in a few seconds it became an impossibility. I ducked down, letting the canoe blow off of my shoulders and into the swamp, and looked back to see how Jean was doing. A tree cracked loudly. I stooped, grabbed the bow of the canoe, and dragged it to the edge of the swamp and into the trees. Jean was right behind. Later she had told me that she could see the winds approaching me as they swept across the swamp, flattening the grasses on its way. We stood in the edge of the forest, soaked and getting cold, but somewhat sheltered from the wind and rain. Eventually we decided to move onward, even though it was still storming, hoping the activity would keep us warm. Occasionally something would fall and clunk loudly on the canoe, but, with the canoe over my head, I could not see much. Ignorance may have been bliss – Jean said that she had been whispering prayers that I would stay safe from the falling trees.

We reached the end of the portage and huddled under an evergreen partially sheltered from the pouring rain, eating gorp and getting colder while waiting for the storm to pass. Eventually it did, and we changed into dry T-shirts, loaded the canoe, and paddled the length of a small lake (Hubbard) to the upcoming 80-rod portage. There we found out that, although the storm had passed, the trail was cluttered with fallen trees. I had already thought that downed trees might be an issue, but I hadn't done a very good job of visualizing the problem. I had pictured myself stepping over tree trunks that fallen in the path, but the reality was that large trees, both deciduous and evergreen, had fallen with their full crowns resting in the trail. There was no going around the tangle of branches and trunks because the rest of the forest was just as impassable. The only way forward was to clear enough of a path to get ourselves, our packs, and our canoe through.

Out came the twenty-five dollar saw. I began clearing a path. Actually, "tunnel" might be the better term to use at times. If the tree trunks were too big, we had to cut enough branches out of the way to be able to clamer through the opening. Sometimes going under a tree was easier than going over. Often it meant removing our packs and pulling them along behind us or handing them across to each other. At one point the trail abruptly ended at a large hole, resulting when a tree uprooted and took the trail with it. At another point, a large log loomed over the trail with little visible means of support. When we went back and portaged the canoe, it was a series of pushing

and dragging the canoe along and then hoisting it back onto my shoulders. I only have so many hoists in me on a given day, so I tried to keep it on my shoulders as long as possible.

I was feeling like an overland version of Humphrey Bogart in The African Queen. The 80-rod portage put us at Copper Lake, and still had three more portages of 100, 180, and 140 rods to go. We made a blunder when we canoed off and unloaded our packs at the entrance to the 100-rod portage, only to discover that we had left our food bag hanging from a tree at the end of the previous portage. While paddling back to get the food bag, we made our second blunder by not taking any raingear with us. It rained hard, and our dry T-shirts got soaked.

The portage out of Copper Lake appeared to be a lot like the previous one, so we decided to clear a path first before we attempted to carry our gear. The most difficult part was a long stretch of tree trunks stacked three-deep on top of each other and running roughly parallel on top of the path. We climbed up on the logs and tightroped the length of a trunk for a few yards. I know I've whined about portages before, but in this case it became a joy to see any stretch of open path ahead of us, no matter how rocky, steep, or sloppy it was.

On Snipe lake, between the 100- and 180-rod portages, we encountered our first human. He was by himself, fishing off his campsite. We asked him if he had come in that day, with selfish hopes that he had already cut a path through the portage for us, but no such luck. We briefly told him of the troubles we were having on the portages, but he didn't seem very concerned. Actually, he seemed a little annoyed that we were disturbing his fishing, so we paddled on.

The 180-rod from Snipe to Missing Link Lake seemed the worst yet, with two large aspen tree crowns lying crosswise in the path. Jean was being optimistic by looking forward to dinner in a restaurant that evening, but what normally would have taken us four hours was taking ten. We had slim chance of making it back to the outfitter. Nature was not helping any either – rain kept coming and going, darkness was setting in, and the mosquitos were thick and annoying and getting thicker. We had to keep re-applying repellent. We were getting tired. Jean twisted her knee. By the time we were carrying the canoe, the trail was hard to see and footing was tricky. Despite all of this, we were both in pretty good moods.

We finished the 180-rod portage into Missing Link Lake around 10:00 PM. Camping seemed like a better option than attempting the final 140-rod portage that day. We canoed in the dark, scanning the lakeshore by flashlight in search of a campsite. The first one we found was already occupied, but we found another one fairly quickly. We hadn't eaten since our early-afternoon gorp break, but all we wanted to do was to climb into a dry tent and sleep. I looped the food bag over the first branch I saw and hoped for no bears. We quickly pitched the tent. Jean took a sponge bath and I had a fast dip into the lake, and by 11:30 we were in the tent, wet-skinned but warm.

Nature seemed to be set on throwing hurdles our way. Thirty minutes after we lay down, another thunderstorm hit. The wind wasn't bad, but the lightning was bright and the thunder was loud and close behind. One lightning strike seemed to be about 100 yards away. We didn't sleep much.

The rain had stopped by morning, and we had stayed dry. We slept in a bit, ate a !eisurely breakfast, wrung out clothing, packed up our things, and broke camp at 10:30. When we reached the 140-rod (and final) portage, it was much like the others. Out came the saw again, and we put on our packs and cut our way to the other end. It was not quite as bad as those from the previous day. When we came back for the canoe, we saw two men canoeing toward the portage. They were carrying an injured third man who turned out to be the canoe guide for a group of six teenagers. He had been struck by a tree, and the same tree had fallen on a teenage boy, injuring his ribs. The guide had recruited these two men from another party, and they had been moving since 4:30 that morning attempting to reach the outfitter and arrange a rescue. We let them "play through", and our final canoeing to the outfitters was a cakewalk compared to the previous day.

It doesn't end there. Tuscarora Outfitters, on Round Lake, had been hit pretty hard, too. The buildings were all still standing, but several trees had fallen on them as well as on the roadways. My heart sank as I saw that trees were lying on top of parked cars as well. Fortunately my own car had come through undamaged. Kerry-the-Outfitter was happy to see us arrive, and we were happy to return his canoe intact. The outfitter's power had gone out, but the faucets were still working and Jean and I were able to shower and change into clean dry clothing.

It seemed a little unfair to drive away and leave the disaster behind, departing with only a few cuts and bruises. As we drove back down the Gunflint Trail, the forest on both sides of the road looked as if someone had taken a machete and lopped off all of the trees at the 20-foot level. Our eastbound lane was largely covered by fallen trees. The westbound lane had been cleared enough to let vehicles pass through, so much of our driving had to be done in the wrong lane. I kept my fingers crossed, hoping that no thrill-seeking motorists were just over the hill or around the next corner, racing lickity-split towards me on a joy ride. None were encountered. The final third or so of the Gunflint Trail seemed largely untouched, and our adventure came to an end when we stopped in Grand Marais at a restaurant around 3:00 for lunch. The fellow at the next table was grumbling at the waitress because she had not automatically brought water. We couldn't relate to his discomfort. **C24**

Gooseberry Falls was going gangbusters.

We'll be back.

Gooseberry Falls was going gangbusters **C4**

BWCA EAST

Boundary Waters Trip 1999
by Di Powell

SAT JULY 3

WE START OUT FROM GRAND MARIAS, AND HEAD UP THE GUNFLINT TRAIL BY 7:30. IT'S A MISTY MORNING, WHEN WE ARRIVE AT TUSCARORA WE FIND OUT THE PAST TWO WEEKS HAVE BEEN VERY WET AND THAT IS EXPECTED TO CONTINUE. GREAT NEWS! !

WE GET OUR GEAR TOGETHER BY 9:40 AND OFF WE GO. BUSY ALREADY THIS MORNING, TWO OTHER COUPLES GOING OUT FROM TUSCARORA AND SOME FROM THE

SEVERAL SITES ARE ALREADY TAKEN SO ON WE GO, TO MORA WHERE WAS OUR 1ST DAYS SCHEDULE ANYWAY. BY THE TIME WE GET TO MORA I AM READY TO SET UP CAMP. WE CHECK OUT I SITE, I'M READY TO TAKE IT!! TIME TO GET OUT OF THE CANOE, BUT MIKE DECIDES WE SHOULD CHECK OUT ONE JUST UP THE LAKE, AS HE RECALLS THIS ONE IS UP A LARGE HILL. SO I GIVE IN AND OFF WE GO. WE DECIDE THIS IS A BETTER SPOT AND NOW THE SUN IS EVEN SHINING!! NICE BREEZE, WHICH SHOULD HELP WITH THE BUGS WE HEAR ARE SOOO BAD THIS YEAR.

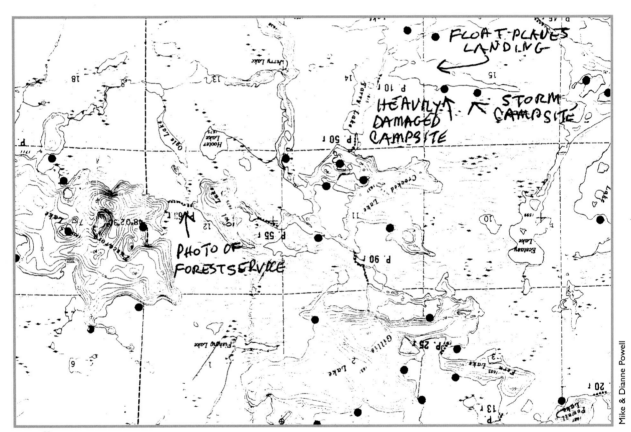

Powell campsite map

ROUND LAKE PUBLIC ACCESS. WE DO THE MISSING LINK AND TUSCARORA PORTAGES. WHAT A MUDDY MESS, SURE MAKES PORTAGING A CHALLENGE. BY NOON WE ARE ON TUSCARORA LAKE, MEET THE FOREST SERVICE WHICH CHECK OUR PERMIT AND TELL US TO WATCH THE SKY, LOOKS LIKE RAIN AGAIN, AND BEFORE WE GET ACROSS, WE MUST HEAD FOR SHORE. RAINS SO HARD YOU CAN'T SEE ACROSS THE LAKE. WE BREAK OUT LUNCH AND AS THE RAIN QUITS WE DECIDE TO KEEP GOING. AFTER FIGHTING WITH THE RAIN PONCHOS ALL MORN BY THE TIME WE GET ACROSS OWL AND CROOKED WE CAN GET RID OF THEM. WE THINK ABOUT CALLING IT A DAY, BUT

DI IS READY FOR SOME RAYS TO SOAK AWAY THE SORE MUSCLES. WE SET UP CAMP FIRST JUST IN CASE THE RAIN COMES THRU AGAIN, BUT IT STAYS CLEAR THE REST OF THE DAY.

MIKE HEADS OUT FISHING, HAS SOME LUCK SO AFTER CLEANING HIS FISH WE JUST SIT BY THE FIRE AND ENJOY THE PEACE AND QUITE. IT'S BEEN A LONG FIRST DAY.

SUN JULY 4TH

NORMALLY WE SPEND THE FIRST 3 DAYS OF OUR TRIP TRAVELING TO OUR DESTINATION, THEN RELAX!! BUT WE

DECIDE TO STAY WHERE WE ARE TODAY AND MOVE ON TOMORROW. IT WAS A WARM NIGHT AND THE SUN IS SHINING SO NICELY THIS MORN. AFTER BREAKFAST OF EGGS, BACON AND TOAST MIKE DECIDES TO TRY HIS LUCK AT EARLY MORNING FISHING. DI CLEANS UP AND HEADS DOWN THE HILL TO BASK IN THE MORNING SUN. AS MIKE PADDLES AROUND THE BEND A DEER HAS JUST WALKED DOWN THE HILL WHERE SHE IS LAYING BACK AND DOES NOT EVEN HEAR IT! HE HEADS ACROSS TO THE OTHER SIDE OF THE LAKE. MIKE YELLS AT ME TO LOOK UP, CAN'T BELIEVE I DIDN'T HEAR HIM. ROCK IN THE FRONT OF THE CANOE REPLACES ME. WISH IT WERE THAT EASY WHEN PORTAGING! BY 11:30 WE MAKE SANDWICHES FOR LUNCH AND WE'D BETTER HURRY CAUSE IT LOOKS LIKE ANOTHER SHOWER IS HEADED IN AND FAST! BY 1:00 WE ARE FORCED INTO THE TENT AND WE ARE RIDING OUT A GOOD STORM. RAIN IS SO HARD YOU CAN'T SEE DOWN THE HILL OR THE LAKE. THIS IS OUR FIREWORKS FOR THE 4TH!! WIND IS WHIPPING THE TENT SO HARD WE ARE UNSURE IF IT WILL STAY STANDING. THUNDER AND LIGHTING ARE CONSTANT, YOU CAN HEAR TREES SMASHING BEHIND US. SURE HOPE THAT IS WHERE THAT SOUND STAYS. THE STORM RAGES ON FOR ABOUT 20 MINUTES THEN JUST RAIN. BY 3:15 WE ARE OUT TO SEE TREES BROKEN OFF ACROSS THE LAKE BUT NOTHING IN OUR SITE. WE COOK SUPPER AND ANOTHER QUICK RAIN SHOWER COMES THROUGH. RAIN CLEARS SO WE HEAD OUT FOR OUR NIGHTLY PADDLE.

WOW!! WE COME TO THE OTHER CAMP SITE WE HAD DECIDED TO PASS STAYING ON AND IT IS DEMOLISHED. AT LEAST 9-10 TREES DOWN RIGHT IN THE SITE WHERE THE FIRE GRATE IS AND WHERE OUR TENT COULD HAVE BEEN. SURE GLAD WE WERE GUIDED TO THE OTHER SITE. AS WE TRY TO WALK AROUND THE CAMP SITE WE DECIDE EITHER THE TENT OR OUR CANOE OR BOTH WOULD HAVE GOT-TEN DAMAGED IF WE HAD BEEN HERE. AT THIS POINT YET WE BELIEVE THIS IS AN ISOLATED STORM. AS WE CON-TINUE OUR PADDLING, MIKE IS FISHING AND EVEN AFTER THE STORM THEY ARE STILL BITING. FISH FOR SUPPER TOMORROW. AS WE HEAD IN, IT'S RAINING AGAIN. WE'RE SOAKING BY THE TIME WE SECURE EVERY-THING FOR THE NIGHT AND HEAD FOR THE TENT. THE RAIN AND THUNDER STORMS CONTINUE THROUGH THE ENTIRE NIGHT AND INTO THE MORN. EVERYTHING IS SOAKED NOW, CAN'T GET A GOOD FIRE GOING OUR WOOD SUPPLY GOT WET BECAUSE WE WERE PACKED UP TO HEAD OUT THIS MORN.

MON JULY 5TH

LOOKS LIKE ANOTHER DAY OF STAYING WHERE WE ARE. HOPE THESE CLOUDS CLEAR OUT WE NEED A DAY TO DRY EVERYTHING OUT SO WE CAN MOVE FOR SURE TOMORROW. FINALLY AT NOON IT CLEARS ENOUGH TO

HANG THINGS OUT TO DRY IN THE BREEZE. SUNS TRYING FROM TIME TO TIME. TIME TO SPLIT SOME WOOD SO WE CAN GET A GOOD FIRE GOING TONIGHT FOR FRYING THE FRESH FISH. EVENING TURNS OUT REAL NICE AS WE HEAD OUT PADDLING. WE POP SOME POPCORN JUST BEFORE SUNSET AND CALL IT A DAY, WE'RE MOVING INTO MORN NO MATTER WHAT!

TUES. JULY 6TH

WE WAKE AT 5, IT HAS COOLED OFF AND IS HARD TO GET GOING. WE FINALLY GET UP AT 6. IT'S WINDY ALREADY WHICH MEANS PADDLING LITTLE SAG WILL BE NO FUN AT ALL AND OF COURSE IT WILL BE HEAD WINDS. DI MAKES BREAKFAST AND MIKE PACKS UP THE WET EQUIPMENT. BY 7:40 WE'RE OFF. VERY WINDY AS WE PADDLE MORA TO THE 45 ROD PORTAGE. TO OUR SURPRISE TREES ARE DOWN AND COVERING THE PORTAGE. NOT IMPASSIBLE BUT OVER AND UNDER AND AROUND. TAKES A LITTLE LONGER BUT WE MAKE IT WITH LITTLE TROUBLE. WHAT A MESS! ONCE AT THE OTHER SIDE WE SEE THE WHITE CAPS ON LITTLE SAG, WE WONDER WHAT'S UP AHEAD ON OTHER PORTAGES AND DECIDE IT'S NOT WORTH GETTING HURT FOR. SO WE HEAD BACK TO WHERE WE CAME FROM. WIND MUST BE BLOWING 25 TO 28 MPH AT LEAST.

BACK WE GO TO OUR SAME CAMPSITE. NO BUGS, NICE ROCK, NO BIG TREES TO FALL (WE HOPE). ONCE WE ARE BACK (2 HOURS LATER) WE HAVE COFFEE AND GET THINGS SET BACK UP, IT'S TIME TO DRY OUT. SOON WE HEAR AIRPLANES, A TWIN AND A CESSNA 182. THESE PLANES CONTINUE TO FLY OUR AREA ALL AFTERNOON. WE THINK THIS IS STRANGE AND FIGURE THEY MUST BE LOOKING FOR SOMEONE OR A DOWNED PLANE, WITH THE STORM ANYTHING COULD HAVE HAPPENED! ABOUT 1:00 AS WE ARE SITTING ON THE ROCK A STATE PATROL HELICOPTER FLIES BY THEN CIRCLES THEN HOVERS JUST ABOVE US. WE WAVE AND OFF THEY GO. NOW WE ARE SURE SOMETHING IS REALLY UP BUT DON'T KNOW WHAT. PLANES WORK ABOUT A SIX MILE RADIUS THE REST OF THE DAY. THEY ARE LOOKING FOR SOMEONE.

WED JULY 7

COOLS DOWN A LOT ONCE THE SUN GOES DOWN AND SHOULD SLEEP WELL. RAINS IN THE NIGHT AGAIN, BUT IS CLEAR BY MORN. FLOAT PLANES IN THE AREA THIS MORNING, MUST BE BRINGING IN THE FOREST SERVICE, TO CLEAR THE PORTAGES AND CAMPSITES. WE ARE RIGHT IN THE FLIGHT PATH, AND IT IS DRIVING MIKE CRAZY SINCE HE IS A PILOT AND WANTS TO BE FLYING WITH THEM. MIKE HEADS OUT FISHING EARLY, WHAT ELSE IS THERE TO DO!! TOO MANY DAYS OF SITTING FOR US. FISHING IS QUIET, WINDY AND COOL, NOW THE SUNS OUT AND IT'S

WARMING UP. MORE PLANES AGAIN TODAY. WIND GOES DOWN AND WE PADDLE AROUND THE LAKE BEFORE SUNSET. THE FOREST SERVICE WAS IN THE PORTAGE AND CUT A PATH.

THUR JULY 8

WE WAKE TO VERY CLOUDY SKIES (I'M BEGINNING TO GET USED TO IT), AFTER LAST NIGHT WE THOUGHT WE'D FINALLY GET A WARM SUNNY DAY. BY THE TIME WE ARE COOKING BREAKFAST THE RAIN COMES AND SETS IN. THIS HAS TRULY BEEN A WET TRIP! ANOTHER DAY OF READING IN THE TENT TO STAY WARM. COFFEE SURE TASTES GOOD AND HELPS WARM THE BONES. TIME TO COOK SUPPER AND AS WE ARE FINISHING UP WE HEAR VOICES, NOW THAT'S A SURPRISE BUT MAYBE WE CAN FIND OUT WHAT IS GOING ON. IT'S THE FOREST SERVICE CHECKING IF WE ARE OK. THEY INFORM US OF MAJOR DAMAGE TO THE PARK. SOME PLACES 90% TREES DOWN, SOME TRAILS NOT PASSABLE. THEY WILL CALL HOME FOR US AND LET FAMILY KNOW WE ARE FINE. THE NEWS HAS BEEN COVERING THE STORM. TUSCARORA IS OUT OF POWER AND PHONE SERVICE, THEY WERE HIT HARD IN THE STORM. TREES DOWN ALL THE WAY UP THE GUNFLINT TRAIL. IT TOOK CREWS 1 FULL DAY TO CLEAR THE ROAD FROM GUNFLING TRAIL TO ROUND LAKE. ALSO LET'S US KNOW WE MAY HAVE VEHICLE DAMAGE DUE TO THE STORM. WE REPORTED THE CAMPSITE WHICH HAD

USFS Beaver Aircraft Pilot Pat Loe off-loading canoe and gear

Mike Powell helping to free pinched chainsaw

DAMAGE. THESE TWO FOREST SERVICE ARE STAYING ON MORA AND HEADING IN TOWARD TERRY THEN INTO CROOKED. (SEVERAL PEOPLE HURT, PARTIES WERE UNACCOUNTED FOR ARE BEING LOCATED BUT CAN'T GET OUT. THE FOREST SERVICE ASK WE STAY PUT FOR A DAY OR SO, SO THEY CAN CLEAR THE PORTAGES AHEAD OF US.

AFTER THEY LEAVE OUR SITE THEY HEAD FOR THE DAMAGED ONE, SOON WE CAN HEAR CHAINSAWS GOING. MIKE HEADS OUT PADDLING I HEAD FOR THE TENT WHERE IT IS WARMER, BEFORE LONG A FLOAT PLANE IS CIRCLING, OUT I GO, SURE ENOUGH IT'S GOING TO LAND RIGHT IN FRONT OF CAMP. WHAT A COOL SIGHT. LET'S OFF CANOE'S AND 2 FOREST SERVICE AND OFF IT GOES AGAIN. THIS IS A AIRSHOW OF A LIFETIME.

BEFORE LONG IN COMES ANOTHER AND AGAIN LANDS RIGHT OUT FRONT. BY NOW IT'S CLOSE TO 8:30 AND THAT'S IT FOR TONIGHT. RAINS ALL NIGHT.

FRI JULY 9TH

ANOTHER RAIN-FILLED DAY! NOW I WISH WE WOULD HAVE TAKEN A FLOAT PLAN RIDE OUT OF HERE LAST NIGHT. I THOUGHT BY NOW IT WOULD HAVE CLEARED. WE SKIP BREAKFAST DUE TO THE RAIN, MAKE EGGS ABOUT 1:00 UNDER THE RAIN FLY. IT CLEARS A LITTLE BY AFTERNOON. WE COOK SUPPER AND PACK UP A FEW THINGS. WE HOPE TO TRY WORKING OUR WAY BACK DEPENDING ON THE CONDITIONS OF THE PORTAGES. WE ARE BOTH TIRED OF THE SITTING AND ITS TIME TO GET MOVING IN CASE WE HAVE A DAMAGED VEHICLE THEN WE HAVE A DAY TO GET THINGS IN ORDER.

SAT JUL 10TH

WEATHER IS A LITTLE BETTER SO WE DECIDE TO PACK UP AND WORK OUR WAY BACK. WE FIND 1 OTHER CAMPER OUT THE WHOLE WAY BACK. SOME PEOPLE WERE TAKEN OUT AND CANOES ARE LEFT BEHIND ON THE SHORES. WITH THE FOREST SERVICE AHEAD OF US WE HAVE PRETTY EASY GOING UNTIL WE GET TO OWL WHERE WE RUN INTO THEM. THIS PORTAGE WAS HIT HARD AND THEY HAVE TRULY HAD TO WORK ON THIS ONE. WE HAVE TO GO OVER AND UNDER TO FINISH THIS ONE. IN SPOTS IT LOOKS IMPOSSIBLE TO ME, THE TRAIL IS TOTALLY GONE. WE ARRIVE BACK AT TUSCARORA IN THE LATE AFTERNOON AND THANKFULLY FIND THAT OUR TRUCK WAS LEFT UNDAMAGED. HOWEVER SOME OTHER VEHICLES AND BUILDINGS WERE NOT SO LUCKY. STILL NO PHONES AND POWER AND IT MAY BE A WHILE.

AS WE DRIVE DOWN TO THE GUNFLINT TRAIL AND THEN AGAIN ONCE WE GET ON TO IT WE REALIZE THE TRUE EXTENT OF THE JULY 4TH STORM. IT IS HARDLY COMPREHENSIBLE. THE DAMAGE GOES ON AND ON AND ON, THEN JUST STOPS AND THEN JUST AS QUICKLY STARTED IN AGAIN.

IT WILL BE THE TRIP OF A LIFETIME (WE HOPE), ONE TO ALWAYS REMEMBER AND SAY WE KNOW WE WERE THERE!

An Incredible Journey
by Susan Wolfram

Finally, at age 44 it was my turn to take a Boundary Waters Canoe Trip. My husband, Tim, had been on quite a few, but with children it was hard for both of us to get away, and until then those trips sounded like too much work to be a vacation. But years of looking at the beautiful pictures and hearing of the wonders of the area won me over, and as a nature lover, I was anxious to experience this untouched wilderness first hand. I - asked Tim to plan a nice peaceful route, not a marathon of portaging and paddling as he had done on his previous trips, but a quiet 4 day trip of relaxing on the lakes.

Tim & Sue Wolfram - July 3, 1999

Sue Wolfram

We drove 6 hours to put in at Brule Lake. After the long car trip, it was great to be in nature– away from it all at last. We found the first available campsite and set up before dark. It was very hot and muggy, but that made swimming in the cool, clean, lakes all the more refreshing. I spent that first night trying to get adjusted to mosquitoes, latrines' and lathering myself in DEET (I had loathed pesticides).

The next morning the weather was still hot and muggy. After breakfast we began our journey to our final destination of Swan Lake, where after 2 portages and some paddling, we would set up camp for 2 days and then just relax and explore from our campsite. Tim thought it would be nice to be in a more out of the way place, where there were fewer campsites and people (a decision I would later regret). This all sounded "do able", although I was skeptical about whether I could handle carrying 40-60 lb. packs almost as big as myself through those 2 portages. The first one to Vernon Lake was encouraging. It was only 1/4 mile, and although we had to double portage (I hadn't thought about that before), I handled it fine and felt fit and confident for doing so. We also discovered a beautiful hidden waterfall off the main path. This canoe trip was really awesome after all! The next portage wasn't so easy; it was 292 rods of difficult terrain (about 200 more than I felt I could handle); and of course doubling portaging this one didn't make me very happy. I informed Tim that this really was too much for me and he should never plan to take me on portages this long and difficult ever again... I couldn't handle it (or so I thought). Little did I know I would be handling much more than

this amount the next day to get out.

The winds shifted. Half way through the end of our double portaging, we heard thunder in the distance. Tim said we had better move quickly, and we did. I certainly did not want to get caught in a forest or on a lake in the middle of a thunderstorm! Little did I know that was the least of our worries The thunder grew closer. That got my adrenaline going and we threw the packs in the canoe and I started paddling frantically down the river that leads to Swan Lake. It was not an easy river to navigate and Tim had to slow me down so he could steer us in the right direction around curves and low branches. Paddling ferociously across Swan Lake, we headed toward the closest campsite directly across from where the river meets the lake. The winds were increasing. This was no time to be picky, and if someone was there already, well..they would have company. No one was there, and we quickly brought the packs to a campsite area at a higher elevation maybe 100 feet from the canoe. Tim and I raced to try to set up the tent, but the winds and rains were so intense and everything happened so fast, there was no time. He grabbed a tarp to put over the packs and then one for me and told me to huddle under it next to a tree stump, while he went to pull the canoe further up on ground so it wouldn't blow away. He didn't tell me that when he had looked up, he saw a black wall moving :across the lake toward us. The rain was horizontal due to the force of the winds, making it now impossible to see, as it would hit directly in one's eyes.

That's when all hell broke lose. As he pulled our canoe further up on shore, a pine tree went over right next to him. Then as he ran back to where I was another group of three pines went over and a very large pine fell just as he crossed its path. I felt a branch on my arm and one hit him in the head as he crawled under the tarp, but we were both all right. The weird thing was that the winds and rain were so deafening, you really couldn't hear these trees falling! I was really worried after Tim got hit on the head and knew we had to get somewhere safe from falling trees. Fortunately the large tree that had fallen, had landed on a rock on an incline creating a small haven underneath its leaning trunk. I suggested we move under there where we might be more protected. We dashed under there with our tarp...the next 30 minutes seemed like years. Tim was in awe of the power of this storm, like none he had ever seen before...I was frozen in fear, like a "deer in the headlights". The winds and rain came down so hard; neither of us could see much of anything. I really didn't want to look. I honestly questioned how we were going to survive this and tried to come to terms with such fears. All I could do was pray, which is what I did for the next 30 hours.

After the storm had passed, Tim went out to survey the damage around us. It looked like a war zone. Multiple giant trees had fallen all around the area that we could see. These weren't little young trees; this storm had toppled mighty pines, hundreds of years old, like toothpicks. I stayed "frozen in the headlights", while my cool-headed husband found his oil turbo handsaw and began sawing and moving tree trunks and branches, so we could get back to our canoe and locate the latrine (minor details!). Two hours later he had cleared a path to our canoe, (which thankfully was still there and undamaged) and found the latrine. We then had to decide to set up camp there or paddle to another site. Neither option appealed to me. I just wanted to be air lifted home right now! We really didn't want to venture out on the lake again, not knowing what else there was to this storm, and reasoned that the trees that were left standing on our campsite, must be pretty hearty and a good bet to be near should more of this storm reappear. We set up camp and ate

some dinner. Tim swam and we saw a moose and her calf trampling through the water. I told Tim that the fun of this trip was gone and I really wanted to head home the next day instead of the day after. I also felt that it was likely the portages we came through would be blocked and we would need more time to get out. Tim knew I wasn't going to be a fun campmate and agreed to head home a day early. We settled into our tent by 9:30 p.m. when the thunderstorms began. Thunder, lightning, and torrential rains continued nonstop until 5:00 the next morning. I know because I didn't sleep for a minute. I lay there in my sleeping bag, shaking from fear, praying my heart out that we or a tree near us wouldn't be struck by lightning, or another tree loosened in the earlier storm, wouldn't topple on us during this one. The next morning the sky remained overcast, and Tim wanted to wait a few hours to see if any weather indicators might appear. I really wished I had the Weather Channel at that point! I felt trapped; I didn't want to leave my tent, for fear of unknown storms on the lakes and portages ahead, but I didn't want to stay there either. I desperately wanted to get back to civilization, but there was no easy way out of this one. After a while, Tim reached the conclusion that although the sky was heavily overcast; it didn't look like a thunderstorm type sky to him. Difficult packing up the tent and venturing into that canoe was, psychologically, one of the hardest things I've had to do, but I had to try or be stranded indefinitely on that campsite on Swan Lake.

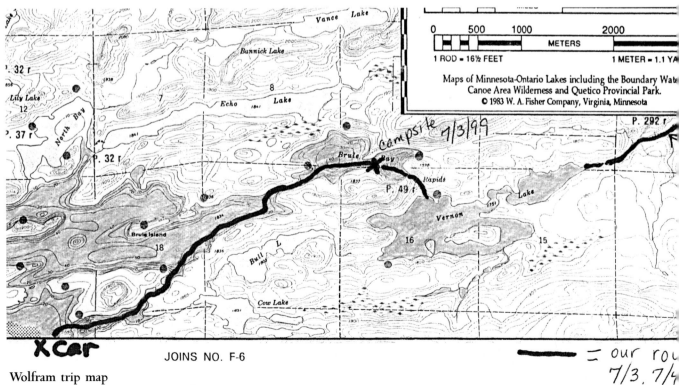

Wolfram trip map

We headed across Swan Lake and along the river, leading to the portage to Vernon Lake. The area was so flooded and strewn with trees; we had a hard time locating the entrance to the portage. After determining it was indeed the portage, we looked a few feet down the path to see nothing but a mass of huge trees and branches. My Daniel Boone-like husband once again got out his turbo saw and began sawing to find and clear the path. After two hours, he made some headway only to find that a small ankle-deep stream we had portaged through yesterday, was now 3 feet deep and quite wide. Even if we could get through that, he said the path was unrecognizable and impassable beyond that point. Huge pines and other trees down as far as the eye could see. He remarked that it looked like a tornado had passed through there. Back to the canoe to pursue an alternate plan. My thought was to just paddle in circles on the lake until someone air lifted us out. Tim said that wasn't likely to happen soon. Now I felt even more afraid and trapped! He said our only other choice was the other way out of Swan Lake. 6 portages and 5 lakes to another entry point to the BWCAW. I was fearful of what those portages would look like; how many would we make it through before we reached an impassable one and would then be stopped for good?! I also knew it was now into the afternoon and we would be trying to beat the darkness as well. Our car was parked at the other entry point, which Tim figured was 12-15 miles away from where we would come out, so he would have to run to get the car, also before dark. It was

a chance we had to take. Paddling across to the portage on the other end, I continued praying God would show us the way out.

This first portage was a difficult one. Unsurprisingly, many trees were down and the portage was flooded and mucky. Tim would saw and move branches to try to find the path and enable us to get our packs and canoes through. It often took both of us lifting and turning the canoe over and under trunks and branches to get to the end. As we reached the end of this first portage, we heard thunder in the distance again. No Dear God..PLEASE, We couldn't face all this amidst another storm. Luckily, that was the last clap of thunder we heard. We just kept moving as quickly as we could. The subsequent 4 portages all blur together in my mind. All were filled with risks and fear of the unknown as to whether we would finally be trapped or caught in another storm. All were frustrating in that it was hard to find the portages from the lakes due to all the misplaced trees and flooding. Each had their moments of looking overwhelming and impassable, but somehow we tackled them one by one, doing whatever it took. We carried our packs and canoe sometimes through mud up to our knees. At one point, I fell backwards into the muck with the heavy pack strapped to me and felt like a bug trapped on its back, struggling to get up. The mosquitoes had multiplied by the millions due to the rains and swarmed us constantly. DEET became a welcome friend. I felt as if my back were breaking. We were not only soaked with sweat, but with water and mud. It was the

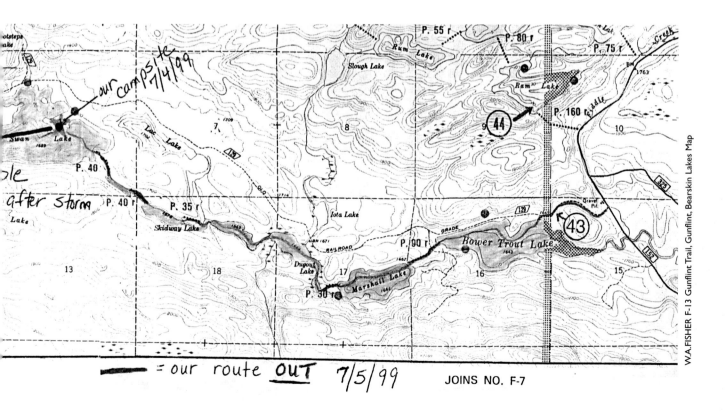

W.A.FISHER F-13 Gunflint Trail, Gunflint, Bearskin Lakes Map

only other experience in my life that I felt was comparable to childbirth. You just keep going despite the relentless, increasing pain. I had enough difficulty maneuvering myself with 60 lb. packs on my back through the maze and trenches; I don't know how Tim carried our 18 ft. canoe through it all! So often we would climb over and under trees, not even sure we were following the portage path. Even though the second trip on each portage was physically exhausting, at least the fear of whether we could find and get to the end of it was only a part of each first trip.

Tim clearing portage between Swan and Vernon Lakes

The last portage was the most frustrating and difficult to find. We were so close; we just had to find it. We slowly combed the shore of the last lake, where Tim figured from his map the portage path had to be, but we could find nothing that looked like a portage (not that anything did). He toyed with the possibility of going down an adjacent river to the road, but the sound of rushing water scared me out of that option. I did not want to have to shoot rapids now to get home (who knew what those rains could have done to the river waters). So we slowly combed the shore once more, and saw what we determined had to be the portage path, even though it now looked like a creek running into the lake. Wading through it, it became clear it was indeed the path. One last trudge through the trenches and we were at the road; not a highly traveled road, with one deserted truck at the entry point. Tim had a partial map of the area and determined he could run 12-15 miles to our car, as he is a runner, with hopes of perhaps passing someone on the way. I was totally terrified at the thought of being left alone at the edge of this wilderness, but knew I certainly couldn't even walk 5 miles after what we had been through, and that it was 7:30 p.m., and we were racing against the setting sun. So Tim prepared to run, and I put on some more DEET, moved the food pack away from me, and got out a flashlight, whistle, and pots to bang, for protection. I tried to remain calm and not give into fears; I knew I might likely have to wait up to 2 hours for Tim's return. I didn't dare panic now.

Forty minutes later, I heard the sound of a truck on the road. It was one of the most wonderful sounds I have ever heard. Words can not express the relief, joy, and elation I felt as that truck pulled into where I was and Tim got out with a couple of "guardian angels" that had picked him up as they headed out from their lake. I wanted to hug them, but given my sweaty, muddy, and DEETy condition, I didn't think it would be appreciated. Tim had not realized that the road to our car dead-ended at a lake and it was really 40-50 miles to our car by road! These wonderful souls loaded up all our gear and drove us back to our car. We then began to realize the magnitude of this storm, as the truck had to zigzag around fallen trees with a narrow pass, that was cut by the utilities people earlier, all the way back to our car. We headed toward the first motel in Tofte. It was 11:00 pm. The hotel clerk took one look at us and offered us the Jacuzzi suite for the cost of the regular room. As we learned of the reality of the storm, I realized how lucky we were to have survived it and gotten out of the area. More importantly I believe for me it was not a lesson in wilderness camping or canoeing, but one I continue to learn and reflect upon regarding having a more real faith in God, and Him teaching me to have faith in my husband and myself; exceeding self-made limits, and taking on and achieving what may seem impossible. I feel today that not many people are as "lucky" as I was to have had such an experience.

Reference to "C" throughout the book indicates a color photo in mid-section.

USFS Wilderness Rangers Brandee Wenzell and Cathy Quinn

Brandee and Cathy are members of an elite team of Forest Service Wilderness Rangers in the BWCAW. Typically the rangers travel in canoes to patrol their districts, enforcing the rules and helping campers in many ways - from locating open campsites after dark to breaking up spousal battles. They pack in radios to call for help if needed.

Maintenance and restoration of campsites and portages is a major responsibility. This involves hard physical work, carrying timbers, logs, rock and tons of soil to repair damage done by campers and severe weather.

The two rangers had Independence Day off. They were at the Forest Service cabin on Brule Lake when the storm hit. The cabin was sheltered from the wind; not knowing how bad it was, they turned on their radio just as an excited ranger, Pete Weckman on Moose Lake, declared "I'm all right but all the trees are gone and the canoe is wrecked!"

Cathy and Brandee hurried to check the campers at the Cascade River campground but found all the roads blocked. Returning to the Brule Lake entrance point, they met a lady paddling her injured husband in from Cone Bay, with lightning close behind her.

The rangers began cutting their way out with chainsaws. After several hours, they heard saws coming from the other direction.

USFS Wilderness Ranger Brandee Wenzell with crushed canoe & slice of blowdown 1686 - Red Pine **C65**

Roger Hahn - Seagull Outfitters

USFS Wilderness Ranger working on Frost Portage

USFS

Brule Lake isn't the worst blowdown area but it did receive some major damage. The west end was spared. Crossing the lake, the wind gained momentum, nailing the east end and stripping the islands of their timber. The portages between Brule and Swan lakes were jammed with broken trees. Jock Mock Bay was hit as bad as any location in the Boundary Waters.

Once the Brule Lake access road was cleared, campers began to arrive. Because most portages were closed, all available campsites were soon taken.

Then, according to veteran ranger Ellen Hawkins, the worst possible scenario occurred. "The campsites filled up with campers and now they overflowed onto off-site locations, taking liberties with rules and regulations. They now assumed the storm excused them from compliance. I could have written 15 to 17 tickets - toilet paper was everywhere!"

For this reason and because of danger from leaning trees, the Tofte Ranger Station discouraged campers from going in when they called for information or arrived to pick up permits.

Rangers Quinn and Wenzell anguished over the damage done to their special place - the BWCAW. Knowing it as well as they did, it was hard to deal with the damage.

After the storm, many campers asked them not about well known sites but about the condition of obscure campsites and portages that were special to them - such as the Lily Lake portage with its huge cedars. According to Cathy, "We have a hard time keeping our sanity, still grieving while answering questions about areas so dear to us."

The two rangers served on search and rescue and chainsaw crews. Following the storm, the weather was bad - wet and windy. Crews worked 12 hour shifts, opening portages and checking each campsite for injured or trapped campers. Brandee's crew rescued many groups of campers, all cheering as the portages were opened.

Brule to Juno Portage

Campers had great difficulty hauling canoes and packs through the blowdown, constantly losing the trail. Branches blocking the way had to be cut with axes and saws.

Cathy found some groups sending youngsters ahead - they could crawl through the downed trees, identify the trail and wave to the others to proceed.

The two rangers also led Hotshot crews. According to Cathy, "There were about 21 Sacramento Hotshots that were split up and generally sent to the toughest areas. They were extremely effective sawyers." Cathy's only complaint was their "loud yelling and throwing fish guts in the lake."

All the crews appreciated the good work done by local outfitters who furnished needed equipment and supplies on schedule.

AMNESIA ON BRULE LAKE

Cathy and Brandee met this nice couple just arriving at the Brule Lake entry on the afternoon of July 4. Cathy describes Sue Hawn as a very brave lady who paddled her injured husband John out of danger - start-

If you can't find a latrine

On some campsites windfalls may make it impossible to reach the latrine. Please keep these two things in mind:

• You don't want to contaminate lakes and streams.

• You don't want to ruin somebody else's trip by leaving toilet paper and human waste near the campsite.

Here's what to do:

1. Pack in litter bags for toilet paper and tampons, and a trowel or small shovel.

2. Choose locations 150' or more from the water and camp area.

3. Dig individual catholes 6" - 8" deep, or start with holes left by tipped over trees.

4. Bury feces and toilet paper at least 6 inches deep (or better yet, pack out toilet paper).

ing from Cone Bay and crossing the lake with lightning and thunder close behind them.

Cathy received the following letter from Sue two weeks after the ordeal:

July 21, 1999

Dear Cathy,

Good to hear from you! I appreciate you taking the time to write. By the sounds of your letter, you are working long, hard days in order to create some sense of order. Meanwhile, you have a constant stream of travelers to deal with on a daily basis. I do hope that at some point when all this becomes a distant memory that you will be given "shore leave" to get away from the grind.

Meanwhile, we are well. John is just fine and each day the soreness suffered from tackling the tree is going away. His head is great although, thankfully, he will never remember the incident. I get to carry that burden. As I look back, which is a whole lot more comfortable, I can be much more philosophical and logical. I decided on the way home that there must be a lesson or something that we learned. I'm not sure about that. I did decide we should never sweat the details of this life so much — just enjoy each moment and continue to work non-stop for the good of human kind. We left the BWCAW feeling grateful for good fortune and that we had not suffered more serious injuries, but I can't get around the great sadness of so much destruction. We both felt that we had lost many good friends in those trees as everyone else feels as well. I find it ironic that the morning of July 4th, the weather was so oppressive, we decided to forego the portage into Davis and crossed the bay to get the campsite which would possibly afford a better breeze. Being old enough to know better (almost 50 and over 50), and longtime travelers of the north (twenty plus years on Brule), we are now cautious and err on the side of caution. Time has taught us well but that won't serve you at all times as we found out. We made camp on the eastern campsite in Cone Bay around 11:00 a.m.

We anticipated the storm just by the sheer feeling in the air, which was confirmed by the distant rumble of thunder to the west of Brule. We made camp ready for weather, stowed gear in the tent, rigged the rain fly and gathered firewood which was covered by an old poncho. As the storm approached, the air became even more unbearable, much like our Iowa weather! The storm chose to build slowly to the west and we were even bold enough to speculate that it would pass by with no activity. It made itself known in a hurry, obliterating all known horizons on the western shore of Brule. We stood and watched at water's edge (old camp training told me to be at water's edge in this storm) as a cloud(?) rolled and raced over the face of the lake and as it approached us, the entire sky above us turned to night and darkness. Immediately following, the world turned to white and all hell broke loose. Wind and rain moving sideways with a vengeance, and Brule in this bay has become an ocean with waves to match the size of the storm. I'm trying to think of words that describe the intensity of the storm and I just come up short. The overall feeling was that everything was rolling and that nothing was stable. It was hard to see because the rain and the wind were so fierce and a large cedar that I was standing under at water's edge was moving back and forth trying to hold its own while the ground beneath was moving, given the stress on the tree's shallow root system. I remember also the tree that hit John moved so quickly and silently. In fact, I don't even remember seeing or hearing two trees fall that landed where the fire grate was. After I got John up (I think he was more in the branches and not pinned under the trunk), we waited out the storm (30-35 minutes???). I knew that he had a concussion and that we'd need medical help. Surprisingly, Brule took no time at all to quiet down. My worst fear at that point was that the lake would be too rough to paddle with just more or less me in the stern. But, Brule stayed calm. It was a good paddle across the lake. Seems that so many crossings on Brule are windy in the summer. I stowed what gear I could up towards the bow to offset our weight in the stern and took off. Once I left cone Bay, I was surprised at the hit and miss effect of the storm. Tree debris was everywhere in the lake and I saw several trees that were smoldering from a lightning strike near the shore. It was a funny quiet on the lake too, almost as if humankind and nature collectively were trying to figure out what just happened. You have to wonder about the wildlife. There was a single loon that sat quietly on the water rather close to the canoe as we paddled by. He didn't appear to be shy, didn't dive and I'm sure he/she felt the same sadness about the lake. On the Grade road to Grand Marais, I saw two baby foxes on the road and a third in the bush. Tiny guys and I wondered where the parents were. The road was in pretty good shape thanks to you and your crew. I think it took me about 45 minutes (?) to make it to town.

At the hospital in Grand Marais, they decided to transport John and another guy who also got hit by a tree to Duluth. Hospital was short staffed and more tree-injury folks kept arriving. The doctor on call wanted John to see a neurologist.

Cathy Quinn motors on Brule Lake

We left Grand Marais about 8:30 and arrived in Two Harbors and Duluth as both towns were in the middle of their fireworks displays. The wife of the other guy nailed by the tree traveled with me and I found myself trying to help keep her calm. Her husband was in bad shape (both legs broken plus his femur) and from what I understand, he was in critical condition. The folks at the Duluth hospital were great and later on that night (1 a.m.) the woman who had traveled with me came in to let us know that her husband would pull through! John checked out fine with the neurologist and outside of taking it very easy, no restrictions. So, back up the North Shore.

After a week of motels, we headed home. We wondered all the way back just how all things had fared. We heard and read lots of things, but your letter detailing some of the spots in the Brule area was really helpful. The Brule to Lily Portage was a beauty. We don't canoe Winchell much due to the heavy traffic but that portage is magic and a great spot to see the tall trees. Majestic, and such a reminder of what the forest looked like before logging. Relieved to hear that Cliff remained intact!! As you said, I remember Brule was hit and miss. I can't imagine Jock Mock Bay without trees and I had feared with its elevation that the Davis Portage would be a wreck - so glad to hear that despite the odds there's still a portage. It sounds like Davis will be a study in contrasts and that we're pretty fortunate compared to some areas of the woods.

Since I work at college, one of the perks is vacation. John and I are trying to figure out a time to come back in September. We had planned on an October trip which we like to do but my travels in October and November will take me to both coasts with no time in between for an October vacation. We don't know at this point if we could get a permit to Brule or whether we should just go to the Homer area. (You can see our homing device lands around the Brule area!) If this works out and we can decide on a time in September, we'll have to plan on a visit with you to talk about this wild summer. Anyway, we at least owe you and Brandee for a dinner for all your help! You're right about stressful situations creating a bond in people - we all love the woods and share that great bond of such a wonderful part of the world. We always feel it is such a privilege to be in the woods, to be in a place that is ancient and fairly untouched by civilization. You are fortunate to call it home and we hope your summer from here on out is without motors, chain saws and with many beautiful days. We both hope to see you in September and stay in touch when you have time.

Blue Skies,

Sue & John

P.S. John built our canoe prior to our wedding eight years ago. Thanks for taking care of it!

Capsized on Jock Mock Bay
by *Todd Kneebone*

Todd Kneebone and his friend from Brainerd, Minnesota experienced a windstorm on Brule Lake that they'll never forget.

"My friend and I and our pet Shelty were canoeing across Jock Mock Bay on Brule Lake when a powerful wind surprised us. It drove us across the bay and bashed us against the rock walls. We were struggling to keep upright when our Shelty suddenly jumped out, tipping the canoe and putting everything in the water.

"We couldn't climb the steep rocks and were battered there, hanging on to the canoe for what seemed like hours. Finally we made our way around the rocks to a landing spot."

Their dog was gone, and no amount of calling could bring her back. When they couldn't wait any longer, they left for Duluth without her. The next day they drove back up Highway 61 and on to Brule Lake, not knowing what to expect. They found their pet exactly where she had jumped out of the canoe, wondering where they had been.

High Winds on Eagle Mountain
by *Andrew Neeley*

Andrew Neeley describes the storm as it roared over Eagle Mountain, the highest point in Minnesota, located in the Tofte Ranger District.

This was the first time I had been to the BWCA in nearly 15 years. The last time was in 1984 when I went on a canoe trip with the Boy Scouts. Ever since then, I have dreamed of going back.

I did it on impulse. When I woke up at home early Saturday morning, I had a great urge to go to the BWCA. I grabbed all my gear and was on the road within an hour. I got to the Tofte ranger station at about 7 p.m., got my overnight hiking permit and rented a few items from Sawtooth Outfitters. I got to the trailhead at about 8:30 p.m.

I solo camped Saturday night (July 3rd) on the Eagle Mountain trail. On Sunday morning, I hiked to the summit of Eagle Mtn., and then went back down and broke camp and headed back to the trailhead, which was 2 miles from my camp. By this time, about 1:30 p.m., about 15 day hikers were on the trail headed to the mountain.

About a third of the way back, I passed a large family group. About 10 minutes later, I crossed a bog that had a boardwalk and at about that time I noticed that it was thundering to the south (down trail). After the bog, the trail climbed a small ridge. The storm hit as I was nearing the crest of the ridge.

The wind first hit the trees at the top of the ridge, and then it rushed downslope towards me. It uprooted a medium sized pine tree about 100 feet to my left. The wind was generally from the south. The wind gusts continued and I decided to run back down the trail to the bog, which had very few trees. I sheltered under a small pine tree growing in the bog next to the boardwalk.

After about a minute, a woman and girl from the family group ran up the boardwalk from the direction of the mountain. They came up to me and seemed uncertain as to where they should go. I am not an expert, but I told them the bog would probably be safer than just about anything else in the area. They had decided to leave the rest of the family and head back when they heard the storm coming, the woman was very concerned about the rest of their family, as they were probably on the mountain by now.

After about 5-10 minutes, two couples came by and also waited out the storm on the boardwalk. At one point the tree that I was standing by started to move as if it was going to uproot and I jumped in the opposite direction of the movement onto the boardwalk, almost knocking over a guy standing there. I was a bit jumpy, to say the least.

After another five minutes or so, the storm abated enough that we decided to try to get back to the trailhead. What followed was about a mile and a half bushwhack through fallen trees. Fortunately for me, several people offered to carry some of my stuff so my pack was much lighter. (My gear is old and not lightweight.)

In most cases, the trees were uprooted and not large, and usually not more than a few in one area. But one section of the trail was absolutely devastated. Large trees were snapped off either at their bases or mid-trunk, and some of the trunks looked like they had been thrown quite a distance from an area just off-trail. That area was at least five acres in size and almost devoid of trees except for a few large half-trunks, their tops totally gone. I think their tops ended up on the trail. Going through the section of trail was more like spelunking, not hiking, as we had to crawl on our hands and knees to go over and under the tangled mess.

After the blowdown area, the going was a bit easier, with only a few spots that were difficult to traverse.

Finally, after two hours, we made it to the parking lot. Fortunately, this area had not been hit bad and none of the vehicles were damaged. In the next half hour the rest of the family group and another couple emerged from the trail. Amazingly, no one was hurt. Apparently they had been on Eagle Mtn. when the storm struck and contrary to (my) logic the storm was not as bad on the mountain as it was in the lowlands.

When everyone had left, I noticed that there was still one vehicle in the lot besides mine. Not feeling up to trying to search for the owners, I left the parking area and went to contact the ranger station in Tofte. The road to Tofte, however, was blocked by fallen trees. A guy with a boat and trailer, headed to Brule Lake, told me the road to Grand Marais was clear.

The route led me past the Eagle Mountain lot, so I checked it again. The vehicle was gone, so everyone made it out. This greatly relieved me.

When I got to Grand Marais I reported in to the ranger station. They were greatly relieved to see me, as I was on the search and rescue list. I also told them that everyone on the trail made it out without injury, and about a new group that was attempting the trail.

Larry and Kirstin Waddell and Chris Cordes are shown with Review Publisher John Olson in front of the 1880's log barn turned sugarhouse at Wild Country Maple Products

Wild Country Maple

The Wild Country Maple Syrup Company, located in the Superior National Forest between the village of Lutsen and Brule Lake, had considerable blowdown. As the state's largest syrup producer, Wild Country maintains more than 12 thousand taps on 60 miles of pipeline on its 320 acres. They have won numerous state and national awards.

Established in Cook County in 1996, Wild Country

moved in and restored three antique log buildings. The biggest, the sugar house, is likely the largest restored antique log building in the state.

The storm toppled hundreds of trees onto Wild Country's lines, requiring many days of chainsaw work and line repair.

The article on the next page tells us about the State of Minnesota tree champions that fell to the storm:

DNR NEWS DIGEST

Foresters say winds destroyed an old sugar maple and the state's largest white cedar and red maple trees.

Friday

JULY 23, 1999

Three champion trees fell during July 4 windstorm

By Terry Collins
Star Tribune Staff Writer

The sight nearly brought tears to Gary Anderson's eyes.

Last week, the forester with the Department of Natural Resources (DNR) saw what was left after three champion "big trees" were blown down during the July 4 windstorm in northern Minnesota.

"I was pretty sad. It's almost like losing a good, dear friend," he said Tuesday. "It wasn't just one, it was three. There was so much damage."

The state's largest white cedar and red maple, as well as a sugar maple that was more than 300 years old, fell in straight-line gusts estimated at more than 100 miles per hour near Boy River, Minn.

"We're completely devastated," said Meg Hanisch, public affairs specialist for the DNR's Division of Forestry. "I don't think they can be salvaged."

TREES continues on B4:
— *DNR has revamped a program for people who may want to nominate a champion tree.*

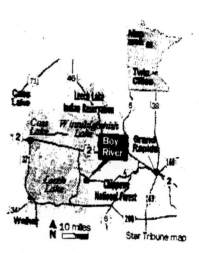

Star Tribune map

TREES from B1

She said that the Northern white cedar measured 86 feet tall, the red maple 90 feet and the sugar maple 83 feet. All of them stood near Big Boy Lake in the Chippewa National Forest in north-central Minnesota.

After the DNR received inquiries about the trees, Anderson, a forester at the Washburn Lake Workstation, verified the damage.

"The trees have no chance for survival," he said. "The red maple is still alive, but it's had such a major loss near the top it probably won't make it; neither will the cedar. And the sugar maple defi-

nitely won't survive."

And that's a shame, said Hanisch, who said a list of Minnesota's "big trees," which contains 52 native species, had just been updated and re-verified in the past two years. DNR follows guidelines of American Forests, the organization that oversees the National Register of Big Trees.

"It's a real loss, especially the sugar maple," said Hanisch, who said the DNR has revamped a "big tree" program for people who may want to nominate a champion tree. For more information, call 651-296-5958.

DNR officials said Tuesday that some state timber sale per-

mits may be extended in northern Minnesota to salvage timber as a result of the storms. Much of the salvage will be done by people who already have permits, said Bruce ZumBahlen, the DNR's forest management section supervisor.

Anderson said the recent downfall should rekindle Minnesotans' interest in finding other champion trees.

"That's the neat thing about trees, their longevity to span many generations," he said. "We're sure there are more out there, we just have to find them."

— *The Associated Press contributed to this report.*

Distributed by The Information & Education Bureau DNR Building, 500 Lafayette Rd., St. Paul, MN 55155-4046
Scott Pengelly, editor, (612) 296-0903

The Bear Rope Saved Us
by Maggie Piehowski

With permit in hand, our annual 4th of July BWCA canoe trip began. Our group consisted of eight seasoned canoeists from the Minneapolis based Rover's Club and a border collie with more boating experience under his belly than most Minnesotans. We had one aluminum canoe (Joel and Sonja), one chamois-colored Kevlar canoe (Judy and Ross), and two well-used Pennobscots that had seen a fair amount of white water (Hank & Maggie in one and Len, Sally & McNeill the dog in the other).

On the morning of Saturday, July 3, we traveled up the Caribou Trail with our windshield wipers flapping.

Sunday, July 4th started off hot and muggy. Several of us went for a morning swim. As the morning progressed, the weather looked a little iffy, a bit like the weather we had experienced the previous day. Sonja and Joel decided to canoe down Winchell, and if the weather held, they would explore by way of Gaskin Lake. The rest of us decided to wait and see what the weather was "going to do". We didn't have to wait long.

With rain imminent, five of the remaining six of us decided to wait out the pending storm in the "big top" tent by playing a rousing game of Hearts. Ross decided to stay

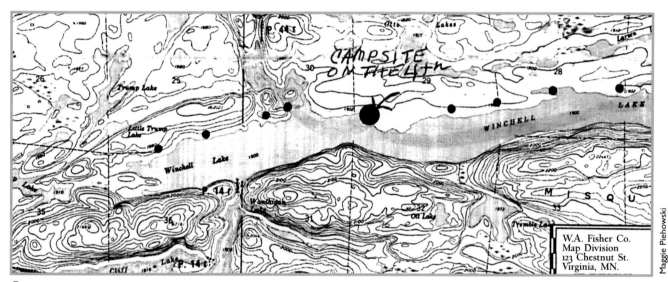

Campers map

W.A. Fisher Co.
Map Division
123 Chestnut St.
Virginia, MN.

Maggie Piehowski

We sat in our cars at the Brule Lake put-in until we had a break in the rain, then we packed up and pushed off. Fog challenged our way on Brule Lake. With some careful squinting and navigating, we found Cone Bay. The Cone Lake "portages" were easily completed by walking the canoes and dragging bottom now and again. The sun finally greeted us and it looked to be a glorious day in the BWCA. We donned mosquito hats for the 160 rod portage to Cliff Lake, zipped over two short portages and arrived at our destination, Winchell Lake.

On Winchell Lake, we found a beautiful site with a rocky point, a Boundary Water's view, enough flat areas to pitch 4 tents and a pair of white cedar for hanging the bear bag. We enjoyed Saturday afternoon sitting on our lawn chairs, reading, trying to fish, exchanging our usual banter, and enjoying the BWCA scenery. Even the mosquitoes were tolerable. The bear bag was set up using a pulley system and 80 feet of old Kevlar/Spectra climbing cord provided by Len. Little did we know what role a double trunk white cedar and the climbing cord would play the following day.

outside. Hank and Sally were at the back of the tent while Len was near the door. Maggie and Judy completed the circle. McNeill was nestled in the corner. Before the first hand could be shuffled and dealt, the wind picked up and the tent was blowing inward upon us. The wind was howling and the tent was flapping madly as we futilely stood up and tried to "hold" the tent outward.

Over the deafening wind and jack-hammer noise of the flapping tent, Len yelled, "we've been hit", but the words were difficult to understand through the din and howl. (We later found out that Len had been hit by the trunk of the white cedar closest to the tent. Luckily, the Spectra cord was fastened to the second trunk, arresting the fall of the trunk that hit Len). Almost simultaneously, Hank was struck across the shoulder by what subsequently proved to be a 3" diameter limb. (There is no way to know how far the limb had fallen or if its fall was broken, but it is reasonable to assume that if it had hit Hank's head squarely, it would probably have knocked him out or worse. The branch did not strike Sally, but it was probably only a few inches above her head). Hank shouted, both to be heard over the storm and to communicate the urgency of the situation, that "I have to get out NOW". At that point we understood that a tree (or part of one) had fallen, that something that could kill us might be hanging by a thread (or bear rope) above us and that we needed to get out instantly.

Len located the tent zipper in the melee and unzipped the opening as the tent collapsed around us. We ducked through the opening and exited into the howling winds and stinging rain. Our world was the eerie green color that is so often described by people who have been in a tornado. Through the driving rain we could see line squalls on Winchell Lake. Green waves were pounding the rocky shore of our campsite.

As the storm continued, Hank and Maggie were trying to hold onto Hank's tent. Judy was using the damaged tent fly as a poncho. She was unable to locate her rain gear in the chaos of the storm and was becoming chilled by the high velocity wind and rain. Len had taken refuge under a canoe. Sally was extracting sleeping bags and clothes from the downed tent and stuffing them into "dry bags". The whereabouts of Ross was uncertain. Mc Neill the dog simply refused to get out of the collapsed tent, even though water was rapidly pooling on the rumpled mass.

The Bear Rope

Maggie Piehowski

We stared at the collapsed tent with the trunk of the white cedar and the 3 inch diameter branch Lying across it. At first we were puzzled as to why no one had been significantly injured (a few minor bruises were the worst anyone suffered) given that we were all inside the tent when the tree hit it. Looking a little closer revealed a sight that was both unique and amazing. The Spectra/Kevlar "bear rope" was holding the tree trunk off the ground, virtually holding the two trunks of the forked tree together at waist level. For those unfamiliar with Spectra/Kevlar, it is a remarkable material used in technical rock and mountain climbing because of its extremely high breaking strength. Kevlar is most widely known for its use in bullet proof vests and light weight canoes. Spectra is another "space age" material often mixed with Kevlar to provide additional flexibility. 5.5 millimeter

Spectra/Kevlar cord (slightly thinner than the standard inch nylon often used for bear ropes) has a breaking strength in excess of 5000 lb. It's not typically used for hanging food bags because it's expensive and few of us bring two tons of food into the BWCA (although on the portages it would often feel like Judy had packed that much). We just happened to be using the Spectra/Kevlar climbing cord because some of our canoeists were also climbers, and the cord was getting too old for climbing use.

What had happened was this. Our "bear bag" set up was of the traditional sort. The Spectra/Kevlar cord was thrown over limbs suitably high in two trees about 40 feet apart, pulled tight, wrapped a couple of times around their trunks and tied at waist level. A pulley and second rope hung from the middle, allowing the food pack to be suspended 20 feet from the nearest tree and 20 feet above the ground. In this case, the double trunked Cedar had split down to the point where it was tied with the Spectra, which was about 4 feet off the ground. The Spectra/Kevlar was strong enough to stop the tree from splitting further. We needed pliers to untie and extract the cord imbedded into the wood. The remarkable result - a completely broken tree trunk, lying straight across the tent, held four feet above the ground by our 5000 lb. test Spectra. We have little doubt that under any other set of circumstances, one or more of us would have been seriously injured. The more we looked at the tree (and since, at the pictures we took of it), the more certain we are that the bear rope saved us from serious injury. Few people can say they've been hit squarely across the back and shoulders by a large falling tree, and walked away from it with a few minor bruises, as happened to Len. Generally, such things happen only in movies staring Schwartzneger or Stallone.

Meanwhile.... Sonja and Joel had paddled east down the north shore of Winchell with a weather-eye intention of a day long paddling loop. As they neared the last point prior to the portage to Gaskin Lake, the sky behind them turned from overcast gray to ominous green-black. The storm bore down as they struck for shore, finding there a low stand of scrub cedar for shelter. With the first squalls the day paddlers hunkered down as again and again the water surface whipped into froth and blew away down the lake. Emotions ranged from doom to wonder to sanguine with the passing of each successive squall.

Overhead the sheltering cedars groaned, creaked and thrashed but held, while sharp cracks and crashing was heard continuously from the forest just behind to the north. After the storm passed, Sonja and Joel continued to the 60 rod Gaskin portage to reconnoiter. Finding the way passable with difficulty, they opted to beat a retreat to camp.

Back at the campsite, the howling winds and rain had subsided. Ross relayed tales of side stepping trees as they came crashing down at the height of the storm, including one very large tree that now lay across the vestibule of one of the tents. Trees had been uprooted throughout the campsite. Of the four tents, only one remained unscathed. We washed mud and debris out of our gear in the lake and hung it out to dry. Tents were jerry-rigged back to some semblance of working order with the help of duct tape, a Fisherman's tool and some engineering ingenuity. Sonja and Joel arrived soaked but fine. The general feeling was good: the storm was over, the group was safe, no one was hurt, we had suitably warm clothes and gear, Judy's gourmet food in our bellies, several sips of gin and Crystal Light (from a plastic container of course), and fairly functional tents.

Although the storm was extremely powerful at our campsite, we at first suspected we had encountered some isolated straight-line winds. In retrospect, Hank had correctly guessed that the winds approached 80 mph. On a humorous note, one of our concerns was that our trash bag blew away in the storm (and the trash bag had our name and permit number on it). We fished the trash out of the lake, combed the perimeter and took the canoes out for trash patrol. We wondered if the storm would be written up in the newspaper. "Maybe the local papers", we concluded, never dreaming the storm would be national news.

Later in the afternoon and early evening, the weather was ambivalent, alternating between drizzling rain and clearing. Clothes were put up and taken off the clothes lines several times before we finally retired for the evening. We saw planes fly low overhead and assumed they were looking for capsized canoes or injured canoeists in our general area.

To say it rained Sunday night would be a gross understatement, since we now know it rained a constant, soaking 8 plus inches. Thoughts of trees crashing, tents collapsing and cliffs eroding from the heavy rain were on the minds of some; others slept soundly "knowing" that the worst of the storm was behind us. The duct-tape and repairs held; we had trickles and streams in our tents, but basically managed to stay warm and dry.

Monday was a bit dreary, but the group decided to head out. We realized that the portages would be a challenge with all the fallen trees, although we were still unaware of the overall extent of the damage in the BWCA at this point. We discussed trying the Lily Lake exit route because it looked more level on the topo map. (That would have been a very bad decision since we subsequently learned that the portages on that route were totally blocked and we would have had to backtrack. We guessed right retracing our route back to Brule Lake). We also knew we had enough food and warm clothes to stay out another day en route if needed.

We packed up the damp gear and began our trip back to Brule Lake. We lifted, pulled and tugged canoes over the 160 rod portage with only one incident - Judy injured her knee while portaging her canoe up, over and around some downed trees. We stopped to help another canoeist extract a fishhook from his hand, then paddled some low-grade whitewater through the Cone "portages".

The dreary day was rapidly turning ugly once we approached Brule Lake. The wind had picked up, waves were forming and thunder was beginning to sound nearby. As we worked our way along the north shore of Brule, the possibility of mutiny existed, or worse yet, the possibility that someone would flip a boat in the blustery weather. We made a rest stop in a protected area, calmed nerves and eased some paddling aches and pains before attempting the main open water crossing. Thought was given to camping on the north shore or at least hugging the shoreline all the way around Brule Lake. However, the entire party appeared resolute to do the crossing, most likely from a REALLY strong desire to get back to the take-out. We just started to make a dash for the shore when the sky cleared, the sun came out, and the lake went as calm as if Jesus and the Apostles were fishing just around the point.

We enjoyed the short remainder of our paddle, got to the take-out and packed up the boats. Groups of canoeists, seemingly oblivious to the effects of the damaging storm, were launching boats and departing as we arrived at the take-out. Our group was still unaware of the widespread path and overall intensity of the storm that ripped through the BWCA on July 4th. Content at having arrived safely to cars unadorned with tree trunks, we decided to head for home.

Not until we navigated the sawed trees along the Caribou and Sawbill Trails, drove through the recently reopened, drenched Highway 61 and developed our pictures of downed cedars, climbing cord and driving green rain did we really begin to realize the extent of the storm and how insanely lucky we had been.

The rest is BWCA history.

The Gunflint Pines Camp dog who helped to clear brush and was bitten for her efforts.

Camper tells harrowing tale

David Nordenstrom of Mora was up at Gunflint Pines on a family fishing trip when the storm came on July 4. He got more than he bargained for.

The little camper resort is next to Gunflint Lodge and Nordenstrom, his dad and brothers were out in their 18-foot aluminum boat on the lake when raindrops began to fall around 2:00 p.m. "We came in just to get our raincoats and go out again, then all of a sudden that thing just hit and wow!" he said, his arms and hands in the air.

Nordenstrom said he and his brothers, BJ and Tom, along with Tom's wife June, took shelter in their camper trailer. "We were sitting there and a big branch came down and went through our awning, then another huge poplar came down and lodged in a tree a foot above our motor home," Nordenstrom said. "We looked out and saw one couple running from their pop-top camper for the lodge with trees coming down behind them as they ran."

Nordenstrom said the wind tore through the area quickly, appearing with no warning and vanishing just as suddenly. "We saw one black cloud, that was all, then it hit," he said.

The family from Mora were in the camp with about 19 other trailer homes and camper trailers. Nordenstrom said most took direct hits from falling trees. Vehicles and other property were also damaged or lost.

"The wind ripped all the docks down and threw all the boats up on the rocks," Nordenstrom said. "But we recovered everything but one tackle box."

Nordenstrom repeatedly stressed the hardship visited by the storm on those who make their living on the trail. "There's nothing left in certain areas about ten or twelve feet up. Those poor people, this is going to devastate that industry-they've got such a cleanup," he said. The owners of a contracting business in Mora, David and BJ abandoned their fishing dreams and began to help clear the debris along with a dozen other adults and even some children and the campground's resident 12-year old spaniel. The dog actually began grasping small limbs in her teeth and pulling them off the paths on the grass.

David Swan and Dori Anderson of Minneapolis were among the helpers. Swan and Anderson were also camping at Gunflint Pines. Having backpacked in the Boundary Waters on previous vacations, they brought their new travel trailer up to the Gunflint this year.

Like Nordenstrom, Swan commented on the sudden onset of the rogue winds. "There was absolutely no warning," Swan said. "But I knew I was in trouble when the rain started coming horizontally." Swan said Anderson stayed the night of the storm in their car because their dogs were so unstrung by the day's events. They left the morning of July 6, but not with their trailer. It took one of those direct hits. "We were planning on leaving today anyway," Swan said. "Just not pulling a U-Haul."

The Nordenstrom family, however, got their fish. "We went out the day after and caught tons of fish!" David Nordenstrom said. "That's what we came for and that's what we got."

Cook County News-Herald

The Lane Family and Gunflint Lodge
by Chris Lane

The Lanes - Chris, Maradee and their eight year-old daughter Maggie - had big plans for their four day Independence Day weekend. Fishing, dining out and just relaxing were on the agenda when they pulled into Nelsons Travelers Rest in Grand Marais. It didn't quite work out that way.

Chris and Maggie fished McFarland Lake on Friday – perfect weather, perfect day. Saturday's fishing trip to Gunflint Lake was washed out; they settled for Grand Portage Monument and lunch at Naniboujou Lodge on the shore. "The weather was rotten but the meal was fantastic," said Chris.

Bad weather continued into Sunday morning, but just as they had decided to head home, the sun came out in Grand Marais. The three jumped in the car and, towing their 14 foot Lund boat, headed for Gunflint Lake.

Half way up the Trail, they realized they had forgotten cigarettes and were low on gas. According to Chris, "The temperature rose 20 degrees beyond Grand Marais. We stopped at Trail Center for gas. The weather was unsettled and the closer we got to Gunflint Lodge, the darker it became. We pulled into Hestons for cigarettes. The owners were watching TV and cautioned us that bad weather was on the way."

Hestons didn't have cigarettes. Gunflint Pines didn't have them either, and there the family was told there was a BIG storm coming. Finally, at Gunflint Lodge they purchased cigarettes at about 1 PM, and then headed for the Gunflint Lake public access.

That's where the action started. "The wind picked up," Chris remembered, "And lightning was constant. After a few seconds the temperature dropped 12 to 15 degrees, causing the car windows to fog up!"

A blast of wind hit them, bending the trees to 45 degrees or worse. A huge poplar broke off and landed just in front of the car; they backed up into a more open area. More trees came down, trapping the car. "Maggie was in the back on the floor, scared to death. The wind continued roaring for 45 minutes."

"When the wind let up we left the car for the

Vehicle and canoe damaged at the Gunflint Lodge

Gunflint Lodge

Gunflint Lodge. At least 50 large trees were down in the area, and all the parked vehicles had trees on them. A Ford 150 truck had a crushed canoe on its topper. We couldn't walk three feet without climbing over or under trees."

At the Lodge, trees were on the buildings and guests were milling around. A woman was beside herself – her husband was on the lake. But it turned out well; everyone cheered when his boat came in to the landing. (Later, he said that he had barely made it to shore on the east end of the lake. While he was there, a person was struck by a falling tree.)

Chris and his family were very impressed with the friendliness and help offered by the Lodge. They were invited to join in the big 4th of July barbecue.

"The Lodge area looked like a moonscape," said Chris. "A Subaru with Colorado plates was completely crushed by a big poplar near a cabin, while the owner reportedly slept through the whole thing."

By 8 PM one lane of the Trail was cleared. The Lane family thanked the owners of the lodge, the Kerfoots, for their hospitality and left for Grand Marais. "We drove through a moonscape with thousands of trees down – weaving through the mess at 10 to 15 mph. The closer we got to Grand Marais, the worse the weather became. In Grand Marais it rained all night."

They left Grand Marais Monday morning and headed south. "We saw water running over Highway 61 at the Cascade Lodge and many other locations. The Knife River was unbelievable, with trees washing down." Chris remembered, "There was no word about the storm on the radio for several days. Finally on MPR they reported the rain but not the wind."

Back at the Gunflint Lodge the staff had rescued 15 stranded canoeists. Two people had their canoe ripped out of their grasp as they stepped out of it – later they found it two miles down the lake.

The storm battered the Lodge owners' homes. Bruce and Sue Kerfoot had 15 trees on their home, while 10 fell on Justine's.

The Spirits of Crooked Lake

A group of local history buffs were an unwitting party to a bizarre incident that occurred at the well-known pictograph cliffs of Crooked Lake.

It was known that those cliffs held a special significance for the early people. The waterway was a primary route for the Native Americans as well as a major fur trade route.

The pictographs painted on the rock face by early Native Americans weren't the only messages left there. The local history group had heard that the early people shot arrows into a rock fissure about 12 feet above the lake. One explanation was that hunting parties shot those arrows, believing that if an arrow stuck in the fissure, good hunting would be assured. Other stories claimed that war parties had fired arrows into the crevice to frighten their enemies.

In late October of 1974 or 1975, the local historians built a raft and ladder on the shore of Crooked Lake, hoping to paddle to the cliffs, position the ladder and climb it to pull out the arrow shafts and points.

While they were paddling to the cliffs, a fierce wind

Climber searching for projectile points 1974

Douglas A. Birk

suddenly came up, forcing them off the lake. They returned the next day, but windy conditions and snow persuaded them to abandon their exploration until the next year.

Next spring they were back again. This time they easily reached the cliffs, but were amazed to see that the rock face had broken off, falling into the lake. –No more fissure, no more arrowheads.

Later, professional archeologists searched the face and lake bottom but "because of silty conditions found no artifacts."

I talked to local Native Americans who were certain that "it was the work of the spirits who guard the special site."

Painted Rock Projectile Point
This single projectile point was presented to Robert Wheeler of the Minnesota Historical Society by William Magie, who said that he recovered it from a fissure in the Painted Rock cliff along with at least 5 others in 1915 or 16.

A   B

Douglas A. Birk

Note from the State Archaeologist

Painting of Picture Rocks of Crooked Lake 1948

Frances L. Jaques

Picture Rocks of Crooked Lake 1974

Voices from the Rapids

Bearskin Lodge and the Gunflint Trail
by Dave & Barb Tuttle

Dave Tuttle, owner of Bearskin Lodge, was struck on the head by a big poplar that also totaled his truck. He made it to the lodge and watched as tree after tree blew down around the lodge, on cabins and on vehicles. **C12**

One car belonging to a couple from Minneapolis just pulled into the parking lot as the wind came up. A giant poplar smashed the top of the car, opening the sunroof, allowing the rain to pour in. Seeing trees falling, the woman feared for her life. She tried to exit the car but the doors were jammed because of the crushed top. Finally she crawled out through a rear window and ran to the lodge with trees falling around her. Her partner, imagining her being "cut in half" by a tree, ran after her.

They both made it to the lodge, thoroughly soaked but in one piece.

The couple called Triple A from the lodge to have their car towed. They were told a truck would be there in 45 minutes – they told Triple A to think again because the entire trail was closed. The following day, customers brought them to Solbakken Lodge where they had been staying. They tried catching the bus from Thunder Bay to the Twin Cities but because of damage to the highway it couldn't get through. They were stranded until they finally hitched a ride with other Solbakken guests. What a trip!

Vehicle totalled at Bearskin Lodge

Tree on dump trunk at Bearskin Lodge

Vehicle totalled at Bearskin Lodge

Crushed vehicle at Loon Lake

Vehicle totalled at Bearskin Lodge

Senator Paul Wellstone with Howard Hedstrom at Bearskin Lodge

After the wind subsided, Dave and his wife Barb surveyed the damage thinking that a few hours worth of chainsaw work would clean it up. But looking around the grounds, they sensed something wrong. There was no canopy; most of the big trees around the lodge were down. "We went from cabin to cabin yelling to check on our guests. Everyone was shaken but OK."

According to Dave and Barb there was lots of wildlife activity right after the storm. "Birds of all kinds filled the air: pileated woodpeckers, hawks and wood ducks. Small animals, squirrels and chipmunks seemed confused, not knowing what to do."

Most of Bearskin's cabins had trees on them. Eight vehicles were totalled–three belonging to the Tuttles. The damage estimate was $200,000. The area around the resort lost about 25% of its trees.

Their resort was the southernmost Gunflint Trail business to be seriously damaged. Brian and Kevin Berglund, two local loggers, helped clean things up. Nearby Bearskin Campground was lightly damaged with no injuries.

The Tuttles have owned the resort since 1973. At that time it was primarily a fishing camp known as Bearskin Camp, established in 1925.

Carson cartoon on Gunflint

The Author's Observations Along the Gunflint Trail

Driving north on the Trail in early January, there are almost no trees down before Trout Lake Resort – and there just a few. At 15 miles, Twin Lake and South Brule Road, damage is more noticeable but there are still long stretches of untouched forest.

At 28 miles the first serious blowdowns are visible, interspersed with untouched areas. Most trees are still standing; it's still a beautiful area. **C17**

At 39 miles, Poplar Lake access and the Laurentian Divide overlook, the damage is suddenly worse. Some trees are standing but I can see far into the forest. Protected areas are still untouched.

At Loon Lake the blowdown continues with a fair number of trees standing. Sheltered areas are very nice, with a good number of very large pines surviving.

Near Gunflint Lake there are large open expanses, but trees remain in sheltered areas. Generally, it is still an amazingly beautiful area in spite of the blowdown. Tuscarora Lake to Seagull Lake to the End of the Trail Campground, there are patches of blowdown and forest.

Generally, the Trail has few large areas of blowdown. Viewed after the first snow, the downed trees present an astonishing jumble, or pattern pleasing to the eye in contrast to many miles of continuous impenetrable forest. It is extremely interesting to see the product of nature's power and still realize the beauty of the area.

Coming home to surreal landscape

by Betty Hemstad

After being wedged between downed trees on the South Hungry Jack Road during the storm in our outback, chainsawing for six and a half hours to help clear the two-mile private road, snaking our way up the Gunflint Trail in semi darkness to Gunflint Lake, we reached the Gunflint Pines Resort.

Our first greeting was the steady drone of a gas generator. Then we saw neighbors and strangers who seemed like friends. Their dimly lit faces reflected only prominent features and their concern for how we were, how we got there, where we had been and what we had seen "down the trail." They didn't say it, but we knew what they were thinking — we were crazy for trying to come back in the darkness after the storm.

There is a force, a feeling not easy to explain, to get home after experiencing and surviving such a horrific storm. Also, we had family in our remote cabin on Gunflint Lake, including two young grandsons who had come for a northwoods Fourth of July. Were they safe? Had our silent giant (a magnificent White Pine) fallen on the cabin? Were they trapped inside?

We could see that the road was totally blocked, but we boldly announced, "We will walk to our cabin from here." Without raising their somewhat hushed voices, our friends made us understand that we could not walk to our cabin from there. They explained what we already knew: that we would be climbing over, around and through downed trees most all night long to get to the cabin, which was about two miles away.

Another idea came to mind — the lake! We could get there by boat. We knew then that we were completely at the mercy of the Smiths, the owners of the resort. I got up my courage and asked, "Wouldn't someone please take us home?"

The silence from around us was deafening. Never having been known for giving up easily, I asked the Smith's college-aged son, Aaron, if he would take us home. Looking into his eyes, I knew the answer — he would. It only took a moment before his sister, Tracy, volunteered to "man" the searchlight to look for logs, docks and other debris floating in the water. Tracy, a relatively new mother, handed her baby to her husband and said, "Let's go."

The trip was surreal. We traveled near the shoreline and saw the devastation as the searchlight moved back and forth. We tried to guess whose cabins we were passing.

We felt like strangers in a land we loved so much. We quickly realized that it was the trees — so many of the trees which had been our friends and served as guideposts for 25 years were gone.

Perhaps the deepest, saddest realization was that even my grandchildren, who were safe on Hungry Jack Lake, and those we found playing Scrabble by candle light in our Gunflint cabin, will never know the forest the way we did.

Surreal landscape

Betty Hemstad - Cook County News-Herald

Blowdown staged along the Gunflint Trail

Jim Cordes

Trees on Gunflint Trail

Blowdown imperils ski season

Senator Paul Wellstone was aghast at the jumble of giant trees littering the back roads around Bearskin Lodge on the Gunflint Trail last week but returning guests seemed to take the changed aspect of the woods in stride.

Wellstone rode with Bearskin Lodge owner Dave Tuttle and Minnesota Department of Tourism Director Steve Markuson to see consequences of the July 4 blowdown.

"This is the only one of my vehicles not trashed by the storm," Tuttle said as the group climbed into his sports utility vehicle. As he drove, Tuttle ticked off his losses.

"The lodge wasn't damaged, but we had fifty trees on cabins," Tuttle said. "We re-roofed ten cabins in one week-we have eleven." Gesturing at the bleak landscape away from the lodge and lake, grasses exposed to sunlight that had grown in shade just a month ago, tree trunks standing yet snapped off about 20 feet from the ground, Tuttle said the scene is reminiscent of World War II bombardment photos.

"We estimate about $150,000 to $175,000 in damage and the trees are still falling. We had one cabin we re-roofed and a tree fell on it just last night," Tuttle said.

The Bearskin trails, at least from the road, were indeed impassable.

Even the ones deemed "not so bad" by Tuttle could not be traversed by man or moose. The 40 miles of ski and hiking trails are key to Tuttle's business, especially in the winter.

The summer business is not as severely impacted, since the water oriented pursuits of swimming, canoeing and fishing go on regardless of the disaster in the woods. Tuttle said that only one of his summer guests cut their vacations short when the July 4 storm hit. "All the rest stayed," Tuttle said, obviously grateful.

Cook County News-Herald

1940's advertisement

Charlotte Eckroot Nelson operates the Windigo Lodge on Poplar Lake, about halfway up the Gunflint Trail from Grand Marais. Nelson has been without power since Sunday. "We've had windows blow out," she says. "The rain came right in, we got them boarded up. Trees everywhere are down. The wind was very very severe. I wouldn't call it a tornado. I didn't see any funnel cloud at all, but it was very intense wind. Very, very strong. I've heard people comment it was like 100 miles per hour."

This is the busiest time of the year for Nelson and other resorters along the Gunflint Trail. Now they'll be scrambling to put their places back in shape for the rest of the brief summer-tourist season. Nelson says the storm emptied her lodge.

Internet

Windigo Lodge article

Storm coverage missing info

To the editor:

Having been a regular summer camping visitor to the Gunflint Trail since 1978, we read with great interest and sadness of the storm that ripped through that area on July 4th. Had we not decided to do something different after 20 years of the same thing, we'd have been right in the middle of it.

While the individual accounts of the great damage reported by various people has been good, there has been a decided lack of information as to damage in certain places, i.e. the national park campgrounds and other points of interest.

There was one article stating that the couple in charge of all the campgrounds on the Trail had visited six of the seven sites. Period. Well.....what did they look like? How bad was the damage? Are they bare of trees now? Are the picnic tables going to have to be replaced? What happened to the outhouses? That's the sort of thing people like us, who live hundreds of miles away and take the paper, want to read.

How are we going to know if we want to go back up there? We came because of the way it looked, among other things. We're not too sure that we would want to go back to a practically treeless area. We know all the trees didn't get knocked down, but you've got to admit, from what the reports that you have printed, most did.

Also, how far down the Trail did the blowdown go? Do you realize no one has said?

Why haven't your two contributors who live on the Gunflint gotten out, like Justine used to, and go see for themselves? Who cares if one of them had a generator so they could have cold beer!

A good reporter writes about what's going on ALL around them, not just in their little world. We don't want to read cute little articles or hear about their children and grandchildren. They are supposed to be writing about what's going on on the Gunflint - the whole Trail.

Tom & Linda Hart
Kilgore, TX

Cook County News-Herald

Missing Storm Coverage

Storm on the West Bearskin
by Richard Cronstrom

The annual West Bearskin Lake Cabin Owners 4th of July Party was terminated when first, green sky was sighted, and then the wind picked up, scattering the attendees.

Member Richard Cronstrom gives us this account:

I noticed the sky turning green, and knew a storm was coming. So I decided to run back to my cabin on a trail along the lake. As the storm increased its fury, the powerful wind, horizontal rain and the surf on the lake were all unbelievable. Trees were beginning to fall. I came to a boardwalk – the wind blew me off! Trees were going down everywhere.

The wind let up briefly and I made it to my cabin. The winds were so strong that I couldn't keep the door and windows shut, so I put 3" deck screws in them with my battery operated drill. I had three trees fall on the cabin and four on the outhouse.

Then the chainsawing began, opening up the lakeshore trail, taking trees off vehicles and removing trees from cabins. We called our team "Fulcrum Engineering" as we made use of many primitive methods for lifting the heavy trees off the paths, cars and cabins. After 3 1/2 days of chainsawing, I left for the Cities until the electric power was restored.

Tree on Cronstrom cabin on East Bearskin Lake

Tree on vehicles East Bearskin Lake

Reference to "C" throughout the book indicates a color photo in mid-section.

He Would Never, Never Leave Me

by Roger & Linda Perreault

Perreault 'adventure story' has danger, bravery and optimism

by Ellen Walker

"It was almost like a novel … a book … an adventure story. I've never seen a storm like it."

Linda Perreault of Coon Rapids dramatically – but precisely – recounts the events of the devastating July 4 storm that ravished the Boundary Waters Canoe Area.

Roger, her husband, can also contribute the details of the day – but only to the point about a minute into the horrific storm that generated winds of up to 100 mph, that toppled an estimated million trees and that, according to some, has forever changed the face and character of the area.

His last clear memory of that day was Linda crying out, "A tree just hit me!"

Later recollections are spotty. He remembers looking into the sky and "I could see trees flying over the road like sticks – like they 'were blown by a fan." He remembers calling out for his wife and the boys. He remembers being uncomfortable and feeling a shot of pain when he tried to change positions.

His memory of the ambulance ride is sporadic. However, his memory of the first part of July 4 is perfect.

His recollection includes the couple's idyllic vacation at Hungry Jack Lodge, located near the end of the Gun-flint Trail. They and three youngsters – daughter Nicolle, 16, son Mike, 14, and Mike's friend Steven Juth, also 14 – had filled the near-perfect days with canoeing, hiking and just enjoying the freedom of living in their motor home away from appointments and telephones.

July 4, says Roger, was to be their last full day at the resort. Roger, Linda and the two boys had hiked the 2-plus miles to Trail's End Center for a late morning breakfast.

"It was really hot and humid," Roger remembers of the weather that morning, "…hazy like it had been all week." Both he and Linda agree there was nothing threatening about the day.

But when they left the restaurant just after noon, "We noticed the temperature had dropped a lot." The difference was enough to prompt them to inquire with the restaurant staff as to whether there had been any storm warnings. No, they were told, none. So they headed back "in no big hurry."

They had covered two miles or more when the storm hit. Linda describes it as being like "something suddenly was overhead. All of sudden it was black." The rain came down in sheets, obscuring their vision even more.

"You could see there was a problem," says Roger, who then yelled to "just run back to camp."

They began to run, but the wind and rain – "It came straight at us," says Linda. – restrained them.

The wind blew Linda sideways. "Remember," she asks Roger, "I kept sliding into the ditch?" Steven pulled her back onto the road several times.

The storm was so intense, says Roger, that even as he told the others to head for camp he was looking for a place to take shelter. The boys ran ahead.

The Perreaults say it's difficult to recapture the drama, fear and intensity of their ordeal. Everything happened so fast. They estimate that less than a minute passed between the time they left the restaurant and that when the boys headed off toward camp.

Then, suddenly, trees were falling.

Linda was startled by a grazing blow to her right shoulder. She turned to see what had struck her, then yelled to Roger, "A tree just hit me!"

She turned back and Roger was gone. "He vanished into the air," she says.

Through squinting eyes, she tried to see if Roger had gone ahead with the boys,

but "I knew he would never leave me – never, never leave me."

She attempts to recreate the scene: Visibility was virtually nil due to the driving rain and darkened sky. Leaves and debris peppered her.

"I couldn't find him. I looked," she emphasizes.

"Then I looked down, and there he was. He'd been hit by another tree." He was lying on his back with a huge birch atop him.

Linda knelt down. "I touched his neck. It was thick, bulging. He made a gurgling noise. His eyes were rolled back in his head." She says his right leg was up near his left shoulder "like a pretzel."

Her first thought was she had to save him. She pushed at the tree to move it off him. But it was no use. She knew she had to go for help.

"I gave him a kiss and told him, 'I'm going.'"

She berated herself during her stumbling, scrambling spurt to camp, she says, because she hadn't kept herself in shape. "The raindrops were big. I had to climb over fallen trees," she says. "I can't do this," she remembers thinking, then driving herself with "I have to do this."

She was becoming exhausted: "My heart was pounding. I couldn't catch my breath, but I thought 'I can't stop.' She noticed the numeral 324 – a fire number – as she tore along the path.

At the camp, she was greeted by more storm victims. "[RVs] had trees on them. Cars had trees on them. The tent campers were flat; they looked like they'd been folded up."

The first person she saw was a Forrest Parsons, the son of the lodge owner. "He's the hero," Linda says. "He saved Roger."

Parsons, a college sophomore home for the summer, was himself in turmoil. His father's almost-new home – built by father and son – had been cleanly sliced in half by a fallen tree. They had been working to salvage items. Much of the house – and more – was lost.

"He had tears in his eyes," Linda recalls softly. "I said, 'Help me! Help Roger!'" She explained what had happened. People gathered around.

The situation was definitely serious: "There were no cell phones, two-way radios, CBs, electricity." The only good thing Linda found was that the children were safe. Frightened, but safe.

"Forest said he'd go to Trail Center and call for help," Linda recalls.

"I begged everyone to go help Roger," she says, remembering that she had become irritated when "they didn't move fast enough."

Again, she compares the situation to a drama: "It was like in a movie. One man finally said, 'Who's going to help this woman's husband?' and then voices said, 'I will!' 'I will.'"

Linda sketched a map and gave the searchers the fire number 324.

The rescue of Roger Perreault is. as Linda describes adventure story."

Parsons had called 9-1-1 from Trail's End; two EMTs were on their way by boat,

the easiest and fastest way to get medical help to him.

Parsons found Roger first. It was about 1:30 p.m. A strange aspect of this story is that, when Parsons found him, Roger was lying on his side and there was no tree lying on him.

The EMTs arrived and prepared Roger for a rendezvous with an ambulance coming from Grand Marais 30 miles away. His right leg was stabilized with a chain saw blade. It was placed between his thighs; then his legs were duct taped. The tailgate of a pickup was removed, and Roger was eased onto it. Duct tape was wrapped around him and the improvised backboard. He was moved to the back of the pickup. By then, Linda had been brought to the site. She and Parsons rode with him.

Roger recalls the EMTs talking to him, joking with him. He knew they were trying to keep him conscious.

"I knew my leg was in bad shape," he says.

"Stay with me. Stay with me," Roger remembers the EMTs saying. They had nothing to keep him out of shock, no pain medications.

"They did have a two-way radio," says Linda, and they were talking to the ambulance that was slowly making its way toward them.

The devastation in the storm's wake impeded all travel. Property owners were being asked to stay out of the BWCA until the initial road clean-up was done. Yet, many were coming, eager to learn the fate of their property. From inside the ambulance, the Perreaults could hear the ambulance driver's voice over the loudspeaker telling people to move their cars aside, that an injured person needed to get to the hospital.

Linda estimates that the pick-up had to stop about every 10 feet and wait while

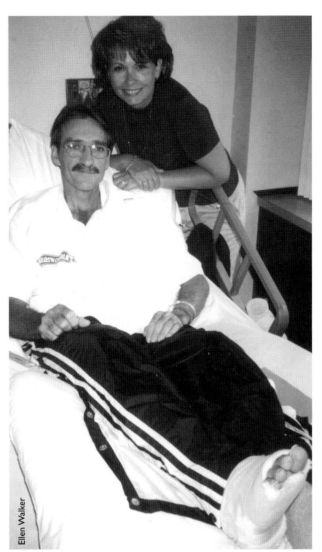

Ellen Walker

DR. ROGER PERREAULT, of Perreault Chiropractic Clinc in Rush City and North Branch, is on the mend following his injuries during the July 4 storm in Northern Minnesota. He and his wife, Linda, say the storm swept upon them in seconds.

workers sawed another tree and hauled it off the road. Another 10 feet and the same process was necessary.

The ambulance's progress was similarly delayed. In advance of it were workers sawing apart the fallen trees. They were followed by a grader that pushed aside the largest pieces. Finally, the ambulance inched forward.

Linda says the pick-up and the ambulance met around 5:30. Roger was transferred and taken to the Grand Marais hospital. In the

storm's aftermath, this was a one-hour trip.

At the Grand Marais hospital, Roger had his most serious injuries assessed. There, his legs were X-rayed. He was given morphine. "They were worried about his lungs," says Linda. "One of my lungs had collapsed," explains Roger.

It was decided that Roger should be transferred to dire situation in the storm's aftermath, no helicopters were available. Roger was transferred to Duluth's St.

Luke's Hospital via ambulance. Linda rode to Duluth with the wife of a man – an amnesia patient – another victim of the storm.

At St. Luke's at least one of Linda's concerns was set aside. The children had been brought to Duluth by the Search and Rescue operation. Amid tears and chatter, they brought each other up to date on what had happened. Steven's parents were there, too.

The St. Luke's staff assessed Roger's injuries – a collapsed lung (a chest tube had been inserted), two fractured ribs, fractures of a neck and a lower back vertebra, nerve injury in the right arm – but it was the right leg that demanded the most and quickest treatment.

The leg had 12 to 15 fractures. In the upper leg, muscles had been ripped; ligaments and tendons, displaced. Surgery began at 12:30 a.m. on July 5. When the surgery ended four hours later, rods had been placed in both the upper leg and lower leg. Pins, screws and staples were also used to repair the damage.

Asked about the hardware he's carrying around in his leg, Roger jokes, "I should get a lifetime pass through airport security."

Roger remained in the orthopedics unit of St. Luke's until July 14 when he was transferred to Fairview Riverside in Minneapolis. Here, he is receiving physical and occupational therapy three hours a day, six days a week.

Each day, he says, he is able to do more, to see improvement.

"Yes," says Linda, "there's improvement every day – not keeps him down."

Roger nods and says that staff members have commented on his upbeat, can-do attitude. He says he remembers awakening the third or fourth night in St. Luke's. "Reality really sank in," he states, "when I saw all those triangle bars, IV tubes, and wanted to move." But he had to have help and he knew then it all would take time.

"It takes patience, but it's all coming back," he says, "and it takes time, just like I tell my own patients."

Roger – Dr. Roger Perreault of the Perreault Chiropractic Clinic in North Branch and Rush City – says he's heard from many of his patients who want to know how he's doing, when he'll be back. And they want to wish him well.

Both of the Perreaults say the many cards, letters and calls they've received from patients, friends and neighbors have strengthened and encouraged them.

The couple brim with optimism, whether discussing the events of the July 4 storm, Roger's recovery or the planned expansion of his business place in North Branch.

"It's all a step-by-step process," he says of it all. He recounts his progress from being barely able to walk 18 feet on July 8 with assistance to July 18 when he walked more than three times that distance with little help.

He says he hopes to be back to work in four to six weeks, although he's not yet sure of how much he'll be doing at first.

"But I'll be back," he says. And you believe it because it's said with all the assuredness, confidence and calmness of the lead character in an adventure novel.

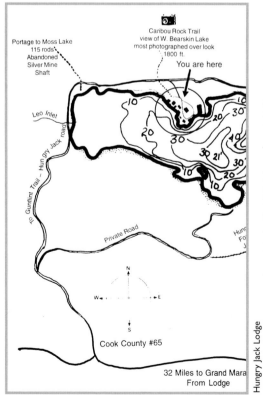

Hungry Jack lake - Gunflint Trail Map

Damage to building at Hungry Jack Lodge **C23**

Gunflint Guide Vince Ekroot

Vince was born and raised near the Trail, guiding his first party at age 12. "Little Vince's" guide service operates in the mid Trail area, generally on 10 to 12 lakes. He is an "independent," working frequently with Rockwood, Bearskin, Clearwater and Windigo resorts. In addition to guiding he conducts 3 or 4 seminars per month during the fishing season.

To operate in the BWCAW a guide pays 3% of his gross earnings to the Forest Service. According to Vince, "About 30 guides operate on the Trail and at least that many near Ely. I prefer to operate in non-congested areas - dead end lakes or lakes outside the BW. My clients include seasoned anglers like Al Linder, to first time beginners. I typically make shore lunch - campfires are extremely important to many clients." **C54**

Vince prefers quantity over trophy fish but his lunkers include a 30 lb. northern - a line class record. His parties generally put back the big ones. "The small ones taste better anyway," he claims.

On Independence Day Vince was at Leo Lake, just off the Gunflint Trail near Hungry Jack Road. Seeing turquoise sky and rain coming across the lake, he made a dash for his truck,

Rainbow caught during Mayfly hatch

Vince Ekroot

making it just as electric lines and poles came down, with wires arcing.

Vince helped with an evacuation from Hungry Jack Road, immobilizing the injured person to a pickup tailgate with duct tape. According to Vince, it took an hour to clear Hungry Jack road to the Gunflint; then 5 - 6 hours before they met the crew clearing the Trail from the south.

Ralph Popein, a summer resident of Poplar Lake, was one of the first down the Trail after the wind. He had this observation: "It was a strange sight, seeing a deputy sheriff leading a line of 20 to 30 cars and trucks winding down through the blowdown, being greeted by an ambulance and as many vehicles with canoes on their way up!"

The Trail was dangerous to drive for some time, with vehicles weaving single lane around down trees and meeting other vehicles.

Vince lost 2 weeks of business. Fishermen accessed only the drive-to lakes; most portages were closed. He has seen less wildlife since the storm, fewer eagles and no osprey.

Vince, his family and friends aren't afraid of future fires. He doesn't welcome USFS controlled burns, recalling some that "got away." His clients are amazed at the blow-

LITTLE VINCE'S GUIDE SERVICE
Vince, Christine, and Christopher Ekroot
69 Brandon Lane
Grand Marais, MN. 55604
(218) 387-2168

1999 RATE SHEET

Year around guided fishing for Walleye, Smallmouth Bass, Bluegills, Lake Trout, Brook Trout, Splake Trout, and Rainbow Trout (season permitting) on mid-Gunflint Trail lakes.

SUMMER:

Everything included except license, bait and shore lunch. 7.5% sales and use tax also included (calculated on $40.00 boat and motor rent).

FULL DAY: (10:00 a.m. until you quit or sunset)
One or two people:......................................$175.00
Three to five people:...................................$250.00

HALF DAY: (10:00 a.m. until 2:00 p.m.)
or
(last four hours of daylight, usually 6:00 to 10:00)
One or two people:......................................$120.00
Three to five people:...................................$155.00

WINTER:

Includes guide service and use of one snowmobile (guide drives it). There are no additional fees for more than two people, but guide will drill holes for only two. 7.5% sales and use tax included (calculated on $40.00 snowmobile rent).

FULL DAY: (8:00 a.m. until sunset)..........$175.00

HALF DAY: (8:00 a.m. until noon)............$120.00

ADDITIONAL INFORMATION:

$50.00 deposit per day required for reservation; 30 day notice required for refund.

Shore lunches cost $5.00 per person and must be arranged for in advance.

Guide will provide bait, but you will be charged for what you use (guide's cost).

IF YOU RESERVE A FULL DAY, YOU WILL BE CHARGED FOR A FULL DAY

Little Vince's Guide Services

Vince Ekroot

down damage but aren't discouraged from coming again.

Some of the well known Ely area guides are or were Paul Okstad, Sr. of Winton, Tommy Chosa of Ely, Tom Murn, Dewey Hardy and Soapy Hedloff, a guide on all the big lakes.

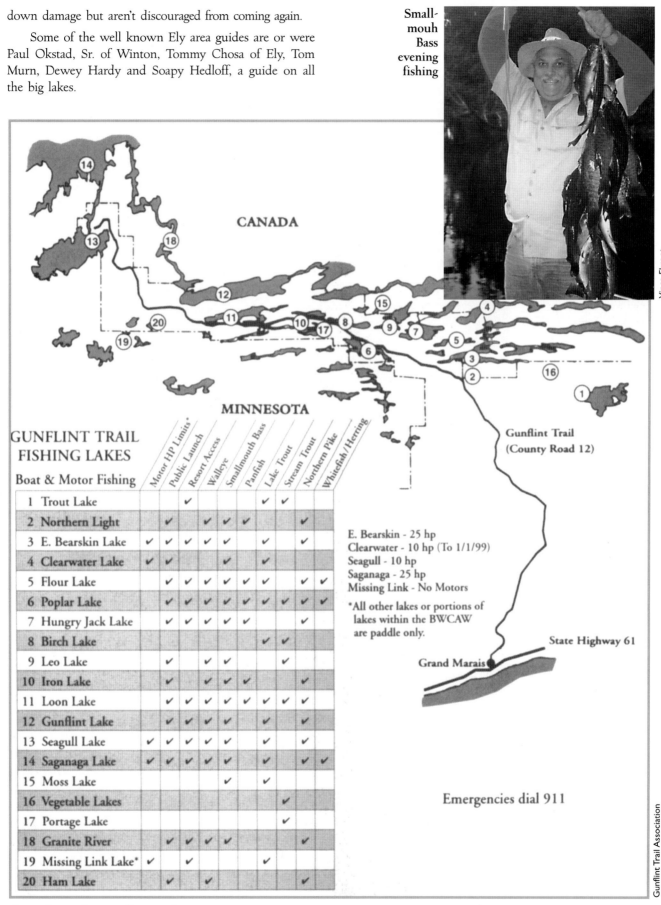

Smallmouh Bass evening fishing

Vince Ekroot

GUNFLINT TRAIL FISHING LAKES

Boat & Motor Fishing

	Motor HP Limits*	Public Launch	Resort Access	Walleye	Smallmouth Bass	Panfish	Lake Trout	Stream Trout	Northern Pike	Whitefish/Herring
1 Trout Lake			✔				✔	✔		
2 Northern Light		✔		✔	✔	✔			✔	
3 E. Bearskin Lake	✔	✔	✔	✔	✔		✔		✔	
4 Clearwater Lake	✔	✔			✔		✔			
5 Flour Lake		✔	✔	✔	✔	✔	✔		✔	✔
6 Poplar Lake		✔	✔	✔	✔	✔	✔	✔	✔	✔
7 Hungry Jack Lake		✔	✔	✔	✔	✔			✔	
8 Birch Lake							✔	✔		
9 Leo Lake		✔		✔	✔				✔	
10 Iron Lake		✔		✔	✔	✔			✔	
11 Loon Lake		✔	✔	✔	✔	✔	✔	✔	✔	
12 Gunflint Lake		✔	✔	✔	✔		✔		✔	
13 Seagull Lake	✔	✔	✔	✔	✔		✔		✔	
14 Saganaga Lake	✔	✔	✔	✔	✔		✔		✔	✔
15 Moss Lake				✔			✔			
16 Vegetable Lakes							✔			
17 Portage Lake							✔			
18 Granite River		✔	✔	✔	✔				✔	
19 Missing Link Lake*	✔		✔				✔			
20 Ham Lake		✔		✔					✔	

CANADA

MINNESOTA

Gunflint Trail (County Road 12)

E. Bearskin - 25 hp
Clearwater - 10 hp (To 1/1/99)
Seagull - 10 hp
Saganaga - 25 hp
Missing Link - No Motors

*All other lakes or portions of lakes within the BWCAW are paddle only.

Emergencies dial 911

State Highway 61

Grand Marais

Gunflint Trail Association

A Guide to the Gunflint Trail

Golden Eagle Lodge
by Dan Baumann

Golden Eagle Lodge
Gunflint Trail
468 Clearwater Rd.
Grand Marais, MN 55604
218-388-2203
www.golden-eagle.com

Dan Baumann, owner of Golden Eagle Lodge, didn't panic when he heard the storm warning come in. As the Gunflint Trail fire chief, he had heard them before. However, he quickly relayed the message of impending severe winds. He called Trail Center, alerted nearby campers on Flour Lake campground, then warned his own campground and cabins. Finally he trotted to his house where his wife Theresa and children were in the basement.

When the power went off, they knew that something was on its way. Suddenly they heard a deafening roar with cracking and breaking sounds. They weren't able to see beyond 50 feet because of wind, rain and flying debris. They saw only the trees by the house go down.

Afterward, the Baumanns weren't ready for what they saw: hundreds of trees down just in the immediate area. Trees were lying on 17 of 26 resort buildings; two buildings were totally destroyed. The Golden

Trees on camper at Golden Eagle Campground

Trees on building at Golden Eagle Lodge

Eagle campground was full of blown over and broken trees - few trees in the wooded campground were left standing. Trees were on camper trailers and cars. Amazingly, no one was killed or badly injured. **C11**

The roads were blocked, so Dan bailed out a boat to check on Flour Lake campground. There, he found trees down but no injuries.

Soon after the storm ended, Dan, an EMT, received an emergency radio call asking him to help a badly injured man on Hungry Jack road. With the roads blocked, Dan couldn't respond - a situation which still bothers him today.

Since the roads were blocked, nobody could leave the resort that day. None of the campers wanted to spend the night outdoors so the Baumanns squeezed them into cabins. With the electricity out, there was free ice cream for all.

The next day, the driveway was cleared as well as the Clearwater road, which had been one of the most severely blocked.

The Baumanns closed their resort for a week, allowing them time to begin the massive cleanup. Tree trunks and slash were piled and burned nonstop for 5 days, after which 2 1/2 dump truck loads of ash were carried away. A big chipper capable of processing 14" diameter trees ran for 36 hours, producing 300 cubic yards of chips.

On Tuesday, July 6, KARE 11 television from the Twin Cities arrived at the lodge with a truck and helicopter to investigate the storm. They interviewed area people and videotaped the blowdown area from above. The tape was shown in the Twin Cities and eventually was incorporated into the USFS "Leave No Trace" camping rules and regulations video. **C34**

The media people were astonished at how upbeat the Gunflint Trail residents were, who "take it as it comes," and have been through terrible storms before.

Many Trail businesses accused the media of overdramatizing the blowdown caused by the storm, and the resulting fire danger. They felt that such sensationalistic coverage would negatively affect their business. As an example, business for Golden Eagle through June 1999 was up 63% over the previous year, but through November it was down slightly. Reservations were down slightly for 2000.

As of December 1999 all BWCAW hiking, cross country and snowmobile trails were open; all Trail businesses were open and operating normally. Canoe country businesses that I talked to were confident that it would be business as usual in the year 2000.

Devastation near Golden Eagle

Golden Eagle Lodge

Kare 11 Helicopter

Dan Baumann

Storm on the Stairway Portage
by Jaye Martin & Karen MacDonald

This is a story about the experiences of Jaye Martin, Karen MacDonald, Carol Voight and two plucky Whippets, Scout and Jem.

On the day of the big storm, we were hiking the Caribou Rock Trail, which starts on the road to Hungry Jack Lake and heads north through the BWCA to Rose Lake and the Stairway Portage on the Canadian border. There were three of us, plus two dogs. We own a cabin together near Grand Marais and had decided to celebrate the fourth of July with a big hike.

We had been hiking about two and a half hours when the storm hit. We'd just come down off the ridge that follows the east shore of Duncan Lake and had arrived at the stream that parallels the

Karen, Scout and Jem   C41

Stairway Portage, but had not gotten across it yet. We were in the woods, so didn't know what the sky looked like, but it had started raining enough that we'd put on rain gear, and there was some distant rumbling. Very suddenly, it went dark, like someone had hit a light switch. The wind came up and trees started going down around us. The noise of the wind and breaking trees was so loud we had to yell to be heard.

We thought the low area we were in was safest, so we huddled on the lee side of the largest cedars we could find and kept our eyes skyward, hoping that if we saw something fall our way, we'd be able to move fast enough. We watched, and heard, a lot of trees go down—huge, mature pines—some snapping halfway up, some at the base. Eventually one of us looked down to see the ground around us undulating. It seemed the trees surrounding us were being uprooted. In looking down, we also realized we were shin deep in rising water and had to move.

At that point, we tried to head back up the trail to higher ground, but there no longer was a trail, just scores and scores of downed trees. To move higher, we had to crawl over and under the trees. In doing so, it occurred to us to take shelter under a fallen tree. Once high enough,

we moved three times before we found shelter large enough for all of us.

The storm lasted 20-30 minutes. Having settled in one place, we realized we were soaked to the skin and shivering with cold. One of our ponchos was completely shredded. Between us, we had books and bathing suits, one windbreaker, one long sleeved shirt, and one pair of windpants that weren't exactly dry. Although we could hardly swallow, we took the opportunity to eat some of our lunch. We contemplated a night in the wilderness, and how we might keep warm.

Once the wind started to subside, I made trips in several directions to get a sense of how bad things were. The forest we'd just hiked through pretty much lay on the ground around us. It was clear we could not make our way out via the trail we had hiked in on.

It was not really possible to move in any direction without scrambling over or under downed trees, and we already knew that was slow and difficult.

During the storm, we hadn't moved far from the stream and we knew the Stairway Portage wasn't far from that. It seemed our best bet was to make our way to the portage, where we increased our chances of finding others, hopefully who had extra gear, clothes, the means to build a fire, or who could paddle out with word that we needed help.

By then the wind had completely stopped; the rain had reduced to a drizzle. It was quiet again, and we thought we heard voices. We yelled for help. The people were on the other side of the stream, which had completely flooded the area we had been in when the storm hit. I scrambled down to where I could communicate with them, let them know how many of us there were, and that we were not hurt.

They immediately came across in two canoes to get us. Their trip was short but it wasn't easy, due to debris in the water and a strong current. In fact, one canoe capsized on the way over but they weren't deterred. One of the men came ashore and helped us move through the downed trees with the dogs, who for the most part had to be carried. When we had all made it down to the canoes, there was tremendous relief, tremendous comfort, in being in the company of others, even though they looked as shaken as we felt.

They brought us back across the swollen stream to the landing. Had we not been so near this major portage, I feel certain we would have been forced to spend the night in the wilderness. Instead, we were able to get a ride out. When we arrived at the portage, we found there were seventeen of us altogether at this spot. Two canoes with four each (the two that had rescued us) and three

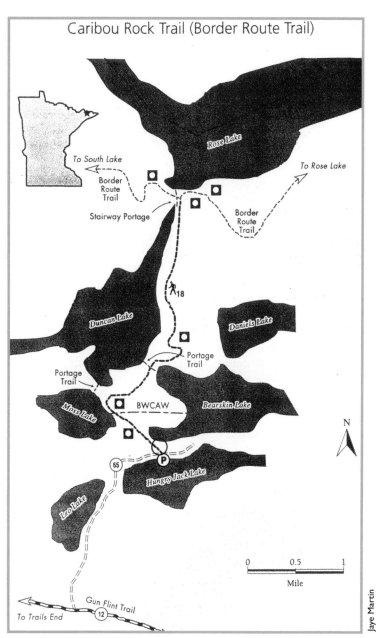

Caribou Rock Trail Map

and warm up. It was very still. The sky even seemed to be brightening. I think we were all taking in the destruction on the shores around us. Many trees were left standing, but what was odd were various areas that looked clear-cut, where nearly every tree had been snapped. At this point, we still thought the storm had been very localized, maybe a tornado had bounced through. As everyone knows now, that was not the case.

At the portage between Duncan and Bearskin Lakes, our progress slowed dramatically. It was a quarter mile portage, one that we had crossed, and explored, that morning on our hike. It had been remarkable for its width, and being lined by towering, majestic pines; now it was unrecognizable. Now most of those pines blocked our path. It took 45 minutes to

canoes with two each. Plus the three of us hikers. We exchanged storm stories and shared our wonder at the speed and power of the storm. No one in the group was hurt. One canoe was slightly damaged from a fallen tree, but that was it. We were all day trippers—no camping gear, little extra clothing, no emergency equipment. But without the extra gear, the canoes had room for us and our dogs. The group of six with three canoes readily agreed to take us, and we all headed out. We felt incredibly lucky; the storm seemed to be over, we had about a two hour trip ahead of us, and plenty of daylight left.

Our group of five canoes made it across Duncan Lake easily. The rain had stopped, and we started to dry out

cross, and with two- sometimes three-people maneuvering the canoes over, under and around stacks of downed trees. During this time we met two young men heading for Duncan Lake, looking for their mother and sister; they were the first of a few we were to encounter, searching for family members or friends.

By the time we got to Bearskin Lake, another party of four, with two canoes, caught up with us. As we all reloaded, the sky darkened and thunder rumbled. With a sense of urgency, twenty-one people scrambled to get seven canoes on a lake in conditions most of us would normally not consider paddling in. We raced for the other shore, converged on the next portage, and hauled people and canoes out of the water as fast as possible. The last one got out just as the first lightening flashed and big drops of rain started coming down hard.

We were then at the carry over to Hungry Jack Lake. The group who initially rescued us had a car there, as well as the group of four that had come up

Portage between Duncan & Bearskin

Jaye Martin and Karen MacDonald

I was reduced to tears by the sight of what the storm had done. In spite of everything they had to deal with at the Lodge, someone immediately got me a can of air/sealant—yet another example of everyone reaching out to each other.

We got the tire filled and headed out; it was two

behind us on the last portage. However, the three couples we'd ridden with had another lake to cross to get to their car. We weren't exactly sure where we were in relation to our car, but it didn't make sense to get on the water again, so we gave them our thanks, and asked the others for a lift. It became clear that they didn't really have room for three adults and two dogs, but they generously insisted that they could squeeze us in anyway.

We made it about twenty yards before we hit our first downed power line. After some debate, we crossed it, only to encounter a fallen tree, of course. It was small enough to drag out of the way, as were the next few we came to. During this time, an older man wandered out of the woods and said his house had been split in two by a downed tree. He seemed shaken, and climbed in with us too.

Within a half mile we came to a point where we could see 15 to 20 trees across the road ahead of us, some of them pretty large. The vehicles were at an impasse without a chainsaw. Though the rain was coming down in sheets, the three of us decided to continue to our car on foot, so once again we said our good-byes and gave our thanks. Before long, we arrived at the driveway to Hungry Jack Lodge. Starting there, the road had been cleared with chainsaws. We ran into a couple looking for some family members, and they told us that a man had been hit by a tree and evacuated, which was why the road had been cleared.

Soon enough, we could see our car ahead. A couple of huge trees were down around it, but fortunately it hadn't been hit, and it had clear passage to the road. When we got closer, we discovered, unbelievably, that we had a flat tire, and we could not budge the lug nuts. I walked back to Hungry Jack Lodge to see if we could get some help. I had been at the Lodge, fishing, a week earlier and

miles to the Gunflint Trail. There were an unbelievable number of trees and wires down, but a path had been cleared for the injured man's evacuation. For some reason, we felt the ordeal would be over once we reached the Gunflint Trail. Therefore, we were stunned when we got there, and it almost seemed worse, even more trees down and across the road. In the direction of Grand Marais, a single lane, partially on the shoulder, had been cleared, again for the evacuation, so we started down the highway, often driving on the shoulder. Before long, we came to a short line of stopped vehicles, and I got out to see what was up and if I could help. It turned out we had caught up with the clearing crew. The injured man was in the back of a pickup truck. Eventually our southbound clearing crew caught up with a crew clearing from the other direction. I think hundreds of trees were cut or dragged out of the road.

An ambulance from Grand Marais came for the injured man. During his transfer, the Cook County sheriff arrived on the scene and he seemed a little taken aback at the scope of the destruction. Evidently, Grand Marais had been enjoying the Fourth, completely unaware of what had happened in the BWCA. At this point, they had closed the Gunflint Trail down at Grand Marais, but not before some eager campers and local residents had already made their way up. Momentarily, we were stuck, northbound cars met southbound on only a single lane "road." At this point it was around 7:30 p.m. Eventually, the police started turning back the cars from town, and then let our line of cars (about 15) head south down the trail.

By 9:00 p.m. we were at our cabin in Colville, with what felt like the necessary comfort of a roaring fire. As much as we remember the intense fear and the sound of snapping trees, we remember the kindness of all the people who helped us that day. Thanks, again, to everyone.

Hurled 15 Feet Through the Air
by Al Hedstrom

Al Hedstrom's Grand Marais store, Better Buy Design, specializes in floor coverings and interior design. Just inside the door of his office stands a hefty 6 foot long piece of a Norway pine branch with chunks of blue tarp imbedded in one end.

For the fourth Independence Day in a row, Al and his friends had found their favorite campsite open on the north shore of Pine Lake. The day was hot, muggy and dead calm. Thunder was rumbling to the northwest. Al explains what happened – "Looking across the lake we saw an intense wall of rain and wind heading our way. Out on the lake not far away we saw a canoe racing full speed for the shore; then they disappeared into the wall. Four loons from different parts of the lake landed close to our site. They laughed and talked together seemingly not knowing what to do. They flew off but were engulfed by the storm."

Then the storm was upon them. Wind blasted their site and trees came down as 8 foot waves hit the shore. Al ran for his video camera, but was picked up and hurled 15 feet through the air. While airborne he could see himself rushing toward rocks, but he missed them. His friend Cindy Lou wasn't as lucky. She was heading for the tent when a falling pine hit her, knocking her to the ground. She sprained a knee and ankle on opposite sides and bruised her rotator cup.

The wind lasted 20 minutes; the rain lasted 40. When it all ended there were 27 trees lying on their campsite and over 100 down close by. Al's coffee cup held six inches of rain. The lake level appeared to rise more than a foot.

Remembering the storm-chased canoe, Courtney James, a member of the Hedstrom party and an EMT, set out to look for them, hoping he wouldn't find them washed up on the shore somewhere. When he found them they said they had been lucky, barely making it to shore.

The battered group was ready to leave but Cindy Lou wouldn't have it, so they stayed. Later that night the shock wore off and she began hurting. The pain lasted all night and into the next day. Monday they set off with her in the bottom of the canoe. They paddled to the entry point, got in their car and headed south through the maze of fallen trees to the North Shore Hospital in Grand Marais where lots of others were being treated, their wet clothes and packs littering the waiting room and hallways.

Asked if they would go in again after that experience, Al said they had already returned several times to their favorite spot.

Shoreline damage

Ely Echo

Escape From the BWCA
by Balazs Hunek

Here is the story of our "Adventure of a Lifetime." It is about being hit by an incredibly powerful storm on Sunday. In spite of that, we managed to escape uninjured through the practically uncrossable portages on Monday. The two of us (Sonia Gomez from Spain and Balazs Hunek from Hungary) went on a three-day long BWCA canoe trip starting on Saturday, July 3rd. Our entry point was #64 and Canoe Lakes. This was my fifth, but Sonia's first trip to the Boundary Waters. It may be her last one due to the HORRIBLE STORM that hit us on Pine Lake.

We set camp in the middle of the south shore of Pine Lake Saturday afternoon. Sunday around noon, we had just started a half day canoe trip to the eastern tip of Pine Lake. Suddenly, especially dark clouds arrived from the west at an alarming speed. We turned back after a little hesitation, because as Sonia said, "I would not have enjoyed the trip so much in the rain."

Propose to close camp site

USFS

Was she right!! Not only would we not have enjoyed it so much, but also we would have been most likely killed in the storm without a shelter! We got back to our campsite by 1 p.m., and it was already raining with quickly increasing wind speeds and towering waves. As we did not have anything better, we got in the tent, and an hour of horror started.

We could still see the wall of even stronger rain coming, but after that we had to seal off all the windows in the tent to avoid flooding it. The wind was constantly gaining power, and the tent was just pushed almost flat on us. Strange and powerful cracking noises were mixed with the howling wind, constant thundering and pouring shower-like rain. Sonia was saying her final good-byes to her family, while I was trying to console her. I just did not want to accept that this was the end for us, and we avoided panic.

Suddenly the rain stopped, but the wind was getting even stronger. As one of the poles of the tent yielded, we had to get out to avoid being buried by it. Trees were cracking and falling behind us, but fortunately none of them landed on us. As the wind calmed down an hour later, we got out on the lake to be amazed by the view. Just above our campsite ALL THE TREES WERE DOWN!! We were the luckiest persons on Earth not to be hit by any of them!

Unfortunately, it was not all of what we had to go through. We still had to get out of the BWCA somehow. As if it had been that easy the day before! Monday at noon, we tried to portage from Pine to Little Caribou Lake

(80 rods = 400 yards), but the trees on the hilltop were all knocked down, making it uncrossable. I hoped that the nearby long portage to Canoe Lake (232 rods = .8 mile) might have been better protected from the storm, so we switched to that one. This was our last chance; we just had to do it at any price! We were not sure if rescue crews would arrive at all, so we had to rely on ourselves.

Probably, we were the first (and maybe the last) group to cross it with a canoe after the storm. There were at least 70 trees lying across or on the portage, ranging from one to four feet in diameter. We were dragging, pushing the canoe and one backpack, climbing on top of these trees sometimes 10 feet high. The worst sections were when two to five trees fell on top of each other, making the obstacles practically insurmountable.

We still do not know how, but we crossed in two hours!! We actually lost the trail the last 20% of the portage, after we had to go around a big bunch of knocked down huge old pine trees. If we had not seen Canoe Lake at that point, we would have been lost for good. Fortunately, we saw the lake 500 feet ahead of us, so we were sliding the canoe down the hillside, cutting our own portage on top of knocked down trees.

Large holes left by the roots of downed trees made our path even rougher. Disturbed mosquitoes, black flies and horse flies were trying to feast on our sweaty misfortune. We were back in the Voyageur ages with no clear portages available. When we got across, we considered going back for our two other backpacks left at the beginning of the portage. Soon we realized that four more hours of extreme portaging would have totally exhausted us. It would have also extremely increased the risk of injury.

We could not afford that, so two of our packs are still sitting there including my camera, sleeping bags, tent, etc. They serve as a warning: "Do not try this now!" Our courage, toughness and strong will made us do it. We knew we needed our canoe, the paddles, some food and some clothes to get out alive. We were drinking the unfiltered lake water from that point on.

Our survival and escape from the BWCA under these conditions required constant belief, toughness and total reliance on each other. We did not give up for a second, even in the most miserable situation. We could not have done it without each other! It is a miracle that we made it back without any serious injury! Now, we feel how tiny we are, and what power nature has on us.

Reference to "C" throughout the book indicates a color photo in mid-section.

Epilogue

As we read through the letters it becomes clear that all will return to the wilderness someday no matter how terrified they were.

With few exceptions they would not trade their experience, all claim to have benefitted in some way.

What a pity that we couldn't all have been there. Seen the storm coming, watched those "old Soldiers" come down. Worked our way out through ruined portages and lived to tell others. To quote Shannon Craig and Paul Jester, "That was living - that was life".

Glossary of Terms

Beaver Aircraft Dehavilland DHC-2 USFS Aircraft.

BW, BWCA, BWCAW Boundary Waters Canoe Area Wilderness.

CL-215 Firefighting aircraft.

Dead-end Lakes a lake with only one portage entering.

District Ranger a USFS employee responsible for administering a specific National Forest District.

DNR Minnesota Department of Natural Resources.

EMT Emergency Medical Technician.

FEMA Federal Emergency Management Agency.

Forest Supervisor, a USFS Employee responsible for administering a specific National Forest

Fond Du Lac Reservation Native American Reservation near Duluth, MN.

Gunflint Trail 60 mile road through the wilderness connecting Grand Marais, MN to Saganaga Lake.

PMA (Primitive Management Area) reserved areas in the BWCAW with no designated campsites and few trails designed for a primitive camping experience.

Permit Document authorizing persons to enter the BWCAW.

Portage Trail between two lakes.

Quetico Provincial Park Ontario, Canadian wilderness area adjacent to our BWCAW.

Ranger Districts the Superior National Forest is divided into the following districts:
    Kiwishiwi - Ely Area.
    Isabella - Isabella Area.
    Tofte - Tofte Area.
    Gunflint - Grand Marais/Gunflint Trail Area.

Root Ball Roots and soil exposed from blowndown tree.

Sag Lake Saganaga Lake.

Sawyer Chain saw operator.

Shots Hotshot crews.

SNF Superior National Forest.

Swamper Person throwing cut wood aside.

Trails End Campground USFS campground at the far end of the Gunflint Trail.

Wilderness Ranger USFS employee responsible for administrating the rules and maintaining certain areas within the BWCAW.

Index